Managing Software Process Evolution

Marco Kuhrmann · Jürgen Münch
Ita Richardson · Andreas Rausch
He Zhang
Editors

Managing
Software
Process
Evolution

Traditional, Agile and Beyond –
How to Handle Process Change

 Springer

Editors
Marco Kuhrmann
University of Southern Denmark
Odense
Denmark

Jürgen Münch
Reutlingen University
Reutlingen
Germany

Ita Richardson
University of Limerick
Limerick
Ireland

Andreas Rausch
Clausthal University of Technology,
  Department of Informatics
Clausthal-Zellerfeld
Germany

He Zhang
Nanjing University
Nanjing
China

ISBN 978-3-319-81060-7   ISBN 978-3-319-31545-4   (eBook)
DOI 10.1007/978-3-319-31545-4

Foreword

Whether we like it or not, the business software is a fashion industry where new fads come and go. All of us can name several of them from the past years and share the war stories about attempting to fix problems with the newest fad at everyone's lips. Today some of these fads are called continuous deployment, lean startups, DevOps, flow and any of the Japanese sounding concepts from the lean vocabulary such as Kanban for some years now. So, who cares about software processes anymore?

Back in the days of my software development in the 1990s in a 10-person software boutique producing production planning software for Nokia factories, I became worried about the quality of our software and shared my thoughts with the chief architect. He made me a quality manager for the company and a few weeks later Nokia performed an ISO 9001 assessment for our boutique and the software. It turned out that we deviated in all other points but at least we had an appointed quality manager to worry about the results. Among others, we did not have processes in place.

Later I made my Ph.D. in Software Process Improvement, became a certified BOOTSTRAP and SPICE assessor, and discovered that if there is a way to improve performance, all sorts of process improvement endeavors are not the way forward. As much as we'd like, the processes are not tangible artifacts, they do not deliver software and when improved, we cannot quantify the results in order to determine whether we are developing better software than yesterday.

The past decade and a half has still been mostly about the processes, methods, and tools; but in a refreshing way. Agile kicked out process developers and empowered developers to become concerned about the business of the company, the actual software development. Agile grew rapidly outside of its origins from small teams to larger teams, to organizations and to global software development. Yes, we still agree to disagree what exactly agile is and what it means in different contexts in precise terms. We have learned that each and every organization must define it for themselves. This has proven to be painful but necessary when the ideas of continuous improvement and learning organizations are nurtured.

I am glad to say that the industry is moving forward, academics are reforming the curriculums, practitioners are more involved than ever before, and improvements or even improvement leaps are being made.

This is where the book at your hand becomes very handy. It shows how software processes evolve and are impacted in various contexts and how this can be managed. In an interesting way the book contributes to the era beyond agile, which will be welcomed by many. Also, I should note that the book does not attempt to anchor itself in one particular domain, context or business situation but offers different perspectives, which will benefit readers with different backgrounds.

The editors have collected 15 chapters from authors that represent both the academic and the practitioner standpoints. Some of the chapters are refreshingly controversial and many provide also concrete guidance on how to make a lasting impact. All of the chapters communicate the same underlying message, which I feel is very important: "We must keep changing the way the software is being developed." I particularly appreciated the sense of urgency to push the industry forward from a multitude of different viewpoints. While all chapters have their merits, I will highlight a few that caught my attention:

Anthony I. Wasserman (Chap. 1) presents the ultimate key question that has puzzled us for a number of years: "How much process is needed by an organization for a particular project?". In many ways he sets the stage for the remainder of the book by arguing that there are only a few places left where high-ceremony (a.k.a. traditional) processes are needed.

Andreas Rösel (Chap. 5) challenges the reader by presenting an approach to guarantee a failure when gigantic improvements should be sought but when we do not dare to take the risk. Many of the anti-tactics he identifies should be an eye-opener for software managers thinking about their improvement efforts.

Christian Prause and his colleagues' (Chap. 8) chapter, on the other hand, is an eye-opener for all those people who think software development is an easy endeavor. They describe their environment insightfully: "Scientific missions have no insurance; a second unit is never built. If the mission goal is not reached, for whatever reason, there is no second chance." Software that needs to operate for decades in the outer space requires all the ceremonies invented but a smart way of executing them.

Kai Petersen's (Chap. 12) contribution should be an absolute read to all researchers and practitioners involved in academia–industry collaboration. In a very practical way, he summarizes the literature on the topic but also adds his personal advice on how the research done by the academics can deliver the maximum value for the company.

Yli-Huumo and his colleagues (Chap. 15) demonstrate how changes in the organization and the way the software is being developed do have a fairly direct impact on the technical debt that hinders the company to progress and move forward in their development. The readers will particularly enjoy the illustrative quotes from the interviews in three large companies.

Coming back to where I started, it turns out that software processes have become ever more tangible and concrete actions can be taken that will show a difference in the bottom line. The editors have put together a book that does a splendid job in fulfilling an evident gap in the current literature by shaping the state of the art in software process evolution scene.

Whether you read this book from start to finish, or piecemeal your approach iteratively, I am sure you will find this book as valuable as I did.

Trondheim, Norway   Pekka Abrahamsson
January 2016   Professor of Software Engineering
                                Norwegian University of Science and Technology

PS: I forgot to conclude the story about the ISO 9001 assessment in the software boutique where I worked. After surviving the shock of being evaluated by Nokia, my company jumped in the process wagon, eventually I departed to pursue academic studies, and the company ended up being recognized by International Quality Crown award in 2008 and Arch of Europe Quality award in 2010. Thus, presenting a happy ending for one process assessment case.

Preface

Imagine this happens to you: Your manager tells you "Agile is the future! Let's go Scrum." He *forces* you to replace the existing development process with Scrum. What would you do? Would you send your developers to a Scrum training course immediately?

It is true that more companies are embracing agile as part of their development process in order to increase speed, accelerate learning, and deliver value rapidly. And many of these companies are applying Scrum. But it is also true that evolution does not follow the principle: "Progressive dinosaurs are the future! Let's go bird."[1]

Evolving the ways through which software-intensive products and services are developed is a challenging endeavor that needs to be done carefully. Where do you start? What do you have to consider?

This book will help you better understand the different aspects and challenges of evolving development processes. It addresses difficult problems, such as how to implement processes in highly regulated domains or where to find a suitable notation for documenting processes. This book emphasizes the need to consider *Software Process Evolution* as an important means for catching up with rapid changes in technical and market environments. It provides insights that might help you manage process evolution. It gives plenty of tips, e.g., how to cope with the threat of disruption from a process perspective. In addition, it provides many examples and cases on how to deal with software evolution in practice.

Why a Book on Managing Process Evolution?

Many organizations need to transform their business to the next level. In order to benefit from leading-edge technologies, catch up with the digital transformation, and continuously innovate and renew business models, companies have to quickly

---

[1]Quote taken from a tweet from David Evans.

adapt and change the ways they develop products and services. As software is the key to this transformation, the ways in which modern software is developed need to change accordingly.

Another important driver for process evolution is the need to mitigate software risks. Basically, a considerable share of software risk is process-based [3]. For example, there have been several incidents which could have been avoided with appropriate coding standards and tools. Although these standards and tools are widely available, they are either not applied or not appropriately applied in many situations. Because this is normally caused by the way work and people are organized and work is carried out it is a software process issue. Companies need to find ways to ensure that process models are properly defined and, furthermore, are appropriately applied while not hindering the creativity of, e.g., designers or developers. To do this effectively, defining and deploying adequate software processes usually requires fostering the evolution of existing processes and their underlying models towards ones that suit better.

Today, there exists a variety of software processes ranging from generic and domain-specific standards, from agile methods to comprehensive process engineering frameworks. Since software processes may contain up to hundreds or even thousands of elements, the management of a software process is a demanding task and, therefore, many companies install whole departments dealing with software process improvement and management. In practice, especially in large organizations, we can observe some interesting gaps:

- Development teams tend to apply agile methods while the hosting organization focuses on "classic" structured development processes [5, 6].
- Implemented development processes in projects differ from what has been defined [4].
- Evolving software technologies and platforms require a parallel evolution of software processes to accommodate the rapid changes. However, this co-evolution does not appropriately take place.

One main reason for these gaps is different mindsets. For instance, program managers and quality assurance people need planned and directed processes for certification, budgeting, and compliance business. Developers need flexibility and processes which support creative work. Business managers need processes that allow for fast results and flexible feature delivery. Moreover, due to technology evolution, business evolves. This requires that emerging markets must be addressed, new technologies should be adopted, and globally distributed development becomes more and more important.

Apart from the big "global players," process evolution is also highly important for small and medium-sized companies. Such companies typically neither have comprehensive process models nor process engineering groups, and often have to trust in a common understanding of principles and applied practices. However, these principles and practices need to be continuously validated against higher level goals (such as business strategies) and potentially changed in order to secure and maintain the company's position in the market place [2]. One example for such a change is the increasing focus on value-delivery [1]. Regardless of the company size, a major challenge that companies face is to provide all stakeholders with flexible processes that:

- Are driven by the needs of the different stakeholders,
- Have clear links to higher level goals of an organization,
- Provide interfaces that are compatible with organizational structures,
- Are supported by tools for modeling, enactment, analyses, and evolution,
- Can be tailored to individual project goals and characteristics,
- Offer adaptability and elasticity to accommodate and support technological and organizational innovations and evolutions.

This book focuses on the design, development, management, governance, and application of evolving software processes that are aligned with changing business objectives, such as expansion to new domains or moving to global production. In the context of evolving business, it addresses the complete software process life-cycle, from initial definition of a product to systematic improvement.

Who Should Read This Book?

This book is aimed at anyone interested in understanding and organizing software development tasks in an organization. The experiences and ideas in this book are useful for both those who are unfamiliar with software process improvement and want to get an overview of the different aspects of the topic, and those experts with many years of experience. In particular, the present book addresses researchers and Ph.D. students in the area of Software & Systems Engineering and Information Systems, who study advanced topics of organizing and managing (software development) projects and process improvements projects. Furthermore, the book addresses practitioners, consultants, and coaches involved in software-related change management and software process improvement projects, and who want to learn about challenges and state-of-the-art techniques and experiences regarding their application to problems in different application domains.

How is the Book Organized?

This book is organized in three parts (Fig. 1). Part 1 focuses on software business transformation, its challenges, and addresses the questions about which process(es) to use and adapt, and how to organize process improvement programs. In Chap. 1, Tony Wasserman discusses short lifecycle projects and how "low-ceremony processes" help shorting project iterations. In this context, in Chap. 2, Diebold and Zehler discuss the "right" degree of agility in rich software processes—how to find and how to achieve this. The challenge of implementing agile software

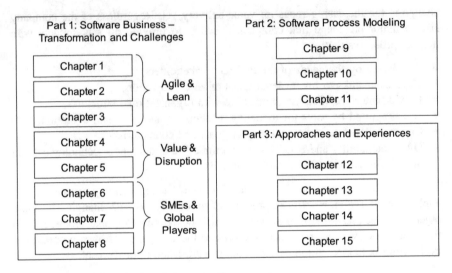

Fig. 1 Overview of the book and chapter outline

development approaches is further discussed by Houston and Rosemergy in Chap. 3, who report an agile transformation of a globally distributed company. As many companies jump to Agile processes hoping for the benefits promised, determining value and value creation is crucial. In Chap. 4, Christof Ebert discusses the principles of value-driven process management and reports experiences. Another perspective is taken by Andreas Rösel, who describes how concepts of design thinking can be applied to disruptive improvements in Chap. 5. Oisín Cawley discusses the trials and tribulations of Global Software Engineering processes in the course of business evolution with a particular focus on regulated software and system development in Chap. 6. The respective Software Process Improvement challenges, approaches, and standards for very small entities and small- to medium-sized companies are presented in Chap. 7 by Mary-Luz Sánchez-Gordón and her colleagues. In their systematic literature review, they give a comprehensive overview of the different improvement approaches and models and show how they find their way into international standards. Standards and their role are also key to the Space business, as presented in Chap. 8, where Christian Prause and his colleagues describe how software processes in the German Space Administration evolve and how they are tailored to the projects.

Part 2 of the book is focused on process modeling. This part starts with Chap. 9 by Dumas and Pfahl, who discuss the appropriateness of the Business Process Model and Notation (BPMN) for software processes modeling. In Chap. 10, Fazal-Baqaie and Engels present an approach to modeling evolving software processes by utilizing method engineering principles. The adaptation of case management techniques for the purpose of improving process model flexibility is demonstrated by Marian Benner-Wickner as his colleagues in Chap. 11.

Finally, Part 3 of the book collects approaches, experiences, and recommendations that help to improve software processes with a particular focus on specific lifecycle phases. The part starts with Chap. 12 in which Kai Petersen reports his experiences in industrial Software Process Improvement projects from the perspective of a researcher. He reports from projects and provides a collection of general lessons learned and recommendations to aid researchers and practitioners to plan and carry out improvement projects in an industry–academia collaboration. Chapter 13 in which Regina Hebig and her colleagues give insights into two large-scale industry projects and demonstrate how co-evolution is manifested and handled in such projects, thus addressing the co-evolution of software processes and model-driven engineering approaches. In Chap. 14, S.M. Didar Al Alam and his colleagues present an approach that helps companies to improve the release readiness of their software products. They show how bottleneck factors that hinder fast releases can be detected and they apply their concept to different Open-Source Software projects. Finally, Jesse Yli-Huumo and colleagues take a broader perspective in Chap. 15, discussing how process evolution affects technical debt. They illustrate their findings with three large-scale software projects.

We wish you an interesting and enjoyable reading experience. A collection such as this book would not be possible without the help of many persons. We would especially like to thank the authors for their insightful articles and their excellent collaboration. In addition, we would like to thank Ralf Gerstner from Springer, who supported us efficiently in completing organizational and contract issues.

Odense, Denmark   Marco Kuhrmann
Reutlingen, Germany   Jürgen Münch
Limerick, Ireland   Ita Richardson
Clausthal-Zellerfeld, Germany   Andreas Rausch
Nanjing, China   He Zhang
January 2016

References

1. Bosch, J.: Speed, data, and ecosystems: The future of software engineering. IEEE Softw. 33(1), 82–88 (2016)
2. Fagerholm, F., Guinea, A.S., Mäenpää, H., Münch, J.: Building blocks for continuous experimentation. In: Proceedings of the International Workshop on Rapid Continuous Software Engineering, RCoSE, pp. 26–35. ACM, New York (2014)
3. Neumann, P.G., et al.: Column: Risks to the Public. ACM SIGSOFT Softw. Eng. Note 40(6), 14–19 (2015)
4. Parnas, D.L., Clements, P.C.: A Rational Design Process: How and Why to fake it. IEEE Trans. Software Eng. 12(2), 251–257 (1986)

5. Theocharis, G., Kuhrmann, M., Münch, J., Diebold, P.: Is Water-Scrum-Fall reality? On the use of agile and traditional development practices. In: Proceedings of the International Conference on Product-Focused Software Process Improvement. Lecture Notes in Computer Science, vol. 9459, pp. 149–166. Springer, Heidelberg (2015)
6. Vijayasarathy, L., Butler, C.: Choice of software development methodologies - do project, team and organizational characteristics matter? IEEE Software (99), 1ff. (2015)

Contents

Contributors

Marian Benner-Wickner is Research Associate at the University of Duisburg-Essen and a professional IT Staff Trainer at CampusLab. His research interest includes software support for case management. After completing a vocational training as an IT specialist (2005), he studied computer engineering at the University of Applied Sciences in Dortmund. During his course of study, he worked on a research project at Fraunhofer ISST. After receiving his M.Sc. in 2010, he started his Ph.D. studies under the guidance of Prof. Volker Gruhn. Contact Marian at:

paluno—The Ruhr Institute for Software Technology, University of Duisburg-Essen, Germany.

E-mail: marian.benner-wickner@uni-due.de

Markus Bibus is Product Assurance Manager at DLR Space Administration for 6 years. He is the responsible product assurance manager in several DLR Space Administration projects such as Laser Communication Terminal, eRosita, ExoMars PANCAM High Resolution Camera, and CAPTARE with focus on EEE parts including FPGA programming, materials and processes. His background includes physics (Diplom, equiv. to M.Sc.), specialized in semiconductor technology and computer science as minor subject. Prior to his current tasks he worked as quality manager and technology engineer in semiconductor manufacturing business, in both research & development and automotive branches. Contact Markus at:

Deutsches Zentrum für Luft- und Raumfahrt, DLR—Space Administration, Königswinterer Straße 522-524, Bonn, Germany.

E-mail: markus.bibus@dlr.de

Matthias Book is Associate Professor for Software Engineering at the University of Iceland. After receiving his doctoral degree from the University of Leipzig, he worked as Research Manager for the German software company adesso, led the Mobile Interaction group at the University of Duisburg-Essen's Ruhr Institute for Software Technology (paluno), and served as acting head of the Software Engineering and Information Systems Chair at Chemnitz University of Technology.

His research focus is on facilitating communication between business and technical stakeholders in large software projects, and on interacting with software systems through novel input modalities such as gestures and voice commands. Contact Matthias at:
Department of Computer Science, University of Iceland.
E-mail: book@hi.is

Oisín Cawley is Lecturer and Researcher in Computing at the Institute of Technology Carlow, Ireland. He worked for 17 years in software development, predominantly for multinational companies, and has held several senior positions. He holds a B.Sc. in Computer Science, an MBA, and a Ph.D. in Software Engineering. Some of his research interests include software development processes and methodologies, particularly within regulated environments. He has a keen interest in improving the learning process for third-level computing students, and introducing young students to computing. He volunteers in his local primary school where he teaches programming to the sixth class children. Contact Oisín at:
Department of Computing, Institute of Technology Carlow, Ireland.
E-mail: oisin.cawley@itcarlow.ie

Ricardo Colomo-Palacios is Professor at the Computer Science Department of the Østfold University College, Norway. Formerly he worked at Universidad Carlos III de Madrid, Spain. His research interests include applied research in information systems, software project management, people in software projects, business software, and software and services process improvement. He received his Ph.D. in Computer Science from the Universidad Politécnica of Madrid (2005). He also holds an MBA from the Instituto de Empresa (2002). He has been working as software engineer, project manager, and software engineering consultant in several companies including Spanish IT leader INDRA. Contact Ricardo at:
Østfold University College, Halden, Norway.
E-mail: ricardo.colomo@hiof.no

Antonio de Amescua Seco has Ph.D. in Computer Science and is Full Professor in the Computer Science Department at Carlos III University of Madrid with more than 30 years of experience in higher education. His main research areas are software architect, project management, process improvement, change management, MOOC. He was the research project leader for the development of the standard of Information System Development Methodology for the Spanish Administration and has participated in projects sponsored by the European Union. He is member of the Chair of the SPI for Ibero-American Space and also member of European Certification and Qualification Association (ECQA). Contact Antonio at:
Universidad Carlos III de Madrid, Madrid, Spain.
E-mail: amescua@inf.uc3m.es

S.M. Didar Al Alam is a doctoral candidate in the University of Calgary's Software Engineering Decision Support Lab. He is also a Lecturer in Computer Science Department, Islamic University of Technology. His main research interests are readiness measurement of software release, planning of software release, decision support, data analytics, and empirical software engineering. Didar received his Master's and Bachelor's degrees in Computer Science and Information Technology from Islamic University of Technology. He held a doctoral scholarship from Alberta Innovates of Technology Futures (AITF) for more than 3 years. Contact Didar at:

University of Calgary, Department of Computer Science, Calgary, AB, Canada.
E-mail: smdalam@ucalgary.ca

Philipp Diebold is working as a researcher in the Process Engineering Department of the Fraunhofer Institute for Experimental Software Engineering IESE in Kaiserslautern (Germany) for some years. His technical focus is mainly on improving software and system development processes with the use of agile development methods such as Scrum or XP. In addition to his Fraunhofer work, he is doing his Ph. D. in the University of Kaiserslautern on introducing more elements from agile development into regulated environments, such as automotive, avionics, healthcare, by integrating agile practices in existing rich processes. Contact Philipp at:

Fraunhofer Institute for Experimental Software Engineering (IESE), Fraunhofer-Platz 1, 67663 Kaiserslautern, Germany.
E-mail: philipp.diebold@iese.fraunhofer.de

Carsten Dietrich is a staff member of the German Aerospace Centre (DLR) in Space Administration. He had set up and implemented the customer-side software product assurance in space projects. After harmonization of ECSS system between software quality assurance and engineering, he is now responsible for the support of software engineering in space projects. Carsten Dietrich holds a diploma in Information Technology (Computer Science) from the Technical University of Braunschweig in Germany. Prior to working for DLR, Mr. Dietrich worked in several other fields, such as project management, system analysis, and quality assurance in national and international automotive and railway–industry projects. Contact Carsten at:

Deutsches Zentrum für Luft- und Raumfahrt, DLR—Space Administration, Königswinterer Straße 522-524, Bonn, Germany.
E-mail: carsten.dietrich@dlr.de

Marlon Dumas is Professor of Software Engineering at the University of Tartu, Estonia, and Adjunct Professor of Information Systems at Queensland University of Technology, Australia. His research interests span across the fields of software engineering, information systems, and business process management. His ongoing work focuses on combining data mining and formal methods for analysis and monitoring of business processes. He has published extensively in conferences and journals across the fields of software engineering and information systems and has co-authored two textbooks in the field of business process management. Contact Marlon at:

University of Tartu, Institute of Computer Science, Tartu, Estonia.
E-mail: marlon.dumas@ut.ee

Christof Ebert is Managing Director at Vector Consulting Services. He supports clients around the world to sustainably improve product strategy and product development and to manage organizational changes. Dr. Ebert serves on advisory and industry bodies and is Professor at the Universities of Stuttgart and Paris. Contact Christof at:

Vector Consulting Services, Ingersheimer Straße 24, 70499 Stuttgart, Germany.

E-mail: Christof.Ebert@vector.com

Gregor Engels received his Ph.D. in Computer Science in 1986 from the University of Osnabrück, Germany. Between 1991 and 1997, he held the position as Chair of Software Engineering and Information Systems at the University of Leiden, The Netherlands. Since 1997, he has been Professor of Informatics at the University of Paderborn, Germany. Currently, he is also director of two technology transfer labs at the University of Paderborn, the C-LAB, a joint venture together with ATOS, and the s-lab—Software Quality Lab. His research interests are model-driven software development, software architecture, and software quality assurance. Contact Gregor at:

University of Paderborn, Database and Information Systems Research Group, Zukunftsmeile 1, 33102 Paderborn.

E-mail: engels@uni-paderborn.de

Masud Fazal-Baqaie studied Computer Science at the Paderborn University with stays at the Carleton University in Ottawa, Canada and the lab IBM Research—Zurich in Switzerland. He is member of the Database and Information Systems Research Group led by Prof. Dr. Gregor Engels and consultant at the s-lab—Software Quality Lab. He is also the vice chairman of the special interest group on process models for business application development at the German Informatics Society (GI). His research interests are provisioning of organization- and project-specific software development processes, global software development, and requirements engineering and management. Contact Masud at:

University of Paderborn, Database and Information Systems Research Group, Zukunftsmeile 1, 33102 Paderborn.

E-mail: masudf@uni-paderborn.de

Volker Gruhn holds the chair for Software Engineering at the University of Duisburg-Essen. His research interests are mobile applications and software processes. Before that he held the chair for Applied Telematics and e-Business at the University of Leipzig. He received a diploma degree (1987) and a Ph.D. (1991) both in Computer Science from the University of Dortmund. Volker Gruhn is author and co-author of about 270 journal and conference articles. He co-founded the software company adesso in 1997, currently deploying more than 1700 people. Volker Gruhn was program chair of the ESEC Conference (in 2001), the German Software Engineering Conference (in 2006) and program co-chair of the ICSE Conference 2008. Contact Volker at:

paluno—The Ruhr Institute for Software Technology, University of Duisburg-Essen, Germany.
E-mail: volker.gruhn@uni-due.de

Regina Hebig is Assistant Professor at Chalmers University of Technology and the Gothenburg University in Sweden since summer 2015. Her research focusses on model-driven engineering, software processes, and quantitative measurement of software size and quality. From 2014 to summer 2015, Regina worked in a French and a European project as a postdoctoral researcher at the University of Pierre and Marie Curie in Paris, France. She received her doctoral degree from the University of Potsdam in 2014 for her research on the evolution of model-driven engineering in practice. Contact Regina at:
Software Engineering Division, Chalmers University of Technology & University of Gothenburg, Sweden. E-mail: hebig@chalmers.se

Daniel X. Houston is a Senior Project Leader at The Aerospace Corporation. His work is applying quantitative methods, particularly using statistics and simulation, to software engineering. His industrial background includes software development, Six Sigma Black Belt, and software measurement. He received M.S. and Ph.D. degrees in Industrial Engineering from Arizona State University. His publications include works on statistical modeling and simulation of software development processes, software process improvement, and the management of software projects, particularly the aspects of risk, product quality, and economics. Contact Dan at:
The Aerospace Corporation, Los Angeles, CA 90009-2957.
E-mail: dan.houston@aero.org

Wolfgang Jobi headed the Product Assurance Department of the DLR Space Administration for over 15 years, and in total has worked there for almost 30 years since the German space agency's foundation in the late 1980s. Even before the ECSS was founded, he drafted the first product assurance standards for use in the agency's missions and is the founder of the computer-aided tailoring methodology for quality and product assurance requirements for space applications. Wolfgang Jobi is a state-certified technician of electronics and holds a diploma in Electrical Engineering from the University of Cologne, Germany. Contact Wolfgang at:
Deutsches Zentrum für Luft- und Raumfahrt, DLR—Space Administration, Königswinterer Straße 522-524, Bonn, Germany, (via Christian Prause).

Andrey Maglyas is a postdoctoral researcher in the Department of Innovation and Software at Lappeenranta University of Technology, Finland. His research interests include software product management, process improvements, and management methodologies. Maglyas has a D.Sc. (Tech) in Software Engineering from Lappeenranta University of Technology and a M.Sc. (Tech) in Management of Information Systems and Resources from Saint-Petersburg State Electrotechnical University, Russia. Contact Andrey at:

School of Business and Management, Innovation & Software, Lappeenranta University of Technology, P.O.Box 20, 53851 Lappeenranta, Finland.
E-mail: Andrey.Maglyas@lut.fi

Rory V. O'Connor is Associate Professor of Computing and the current Head of the School of Computing at Dublin City University, Ireland where he lectures in Software Engineering. He is a Senior Researcher with Lero, The Irish Software Research Centre. He is also Ireland's Head of Delegation to ISO/IEC JCT1/SC7 and editor of standard ISO/IEC 29110 part 2. In addition, Prof. O'Connor serves as the Editor in Chief of the Elsevier Journal Computer Standards and Interfaces. His research interests are centered on the processes where software-intensive systems are designed, implemented, and managed. His website address is www. roryoconnor.com, or Contact him at:
Dublin City University, Dublin, Ireland.
E-mail: rory.oconnor@dcu.ie

Kai Petersen is Associate Professor at Blekinge Institute of Technology (BTH). His research focuses on software processes, software metrics, lean and agile software development, quality assurance, and software security in close collaboration with industry partners. Kai was ranked among the 18 most productive scholars in lean and agile software development based on publications in journals of a total of 448 researchers by Sun et al.: Assessment of institutions, scholars, and contributions on agile software development (2001–2012) in Journal of Systems and Software. Kai has authored over 70 publications in peer-reviewed international journals, conferences, and books. Contact Kai at:
Blekinge Institute of Technology, Sweden.
E-mail: kai.petersen@bth.se

Dietmar Pfahl is Associate Professor of Software Engineering at the University of Tartu, Estonia, and Adjunct Professor of Software Engineering at the University of Calgary, Canada. His research interests include data-driven product and process analysis, management, and improvement. His work involves the application of data mining and machine learning techniques to build decision support models. He has 100+ refereed publications in software engineering conferences and journals. He is a Senior Member of both ACM and IEEE. Contact Dietmar at:
University of Tartu, Institute of Computer Science, Tartu, Estonia.
E-mail: dietmar.pfahl@ut.ee

Christian R. Prause is the head of the software product assurance field in the DLR Space Administration and is responsible for software product assurance in all major projects. For advancing the field and its application in projects, he leads dedicated improvement projects and participates in ECSS standardization committees. Before joining DLR in 2012, he was a developer, a software quality manager, and a project manager at Fraunhofer FIT. He graduated (Dipl.-Inform.) from the University of

Bonn, and received his Ph.D. (Dr. rer. nat.) in Computer Science from RWTH Aachen University. Contact Christian at:
Deutsches Zentrum für Luft- und Raumfahrt, DLR—Space Administration, Königswinterer Straße 522-524, Bonn, Germany.
E-mail: christian.prause@dlr.de

Andreas Rösel is Principal Consultant with SAP since 2011, and since 2014 he has been IT Process Officer. His experience of some 30 years also includes being Principal Consultant for DNV IT Global Services & Q-Labs, Software Technology and SEPG Leader at Heidelberg Printing Machines, Department Head of the Advanced Software Center at ABB and beforehand as SPI consultant, Software Architect, Software Engineer and Lecturer in Germany and Australia. Andreas holds an MSc in Software Engineering and an Engineering Degree in Electronics. He has a keen interest in combining innovation, agility and processes and has published and presented at conferences including ESEPG, SPICE-Days, Object World, Comdex, BITKOM. Contact Andreas at:
SAP AG, Walldorf, Germany.
E-mail: andreas.roesel@sap.com

Stephen W. Rosemergy is Software Architect and Software Engineering Practice Expert at The Aerospace Corporation. Steve has more than two decades of experience in developing software-intensive systems for both commercial and nonprofit sectors and has been a practitioner of agile methods since 2005. Steve is a graduate of both the School of Computer Science and the Heinz School of Information Systems at Carnegie Mellon University. Contact Steve at:
The Aerospace Corporation, Los Angeles, CA 90009-2957.
E-mail: steven.rosemergy@aero.org

Günther Ruhe is the Industrial Research Chair in Software Engineering at the University of Calgary. His research focuses on product release planning, software project management, decision support, data analytics, empirical software engineering, and search-based software engineering. Ruhe received a habilitation in computer science from the University of Kaiserslautern. Since 2016, he is the Editor in Chief of the Elsevier journal Information and Software Technology. He is a Senior Member of IEEE and a member of ACM. Contact Günther at:
University of Calgary, Department of Computer Science, Calgary, AB, Canada.
E-mail: ruhe@ucalgary.ca

Mary-Luz Sánchez-Gordón is a Ph.D. student in Information Science and Technology at Universidad Carlos III de Madrid, Spain. She holds a Master's degree in Information Science and Technology from the same university. She studied computer engineering at Universidad Central del Ecuador, Quito, Ecuador. She also got her Master's degree in Education at this university. She has more than 10 years of experience in the software industry and 5 years in research and teaching in Ecuador. Her research interests are software process, software process improvement, and knowledge management. Contact Mary-Luz at:

Universidad Carlos III de Madrid, Madrid, Spain.
E-mail: mary_sanchezg@hotmail.com

Andreas I. Schmied is Managing Solution Architect at Capgemini since 2008. He has been involved in various IT projects along the development, production, and sales processes within the automotive industry. His work leads him into various roles, ranging from consultancy and development to engagement management, with a special interest in model-driven architectures that resonate with multi-cultural specifics. Andreas received a Ph.D. in Computer Science from Ulm University, Germany, for his work on the composition of software transformation processes. Contact Andreas at:
Capgemini Deutschland GmbH, Löffelstraße 46, 70597 Stuttgart, Germany.
E-mail: andreas.schmied@capgemini.com

Kari Smolander is Professor of Software Engineering in Department of Computer Science, Aalto University, Finland. His current research interests are software development practices and include especially the ongoing change in software and systems development practices and software development organizations related to digitalization. Smolander has a Ph.D. (2003) in Computer Science from Lappeenranta University of Technology, Finland. Contact Kari at:
Department of Computer Science, Aalto University, P.O.Box 15400, FI-00076 Aalto, Finland.
E-mail: kari.smolander@aalto.fi

Anthony I. Wasserman is Professor of Software Management Practice at Carnegie Mellon Silicon Valley, and the Executive Director of its Center for Open Source Investigation (COSI), focused on evaluation and adoption of open-source software. Earlier in his career, he was Professor of Medical Information Science at the University of California, San Francisco. He then started Interactive Development Environments (IDE), and served as its CEO for 10 years. He subsequently managed software and product development groups for several small companies before returning to academia in 2005. Tony is a Fellow of the ACM, a Life Fellow of the IEEE, and a Board member of the Open Source Initiative. He is a graduate of the University of California, Berkeley, and earned his Ph.D. in Computer Sciences from the University of Wisconsin, Madison. Contact Tony at:
Integrated Innovation Institute, Carnegie Mellon University, Silicon Valley, Moffett Field, CA 94035, USA.
E-mail: tonyw@sv.cmu.edu

Ingo Weisemöller worked as a scientific employee at the TU Darmstadt and the RWTH Aachen from 2006 to 2011, focusing on model-based and generative software development, domain-specific languages, and model transformations. In 2012 he graduated with his dissertation thesis "Generation of Domain Specific Transformation Languages." Since 2012, he is working as Software and Systems Designer at the Carmeq GmbH, Berlin. His activities at Carmeq include development, operation, and maintenance of tools for model-based software engineering, primarily in the application and development of AUTOSAR, as well as software architectures, processes, methods, and data formats in automotive software development. Contact Ingo at:

Carmeq GmbH, Carnotstr. 4, 10587 Berlin, Germany.
E-mail: ingo.weisemoeller@carmeq.com

Jesse Yli-Huumo is a Ph.D. student in the Department of Innovation and Software at Lappeenranta University of Technology, Finland. His research interests include technical debt, process improvements, and software development methodologies. Yli-Huumo has an M.Sc. (Tech) in Software Engineering from Lappeenranta University of Technology. Contact Jesse at:

School of Business and Management, Innovation & Software, Lappeenranta University of Technology, P.O.Box 20, 53851 Lappeenranta, Finland.
E-mail: Jesse.Yli-Huumo@lut.fi

Thomas Zehler is working as a researcher in the Process Engineering Department of the Fraunhofer Institute for Experimental Software Engineering IESE in Kaiserslautern (Germany) for several years. His technical focus is mainly on software and system process improvement of development processes, especially using common best-practice models, such as CMMI or SPICE. His favorite domain is automotive, and he is a certified Automotive SPICE Provisional Assessor. Contact Thomas at:

Fraunhofer Institute for Experimental Software Engineering (IESE), Fraunhofer-Platz 1, 67663 Kaiserslautern, Germany.
E-mail: thomas.zehler@iese.fraunhofer.de

Disclaimer

Any of the trademarks, service marks, collective marks, registered names, or similar rights that are used or cited in the book are the property of the respective owners. Their use here does not imply that they can be used for any purpose other than for the informational use as contemplated in this book.

The following table summarizes the trademarks used in this book. Rather than indicating every occurrence of a trademarked name as such, this report uses the names only in an editorial fashion and to the benefit of the trademark owner, with no intention of infringement of the trademark.

Automotive SPICE®		Verband der Automobilindustrie e.V. (VDA)
BPMN™	Business Process Model and Notation™	Object Management Group®
CMM®	Capability Maturity Model	Software Engineering Institute (SEI)
CMMI®	Capability Maturity Model Integration	Software Engineering Institute (SEI)
IDEAL^SM	The IDEAL^SM Model	Software Engineering Institute (SEI)
MS Office®	MS Word®, MS Excel®, and MS PowerPoint®	Microsoft® Corporation
PSP^SM	The Personal Software Process^SM	Software Engineering Institute (SEI)
SAP HANA®		SAP SE
SPEM™	Software & Systems Process Engineering Metamodel™	Object Management Group®
TSP^SM	The Team Software Process^SM	Software Engineering Institute (SEI)
UML®	Unified Modeling Language®	Object Management Group®
V-Modell® XT		Federal Republic of Germany

Chapter 1
Low Ceremony Processes for Short Lifecycle Projects

Anthony I. Wasserman

Abstract Modern software applications, particularly those for mobile devices and web applications, are fundamentally different from traditional applications. Many of those applications are developed by startup businesses, which are under time and financial pressure to release their applications as quickly as possible. They have chosen to use agile methods for their development activities, largely because the administrative overhead for the process is low and the release cycle for the product is short. In this chapter, we contrast software processes based on the amount of management overhead ("ceremony"), describing the characteristics of startup businesses and their use of low-ceremony processes.

1.1 Introduction

Software development processes have long been a central topic of software engineering, starting with the very first NATO-sponsored workshop that defined the term *Software Engineering* [8]. Within the software engineering research community, it is widely believed that a well-organized and repeatable process can improve both the predictability of development schedules and the quality of the resulting software system. However, the increasingly wide diversity of software projects has led to ongoing debates over which types of software process are most effective and over the appropriate degree of rigor in the process itself.

In 1996, this author wrote [11]: "Having some defined and manageable process for software development is much better than not having one at all." That observation was made in recognition of the vast differences among applications in project criticality, modifiability of the deployed software, and project size. The nature of software for embedded systems avionics and medical devices requires detailed attention to every step of the process, while the process needs for less critical applications are less rigorous. This author believes that the observation remains true today, especially

A.I. Wasserman (✉)
Integrated Innovation Institute, Carnegie Mellon University – Silicon Valley,
Moffett Field, CA 94035, USA
e-mail: tonyw@sv.cmu.edu

© Springer International Publishing Switzerland 2016
M. Kuhrmann et al. (eds.), *Managing Software Process Evolution*,
DOI 10.1007/978-3-319-31545-4_1

considering the ability of development organizations to update deployed applications and the widespread adoption of rapid development processes for smaller applications.

Processes used today for application development range from highly formalized approaches with extensive management oversight to those with little or no structure at all. We may think of those extremes as "high ceremony" (HC) and "low ceremony" (LC), recognizing that there is a broad spectrum of development approaches and a vast middle group between the extremes.

A central question in software engineering is: "How much process is needed by an organization for a particular project?" Where a large, complex system is being developed under contract, perhaps as a collection of independent software-intensive subsystems, those responsible for the system want the development organization to follow numerous best practices during the development process, with the goal of gaining management insight into the process and identifying delays or other issues as early as possible. That approach is HC, almost by definition. By contrast, many small projects, particularly those being developed by one or two people, are LC and are focused almost entirely on iterative coding and product release, with very little attention given to the process beyond what may be embedded in the team's development environment.

In general, one can envision a sliding scale for the ideal amount of process used for a software project. The degree of process needed is dependent on the complexity of the system, the business risk, and the number of people involved in the project. Ideally, an organization should avoid a process mismatch, both to avoid too much organizational overhead for simple projects and to gain enough ongoing insight into more complex ones.

1.2   Background and Context

For many years, the "waterfall" model prevailed as the preferred process model, with the process ideally flowing sequentially from specifications through design, programming, and testing prior to release of the software. Each phase had certain defined activities and intermediate deliverables.

However, many projects following a waterfall approach ran into trouble. For applications that were fundamentally different than anything that had previously been developed by an organization, it was very difficult to estimate the needed effort and thus the time and budget needed to build it. Changes in requirements at late stages of the project often led to a large amount of rework. Finally, it was difficult to determine the quality of the software until very late in the process.

1.2.1   The Software Engineering Institute

The Software Engineering Institute (SEI) was founded in the late 1980s, in part to address these problems, which arose in numerous complex software and systems project under development for the US military. The SEI leadership believed that the quality of an organization's software development process was at the heart of addressing the problems. Accordingly, they defined the Capability Maturity Model (CMM) to define the key process areas that should be followed by a systems development organization and to define "maturity levels" for those organizations [6, 7]. One key idea is that organizations with more mature processes were more likely to succeed in delivering systems that met their requirements on schedule and on budget.

Over the years, the CMM has evolved into the Capability Maturity Model Integration (CMMI), with three different areas, of which the CMMI for Development is intended for product and service development. The most recent (1.3) version of the CMMI includes 22 different process areas [5] covering five different levels of process maturity. Addressing and attempting to improve performance on all of these process areas requires a significant organizational effort, which is most appropriate for large software and system development activities involving many people over a long period of time, typically years.

The CMMI is an excellent framework for evaluating HC processes, where an organization's process addresses all of the areas and activities recommended for achieving a Level 3 (or higher) Maturity according to the CMMI. These activities may be summarized and grouped into four categories as follows:

1. Multiple levels of management review of the process and the progress of the project, often as part of a larger software development program.
2. Submission and review of intermediate non-code deliverables, such as functional specifications.
3. Required team conformance to organizational or third-party development process standards or tool use, and
4. Gathering metrics about the process for use by a program management office (or similar organization).

The high-ceremony process of the CMMI, with its associated management overhead and training requirements, has increasingly limited it to use in contract software settings for large software-intensive systems, where the contract manager uses the CMMI to select the contractor and evaluate the contractor's performance. Companies wishing to show the maturity of their software engineering processes can be evaluated by an Assessor, who conducts an assessment of the company's capabilities.

Large contract software projects, such as those addressed by the CMMI, are a very small percentage of all software projects. Other projects normally follow a process that addresses far fewer of the key process areas described in the CMMI. A week-long project by a single developer may have very little process overhead. When the complexity of the software is high, the cost of errors is high, and the ability to update installed software is low, both its developers and its users are likely to be risk-averse.

In that setting, HC processes are valuable, and the development organization must adopt (and continually improve) the way that it develops, enhances, tests, and releases software.

In the past, such applications have been updated infrequently. Many commercial applications were regularly updated no more than twice a year, and many users of the applications chose not to update to later versions because of the additional work needed to replace the software and potentially other applications that would be affected by the change. The infrequent release schedule placed a lot of pressure on the creators of the software. The product manager had to decide which new features, enhancements, and bug fixes would be included in each release, knowing that no changes could typically be made for six months after the release. Similarly, the QA organization had to be very thorough in detecting problems and getting them fixed by the developers prior to freezing the software for release.[1]

1.2.2 The Emergence of Agile Methods

As a result, software developers looked for a more effective development process. The spiral model, developed by Boehm [3], addressed many of these issues by defining an incremental and iterative process where new features were successively implemented and tested. The spiral approach has been tremendously influential in modern "agile" software development practices, which are central to LC processes.

Agile software methods evolved from the 12 principles of the Agile Manifesto [1]. Agile development processes, such as Scrum [10], have now largely displaced waterfall methods in commercial software product development organizations, and thus disrupted software development processes. Even organizations that continue to adhere to the older approach have sought ways to make their processes more agile.

1.2.3 Outline

In the remaining parts of the chapter, we first review the evolving nature of software applications in Sect. 1.3, and contrast modern and traditional applications in Sect. 1.4. We describe the qualities of startup businesses that lead them to favor low-ceremony processes in Sect. 1.5, and their use of agile and iterative development processes to frequently deliver new versions of the application in Sect. 1.6. Finally, we note the evolution of processes as startups grow into more established businesses, with the attendance growth in staff and in business risks in Sect. 1.7.

---

[1]This problem was more severe when software developers had to incur the expense of sending physical media to their customers, and has been partly mitigated by the ability to download critical updates over the Internet.

1.3 Types of Modern Applications

Historically, software was developed to run on servers and on desktop computers under control of the product's users, where the end user (or a system administrator) would use the provided software installation program to set up the software for use. The application developers would package the software into an installer to enable customers to perform the installation from physical media, or a downloaded file. While that approach is still widely used for packaged software, the vast majority of today's applications are either hosted in the "cloud," developed to run on mobile devices, or embedded in a device. All of these types of applications are developed and updated differently from traditional packaged software.

1.3.1 Hosted Applications

Hosted applications run in an environment defined by the application developer, perhaps using their own servers (as with Google, Facebook, and World of Warcraft), or, alternatively, a cloud computing service (e.g., Amazon Web Services or Rackspace) that provides computing resources (servers, storage, etc.) on demand.

Hosted applications provide some significant advantages to the application development organization. In particular, they are in control of all running instances of their application, so they are able to avoid the traditional situation where users are slow to upgrade to newer versions of the application. Application development organizations can create a collection of hosts for application testing, staging, and production, and update those hosts as frequently as they wish, even if the update is a trivial change to the application, such as fixing a typographical error. They can also host different versions of the application on different hosts, perhaps to analyze user behavior with slightly different versions of the software (A/B testing). They can also use different hosts in different geographical areas, not only to reduce network traffic, but also to manage geographically specific aspects of the software, such as privacy regulations or native languages.

Many organizations providing hosted services are adopting processes that provide continuous integration, using a tool such as Hudson or Jenkins [4]. With the appropriate toolset and release process, they are able to update their application multiple times per day if so desired.[2]

1.3.2 Mobile Applications

Mobile applications (apps) are installed on a user's mobile device, and may run locally on the device, or more commonly, as a hybrid app where the software installed on the

---

[2]Highly frequent updates can present problems for the development organization, and may indicate a poor (or absent) process for testing.

device communicates with remote servers for data retrieval, business transactions, and multi-user coordination. Web browsers, mobile commerce, and chat apps are representative of such hybrid apps. In this situation, the app developer sets up the infrastructure for running the app, but then submits it to an app store for review and approval. All of the mobile operating system providers, as well as some third parties, provide an app store for apps running on a particular mobile platform. The app review process encourages (and may force) apps to conform to user interface guidelines and to avoid specific types of application (e.g., radical political movements and pornography). The user of a mobile app will be notified of the availability of a new version of any app installed on their device, and can choose to download and install the new version.

As a rule, device users almost always install updates when they become available, and the expectation of the app developer is that users will be running the latest version of the app. As with hosted software, such an assumption reduces the need for app developers to support multiple versions of the app, and leaves them free to offer updates as frequently as they desire. However, each update needs the approval of the relevant app store(s) before it can be made available to users.[3] As a result, the update frequency for mobile apps is not as rapid as for many hosted apps, but both are updated far more frequently than traditional packaged apps.

1.3.3   Embedded Applications

Embedded applications are found in a wide variety of electronic devices, including networking equipment, wearables, telematics for automobiles, and medical devices. In the past, the software in such devices was not changed throughout the lifetime use of the device. Now, however, it is possible to do over-the-air (OTA) updates to the software, and a large share of modern devices include the capability to update the embedded firmware and/or any associated application. Since many of these embedded applications are used for mission-critical or life-critical purposes, they are not updated as frequently as are hosted applications and mobile apps. Hence, they tend to follow a more deliberate development and testing process. However, they are an important class of modern applications that is likely to become increasingly important as software becomes an important component in many types of equipment, including home appliances and automobiles.

1.4   Modern Applications vs Traditional Applications

Modern applications (and their development processes) differ significantly from traditional applications. We explore the major differences in this section.

---

[3]There are techniques that can be used to bypass the update approval process, but the vast majority of apps follow the process.

First, modern applications are almost always distributed, going well beyond the client–server architectures that became popular in the 1980s. The back-end, or server side, may run on one or more servers, and the front-end, or client side, may allow a user to access the back-end of the application in many different ways, including web browsers, mobile devices, and programmatic means. The primary back-end server may provide little more than a load balancing function, passing the client request to a server that performs the desired function, often calling upon other services in the process.

Next, modern applications rely upon multiple technologies and languages, necessitating the use of a diverse team with different skills. Web application development has long followed a front-end/back-end division, where one team is responsible for the design of the user interface and experience, and another team is responsible for the application functionality. In many data-driven web applications, the content of the user interface, i.e., the displayed HTML output, is produced by the back-end code, following the user interface model created by front-end designers. Similar issues arise in the development of mobile apps, where it is common for a small native app running on the device to connect to the main functionality of the application running on remote servers. In both cases, various members of the team have different areas of expertise and may write code in multiple languages. Teams may also rely on additional expertise for database design, application scalability, and testing.

Indeed, testing of modern applications is much harder than with traditional applications. Not only are there vast differences among the user environments (different software versions of browsers and devices), but there are often transient errors in network connections, as well as different types of network communication, e.g., the telecom network and a WiFi network. As a result, it is often impossible to replicate problems, since it is infeasible to duplicate in a test environment all of the situations that may occur in a distributed application running "in the wild."

Modern applications are often subjected to wide variations in load. Publicity about a website or mobile app may drive vast amounts of unanticipated traffic and cause the site or app to fail or to suffer from severe performance degradation.[4] This problem may arise even in situations, such as the Olympics or the World Cup, where the site developer has tried to anticipate and estimate such traffic. This situation may arise even when the application is hosted on a cloud computing platform, e.g., Amazon Web Services or Microsoft Azure, where it is possible to allocate and de-allocate resources dynamically.

Next, modern applications are typically built upon third-party components that provide database management, messaging, search, and other essential functions of the application. Whereas traditional desktop applications made relatively little use of such components, the development philosophy for modern applications is to write as little code as possible, relying upon proven software, often open source. Along the same lines, modern applications also rely heavily on third-party services to provide essential functionality. Such services provide, for example:

---

[4]Distributed denial of service (DDoS) attacks have similar impact.

1. Content caching to reduce latency time for displaying content, e.g., images.
2. Enablement of electronic commerce, such as PayPal and credit card processing.
3. Site traffic analysis, including user tracking.
4. Advertising servers, which deliver customized ads to the client.
5. Support and discussion forums.
6. Connections to social media sites, e.g., Facebook and Twitter, for messaging, login, email, and more.

In each of these cases, there is a well-defined protocol, typically an application programming interface (API), by which the application can use the third-party service as part of a business agreement. The quality and robustness of these third-party services are well-established, and are often provided by a well-known company, such as Akamai or Zendesk, that supports and updates the service.

Using such services significantly reduces the development effort and required testing for the application developer, but carries the risk that the third-party service might fail and disrupt the application.

1.5 Startups and Processes

Many of the developers of hosted and mobile applications are startups, which may be characterized as young companies with fewer than 50 people, often fewer than 10. Such companies are looking for a scalable and repeatable business model [2], and have few processes for any aspect of their business, though their software developers may have developed a set of best practices in their previous work. While having organized software development and release processes will be important for these startups as they grow, that need is overshadowed at the outset by the need to bring their products to market as quickly and as inexpensively as possible. Product release and acquisition of users are essential to the initial success of their business, and are often the critical factors in being able to obtain funding from investors.[5]

Many startups join accelerators, organizations that aim to improve the startup's chances of success by providing mentorship and introductions to potential investors. These programs, typically lasting three to four months, focus on helping the new company develop a "minimum viable product" (MVP) and on crafting a presentation that will attract an investment to support their future growth. As a result, many startups, particularly those with just a few people, are completely unsystematic in developing their MVP, following coding practices most accurately described as "hacking." Products developed this way are often poorly architected, lack documentation, and do not adapt well to creating successive releases following a product roadmap.

However, even with the severe time pressure to build the MVP, obtain funding, and attract users, startups must include numerous activities as they define, design,

---

[5] Some of the largest and best-known modern applications such as Facebook, Amazon.com, WeChat, eBay, Salesforce.com, and Google were initially built by small teams, and have since evolved into large enterprises that have systematized many aspects of their development processes.

develop, and deliver their software products. These process-related activities include the following:

1. Addressing key customer needs, which usually requires requirements gathering through interviews with potential users and customers [2]; this task is typically handled by a product manager, who prioritizes the requirements and communicates with the developer(s).
2. Delivering functioning code early and often.
3. Using proven software components wherever possible, minimizing the need to write new code.
4. Focusing on the user experience, which is much more critical in hosted and mobile applications than in traditional desktop applications.
5. Addressing robustness, scalability, performance, and power consumption for their application.

One key aspect of the process is to create a development environment that both supports collaboration among members of the development team and augments the coding activity. For example, Google provides Android Studio, a software development kit (SDK) for Android applications that builds on the Eclipse development environment. The SDK contains many elements that simplify the creation of the Android user interface and the connection to runtime libraries.

Programming support such as that provided by Eclipse is complemented by tools for version control, configuration management, and collaboration, simplifying the task of building versions of the evolving product. This set of tools encompasses issue tracking, project management, and build management, and are typically complemented by user interface design tools, testing tools, and more, depending on the nature of the application.

Here the differences from the CMMI model become apparent. While the CMMI identifies 22 different process areas, the typical startup may only address four of them: requirements development, configuration management, product integration, and product quality assurance. An important shortcoming of the CMMI is its failure to directly address both the necessary skills for the development team and the use of automated tools to support the development process. A complete, integrated development environment, covering the various steps needed to develop and release a product, can save substantial amounts of time and effort in creating a software product. In short, the CMMI is "overkill" for a startup from a process perspective, but also ignores the critical role of team talent and development environments in creating a productive setting for product development.

1.6 Agile Development Processes

The set of critical activities listed above strongly suggests that startups must use a very different approach to software development than is typical of waterfall-based processes. That approach must balance severe time constraints with some fundamental principles and best practices for software development.

Over the past 15 years, startups (as well as many established companies) have adopted an "agile" approach to software development, based on the principles set forth in the Agile Manifesto [1], which can be summarized as follows:

1. Capture requirements at a high level.
2. Keep [eventual] users involved.
3. Allow the team to make decisions.
4. Develop incremental releases, then iterate, with a focus on frequent delivery.
5. Complete each feature before moving on to the next one.
6. Integrate testing throughout the product life cycle.
7. Maintain a cooperative and collaborative approach among all stakeholders.

Note that there is an implied process associated with the principles in the Agile Manifesto, but that the degree of management is intentionally light. In this sense, these principles are at the heart of an LC process.

In addition to the process-related concerns addressed by the agile approach, the character of modern hosted and mobile applications has driven new philosophies about software development. Among the most notable changes from traditional approaches are the following:

1. Documentation is sharply reduced.
2. Working code is emphasized.
3. Continuous user involvement is essential.
4. The integrated development environment takes on greater importance.

Of the numerous development methods to have emerged from the transition to agile methods, Scrum has gained the widest acceptance. In the Scrum approach, a designated product owner has responsibility for defining features and priorities for development and represents the customer for the emerging product. The product owner is also responsible for tracking the features to be implemented, known as the product backlog, and expressed as a set of user stories. The development team is coordinated by a Scrum Master, who serves as a "coach" whose goal is to encourage the team to improve their practices and performance. The team is self-organizing, and is responsible for implementing user stories, thus adding new functionality to the product.

The product development process is a sequence of "sprints," where the team implements a set of user stories from the product backlog based on the importance of the stories from a customer perspective. Each sprint may last a week or two, allowing the team to view their ongoing progress through brief daily meetings and other communication. Short sprints assure frequent releases of the product, which can lead to valuable feedback during the ongoing development process. Such an approach is the complete opposite of the waterfall approach, where customer feedback is only gathered at the very end of the development process.[6]

---

[6]Some traditional software product companies are beginning to release alpha and beta versions of their products, with the goal of obtaining such feedback before the final version of the product is "frozen."

Along the same lines, the concept of Lean Software Development aims to reduce "waste," i.e., unneeded activities, from the development process [9]. Naturally, there is some disagreement as to which activities are wasteful, but the overall point remains that organizations, especially small ones, must focus on a handful of key activities that are essential to their primary goals of continuous development and release.

1.7 When Startups Grow up

Successful startups grow into larger businesses. While that is a highly desirable transition for the company's founders and early-stage employees, the success brings a set of new challenges. Many of these challenges go beyond software development processes, but have both a direct and an indirect impact on processes.

First, the people who join an established business are different from those who start the company or take a risk on the company when its future survival is still highly uncertain. It takes time for new developers to learn the technology of the existing product, and to fit into the emerging company culture. More importantly, though, building a well-functioning development team means increased systematization of the development and release activities, and often re-architecting of the product to meet future needs. Second, the company has customers and users, who have wishes and expectations about product direction and new features. These concerns will influence the product roadmap, the engineering activities, and the release schedules. Third, business issues, including issues related to hiring, sales, and funding, all place time demands on people, with the result that developers spend less time writing code. Finally, the structure of the company changes, as departments emerge from the initial core team, with likely changes to company leadership. It is not uncommon for founders to leave the company or to take on new roles at this stage.

Above all, the product development team becomes more constrained in what they can do. In the early stages of the company, when there are few, if any, customers, the product team can pivot from one product idea to another, and can pursue the evolving vision of the product owner. Once there are users and customers, that freedom is sharply reduced, and the process for development changes from one driven by the product owner to a more inclusive approach reflecting the potentially conflicting needs and wishes of many people.

At the same time, though, the company is likely to retain its agile approach to product development. First, that approach is part of the company's culture and heritage. Second, the recruiting process for new developers will require previous experience with agile approaches. Third, the company has developed a development environment and internal procedures that enables them to continue following an agile process.

Finally, most customers welcome the regular delivery of new functionality, as long as the new features do not "break" existing features and functions. That is a big change from the historical approach where companies building software for enterprises (companies, government, universities, etc.) would make one major and one minor release each year. Minor bug fixes were deferred to a future release and the development organized hoped that no emergency patches would be needed in the interim, since they were expensive.

1.8 Conclusion

In summary, high-ceremony processes are increasingly limited to a niche category of software development, where contractors use a set of key process areas to assess the qualifications of competing suppliers. Those organizations competing for contracts in that environment must put extensive (and possibly expensive) processes in place so that they can win business against their competitors.

Product development businesses do not have the constraints imposed by a supplier assessment process, as used by the CMMI and similar evaluation approaches. Their goal is to build a successful and profitable business by delivering high quality products to a marketplace. That requirement forces them to build their products as efficiently as possible, and to have a product development process that addresses market and customer needs and wishes. These companies have found that agile processes for development are much more effective than are traditional waterfall-based processes for today's applications, as long as they adhere to the principles of agile development and do not devolve into an uncontrolled set of changes to their applications.

The nature and structure of these modern applications is central to the success of agile methods. These applications are no longer monolithic, but rather a distributed system where the development team focuses on core functionality, and integrates that code with third-party components to build out the complete application.

The low-ceremony processes that emerged from the agile approach to software development are well-suited to this style of incremental development, since it enables large software products to be developed iteratively as a sequence of short-term projects. As a result, many existing development organizations are seeking to make their processes more agile so that they may develop successive versions of their products more efficiently. For this reason, combined with the smaller size of many modern applications, low-ceremony processes are likely to prevail for future software development processes.

References

1. Agile Alliance: Manifesto for Agile software development. http://agilemanifesto.org (2001)
2. Blank, S., Dorf, B.: The Startup Owner's Manual: The Step-By-Step Guide for Building a Great Company. K & S Ranch, Pescadero (2012)
3. Boehm, B.: A spiral model of software development and enhancement. Computer **21**(5), 61–72 (1988)
4. Burns, E., Prakash, W.H.: Continuous Integration in Practice. McGraw Hill Osborne Media, New York (2013)

5. Chrissis, M.B., Konrad, M., Shrum, S.: CMMI for Development: Guidelines for Process Integration and Product Improvement, 3rd edn. Addison-Wesley Professional, Reading (2011)
6. Humphrey, W.S.: Characterizing the software process: a maturity framework. IEEE Softw. 5(2), 73–79 (1988)
7. Humphrey, W.S.: Managing the Software Process. Addison-Wesley Professional, Reading (1989)
8. Naur, P., Randell, B.: Software engineering. Technical report, NATO Science Committee (1969)
9. Ries, E.: The Lean Startup. Crown Business, New York (2011)
10. Sutherland, J.: Scrum: The Art of Doing Twice the Work in Half the Time. Crown Business, New York (2014)
11. Wasserman, A.I.: Toward a discipline of software engineering. IEEE Softw. 13(6), 23–31 (1996)

Chapter 2
The Right Degree of Agility in Rich Processes

Philipp Diebold and Thomas Zehler

Abstract Many companies that change their development process to agile later adapt these methods to their specific needs, take a step back to traditional processes, or do not continue their agile initiative. Particularly in light of the huge diversity of domains from information systems to embedded systems, it is necessary to find the right degree of agility for each context. Our goal is to describe how agility can be integrated into rich processes. Bringing the advantages of these two organizational worlds together should result in a useful, pragmatic, and feasible solution. This integration can be performed using two different approaches: revolutionary and evolutionary. In the revolutionary approach, an agile method is introduced to replace the current development process. In the evolutionary approach, the existing process is enhanced with appropriate and beneficial agile aspects. Both of these approaches have advantages for specific domains or contexts. After comparing the two approaches and related implementations of the revolutionary approach, this chapter focuses on the integration of agile practices, a specific evolutionary approach, due to the lack of existing research. With our comparison on the basis of the advantages and disadvantages of these two integration approaches, their detailed description, and some related implementations, we provide a foundation for further investigation in the field of combining agile and rich processes to find the right degree of agility.

2.1 Introduction

Modern society and our daily lives are characterized by a rapidly changing, fast responding world. Particularly in information system domains, with their development of apps for smartphones or other devices, time to market is one of the most important development factors (in addition to customer satisfaction).

P. Diebold (✉) · T. Zehler (✉)
Process Management, Fraunhofer Institute for Experimental Software Engineering (IESE),
Fraunhofer-Platz 1, 67663 Kaiserslautern, Germany
e-mail: philipp.diebold@iese.fraunhofer.de

T. Zehler
e-mail: thomas.zehler@iese.fraunhofer.de

© Springer International Publishing Switzerland 2016
M. Kuhrmann et al. (eds.), *Managing Software Process Evolution*,
DOI 10.1007/978-3-319-31545-4_2

For this reason, issues such as long development time, customer involvement only at the beginning of a project, no transparency, and expensive changes have emerged as problems and, around the turn of the millennium, had a tremendous impact on how software development is done. A community came up with the idea of agile software development to solve these development problems [9]. This way of development started in certain companies that improved their development process using agile software development in their specific context [36, 37]. Then other companies jumped on the bandwagon to get the same improvement. Since that time, the popularity of this way of development has started to grow, companies have tried various methods in agile software development, and now agile development has become mainstream [32].

Besides this process-related trend, software development has also become increasingly important for embedded software, embedded systems, cyber-physical systems, or systems of systems in recent years. This means in effect that the importance of combining hardware and software as well as that of combining several systems (including software as part of the systems) from the domains of information and embedded systems has also increased.

In these different areas of growth, agile software development and its various agile methods tend to be stretched to their limits because they were originally designed for information (software) systems [7] and not for embedded systems or the combination of systems. For example, more or less all agile methods include preconditions such as small teams ideally located in one common room [48], which is a challenge considering today's global and distributed development with outsourcing and subcontracting [39, 42]. This also complicates collaboration and communication, which cannot be carried out by exchanging artifacts or documents because these are not in the focus of agile development. For this reason, embedded domains still use traditional rich development processes with their particular benefits and have only a minor tendency to use agile processes in some parts [24].

The usage of different processes is mainly due to the huge diversity between the various domains or subdomains. Today, almost every domain somehow is involved with software, e.g., develops or uses it in some way or another. Nonetheless, different aspects such as domain requirements or various regulations that may also affect the development process characterize these domains. For example, in the development of safety-critical embedded systems such as medical devices, compliance with specific laws or process-related ISO standards, e.g., IEC 62304 [29], is required.

These different aspects (1) agile benefits, (2) agile problems in domains that are still working in plan-based ways, and (3) the varying characteristics of different domains led to the idea of making use of the benefits of both areas, rich as well as agile processes. Since none of them can be seen as a silver bullet for solving all problems, the two areas need to be integrated somehow because it is common that development projects need both agility and discipline [13]. For the remainder of this chapter, we use the term "agility" based on Boehm and Turner's [13] idea of flexibility, change, and reaction, as will be further elaborated in Sect. 2.2, where a detailed definition of agile software development will be given. For integrating agility into rich processes (which is more common than the other way around), there are generally two different types of approaches: the revolutionary approach and the evolutionary approach. In the revolutionary approach, agile methods are introduced and afterwards adapted to the specific context needs. In contrast, in the evolutionary approach, appropriate agile elements, e.g., agile practices, are integrated into the currently used development process. Even though both of these approaches support finding the right degree of agility in rich processes, their success depends on the specific context, such as the company, the specific project, or even the respective development team. Thus, the exact degree of agility for a process needs to be defined according to these aspects.

In this chapter, we address the topic of integrating agile methods and rich processes and discuss how to find the right degree of agility in rich processes. We will first present some background information on rich processes as well as agile methods. Based on this, the different approaches for integrating agile and rich processes will be described, and advantages and disadvantages will be discussed and extended with detailed implementations. Since the revolutionary approach is already covered in the literature and in practice, we present related work from these areas. In contrast, for the evolutionary approach, which is not covered much in research, we focus on the detailed implementation idea of agile practices as our integration approach. Finally, the chapter concludes with some aspects for future work regarding the integration of the two areas and our specific approach.

2.2   Background and Context

With regard to systematic procedures, which are one of the characteristics of engineering [28], software development lifecycles as well as processes feature prominently in software engineering. Lifecycles describe the general way of software development, such as development based on a waterfall or iterative lifecycle, or the spiral model by Boehm [12]. How the different lifecycles are organized in detail is most often defined in software development processes that are aligned with a specific lifecycle. In 1987, software processes were first deemed worth mentioning in a separate publication [37] because they were gaining more and more importance.

This chapter gives an introduction to the current state in the two different areas of software development processes currently existing, namely rich and agile software development processes. Besides some necessary definitions for aspects that will be regarded later on, this chapter contains basic information about the characteristics of these processes.

2.2.1   Rich Processes

The first of the two areas of software development processes that will be described are the so-called rich processes. These processes describe the traditional way of developing software. Based upon the concepts drawn from other engineering disciplines, these processes follow a sequence from requirements and design to implementation and quality assurance (incl. testing). Based on the considerations of Boehm and Turner [13], we define rich processes as follows:

Definition 2.1 (*Rich Process*) *Rich Processes* are systematic approaches that define how software or systems are developed over their whole lifecycle using the following engineering principles: focus on repeatability and predictability, permanent improvement processes, extensive documentation, up-front system definitions, and detailed plans (incl. workflow, roles, responsibilities, and work products).
(*Synonyms: Plan-based Processes, Structured Processes*)

Some examples in the area of the rich processes are the Rational Unified Process, most of its existing adapted variations, the German V-Model XT, as well as the Personal Software Process (PSP; [26]) and the Team Software Process (TSP; [27]), both created by Watts Humphrey in the 1990s. Still, the majority of rich processes are context-specific in-house approaches, which are not published at all.

As already mentioned briefly in the above definition, one of the main characteristics of these processes is their focus on a plan that is defined for the overall project before the actual start. This plan is usually built around some milestones that focus on documentation to verify the project's progress. The project is broken down step-by-step into tasks or activities that are analyzed in terms of concurrencies and dependencies in order to provide a schedule. The resources are allocated, the project starts and is then monitored regularly and controlled throughout the development. From our point of view, the following properties characterize rich processes:

- Fairly detailed planning, e.g., including project planning, resource planning, and milestones [34].
- A largely complete and detailed requirements specification [34].
- Systematic handling of requirements changes, e.g., changes only by means of defined change request processes.
- A sophisticated architecture that covers the majority of the requirements.
- Rather little customer involvement, predominantly during requirements elicitation [34].
- Often a systematic approach to quality assurance (verification and validation) and ongoing risk management.
- Regular process monitoring, controlling, and educating [34].

Rich processes are preferably used in practice when the majority of the requirements of the final product can be specified in the beginning [34]. This assumes that the project is predictable and it is therefore possible to plan and design the whole project up-front from beginning to end. The implementation is supported by concrete, standardized procedures that increase project transparency, improve project management, and sustainably increase the probability of success [46].

Summarizing, it can be observed that the majority of development processes belonging to the area of rich processes are rather "heavyweight" due to the detailed definition and performance of fine-grained activities, many different roles, and a lot of required documentation, e.g., customer requirements specification, functional specification document, technical architecture, and so forth. The advantage of this up-front planning is that it is suitable both for tenders and for contracts that need to cover a specific scope specified before the beginning of the project. Other strengths of rich processes, which are a consequence of their standardization, are the comparability and repeatability of stated activities. By defining how specific development activities are performed and how work products are formatted (e.g., by specifying templates), it is possible to move personnel quickly between different projects without the need for retraining [46].

Nonetheless, these different characteristics or at least parts of them are also reasons for criticism because they cause certain problems or lead to unattractiveness: The required documentation artifacts in rich processes, for instance, create a feeling of software bureaucracy [40]. Additionally, the customer involvement predominantly at the beginning often means limited feedback in later development stages; in the worst case only when the software has been fully developed [34]. This raises the issue of how to deal with (requirements) changes in later stages or even at the end of the project because formal change requests mean rework of all lifecycle phases, which leads to high costs [6]. This also makes rich processes somewhat sluggish because of the up-front detailed planning and activities that need to be followed.

Due to these different points of criticism, especially the issue of inflexibility, alternatives were needed in the software process world. Thus, agile software development emerged in the new era of software development processes.

2.2.2   Agile Processes

In contrast to the rich processes described above, the area of agile processes is relatively new. It became famous around the turn of the millennium when more and more different agile methods were invented [1]. This is called agile software development and can be defined as:

Definition 2.2 (*Agile Software Development*) *Agile Software Development* is the way of working in an agile manner, meaning in alignment with the core values and their refined agile principles of the Agile Manifesto [9], for example by using agile methods or, more specifically, agile practices.
(*Synonyms: Agile Software Engineering*)

The mindset of agile software development is completely different from that of development using rich processes and forms a kind of counterpart. All agile aspects (e.g., methods, practices, etc.) should focus more on:

1. Individuals and interactions between them.
2. Working software.
3. Strong customer collaboration.
4. Response to change.

These four core values are the foundation of agile software development and are defined in the Agile Manifesto [9] as an agile mindset independent of the large and growing number of agile methods. In addition, the Agile Manifesto also refines these into so-called agile principles:

Definition 2.3 (*Agile Principles*) *Agile principles* are the high-level ideas behind agile software development as refinements of the core values defined in the Agile Manifesto [9].

Based on the principles defined in the Agile Manifesto, all commonly known agile methods can be described as follows:

- Self-organizing teams.
- Evolutionary development with short iterations and release cycles.
- Active involvement of the customer with feedback.
- Simple reactions and quick changes without formal change requests.
- Simple design.
- Testing as a central point in the development.

All these characteristics result in slim and lightweight processes with few roles and artifacts as well as a minimum workflow. Especially the advantages of higher flexibility in combination with faster working software (elements), easier and efficient communication, as well as high transparency bring benefits to customers and other stakeholders.

Besides these characteristics, there are also certain preconditions that are needed to work with agile software development or to use the benefits of this type of development. Ideally, the development is structured into small teams (up to 10 people) who have the necessary qualifications and are located in one shared room. One of the main preconditions, which is often ignored and thus often results in problems, is the acceptance of this development idea and method(s) by the different levels of management [14].

Besides these management problems, which are often caused by the usage of traditional lifecycle models and the fear that changing the whole development process would require high effort, contracting is problematic in agile development [45]. The reason for this is that contracts are normally made on the basis of a mostly complete specification, which is often not available in agile projects. On the other hand, customers are skeptical regarding payment by working hours [38]. Despite refactoring, maintenance is an important topic because the less planned and continually evolving (architectural) structure causes high complexity and hard-to-understand software or system structures. All in all, the rising number of large projects (with long duration, high costs, and high risks) with larger teams often working in distributed environments complicates the use of agile development, e.g., by creating difficulties in communication [39, 45].

Even though agile software development has not only advantages, but also disadvantages, a large number of agile methods have been developed, modified, and enhanced in the last 15 years. The evolvement and history of the main agile methods are illustrated in [1]. In general, an agile method is defined as follows:

Definition 2.4 (*Agile Method*) *Agile Methods* are methods that define how software or systems are developed over the whole lifecycle or major parts of it using a specifically named set of agile practices.
(*Synonyms: Agile Processes, Agile Approaches*)

The most common examples from the huge list of existing agile methods are Scrum and eXtreme programming (XP). Nonetheless, as presented in all of the previous definitions, Scrum as the most frequently used agile method is not the same as agile development in general, which is a common mistake.

Similar to most software engineering methods, agile methods are defined in more specific details, building especially upon a set of very detailed and finely granular practices as defined above. Thus, we define agile practices as follows:

Definition 2.5 (*Agile Practice*) *Agile Practices* are established instructions, e.g., tasks, activities, technical aspects, or guidelines, with a specific focus or with an aspect in the development of software that is performed according to address one or less agile core values and agile principles.
(*Synonyms: Agile Techniques*)

The most common examples for practice are the 12 core practices of XP, which initially define a set of practices as the XP method. This is in contrast to most of the other methods, which define them implicitly. All these definitions and their connections are summarized in Fig. 2.1. The foundation for agile aspects used in practice, such as agile methods and agile practices, is the Agile Manifesto [9]. Here the core values form the basis for the more detailed and refining principles. The

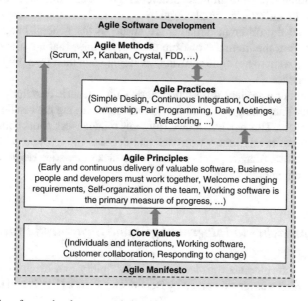

Fig. 2.1 Agile software development: relationships among different agile aspects

agile methods as well as the agile practices are both grounded on aspects defined in the Agile Manifesto. Agile methods, which are often frameworks for a set of agile practices, can be seen as being aligned more with the idea of agile development because most often they cover the whole lifecycle. In contrast, agile practices are meant for certain parts of the lifecycle; therefore, they might sometimes not be aligned with all the principles and core values.

2.3 Integration of Agile and Rich Processes

As already mentioned in the introduction and motivation of this chapter, combinations or integrations of agile and rich processes are needed in industry. Even though most of the companies from information systems domains claim to be using agile methods [47], most often Scrum, [19] as well as [22] confirm the experience made by many experts that these methods are adapted to the specific needs of the companies' and projects' contexts. Especially in embedded systems domains, which need to deal more with regulatory requirements than information systems, agility is not in such widespread use. Regulatory requirements, which are partly also domain-specific, include laws or standards that companies need to comply with. Since we deal with software or system development processes, we focus on process-related regulations, e.g., ISO/IEC 15504-5, CMMI [17], and others. However, there are also other standards that influence the development process, for example because they prescribe the use of specific techniques, such as the safety standard ISO 26262 [44] in the automotive domain. Due to all these different regulations, combining these various regulations with agility is a complex topic.

However, all the different domains are aware of the general benefits of agile development from the literature or from other companies that are already using it. Thus, they also want to use agile software development in their own projects to profit from these benefits.

To give a better overview, this section starts with a generic description of the two approaches for integrating agile and rich processes, including their main advantages and disadvantages. This will be followed by some related work about concrete implementations of the revolutionary approach and detailed information on how to deal with the integration of agile practices, due to the lack of existing research regarding this combination approach.

2.3.1 *Approaches to Integrate Agile and Structured Processes*

The trend that development projects need both agility and discipline (from rich processes), which was already noted by Boehm and Turner [13], is still ongoing and may not even have reached its climax yet. For this reason, this subsection focuses on the integration of agile methods and rich processes.

There are the two completely opposite approaches for how to technically[1] integrate the different areas, which are presented on a high level in Fig. 2.2, including their main flow: the revolutionary approach (Fig. 2.2, left part) and the evolutionary approach (Fig. 2.2, right part). To illustrate these two approaches in a graphical representation, we used colored puzzles because these offer a good way to represent different agile aspects, such as agile methods and agile practices. The complete puzzles represent the full development process or method, whereas the different puzzle pieces represent parts of them, such as specific techniques, e.g., for requirements engineering or coding.

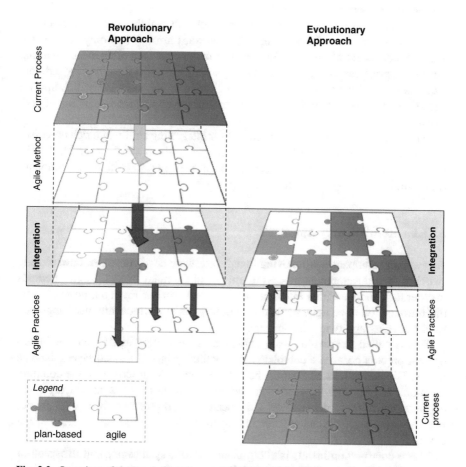

Fig. 2.2 Overview of the revolutionary approach (*left*) and the evolutionary approach (*right*) of the integration of agility into rich processes

---

[1]Not focusing on organizational improvement, e.g., by management versus developers.

In addition to horizontal separation, there is also vertical segmentation, containing five different layers representing different aspects of the development process (most of them already introduced in Sect. 2.2). The first and the last layer represent the current development process. In our figure, it is represented as a rich process because we are mainly focusing on the idea of bringing more agility into the current processes and therefore we start from the worst case: completely plan-based development. The second layer covers whole agile methods. In contrast, the fourth layer contains several different agile practices. In general, this layer covers all existing agile practices, but Fig. 2.2 only illustrates some of these, specifically those practices that are used for the final integration. The middle layer contains the integration of agility (agile methods in the revolutionary approach and agile practices in the evolutionary approach) into the current development process.

The figure shows that the revolutionary approach mainly covers layers one to three with a flow from the top (Fig. 2.2, downward arrows) and only brushes the fourth layer because of the adaptation of agile methods, which often means omitting some agile practices. Since the evolutionary approach works the other way around, it covers layers three to five with a flow beginning at the bottom (Fig. 2.2, upward arrows). Thus, both approaches end up at the third layer with the integration of both areas.

The details of how these two approaches for integrating agility into rich processes work will be explained in the following subchapters, which will focus on the details, advantages, and disadvantages of each approach. We will start with the revolutionary approach, followed by the evolutionary approach.

2.3.1.1 Revolutionary Approach

Today, many companies are moving to agile software development or have already switched their development process to use one of the many available agile methods in order to introduce agility into their development process. From our point of view, this introduction of an agile method is currently the most frequently used approach for introducing agility into a company.

This is called the revolutionary approach of integrating agility into the development process because a complete agile method (Fig. 2.2, second layer), such as Scrum, is practically used "out-of-the-box," meaning as described in the common literature, and replaces the current development process (Fig. 2.2, first layer) in the entire organization or department. This means that all processes from e.g., project management, requirements engineering up to implementation and integration are covered.

This is done predominantly in a "big-bang" sort of way, meaning that all aspects of the specific agile method are integrated directly into the company-specific development process. This integration approach, which can be seen as replacing the current process with an agile method, uses the method as given and does not adjust it, e.g., in order to address company- or project-specific needs.

In most cases, this results in various problems or challenges [34] because there are only few agile methods and even fewer domains or companies whose context is an exact fit for such a method, e.g., web development with frequent user feedback. This is why the revolutionary approach is most often followed by a second step with various adjustments of the agile method [22]. These are necessary to address company-specific aspects in the development process (Fig. 2.2, third layer). These adaptations range from changing variables in the agile method (e.g., sprint length) via replacing various aspects of the method with previously used aspects to merely removing various aspects (Fig. 2.2, fourth layer), such as daily stand-ups.

There are numerous examples, even from large companies such as SAP [25] or Yahoo [15], which have introduced agility exactly according to this procedure. Such concrete examples of the revolutionary approach used by large and well-known companies will be provided in Sect. 2.3.2. This chapter about revolutionary implementations will close with another case study with data from method adaptations by several companies and possible method adaptations that appeared after a revolutionary integration.

2.3.1.2 Evolutionary Approach

In contrast to the revolutionary approach, which is the most frequently used approach for integrating agility into a company, several experts have claimed [13] and empirical studies [22] have shown that appropriate enhancement for the specific context is more beneficial. Thus, the evolutionary approach for integrating agility into rich processes is used to address this issue.

The approach is called evolutionary because the current development process (Fig. 2.2, fifth layer) is enriched by a set of (from one to many) agile practices (Fig. 2.2, fourth layer) that are appropriate for the specific context, including company, project, and so forth. Therefore it directly ends up being a mixed process, with elements from the original process (most often rich) and elements from agile software development (Fig. 2.2, third layer), the appropriate agile practices. For frictionless performance of this approach, the current development process and the objective for the transition to agile are analyzed, suitable agile practices are identified, and those whose introduction represents an added value for the company, department, or project are integrated incrementally.

This can be compared to a modular system of individual building blocks (in our case: appropriate agile practices) that are selected according to certain criteria from a comprehensive pool of building blocks (in our case: the set of all agile practices). The consideration of company-specific aspects during the selection phase is very important to avoid rolling out inappropriate agile practices.

Because this approach for integrating agility into rich processes is not the most frequently used one, not much has been published about the procedure, about any case study, or even about specific approaches. However, from our point of view, this is a promising integration approach, especially for domains that are restricted by some kind of regulations. Therefore, Sect. 2.3.3 will focus on describing how to integrate agile practices into rich processes, respectively into their process descriptions/models.

2.3.1.3 Discussion of Advantages and Disadvantages of both Approaches

Based on the detailed descriptions of the two different approaches for integrating agility into current (most often) rich processes, we identified several advantages and disadvantages. These were classified into categories and are presented in Table 2.1 to allow easy comparison. In general, the comparison of the advantages and disadvantages in Table 2.1 shows that both approaches have their respective advantages and disadvantages. Therefore, the table shows that the different approaches work best in different contexts. When looking at the plain numbers of advantages and disadvantages, the evolutionary approach seems to dominate. Nonetheless, there is more to it than just the numbers because the different aspects also need to be weighted and are either positive or negative in different domains or contexts. Regarding availability, both approaches are assessed as positive because various agile methods and practices are available, although there are more practices than methods. Of these available agile aspects, documentation for the revolutionary approach is better because only a few of the many agile practices are documented well. The type of introduction or procedure for the two approaches varies and each approach performs better in different contexts. This is because the evolutionary approach is the more context-specific approach (by default) and can also be introduced step-by-step, unlike the revolutionary "big-bang" approach. This also makes the evolutionary approach more flexible. Only the documentation of the procedure is better in the revolutionary approach, which results from the good documentation of agile methods. A similar result is shown for the different advantages and disadvantages regarding organizational issues. This is because the revolutionary approach requires considerably more involvement of different people, including the management, and calls for major changes within a short time. The longer time and stepwise introduction of the evolutionary approach also increase the willingness of people to participate, which is partly due to the regular feedback and adaptation loops. Some of these organizational issues are strongly connected to management commitment, which is necessary for introducing agile methods. For agile practices, this depends on whether the single practice has only local effects or greater ones, e.g., on the whole development process. Compliance issues are only relevant for domains that are confronted with different regulations, but even then evolution is better than revolution because of the integrated customizability of the approach and the fact that, unlike agile methods, it does not require adaptation. Summarizing the advantages and disadvantages of the two approaches, the overall impression from the beginning has been confirmed with respect to better performance of the evolutionary approach. But the details in the discussion show that the differences are not as great as the numbers would lead us to expect.

Table 2.1 Comparison of the advantages (+) and disadvantages (−) of both integration approaches

Categories	Revolutionary approach: +/−		Evolutionary Approach: +/−	
Availability	+	Various agile methods available	+	Many various agile practices available
Documentation	+	Adequate documentation of best-known methods	+	Some individual practices are well documented
			−	Much of the practices are documented less or in an unstructured manner
Type of introduction	−	Introduction of methods is done in a "big-bang," with the risk that aspects may also be used that individually make no sense for the company	+	Company-specific adaptation and stepwise integration of individual agile practices is possible
	−	Major change of the complete development process from rich to agile is necessary	+	Integration of individual practices into the existing rich process (only minor changes required)
	+	The procedure for the introduction is defined by the introduction of characteristics of the method	−	Currently, there is no "blueprint" for how to select and adapt (tailor) appropriate agile practices to use them in a company from scratch
Flexibility of application	−	By default, methods are not tailored to concrete context needs, so adaptation is necessary	+	Stepwise selection of appropriate practices is possible, so it can be adapted better to specific needs
Organizational issues	−	The predominant part of the organization has to change towards agile	+	Need for change is initially restricted to the persons affected by the agile practices
	−	Rapid anchoring of the agile mindset throughout the organization is required	+	Organizational change to agility can proceed much slower because of stepwise introduction
	−	Reservations regarding major changes are more pronounced than for smaller, incremental changes	+	The willingness to participate in the change process is higher
			+	Small, iterative changes with regular feedback and adaptation loops are better suited for a successful change process
Management commitment	−	Is mandatory to fundamentally change the development process from rich to agile	+	Is not necessary if the effects of single agile practices are local
			+	Is necessary for agile practices with greater impact on the development process, e.g., if delivery times are affected
Compliance issues	−	If compliance is violated by the introduced agile method, individual aspects have to be added, changed, or deleted afterwards	+	Early consideration of compliance issues during the selection of the practices; no subsequent tailoring is required

2.3.2 Revolutionary Implementation

In this section, we will present experiences with respect to actual implementations of the revolutionary approach, which are mainly based on existing related work. We will present some industrial case studies that show their concrete revolutionary implementations and discuss some adaptations of Scrum, the most commonly used agile method.

Example 1 Our first example of an implementation of the revolutionary approach is that of SAP, a large German software company developing business information systems [25]. A few years ago they recognized that their development process was evolving along with the size, complexity, and scope of their products, but at the same time, development efficiency was becoming more difficult to attain. The processes for managing the growing number of projects grew as well, but the results did not meet the expectations. Thus, SAP decided to change their development model from a waterfall approach to agile software development, specifically Scrum. To accomplish this changeover, they restructured the organization from large functional silos to small, cross-functional, self-organizing teams, split work into small batches, split development time into fixed iterations, and broke the high-level release backlog up into detailed backlogs. Still, they faced problems such as getting inferior quality. For this reason, they adapted Scrum to their specific needs, for example by adding additional agile skills, e.g., test-driven development or pair programming.

Example 2 Yahoo as a well-known software company provides another example of this approach to agility integration [15]. Until 2004, their developers had used a managed software product development process very similar to the waterfall approach, including many (quality) gates and sign-offs, which resulted in huge dissatisfaction and high levels of burnout and turnover. Because of this and ignorance of the more traditional rich process, after some initial negative experiences and skepticism regarding agile development in discussions with agile experts, they tried Scrum with some volunteers in a pilot program launched in 2005, including two different cases, to see its benefits. One of these two teams failed because they saw agile as a way to correct deficits, which resulted in many challenges. However, at the end of the initial pilot period, a positive conclusion was drawn. The feedback from the team that liked the process and the experience was mostly positive, and the management also saw positive results [10]. Beyond that, other teams were beginning to express interest in developing in an agile way. So the program was expanded and a few years later, when agile development was at its height, many teams in the company reported using Scrum. However, in part the initial release planning they used was still very much a waterfall process [16]. Based on this large roll-out of Scrum, Yahoo recognized that their main problems lay in scaling the success of single agile teams. Therefore, they tried several adaptations in parallel. During these different adaptations, which were mainly refinements, they found some other problems, e.g., backlog controlling, which they needed to face. Even though they are still doing agile development and benefit from its advantages, during their top–down integration they adapted the methods to their specific needs, e.g., mandatory sprint breaks after five or six sprints, and partially integrated aspects from previous development processes.

Example 3 Our third example of this kind of revolutionary implementation is again an introduction of Scrum into the identity management business unit of the BMC group [41]. Several years ago, certain specific teams started working on their own in a Scrum fashion. Because this worked quite well for these teams, they transformed their whole organization (this business unit) into agile, specifically using Scrum as a method. Nonetheless, they had some problems within their distributed development environment that they needed to face. After gathering and analyzing all the data, they came up with some changes and specific adaptations to their Scrum implementation. They mainly built a regular "Scrum-of-Scrums," called "Nested Scrum," and additionally created a validation team for dealing with planning and integration aspects. This is a perfect example of our revolutionary approach because during their final process implementation, they did, for example, reintegrate further planning aspects from rich processes development that they had used before their process change.

Practitioner Perspective In addition to these detailed descriptions of implementations of the revolutionary approach in industrial companies, Diebold et al. [22] performed a multi-case study about how practitioners modify Scrum such that it fits their respective company or project context. Most of the companies covered in this case study introduced original Scrum. However, when this was compared with the current process, several deviations, variations, and adaptations were revealed. Thus, all of the considered companies introduced agility using a revolutionary approach.

All in all, these different examples of the introduction of an agile method and/or the final variation compared to the original method or approach found in the literature show how often revolutionary approaches for integrating agility into the development process are employed.

2.3.3 Evolutionary Implementation

As already stated at the beginning of this chapter, not much literature exists about the evolutionary approach. This is the reason for us to focus on this approach and to describe the implementation of one evolutionary approach, focusing on agile practices, their concepts, and their integration. The agile practices are the core concept of every evolutionary approach. Although agile practices are so important for the integration of the two areas, most practitioners and researchers focus on agile methods in their publications instead of on agile practices, which is a huge gap in agile software development. In the academic literature, only very little is being published and then only about some specific, very common practices, such as Pair Programming [49]. A first systematic review of the (academic) literature specifically focusing on agile practices was published as a mapping study [19]. In contrast to this academic literature, the internet provides a little more information about agile practices. For example, some lists or collections of agile practices are provided in blogs or on other websites, e.g., "The Big List of Agile Practices" [3] or "Guide to Agile Practices" [2].

Nonetheless, almost all of the existing lists of agile practices are either incomplete, as they just cover a small set of agile practices, unstructured, or without any description. To support evolutionary implementation with agile practices, our approach needs a repository containing all common agile practices in a structured and unique description or schema. Therefore, the following paragraphs will present details about our schema for describing agile practices in a repository to support our evolutionary implementation: a graphical schema representation, a detailed explanation of the elements of the schema, and an example.

Our schema for describing and presenting agile practices, presented in Fig. 2.3, is based on a UML representation [36] in order to allow using inheritance and aggregations (similar to UML class diagrams). In general, the graphical representation shows the different elements for describing agile practices in detail. During the development and piloting of this schema, some of the elements evolved into being mandatory and others into being optional. This is represented by the UML cardinalities of the different elements at the top level. Detailed descriptions of the different schema elements are provided in Table 2.2.

One of the mandatory elements in the schema, which is also very important for the integration of practices into processes, is the lifecycle process. This element can serve as a classification mechanism for the practices. For this reason, we reused the common classification from ISO/IEC 12207 [30], which also serves as a foundation for several other standards and their process classification, such as ISO/IEC 15504 [31]

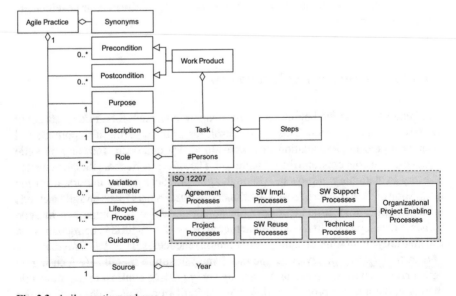

Fig. 2.3 Agile practices schema

Table 2.2 Detailed description of the schema elements, including information about whether they are mandatory (M) or optional (O), their description, and their connection to the common process modeling language SPEM

Schema elements	M/O	Description	SPEM
Name	M	Information about how the different practices are called	✓
Synonym(s)	O	Information about possible other names for this agile practice. This content can be seen as a kind of alternative to the name element	–
Precondition	O	Information about aspects that need to be fulfilled before the described practice can start. The most prominent kinds of preconditions are specific work products, which are, for example, used by the practice as its input	(✓)
Postcondition	O	Information about aspects that need to be fulfilled after the described practice is finished. Similar to the precondition, work products that are created or changed by the practice are examples of the output of this element	(✓)
Purpose	M	Short description that provides information about the main aim that is achieved by this practice. Should only be a few (1–2) sentences long	✓
Description	M	Detailed description of the agile practice. In addition to the purpose (short description) that is covered, it describes how the specific practice works. Thus, the description element could be refined by a set of tasks. If there is a need to further refine such a task in more detail, a task can subsume a number of steps	(✓)
Role	M	Detailed description of specific role(s) needed to perform the agile practice or some subtasks. For this reason, the schema also shows a connection to the tasks (sub-elements of the description). Because sometimes a role is not enough, the role element is refined by the number of persons performing the specific role; e.g., Pair Programming needs two developers	✓
Variation parameter	O	The variation parameter describes the possibilities of changing or adapting the described practice regarding specific aspects. The most prominent example is the interval length of an iteration, which is given in the Scrum Guide [43] as 4 weeks max., but is often changed to other intervals	–
Lifecycle process	M	Information about the different lifecycle processes that are addressed or covered by the agile practice. We decided to go for ISO12207 [30], its processes categories, and processes because it is a common standard that is also used by other regulations	–
Guidance	O	Sometimes it is possible for a practice to be supported by some kind of guidance that includes additional information. Examples of such kinds of guidance are guidelines, templates, checklists, tool mentors, estimates, supporting materials, reports, concepts, etc. [35]	✓
Source	M	Defines the origin where we found the description of the practice. This may be a literature source, a website, or any other kind of source. To see how recently this practice was developed, adapted, or updated, we also consider it beneficial to provide the year this source was published	✓

Table 2.3 Example instantiation of the agile practices schema: pair programming

Schema elements	Description
Name	Pair programming
Synonym	Pairing; peer programming
Precondition	Available requirements and architecture/design
Postcondition	Code with high quality and shared knowledge regarding the written code
Purpose	Pair programming is a dialog between two developers simultaneously programming and trying to implement better software [8] with additional knowledge sharing
Description	In pair programming, two programmers develop software together as a pair on one workstation. The driver writes code while the other person, the observer, reviews each line of code as it is typed in
Role	(Two) developers
Variation parameter	Experience of the two developers: expert–expert, expert–novice, novice–novice
Lifecycle process	SW implementation processes: software implementation process, software construction process
Guidance	–
Source	[8]

or Automotive SPICE [5]. Additionally, such a classification also offers the possibility to visualize all the practices in the categories, as done, for example, with landscapes in the German V-Model XT [46].

Based on these different descriptions, Table 2.3 presents Pair Programming as an example of the filled schema because it is one of the best documented and known agile practices. Even if this common example presented below gives an idea of how to use the *Agile Practices Schema*, it is not that easy to fill this schema consistently for all existing agile practices, e.g., the 40 h week from XP. For example, the description element cannot always be refined by tasks (Table 2.3).

During the development of this schema, it was important for the overall idea of integrating agile practices into processes, respectively their models or descriptions, to include an easy connection to common process modeling notations [23]. For this reason, we chose the Software & Systems Process Engineering Metamodel Specification (SPEM; [35]) as a connected modeling notation. The direct connections between elements (Table 2.3) are elements on the highest level of the schema that are also SPEM elements, whereas indirect connections are elements of our schema that are refined by elements that are also part of SPEM, e.g., work products as refinement of the pre- and postconditions or tasks as refinements of the description.

This link with a common process modeling language provides the necessary precondition for facilitating the integration of different agile practices into software development processes. The reason is that agile practices contain their information in a structured way, using work products as input and output with some kind of tasks in between, which can be directly integrated into the process in a number of ways (addition, replacement, etc.).

At the moment we are building, verifying, and finalizing a list of all existing agile practices aggregated from the different lists in existence, which will be published later on. All practices contained in this list should be described step-by-step using our schema to ensure that they are all described uniformly for the integration approach. Finally, the last step regarding agile practices that has to be explored is the missing objective evidence regarding their impact, which would be helpful for guiding the decision on which agile practice(s) to integrate.

2.4   Conclusion

This chapter dealt with the topic of the degree of agility that can be achieved in rich processes by integrating both rich and agile software development. This is motivated by the fact that there is no silver bullet for development processes, by the diversity of different domains, and by the possible benefit for both areas, meaning it is "necessary [...] having methods available that combine agility and discipline (plan-driven)" [13]. To discuss the idea of possible integration approaches, some terms were defined, such as agile methods versus agile practices. Regarding the integration of the two areas, two approaches—the revolutionary and the evolutionary approach—were defined and illustrated. These two approaches were discussed and compared in terms of their advantages and disadvantages.

The comparison showed that the evolutionary approach is more appropriate in various scenarios than the revolutionary approach, which is mainly the case because it works in a more context-specific way and can thus be adapted to the relevant needs. This makes introduction easier, allows more flexibility. Corresponding to that, Boehm and Turner [13] also state that extending a simple method or a rather small set of practices is better than tailoring an extensive method. This confirms the overall results of the comparison between the two approaches.

Although the revolutionary approach fits in other scenarios than the evolutionary one, we presented some related work regarding different revolutionary implementations from industrial practice. For the evolutionary implementation, we focused on the approach of integrating single agile practices into the current development process, presented a schema for describing the practices and easily integrating them into the process, and demonstrated this with an example.

Regardless of which approach is performed and which agile methods or agile practices are used in this approach, everything focuses on creating the right process for a particular context, as proposed in the past by Armbrust and Rombach [4]. At the end of this integration procedure, the final process is often published as a new specific process or method, e.g., Moonlighting Scrum [21] for specific team characteristics (distributed teams with part-time developers) or Agile V-Model [33] for specific domains, e.g., Medical. This method development confirms the statement that balanced methods have been successfully used and combined in a variety of situations [13]. But one question remains: Do we need more "specific" agile methods or would context-specific tailoring be more fruitful?

There is no single, general answer regarding how to find the right degree of agility because there is no silver bullet solution; solutions need to be defined for each specific context. Therefore, the best-suited degree of agility must be found for the respective context, e.g., by selecting the most appropriate agile practices. The two different integration approaches presented in this chapter provide support for selecting the right degree, especially the evolutionary approach, which works with fine-grained agile practices. Even if these two approaches with their detailed aspects regarding evolution with the practices are a first step, some work still remains to be done to improve support for selecting the right degree of agility.

2.5 Further Reading

For some of the aspects discussed in this chapter, further readings provide references, discussions, and future aspects.

First of all, the naming of the two different approaches—evolutionary and revolutionary—originates from the area of change management and is very common in this domain. Nonetheless, we also thought of other names that could be used interchangeably, see Table 2.4.

Even though the agile evangelists[2] believe that agile is so flexible that no definition is necessary or that a definition would not make much sense in this rapidly changing area, we believe that the different levels of agility (as partially started in [9]) need to be defined properly. During the elaboration of these different definitions of agile aspects, we also used [18] and their way of developing their definition as a kind of guidance for coming up with the different short definitions presented in Sect. 2.2.2. Furthermore, the definitions of agile practices and agile methods are inspired by [11].

The work regarding the synthesis or consolidation of agile practices started with a systematic mapping study [19] on a high level of categories for these practices. This was followed, on the one hand, by a multi-case study specifically for Scrum [22], which identified and reasoned on which Scrum practices are used or not used. On the other hand, we are currently building a set of all existing agile practices from common sources that mention agile practices or their synonyms (mainly websites or blogs).

Table 2.4 Naming and synonyms for the two different approaches	Revolutionary approach	Evolutionary approach
	Top-Down approach	Bottom-Up approach
	Big-Bang approach	Step-by-Step approach
	Up-Front approach	

---

[2]See Online http://www.arrowsgroup.com/services/agile-evangelist.

Furthermore, we are currently working on an "Agile Capability Analysis" as part of our evolutionary implementation to get a methodological foundation for selecting the most appropriate agile practices for a specific context. This analysis method should be based on the repository of these practices and the necessary company context, which could be characterized by several factors such as project size/type, criticality, or team size, as stated by Boehm and Turner [13]. Their approach also includes a model for defining the impact of the single agile practices [20] on these factors. To provide better support for this analysis and even for every evolutionary approach, knowledge or evidence about the impact of agile practices, e.g., on specific quality characteristics, costs, and time, would be beneficial. All this will result in a more detailed refinement of our evolutionary implementation.

Besides this more specific future work regarding our approach, there is still some open work regarding the alignment of the more technical integration approaches presented in this chapter and regarding organizational integration, which is often known as "change management" and can also be performed in a revolutionary as well as in an evolutionary manner.

Acknowledgments First of all, we would like to thank to Sofia Vidal for her support and help during the development and piloting of the Agile Practices List and Schema. In addition, we would like to thank Sonnhild Namingha and Jens Heidrich for their valuable comments and feedback. This research was conducted partly in the context of a Software Campus project funded by the German Ministry of Education and Research (BMBF grant no. 01IS12053).

References

1. Abrahamsson, P., Warsta, J., Siponen, M.T., Ronkainen, J.: New directions on agile methods: a comparative analysis. In: Proceedings of the International Conference on Software Engineering, pp. 244–254. IEEE, Washington, DC, USA (2003)
2. Agile Alliance Inc.: Guide to agile practices. http://guide.agilealliance.org (2013)
3. Appelo, J.: The big list of agile practices. http://noop.nl/2009/04/the-big-list-of-agile-practices.html (2009)
4. Armbrust, O., Rombach, D.: The right process for each context: objective evidence needed. In: Proceedings of the International Conference on Software and Systems Process, pp. 237–241. ACM, New York, NY, USA (2011)
5. Automotive SIG: Automotive SPICE process assessment model. In: The Procurement Forum (2010)
6. Balaji, S., Murugaiyan, M.S.: Waterfall vs. V-Model vs. Agile: a comparative study on SDLC. Int. J. Inf. Technol. Bus. Manage. 2(1), 26–30 (2012)
7. Baskerville, R., Pries-Heje, J.: Racing the E-Bomb: how the internet is redefining information systems development methodology. In: Proceedings of the IFIP TC8/WG8.2 Working Conference on Realigning Research and Practice in Information Systems Development: The Social and Organizational Perspective, pp. 49–68. Kluwer, B.V., Deventer, The Netherlands (2001)
8. Beck, K., Andres, C.: Extreme Programming Explained, 2nd edn. Addison-Wesley Professional, Reading (2004)
9. Beck, K., Beedle, M., van Bennekum, A., Cockburn, A., Cunningham, W., Fowler, M., Grenning, J., Highsmith, J., Hunt, A., Jeffries, R., Kern, J., Marick, B., Martin, R.C., Mellor, S., Schwaber, K., Sutherland, J., Thomas, D.: Manifesto for agile software development. http://www.agilemanifesto.org (2001). Accessed 29 May 2007

10. Benefield, G.: Rolling out agile in a large enterprise. In: Hawaii International Conference on System Sciences, pp. 461–461. IEEE Computer Society, Washington, DC, USA (2008)
11. Bleek, W.G., Wolf, H.: Agile Softwareentwicklung – Werte, Konzepte und Methoden. dpunkt.verlag (2008)
12. Boehm, B.: A spiral model of software development and enhancement. IEEE Comput. **21**(5), 61–72 (1988)
13. Boehm, B., Turner, R.: Balancing Agility and Discipline: A Guide for the Perplexed. Addison-Wesley Longman Publishing Co., Inc., Boston (2003)
14. Chow, T., Cao, D.B.: A survey study of critical success factors in agile software projects. J. Syst. Softw. **81**(6), 961–971 (2008)
15. Chung, M.W., Drummond, B.: Agile at Yahoo! from the trenches. In: Proceedings of the Agile Conference, pp. 113–118. IEEE, Washington, DC, USA (2009)
16. Chung, M.W., Nugroho, S., Unson, J.: Tidal wave: the games transformation. In: Proceedings of the Agile Conference, pp. 102–105. IEEE, Washington, DC, USA (2008)
17. CMMI Product Team: CMMI for development, version 1.3. Technical report, CMU/SEI-2010-TR-033, Software Engineering Institute, Carnegie Mellon University, Pittsburgh, PA. http://resources.sei.cmu.edu/library/asset-view.cfm?AssetID=9661 (2010)
18. Conboy, K.: Agility from first principles: reconstructing the concept of agility in information systems development. Inf. Syst. Res. **20**(3), 329–354 (2009)
19. Diebold, P., Dahlem, M.: Agile practices in practice: a mapping study. In: Proceedings of the International Conference on Evaluation and Assessment in Software Engineering, pp. 30:1–30:10. ACM, New York, NY, USA (2014)
20. Diebold, P., Zehler, T.: The agile practices impact model – idea, concept, and application scenario. In: Proceedings of the International Conference on Software and System Processes, pp. 92–96. ACM, New York, NY, USA (2015)
21. Diebold, P., Taibi, D., Lampasona, C.: Moonlighting scrum: an agile method for distributed teams with part-time developers working during non-overlapping hours. In: Proceedings of the International Conference on Software Engineering and Advances, pp. 318–323. IARIA XPS Press (2013)
22. Diebold, P., Ostberg, J.P., Wagner, S., Zendler, U.: What do practitioners vary in using Scrum? Agile Processes, in Software Engineering, and Extreme Programming. Lecture Notes in Business Information Processing, vol. 212, pp. 40–51. Springer International Publishing (2015)
23. Garcia-Borgonon, L., Barcelona, M., Garcia-Garcia, J., Alba, M., Escalona, M.: Software process modeling languages: a systematic literature review. Inf. Softw. Technol. **56**(2), 103–116 (2014)
24. Graaf, B., Lormans, M., Toetenel, H.: Embedded software engineering: the state of the practice. IEEE Softw. **20**(6), 61–69 (2003)
25. Heymann, J., Kampfmann, R.: SAP's road to agile software development. In: Future Business Software. Progress in IS, pp. 111–116. Springer International Publishing (2014)
26. Humphrey, W.S.: The personal software process. Technical report CMU/SEI-2000-TR-022, Software Engineering Institute, Carnegie Mellon University, Pittsburgh, PA (2000)
27. Humphrey, W.S.: The team software process. Technical report. CMU/SEI-2000-TR-023, Software Engineering Institute, Carnegie Mellon University, Pittsburgh, PA (2000)
28. IEEE: IEEE standard glossary of software engineering terminology. IEEE Standard 610.12-1990, Institute of Electrical and Electronics Engineers (1990)
29. ISO/TC 210: Medical device software – software life cycle processes. International Standard IEC 62304:2006, International Organization for Standardization (2006)
30. JTC 1/SC 7: Systems and software engineering – software life cycle processes. International Standard ISO/IEC 12207:2008, International Organization for Standardization (2008)
31. JTC 1 SC 7: Information technology – process assessment – part 5: an exemplar software life cycle process assessment model. International Standard ISO/IEC 15504-5:2012, International Organization for Standardization (2012)
32. Maurer, F., Melnik, G.: Agile methods: moving towards the mainstream of the software industry. In: Proceedings of the International Conference on Software Engineering, pp. 1057–1058. ACM, New York, NY, USA (2006)

33. McHugh, M., Cawley, O., McCaffcry, F., Richardson, I., Wang, X.: An agile v-model for medical device software development to overcome the challenges with plan-driven software development lifecycles. In: International Workshop on Software Engineering in Health Care, pp. 12–19. IEEE, Washington, DC, USA (2013)

34. Nerur, S., Mahapatra, R., Mangalaraj, G.: Challenges of migrating to agile methodologies. Commun. ACM **48**(5), 72–78 (2005)

35. OMG: Software & Systems Process Engineering Metamodel Specification (SPEM). Omg standard, Object Management Group (2008)

36. OMG: Unified Modeling Language (UML) ver 2.4.1. Omg standard, Object Management Group (2011)

37. Osterweil, L.: Software processes are software too. In: Proceedings of the International Conference on Software Engineering, pp. 2–13. IEEE, Los Alamitos, CA, USA (1987)

38. Paetsch, F., Eberlein, A., Maurer, F.: Requirements engineering and agile software development. In: Proceedings of the International Workshops on Enabling Technologies: Infrastructure for Collaborative Enterprises, pp. 308–313. IEEE, Washington, DC, USA (2003)

39. Ramesh, B., Cao, L., Mohan, K., Xu, P.: Can distributed software development be agile? Commun. ACM **49**(10), 41–46 (2006)

40. Scacchi, W.: Process Models in Software Engineering, pp. 993–1005. Wiley, New York (2002)

41. Smits, H., Pshigoda, G.: Implementing scrum in a distributed software development organization. In: Proceedings of the Agile Conference, pp. 371–375. IEEE, Washington, DC, USA (2007)

42. Sureshchandra, K., Shrinivasavadhani, J.: Adopting agile in distributed development. In: Proceedings of the International Conference on Global Software Engineering, pp. 217–221. IEEE, Washington, DC, USA (2008)

43. Sutherland, J., Schwaber, K.: The scrum guide. The definitive guide to scrum: The rules of the game. Scrum.org-October (2013)

44. TC 22/SC 32: Road vehicles – functional safety. International Standard ISO 26262:2011, International Organization for Standardization (2011)

45. Turk, D., France, R., Rumpe, B.: Limitations of agile software processes. In: Proceedings of the International Conference on eXtreme Programming and Agile Processes in Software Engineering, pp. 43–46. Springer (2002)

46. V-Modell XT Team: V-Modell XT. National standard, Federal Ministry of the Interior, Germany, Berlin (2013)

47. Version One Inc.: 9th annual state of agile survey. https://www.versionone.com (2015)

48. Williams, L., Cockburn, A.: Agile software development: it's about feedback and change. IEEE Comput. **36**(6), 39–43 (2003)

49. Williams, L., Kessler, R., Cunningham, W., Jeffries, R.: Strengthening the case for pair programming. IEEE Softw. **17**(4), 19–25 (2000)

Chapter 3
Assessing Product Development Agility

Daniel X. Houston and Stephen W. Rosemergy

Abstract Agile software development grew out of a variety of alternative software development methods that shared a common set of values and principles. After two decades with these alternative methods, agile software development remains loosely defined, but has been widely accepted. This acceptance has gained the attention of other fields with discussions of applying agile to their work, for example agile systems engineering and agile program management. However, within the larger field of product development, agility was defined in terms of software development, both in practice and in principle. This chapter focuses on a set of general agile characteristics derived from the agile values and principles embraced by many software developers. This set of characteristics provides a basis for (a) assessing difficulties in software development projects employing agile practices, (b) applying concepts of agility to other disciplines beyond software development, and (c) measuring agility. In addition to deriving general agile characteristics, this chapter relates two stories of agile methods adoption that illustrate both the need for and the utility of general agile characteristics.

3.1 Introduction

According to the American Society for Quality, the quality movement can be traced to the trade groups of medieval Europe in which craftsman organized into guilds that used strict rules for applications of their crafts. During the industrial revolution, factories produced more specialized work and, in the late nineteenth century, factory planning became a discipline for increasing productivity. In the early twentieth century, process improvement was formalized with time and motion studies and statistical quality control. In the mid-twentieth century, emphasis shifted to the quality of both production and produced items in the Toyota Production System, Total Qual-

D.X. Houston (✉) · S.W. Rosemergy
The Aerospace Corporation, Los Angeles, CA 90009-2957, USA
e-mail: dan.houston@aero.org

S.W. Rosemergy
e-mail: steven.rosemergy@aero.org

© Springer International Publishing Switzerland 2016
M. Kuhrmann et al. (eds.), *Managing Software Process Evolution*,
DOI 10.1007/978-3-319-31545-4_3

ity Management, ISO 9000 series of quality management standards, Six Sigma, and Lean Product Development [1].

Viewed in the broadest context of development and production processes, contemporary system and software development share the ancestry of the quality movement. In balancing concerns for product quality, technical features, cost and timely completion, and productivity, emphasis has varied over the centuries, especially in the last century. The nascent agile movement that was underway in the early 1990s in business and manufacturing [13] had a coincident expression in alternative software development methods that later came to be grouped under the label "agile." This movement exhibited another emphasis in product development, one focused on flexibility and leanness [8]. Conboy [8] systematically developed a definition of agility based on these two concepts of flexibility and leanness. In this chapter, we take an alternative approach and develop general characteristics of agility based on experiences with the alternative software development methods that were distilled in the Agile Manifesto of 2001 [3].

3.2   Background and Context

The agile movement in product development has been fueled particularly by the field of software development. Software development was dubbed "software engineering" in 1968 and major advances in the ways of producing software took on the character of large engineering programs with the specification of requirements, design of architectures and details, and implementation followed by stages of integration and testing. The ability for an organization to develop software according to engineering methods was canonized in standards and in levels of capability maturity. However, the poorly understood dynamics of product development that challenges most engineering endeavors were especially troublesome in software projects, which—due to software's less tangible nature—seem to amplify the effects of "inadequate" prescriptive planning.

During the 1990s, some software developers reacted against the generally accepted engineering approach and tried various alternative practices and techniques. Methods such as eXtreme Programming, Scrum, Feature Driven Development, and Crystal Clear arose in this period, each with its own discipline for developing software. As these methods and their practices were published, software development groups began to embrace them. The authors of the various alternative methods convened in 2001 to produce the well-known Agile Manifesto, with a set of values and principles that called for a re-evaluation of software development processes. A later entry was Lean Software Development, which abstracted principles from the Toyota Production Systems and applied them to software development.

After 2001, the various alternative methods began to be referred to as agile methods with development groups referring to themselves as "agile." As the agile movement gained prominence, less and less attention was given to the disciplines underlying each of the methods. Thus the agile software development movement has exhibited a tendency toward homogenization of the different methods that gave rise to it. Today, agile software development is a mindset with a set of values, principles, and practices, but does not prescribe a particular process or set of processes.

With increasing acceptance of agile values, principles, and practices, several phenomena have occurred.

- Concept adaptation. In recent years, the idea of agile development has been applied widely, both within and outside the field of product development. Within product development, agile concepts have been applied to software requirements, systems engineering, product architecture, project management, and process improvement. Outside the field of product development, agile concepts have been applied to enterprises, business intelligence, supply chains, defense acquisitions, research methodology, and so forth.
- Agile precedents. Students of agile methods have found software development programs that preceded the current agile movement, but can now be described as agile. Duvall [11] provides eight examples of DoD programs that exhibited agile characteristics well before the agile movement in software development. Reagan and Rico [23] provide a similar list.
- Research growth. Because agile software development was largely a practitioner-led movement, it received almost no attention from academic researchers prior to 2001. Between 2001 and 2005, 36 empirical studies were found [12]. A 2012 study of agile methods research demonstrates growing research attention [10].

These phenomena all affect the meaning of "agile." Broad application of agile concepts has resulted in semantic inflation: agile development no longer refers clearly to the software development methods from which it arose. Similarly, searches for precedents have found agile characteristics in development programs of previous decades. On the other hand, research counters semantically inflationary effects by requiring clear definitions for the sake of answering questions such as "What constitutes agility?" "Under what circumstances is agility beneficial?," and "How does one become agile?" This chapter is motivated by the first question and seeks to address that question with derivation of a set of agile characteristics and a proposal for using the characteristics to answer other research questions.

3.3 Software Development Dynamics and the Need for Agility

The agile movement in software development arose out of need to harness the dynamics of software development beyond what software engineering had accomplished. The dynamics that drive product development projects out of control are amplified in software development because software is less tangible and unconstrained by physics. Therefore, functional specifications are more likely to over-reach what can be accomplished realistically with available resources while underestimation is more likely. Furthermore, functional changes are expected to be easier in software than in hardware. This section offers a brief explanation of software development dynamics

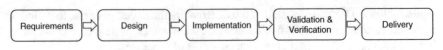

Fig. 3.1 A plan-driven process

that is intended to demonstrate the need for the agile movement and provide some hints as to what allows agility to work.

In the engineering or plan-driven approach to developing software-intensive systems, plans are made for producing a system with specified functional capabilities and a sequence of steps is followed, at least at a high level (Fig. 3.1). However, Fig. 3.1 does not show the rework cycles, both within and between development phases.

Rework cycles in product development have been studied extensively in the System Dynamics Modeling community. The underlying problem with most product development plans is that they measure progress based on the plan and are unable to account for product quality and undiscovered rework in their progress measures. Consequently, quality shortcomings accrue until the need for rework delays progress. The product development rework cycle (Fig. 3.2) has come to be recognized as the central structure for modeling development projects because it is the most important feature for explaining project behavior.

Consider the rework cycle in a plan-driven process. For rework that is found in-phase, for example design errors found in the design phase, delays are incurred, but the cost of rework can be relatively low. For problems found in later phases (highlighted arrows in Fig. 3.2), the delays are much longer and the rework costs much higher. For example, a misinterpretation of a requirement that is not discovered until V&V testing means reworking artifacts in all phases from requirements through V&V. Changes to requirements during development produce rework that propagates through the development process. To complicate the project, delays put the project under schedule pressure. Developers working under schedule pressure are more likely

Fig. 3.2 The product development rework cycle

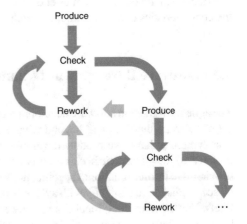

Fig. 3.3 An agile process

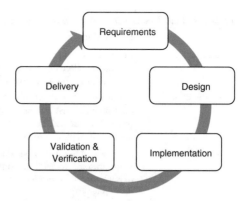

to make errors and to skip quality-inducing steps, such as peer reviews of work, thereby increasing the cycling of rework.

Agile software development, first and foremost, accepts changes as a fact of life and seeks to incorporate them in an ordinary workflow. Thus, the moniker, "agile." To accomplish the goal of an agile development process, the development cycle is scaled down to produce a smaller working product in a shorter amount of time. The sequence of phases is visited in every delivery cycle (Fig. 3.3). By approaching development incrementally and delivering an increment of system capability, say every few months, the rework cycles are dramatically shortened. Rather than building up schedule pressure over many months and incurring all its corrosive effects, delays are absorbed prior to each release by delivering only as much working functionality as possible. Thus, agile trades off a commitment to a delivery date against a plan-driven commitment to required functionality.

3.4 Development Challenges and Agile Methods

Since the Agile Manifesto, its proponents argue that the key to building better software is to view it not as a destination, but as a journey supported by underlying values and principles that deemphasize (but do not eliminate) practices and work products associated with project management best practices [7]. After more than two decades of discussion, debate, and informative evidence, we continue to debate the merits of agile software development. Both proponents and opponents agree that agile methods provide benefits in the forms of improved communication, team coordination, increased customer focus, less process overhead, and improved predictability [18].

Nonetheless, practitioners report issues (Table 3.1) that may be perceived as insurmountable challenges to agile software development teams, most notably project scaling, use of geographically distributed teams, cultural barriers to successful adoption, and applicability of agile principles to other technical domains [4, 8, 18]. Even though these challenges are reported often, examples of overcoming them success-

Table 3.1 Perceived issues that plague agile teams [17]

Issue	Description
Project scaling	Increasing team size also increases the amount of interaction required to coordinate, allocate, and integrate work between team members. Coordinating change across a large team is difficult [18]
Distributed teams	Frequent team interactions are not always possible with geographically distributed teams; remote teams lack the necessary accessibility to the product owner and are unable to develop and maintain the level of contextual expertise required to support the project [8, 18]
Culture change	Adoption of agile methods decentralizes day-to-day decision-making. Decentralized decision-making breaks down functional/hierarchical silos; organizational hierarchies are large impediments to decentralized decisions [19]
Technical domain	Agile methods are not applicable to non-software development or multidiscipline projects [8]

fully are available [6]. The following story illustrates the use of agile software development principles in addressing one of the most common challenges, geographically distributed teams.

3.4.1 Project Scaling and Geographic Distribution

Company A was a mid-size (8000 employees) software company that developed small-business software products. Based out of San Jose, California, they also employed an offshore team located in Hong Kong. This team provided specialized expertise in support of product internationalization. The remote team used Scrum very successfully for integrating application content and layout to support foreign language usage in U.S. markets. The San Jose team was happy with both the responsiveness and quality of the work delivered by the remote team. With the expanded language support of their products, demand for products tailored to locales outside the United States increased.

3.4.1.1 Transitioning to Global Product Development

Because Company A architected their system as a product line, whereby core assets could be quickly applied for new variant products [15], they were confident that their product was well positioned to address global markets. Having proven their ability to support Internationalization, Company A expanded the scope of the team in Hong Kong, to address International markets, starting with Asia (Fig. 3.4).

The two teams met in San Jose, agreed to continue using Scrum for their development method, e-mail and Skype for collaboration, and a common infrastructure for

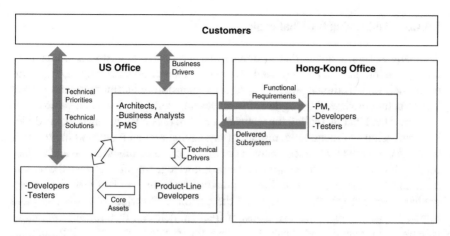

Fig. 3.4 Company A globalization

storing source code and documentation, instead of transferring files between sites. The San Jose team would host daily meetings, and because of time-zone differences, the Hong Kong team would shift their workweek by one day (Tuesday through Saturday).

3.4.1.2 Global Software Development Challenges and Agile

Although work progressed on schedule for each of the teams, trouble began as the San Jose team integrated and tested the software developed by the remote team. As both the frequency and severity of problems rose, tension between the two teams mounted. Daily standup meetings increased in length from 20 min each to 1.5 h, with most of the time devoted to reporting on status.

In trying to understand their problems, the company initially assumed that the scope of their endeavor (large-scale software development) and geographically distributed development were a mismatch with their agile method. They called for a face-to-face meeting of key contributors in San Jose where the two teams gathered at a local hotel to share their concerns. Their findings, which were consistent with other software development companies managing geographically distributed projects [19], did not point to agile development practices as the source of their problems. Rather, they indicated a failure to adhere to the principles of agile software development as they expanded their efforts. Specifically, the San Jose team had ignored the impacts of their locale-specific organizational constructs and delegated responsibility in what seemed the most expedient manner, not cognizant of the effects on the remote team. Changes were neither well-coordinated nor welcomed across teams, and interactions between teams became increasingly transactional, with emphasis placed on status rather than cooperation and collaboration.

3.4.1.3 Addressing the Challenges

Company A soon realized that in order to be responsive to customer needs, both locally and internationally, they needed to realign their efforts. In doing so, they evaluated their organizational structure, project responsibility partitioning, and project infrastructure in view of the agile software development principles and values.

They found that by scaling the teams in the most expedient manner, that is dividing responsibility functionally, instead of organizing around motivated individuals, they had inadvertently formed organizational barriers to communication and collaboration. Furthermore, collaboration and tacit knowledge transfer between the remote team and the customer was no longer practical because they had placed an intermediary between the remote team and the customer. So while both the local and remote teams embraced the principles of frequent delivery, face-to-face communications, and measured and constant progress, the remote team became information-constrained and were trusted only to organize themselves around the functions they were to deliver to the project. Both teams depended on each other to deliver, but neither team, particularly the remote team, had the authority or access to evolve the requirements, architecture, and designs.

After realizing their mistake, Company A revised its organizational structure (Fig. 3.5). The new organizational model established three distinctly separate development teams, one at each locale, and a product-line team, managed by a single team distributed across the two locales. In addition, Company A co-located architects, business analysts, and project manager in each locale—with responsibility partitioned by customer product, rather than by functional responsibility [20].

To anchor implementation efforts across teams, the Product-Line Development team established a continuous integration environment and collaboration environment to link communication, configuration management, and testing, and deployment of software releases [20]. Scrum Master roles were tailored to facilitate cross-team

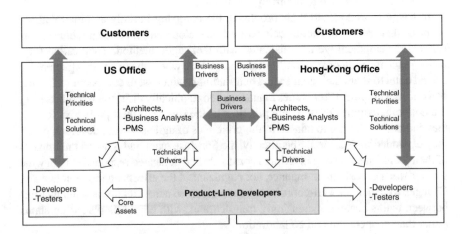

Fig. 3.5 Company A's revised organizational model

coordination and collaboration, surface problems during coordination meetings, and to remove barriers [2].

The preceding story demonstrates that impediments to agility can be difficult to identify, much less, solve. Had this organization not revisited the principles and values of agile software development, they might have concluded incorrectly that agile methods could not work for their business or that globalization was incompatible with their business objectives. Not all software development is well suited to agile practices and not all software organizations are disposed to employing agile methods. Nonetheless, the story suggests that periodically revisiting principles of agile software development can help a software business using agile practices recognize ways in which development problems can be addressed. Taking this a step further, we propose that the values and principles of agile software development can be generalized so that they can be applied to other disciplines in product development. The following section pursues the question of the nature of product development agility in an effort to identify a set of general agile characteristics derived from software development experience.

3.5   The Nature of Product Development Agility

The task of characterizing product development agility can be pursued in different ways. Conboy [8] takes a conceptual approach to developing a definition and taxonomy of agility by starting with its conceptual underpinnings and progressing through 16 steps. This chapter takes another approach that builds on the distilled experience of agile software development. The agile software development values and principles are distillations of the experiences of the practitioners of agile methods. Although the methods, and the practices that comprise them, are the building blocks of the agile software development movement, the values and principles have provided the movement a unifying identity.

3.5.1   Agile Values, Principles, and Practices

The self-dubbed agile alliance defined itself through values and principles. These were published as fixed lists [3], in contrast with practices often embraced by agile methods. Although lists of agile practices are available, the lists are not definitive because agile software development is not limited to any particular practices. In fact, whatever practices promote agility in a given circumstance may be regarded as agile practices. Furthermore, some agile practices originated decades earlier in the history of software development. Therefore, any published list of agile software development practices remains open-ended, guided by the values and principles as well as empirical success. For this reason, we focus on the values and principles for deriving general characteristics of agility.

Table 3.2 Agile software development principles

Issue	Description
Continuous value delivery	Our highest priority is to satisfy the customer through early and continuous delivery of valuable software
Welcome change	Welcome changing requirements, even late in development. Agile processes harness change for the customer's competitive advantage
Frequent delivery	Deliver working software frequently, from a couple of weeks to a couple of months, with a preference to the shorter timescale
Business-developer collaboration	Business people and developers must work together daily throughout the project
Motivation centricity	Build projects around motivated individuals. Give them the environment and support they need, and trust them to get the job done
Face-to-face conversation	The most efficient and effective method of conveying information to and within a development team is face-to-face conversation
Progress measure	Working software is the primary measure of progress
Constant pace indefinitely	Agile processes promote sustainable development. The sponsors, developers, and users should be able to maintain a constant pace indefinitely
Technical excellence	Continuous attention to technical excellence and good design enhances agility
Simplicity	Simplicity—the art of maximizing the amount of work not done—is essential
Self-organizing teams	The best architectures, requirements, and designs emerge from self-organizing teams
Reflect and adjust	At regular intervals, the team reflects on how to become more effective, then tunes and adjusts its behavior accordingly

Table 3.2 lists the principles of agile software development, preceded by phrases used in Table 3.3. Table 3.3 relates the values and principles, indicating the degree to which the principles address or explicitly support the values. For example, "continuous value delivery" strongly supports "working software." Séguin et al. [25] performed a similar assessment of correspondence between the principles and values. In terms of correspondence, Table 3.3 agrees with their results in 96% of the cells.

Table 3.3 indicates that the values are not supported equally by the principles. Not only does each value statement represent a prioritization, but the set of principles represents a prioritization of the four values: "individuals and interactions" and "working software" are more supported by the principles than "responding to change" and "customer collaboration."

Agile software development started with practices that sought to improve the production of software. Some of the practices, such as pair programming and story point estimation, were created to satisfy a specific objective. Others, such as iterations and test-driven development, were refined from ideas used in early computer program-

Table 3.3 Agile values and principles matrix (●: major, ◐: moderate, and ○: minor support)

Agile software development principles	Agile software development values			
	Individuals and interactions over processes and tools	Working software over comprehensive documentation	Customer collaboration over contract negotiation	Responding to change over following a plan
Continuous value delivery		●	◐	◐
Welcome change			●	●
Frequent delivery		●		◐
Business-developer collaboration	●		◐	
Motivation centricity	●			
Face-to-face conversation	●		○	
Progress measure		●		
Constant pace indefinitely	◐		◐	
Technical excellence		●		
Simplicity		●		◐
Self-organizing teams	●	◐		
Reflect and adjust	●			◐

ming. Still others, such as coding standards and software configuration management, were simply included from accepted software engineering practice. As practices were created or appropriated, and refined, they were collected and their use integrated into methods or processes. Agile software development practices continue to evolve, guided by the values and principles.

With alliance of the "agilists" and identification of the various alternative software development approaches as "agile," the practices formerly identified with each method have become pooled as agile software development practices. Consequently, when members of a software development group describe themselves as "agile," they must further explain the practices they employ. Referencing a specific agile method may be helpful also.

3.5.2 Deriving General Agile Characteristics

The matrix of Table 3.3 indicates intersections that can be aggregated and abstracted to produce general characteristics of agility beyond software development. Abstracting these characteristics should also remove overlaps in the values and principles. The following list of general agile characteristics (GAC) was abstracted from the agile values and principles.

- Interpersonal interaction
- Working product or service
- Customer/user collaboration
- Responsiveness to change
- Continual delivery of customer value
- Self-organizing, multifunctional collaboration
- Leadership by the motivated
- Technical excellence and simplicity

Table 3.4 uses a checkmark (✓) to relate these characteristics to the agile software development values and principles (a) to demonstrate that the characteristics cover the values and principles, and (b) to define the meaning of each characteristic in terms of the values and principles.

3.5.3 Comparison of General Agile Characteristics with Other Sources

Turner [31] has also produced a list of key characteristics of agile software development though he does not provide a derivation for his list.

- Learning attitude
- Focus on customer value
- Short iterations delivering value
- Neutrality to change (design processes and system for change)
- Continuous integration
- Test-driven (demonstrable progress)
- Lean attitude (remove no-value-added activities)
- Team ownership

This list compares well with the preceding list, though the two lists have a few differences. Turner's list does not explicitly include product characteristics of technical excellence and simplicity, but it does include "learning attitude," which may refer to learning about both the product under development and the development processes employed. Also, Turner's list does not mention leadership motivation. His list does introduce lean attitude as a willingness to remove non-value-added activities.

Table 3.4 General agile characteristics defined from agile software development values and principles

Agile software development values and principles	General agile characteristics						
	Interpersonal interaction	Customer/user collaboration	Responsiveness to change	Continual delivery of customer value	Self-organizing, multifunctional team	Leadership by the motivated	Technical excellence and simplicity
Individuals and interactions	✓	✓					
Working software					✓	✓	✓
Customer collaboration	✓	✓	✓	✓			
Responding to change		✓	✓	✓	✓		
Continuous value delivery		✓	✓	✓			
Welcome change			✓				
Frequent delivery				✓			
Business-developer collaboration	✓				✓	✓	
Motivation centricity					✓	✓	
Face-to-face conversation	✓	✓		✓			
Progress measure				✓			
Constant pace indefinitely	✓		✓	✓			
Technical excellence	✓						✓
Simplicity	✓						✓
Self-organizing teams	✓				✓	✓	
Reflect and adjust	✓				✓	✓	✓

Diebold and Zehler, Chap. 2, also produced a list of characteristics that they claim describe all known agile methods. They say that these characteristics are based on principles defined in the Agile Manifesto, but do not offer a derivation.

- Self-organizing teams
- Evolutionary development with short iterations and release cycles
- Active involvement of the customer with feedback
- Simple reactions and quick changes without formal change requests
- Simple design
- Test as central point in the development

This set of characteristics compares well with the derived set of GAC. With the exception of Interpersonal Interaction and Leadership by the Motivated, a one-to-one correspondence can be drawn between the derived general characteristics and Diebold and Zehler's set.

Conboy's [8] Taxonomy of Information Systems Development (ISD) agility provides another example of a set of characteristics of agility.

1. To be agile, an ISD method component must contribute to one or more of the following:

   a. Creation of change
   b. Proaction in advance of change
   c. Reaction to change
   d. Learning from change

2. To be agile, an ISD method component must contribute to one or more of the following, and must not detract from any:

   a. Perceived economy
   b. Perceived quality
   c. Perceived simplicity

3. To be agile, an ISD method component must be continually ready, i.e., minimal time and cost to prepare the component for use.

Conboy derived his taxonomy rigorously from definitions of "leanness" and "flexibility" rather than from agile values and principles. Consequently, it has a different structure than the previous sets of characteristics of agility. Nonetheless, it provides a useful set of characteristics for comparison.

Comparing the four sets of agility characteristics, several observations can be made.

- Only the GAC explicitly lists "interpersonal interaction," a strong motivator in the agile software development movement for increasing agility by reducing documentation. Table 3.3 illustrates that this value underlies six of the principles, so the other sets of characteristics likely treat this implicitly as an enabler of other characteristics.

- Turner [31] and Conboy [8] each include similar characteristics that the other two sets do not include. Turner includes "lean attitude (remove no-value-added activities)" and Conboy includes "perceived economy." These do not trace directly to agile values and principles, but do trace to an agile method, Lean Software Development, and to one of Conboy's starting concepts, "leanness."
- Another characteristic that Turner and Conboy include, but is not included in the other two sets, is learning: "learning attitude" (Turner) and "learning from change" (Conboy). In addition to Conboy's derivation, this characteristic is traced to the agile principle of "reflect and adjust."

3.6   Agility and Other Endeavors

A general set of characteristics provides a basis for discriminating between conformance and nonconformance to an ideal: a product development program can be described as agile to the extent to which it exhibits the characteristics. Thus, one can use such a set of characteristics to assess, at least qualitatively, whether a development program is behaving as an agile program is expected to behave. Because the set of characteristics is generalized, this included not only software development, but also other types of development programs. Furthermore, the set of characteristics could serve as a basis for developing a quantitative measure of agility.

To illustrate how we can use these characteristics to evaluate the degree of agility, we will examine the use of agile methods in the context of another domain: highly regulated systems development.

3.6.1   Development Process Agility in Highly Regulated Environments

Company B was a small (200 employees) bio-tech software start-up based in North America. Their primary product offering was an enterprise medical informatics diagnosis and digital record keeping software system. In spite of its relative size, Company B dominated the clinical informatics industry by virtue of its patented high-performance image streaming and business process automation technology. Company C was an established international medical device company, with over 100,000 employees worldwide. In addition to medical imaging devices, Company C sold enterprise business process automation tools, similar to that of Company B. However, Company C's product offering was not competitive due to Company B's patented streaming technology, which gave Company B a market share advantage of more than 40 % over Company C.

In order to gain market share in the clinical informatics industry, Company C acquired Company B. Company C had a reputation for delivering high-quality, innovative products to the marketplace. Moreover, because the European medical industry is highly regulated, Company C had established corporate-wide engineering policies, documented practices, and work product standards that ensured both transparency and compliance with IEC 62304 standards for medical device software development [14]. In contrast, Company B had used test-driven development (TTD) methods, with an emphasis on test automation. Having already built a testing infrastructure to accommodate both regression testing and just-in-time product enhancements, Company B delivered new capability for customer evaluation every four weeks. Company C, concerned for the success of their acquisition and the perceived risk of delivering new capability compliant with IEC and ISO standards, (a) investigated the possibility of imposing any mandates on the TDD team and (b) sought to learn from the software development successes of Company B.

Through interviews with Company B's software development team, and assessments of their product related work products, Company C found the following strengths:

1. While company B placed less emphasis on developing detailed documented requirements, they were able to trace driving requirements from user stories, to test cases, to documented design decisions (through both their feature tracking tools and the source code), and finally to test results.
2. Architectural decisions and constraints, while discussed only in face-to-face forums, were well understood by all internal stakeholders (well beyond the software engineers).
3. Product implementation followed establishment of requirements mandates and constraints through the creation and execution of tests, each of which served as a mechanism for demonstrating technical progress and achievement of both quality attributes and functional requirements alike.
4. Customers drove feature innovation, based on real-world use and evaluation of prototypes. Company B's mechanism for evaluating product features with customers, early and often, pruned unimportant features from the product line.

On the other hand, Company C found that although Company B products were not subject to medical device regulatory standards (ANSI, AAMI, IEC, and ISO) [24], they were not compliant with corporate IT safety standards (IEC 60950-1). Also, they found no mechanisms for demonstrating compliance with regulatory requirements if they chose to integrate their medical imaging products directly with Company B products.

3.6.2   Addressing Regulatory Concerns with an Agile Process

Company C's evaluation of Company B's practices and work products found that B's practices served as a motivating force for innovation, collaboration, and the delivery of both high-quality and marketplace-relevant products. They also determined that dismantling B's approaches could put the company acquisition at risk. The biggest

Fig. 3.6 Pre-acquisition company product development comparison using general agile characteristics

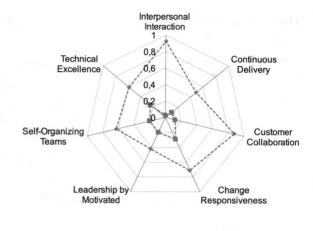

<!-- radar chart labels: Interpersonal Interaction, Continuous Delivery, Customer Collaboration, Change Responsiveness, Leadership by Motivated, Self-Organizing Teams, Technical Excellence; scale 0, 0,2, 0,4, 0,6, 0,8, 1 -->

--◆--Company B Pre-acquisition   --■--Company C Pre-acquisition

challenge they faced was incorporating ISO and IEC medical device safety compliance standards, so they approached B's development team and asked them how they could demonstrate compliance with these regulatory standards while maintaining the general characteristics of agility.

Company B's development team reviewed both the regulatory standards and Company C's compliant practices against the general agile characteristics. Next, the team engaged Company C's compliance experts and developers to assess all development practices (of both companies), using the agile general agile characteristics (Fig. 3.6). Understanding that relative agility was not reflective of product quality, together they found significant differences with respect to development practices, each of which either promoted or inhibited the general agile characteristics. Next, the team evaluated the regulatory constraints and requirements to determine the extent to which they might inhibit (or possibly promote) development agility. Together they determined the following points.

1. They could, with careful attention, maintain performance that exhibited all the general agile characteristics.
2. TDD provided the infrastructure for demonstrating compliance with regulatory requirements but required some enhancements to be fully compliant.
3. With the help of good coaching and an embedded subject matter expert, they could demonstrate traceability to regulatory and safety standards at each delivery, and the acquiring organization could adopt agile practices.
4. Integration with external safety critical software/hardware would need to be decoupled architecturally to ensure that their certification would not impede the deployment of new products.

Fig. 3.7 Pre-acquisition and post-acquisition company product development comparison using general agile characteristics

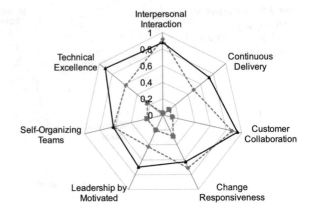

-•••Company B Pre-acquisition -■••Company C Pre-acquisition
-•-Post-acquisition ACE

3.6.3 Epilogue: Further Adoption of Agile Approaches

After finalizing the acquisition of Company B, Company C created a new business unit to house its medical informatics product suite, and then incrementally migrated its existing customer base to the acquired product suite. Within two years, the financial performance of the new business unit eclipsed the combined performance of all Company C's other medical business units.

Under stakeholder pressure to improve the financial performance of the other business units, Company C embarked on a two-year plan to adopt agile methods on all software-intensive systems. To this end, they created an Agile Center of Excellence (ACE) led by a long-time Company C leader. Because the company was more than 100 years old, this action met with initial resistance and distrust. After four years of coaching and mentoring both leaders and individual contributors (more than 5000 employees), the company has strongly embraced agile approaches to product development, as shown in the results of an assessment against general agile characteristics (Fig. 3.7). In terms of business value, the company attributed its profits to their "Agile Renewal."

3.7 Measurement of Agility

The preceding story demonstrates the value of using GAC as a basis for measuring agility. Measurement of agility has been a topic of discussion in product development [29] and production research [30] for over a decade. In software development circles, a number of agility measures have been discussed in various forms and for various purposes.

- Datta [9] has proposed an Agile Measurement Index based on five software project dimensions, for use in selecting a development methodology.
- Bock [5] suggests Agility Index Measurements for comparing capabilities of software development teams using seven scales.
- Seuffert [26] uses an 11-item questionnaire to measure degree of agile adoption.
- Kurian [16] produced a fuzzy model for measuring agility based on seven project characteristics.
- Lappo and Andrew [17] categorize agile goals and offer an example of collecting data for assessing a goal.
- Shawky and Ali [27] produced a measure of change rate, or entropy as an indicator of agility.
- Qumer and Henderson-Sellers [22] developed a four-dimensional framework (4-DAT) for evaluating the degree of agility in agile methods.

Of these six proposals, the first, the fourth, and the seventh hold the most promise. They are based on project characteristics, recognize degrees of agility, can produce leading indicators, and can be extended beyond software development. However, the first of these three have two shortcomings: (1) neither use characteristics that have been verified as dominant variables for measuring product development agility; and (2) the scales and mathematical models employed by each require validation for their ability to produce meaningful measures. Using the Agile Manifesto as a starting point, Tables 3.3 and 3.4 have sought to address the first shortcoming with a set of characteristics that are clearly traceable to a widely accepted set of values and principles that define agile software development. The second aforementioned shortcoming remains to be addressed.

The seven proposals indicate needs for measuring agility and hint at some of the potential benefits. One of the benefits would be overcoming the popular misconception of a binary approach to agile development: either a development organization is agile or it is not. Measureable definitions of agility would recognize that organizations demonstrate degrees of agility and would facilitate discussion of those degrees.

Another benefit of measuring agility is technical definition. "Agile" is a word so broadly used that its meaning has been overly inflated. Ironically, it fails to carry substantial meaning for people who must manage technical development processes. Measurement of agility would provide a technical basis for the term and support clear communication about the merits, shortcomings, and suitability of development processes. Measurement of agility would lend objectivity to a number of practical concerns, from guiding and supporting process improvement decisions, to choosing a development method for a specific project, and to choosing the best group for a development project.

Each agile software development method is usually recognized by its practices, but practices may be modified to fit a particular circumstance (a combination of development organization, customer, software type, product domain, contract, regulations, and so forth). In a multi-case study of Scrum projects, Diebold and Zehler,

Chap. 2, found deviations, variations, and adaptations of Scrum. When such variations are undertaken, the question may arise as to the ability to perform agilely. As the preceding story illustrates, measuring agility from a set of characteristics can produce valuable results.

3.8 Conclusion

Product development always requires balancing concerns for cost, duration, features, and product quality. Although business and manufacturing had begun developing agile production concepts, the authors of the agile manifesto took a step forward by producing a set of values and principles based on a decade of experience using various alternative software development practices and methods. From those values and principles we have distilled a set of general agile characteristics and demonstrated the usefulness of these characteristics in facilitating software-intensive systems success. As general characteristics, they can be applied to other product development domains. More importantly, they provide a basis for judging the agility of a particular development process. The stories in this chapter suggest that qualitative assessments are the usual means of judging process agility, but some work has pursued quantification. More work is necessary to develop good measurement scales based on general agile characteristics.

3.9 Further Reading

Balancing Agility and Discipline: A Guide for the Perplexed, by Barry Boehm and Richard Turner, shows that agile and disciplined methods lie on a continuum. They have worked out guidelines for determining where on the continuum a project lies and how agile or disciplined a method must be.

For readers interested in degrees of agility, we recommend the following works cited in the References section: Conboy [8], Chow and Cao [6], and Qumer and Henderson-Sellers [22]. Qumer and Henderson-Sellers [21] provide more background on the 4-DAT analytical framework for evaluating methods from the perspective of agility in their article. Sheffield and Lemétayer [28] discuss factors that indicate software project agility and project success.

"The Right Degree of Agility in Rich Processes," by Diebold and Zehler, is the Chap. 2 in this volume. It discusses two approaches, evolutionary and revolutionary, to integrating of agile software development practices into a structured process.

References

1. American Society for Quality: ASQ history of quality. Available from http://asq.org/learn-about-quality/history-of-quality/overview/overview.html
2. Bass, J.: Scrum master activities: process tailoring in large enterprise projects. In: Proceedings of the International Conference on Global Software Engineering, pp. 6–15. IEEE, Washington, DC, USA (2014)
3. Beck, K., Beedle, M., van Bennekum, A., Cockburn, A., Cunningham, W., Fowler, M., Grenning, J., Highsmith, J., Hunt, A., Jeffries, R., Kern, J., Marick, B., Martin, R.C., Mellor, S., Schwaber, K., Sutherland, J., Thomas, D.: Manifesto for Agile Software Development. http://agilemanifesto.org (2001)
4. Begel, A., Nagappan, N.: Usage and perceptions of agile software development in an industrial context: an exploratory study. In: Proceedings of the International Symposium on Empirical Software Engineering and Measurement, pp. 255–264. IEEE Computer Society, Washington, DC, USA (2007)
5. Book, D.: Improving your processes? Aim high. http://jroller.com/bokmann/entry/improving_your_processes_aim_high
6. Chow, T., Cao, D.B.: A survey study of critical success factors in agile software projects. J. Syst. Softw. 81(6), 961–971 (2008)
7. Chrissis, M., Konrad, M., Shurm, S.: CMMI. Guidelines for Process Integration and Product Improvement, 2nd edn. Addison Wesley, Boston, MA (2007)
8. Conboy, K.: Agility from first principles: reconstructing the concept of agility in information systems development. Inf. Syst. Res. 20(3), 329–354 (2009)
9. Datta, S.: Agility measurement index: a metric for the crossroads of software development methodologies. In: Proceedings of the Southeast Regional Conference, pp. 271–273. ACM, New York, NY, USA (2006)
10. Dingsøyr, T., Nerur, S., Balijepally, V., Moe, N.B.: A decade of agile methodologies: towards explaining agile software development. J. Syst. Softw. 85(6), 1213–1221 (2012)
11. Duvall, L.: Be quick, be useable, be on time: lessons in agile delivery of defense analytic tools. 21st Century Defense Initiative Policy Paper (2012)
12. Dybå, T., Dingsøyr, T.: Empirical studies of agile software development: a systematic review. Inf. Softw. Technol. 50(9–10), 833–859 (2008)
13. Goldman, S., Nagel, R., Preiss, K., Dove, R.: Iacocca Institute: 21st Century Manufacturing Enterprise Strategy: An Industry Led View. Iacocca Institute, Bethlehem (1991)
14. ISO/TC 210: Medical device software – software lifecycle processes. International Standard IEC 62304:2006, International Standards Organization (2006)
15. Krueger, C.: Software product line reuse in practice. In: Procedings of the IEEE Symposium on Application-Specific Systems and Software Engineering Technology, pp. 117–118. IEEE, Washington, DC, USA (2000)
16. Kurian, T.: A fuzzy based approach for estimating agility of an embedded software process. http://www.siliconindia.com/events/siliconindia_events/Global_Embedded_conf/Globa_Embedded_Conf_PPT_final_tisni.pdf (2011)
17. Lappo, P., Andrew, H.: Assessing agility. Extreme Programming and Agile Processes in Software Engineering. Lecture Notes in Computer Science, vol. 3092, pp. 331–338. Springer, Berlin (2004)
18. Murphy, B., Bird, C., Zimmermann, T., Williams, L., Nagappan, N., Begel, A.: Have agile techniques been the silver bullet for software development at Microsoft? In: Proceeding of the International Symposium on Empirical Software Engineering and Measurement, pp. 75–84. IEEE, Washington, DC, USA (2013)
19. Niazi, M., Mahmood, S., Alshayeb, M., Rehan Riaz, M., Faisal, K., Cerpa, N.: Challenges of project management in global software development: initial results. In: Proceedings of the Science and Information Conference, pp. 202–206. IEEE, Washington, DC, USA (2013)

20. Phalnikar, R., Deshpande, V., Joshi, S.: Applying agile principles for distributed software development. In: Proceedings of the International Conference on Advanced Computer Control, pp. 535–539. IEEE, Washington, DC, USA (2009)
21. Qumer, A., Henderson-Sellers, B.: An evaluation of the degree of agility in six agile methods and its applicability for method engineering. Inf. Softw. Technol. **50**(4), 280–295 (2008)
22. Qumer, A., Henderson-Sellers, B.: A framework to support the evaluation, adoption and improvement of agile methods in practice. J. Syst. Softw. **81**(11), 1899–1919 (2008)
23. Reagan, R., Rico, D.: Lean and agile acquisition and systems engineering, a paradigm whose time has come. Defense Acquisition University, Defense AT&L (2010)
24. Rottier, P., Rodrigues, V.: Agile development in a medical device company. In: Proceedings of the Agile Conference, pp. 218–223. IEEE, Washington, DC, USA (2008)
25. Séguin, N., Tremblay, G., Bagane, H.: Agile principles as software engineering principles: an analysis. Agile Processes in Software Engineering and Extreme Programming. Lecture Notes in Business Information Processing, vol. 111, pp. 1–15. Springer, Berlin (2012)
26. Seuffert, M.: Agile Karlskrona Test. http://mayberg.se/archive/Agile_Karlskrona_Test.pdf (2009)
27. Shawky, D., Ali, A.: A practical measure for the agility of software development processes. In: Proceedings of the International Conference on Computer Technology and Development, pp. 230–234. IEEE, Washington, DC, USA (2010)
28. Sheffield, J., Lemétayer, J.: Factors associated with the software development agility of successful projects. Int. J. Proj. Manag. **31**(3), 459–472 (2013)
29. Sieger, D.B., Badiru, A.B., Milatovic, M.: A metric for agility measurement in product development. IIE Trans. **32**(7), 637–645 (2000)
30. Somanath, N., Sabu, K., Krishnanakutty, K.V.: Measuring agility of organizations - a comprehensive agility measurement tool (camt). Int. J. Innov. Res. Sci. Eng. Technol. **2**(1), 666–670 (2013)
31. Turner, R.: Toward agile systems engineering processes. CROSSTALK the Journal of Defense Software Engineering, pp. 11–15 (2007)

Chapter 4
Value-Driven Process Management

Christof Ebert

Abstract To survive in a fast-changing environment, almost all companies strive for continuous efficiency improvement, reducing the cost of non-quality and optimizing product strategies. Simultaneously, it is thus crucial to improve product strategy and the product development processes. However, such improvement programs often fail due to lack of leadership and organizational misalignment. Operational constraints such as project pressure, client interaction, and strategic dependencies are often neglected, thus making a proposed change program a mere theoretic exercise—without much buy-in from the trenches. Despite access to a substantial body of knowledge of methods such as Capability Maturity Model Integration (CMMI) and Six Sigma, many organizations still struggle in practice. Most organizations fail to align necessary transformations with concrete business objectives. This chapter shows how to set up and drive a value-driven process environment based upon explicit business objectives and how to deliver sustainable value. It goes beyond theoretical method frameworks and emphasizes hands-on change management. Value-driven process evolution underlines the need continuously to manage the transformation based on business objectives and operational constraints. From these, a specific and tailored approach toward achieving engineering excellence is derived. A case study shows how value-driven process management was used over a period of several years. Improving productivity and efficiency is selected as a hands-on example how practically to implement value-driven process evolution.

4.1 Introduction

Today's market for technical products is more competitive than ever. Many enterprises compete in a fluctuating and increasingly saturated market for narrow margins. Especially when the market fluctuation is running into "hard times" such as the economic crisis a few years ago or today's brutally competitive struggles, many companies find themselves in a fight for mere survival—and the urgency to reduce costs and optimize profits increases. Consequently, product development becomes

C. Ebert (✉)
Vector Consulting Services, Ingersheimer Straße 24, 70499 Stuttgart, Germany
e-mail: Christof.Ebert@vector.com

© Springer International Publishing Switzerland 2016
M. Kuhrmann et al. (eds.), *Managing Software Process Evolution*,
DOI 10.1007/978-3-319-31545-4_4

the focus of profit optimization, because many cost drivers of the final product, such as rework due to poor quality or production costs due to uncontrolled variants, are defined during development. Cost-reduction programs in product development often conflict with existing process improvement programs or limit activities of quality assurance such as peer reviews—but why? In some cases, these decisions are based on gut feelings, and, in other cases, there are simply no clear objectives or any convincing evidence on the positive effects of such activities within an organization.

Efficient software development and lifecycle management is a major asset on a global scale. In industrial and consumer sectors, it is increasingly software that defines the value of products. Today, value generation in the automotive and medical industries already depends over 50% on innovative software-driven technologies. Not surprisingly, engineering investments are heavily spent on software development of applications and products. In our fast-changing world, a company will only succeed if it continually challenges and optimizes its own engineering performance. At the same time, engineering of technical products is currently undergoing a dramatic change. Ever more complex systems with high quality must be developed at decreasing costs and shortened times to market. Competition is growing, and the entry barriers to established markets are diminishing. The result is more competitors claiming that they can achieve better performance than established companies. An increasing number of companies are aware of these challenges and are proactively looking at ways to improve the efficiency and productivity of their product strategy and development processes.

Business processes determine how things are done—end to end. They provide guidance to those who do and focus on what to do. Guidance means understanding and ensures repeatability. Focus means achieving targets both effectively and efficiently, without overheads, friction, and rework. Good processes are as lean and agile as possible, while still ensuring visibility, accountability, and commitment to results. Insufficient processes reduce business opportunities and performance due to not keeping commitments and delivering below expectations. Processes must be usable by, and useful to, both practitioners and managers. They must integrate seamlessly, and they must not disturb or create overheads. Often, processes gradually evolve, but without a big picture of overall business needs. They organically grow and gradually morph into a ballast rather than a value-driver.

Improvements must target value! There is no performance gain, if not measured and traceable to clear value improvement. One can always improve figures by polishing statistics and number-crunching, but this is lying to yourself and your stakeholders. We talk here about tangible value improvement in an economic sense.

What exactly is value? We can express value with in the economic perspective that we use in this chapter. The value of a product is an economic category that forms the basis for comparing and charging totally different supplies and services in a particular quantitative relationship to each other [4]. Value is a perception and exists only in the eyes of the beholder. Therefore, value is always quantifiable and expressed in monetary terms, i.e., the price, and is determined by the supply and demand. Business value is the value of a product for a business. It depends on the customer value, which is the perceived value in a market.

Organizations thus must *simultaneously* improve product strategy and related business processes, such as product development. However, such improvement programs often fail due to lack of leadership and organizational misalignment. Operational constraints such as project pressure, client interaction, and strategic dependencies are often neglected, thus making a change program a mere theoretic exercise—without much buy-in from the trenches. Despite access to a substantial body of knowledge of methods such as Capability Maturity Model Integration (CMMI) and Six Sigma, many organizations still struggle in practice. Most organizations fail to align necessary transformations with concrete business objectives.

Process management will fail if companies do not consider changing business requirements, such as digitalization. By focusing on the essence of the processes, integrating process elements with each other and providing complete tool solutions, organizations can tailor processes to meet specific needs and enable localized and problem- or skill-specific software practices, while still ensuring that the basic objectives of the organization are achieved.

This chapter shows how to set up and drive a change program based upon explicit business objectives and how to deliver sustainable value. It goes beyond theoretical-method frameworks and emphasizes hands-on change management. Value-driven process evolution underlines the need continuously to manage the transformation based on business objectives and operational constraints. From these, a specific and tailored approach toward achieving engineering excellence is derived. A case study shows how value-driven process improvement was used over a period of several years. Improving productivity and efficiency is selected as a hands-on example of how practically to implement value-driven process evolution.

> Let me close this section with a small side note for further reflection. As with all economic expressions and sober performance measurements, we should not overlook the much more relevant humanistic perception, as, for instance, that expressed by Antoine de Saint-Exupery, who observed *"Grown-ups like numbers. When you tell them about a new friend, they never ask questions about what really matters. They never ask: 'What does his voice sound like?' 'What games does he like best?' 'Does he collect butterflies?' They ask: 'How old is he?' 'How many brothers does he have?' 'How much does he weigh?' 'How much money does his father make?' Only then do they think they know him."* [6].

4.2 Implementing Value-Driven Process Management

Today, software is the major asset of many companies. In the industrial and consumer sectors, it is increasingly software that defines the value of products. For instance, value generation in automotive already depends over 50% on innovative software-driven technologies. Not surprisingly, engineering investments are heavily spent on the software development of applications and products. In our fast-changing world, a company will only succeed if it continually challenges and optimizes its own engineering performance. At the same time, the engineering of technical products is currently undergoing dramatic changes, such as for digitalization and enhanced services. Ever more complex systems with high quality must be developed at decreasing costs and shortened times to market. Competition is growing, and the entry barriers to established markets are diminishing. The result is more competitors claiming that they can achieve better performance than established companies. An increasing number of companies are aware of these challenges and are proactively looking at ways to improve the efficiency and productivity of their development processes.

Development processes along the product lifecycle determine how things are done—end to end. They provide guidance to those who do and focus on what to do. Guidance aims at understanding and ensures repeatability. Focus means achieving targets both effectively and efficiently, without overheads, friction, and rework. Good processes are as lean and agile as possible, while still ensuring visibility, accountability, and commitment to results. Insufficient processes reduce business opportunities and performance due to not keeping commitments and delivering below expectations. Processes must be usable by, and useful to, both practitioners and managers. Usable means that the process must be applicable in its intended purpose and environment. Useful means that it creates value if executed according to its intended purpose. Processes must integrate seamlessly, and they must not disturb or create overheads.

Process improvement will fail if we do not consider these basic requirements. By focusing on the essence of the processes, integrating process elements with each other, and providing complete tool solutions, organizations can tailor processes to meet specific needs and enable localized and problem- or skill-specific software practices, while still ensuring that the basic objectives of the organization are achieved.

To improve continuously and thus stay ahead of the competition, organizations need to change in a deterministic and results-oriented way. If you do not know where you are and where you want to go, change will never lead to improvement. Looking toward improved process maturity will help in setting up an improvement trail.

The concept of process maturity is not new. Many of the established quality models in manufacturing use the same concept. This was summarized by Philip Crosby in his bestselling book *Quality Is Free* in 1979 [2]. From his broad experiences as a senior manager in various industries, he found that business success depends on quality. With practical insight and many concrete case studies, he could empirically link process performance to quality. His credo was stated as *"Quality is measured by the cost of quality which is the expense of nonconformance—the cost of doing things wrong."* Or doing the wrong things—as the author with his strong business perspective observed in many companies which actually had leading processes and still failed in business.

Over half of all process improvement programs fail, as the author have observed in many companies over the past two decades [4]. Why is that? It is for two reasons, namely:

- Lack of systematic change management
- Insufficient leadership

Both observations have one common denominator. Many improvement activities have insufficient objectives and, for that reason, no motivation to change and no possibility to complete the implementation of changes. Projects without clear goals will miss their goals clearly, as Tom Gilb once stated. Value-driven process evolution is a goal-oriented improvement approach toward measurable and sustainable performance improvement. It has several components that distinguish it from the more traditional approach with a focus on certification and therefore insufficient buy-in from stakeholders:

- Align with business needs
- Incrementally deliver tangible progress
- Broaden the scope of the improvement project from engineering to a product and customer perspective
- Use methods such as Six Sigma as tools and best practices, but not as ends in themselves

Process improvement frameworks, such as Six Sigma and the Capability Maturity Model Integration (CMMI), offer the benefit of improving on a determined path, to benchmark with other companies, and to apply worldwide supplier audits or comparisons on a standardized scale. Combined with value-driven process improvement, they provide the "tools" to implement changes, whereas value-driven process improvement ensures staying on track and delivering the right results in due time.

Fig. 4.1 Value-driven process improvement: seven steps to success

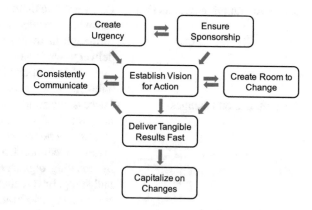

Figure 4.1 shows the basic steps in value-driven process improvement, starting from business objectives and ending with sustainable results being delivered. There are seven steps to emphasize:

1. Create Urgency

Derive concrete change needs from the organization's business goals. The status quo must appear more dangerous than the journey to the new state. Employees and management must feel the pressure resulting from business needs.

2. Ensure Sponsorship

Sustainable change starts at the top and then grows top-down. Change needs to be pushed by senior management. "You need to be the change that you want to see in the world."

3. Establish Vision for Action

Establish a compelling vision. The change vision must energize employees toward being part of the change. Ensure a sound methodology and the right actions. You have just one shot.

4. Create Room to Change

Change needs resources and competences. Organize change as a project with a small energetic team. Provide a budget and ensure expert support. Agree on project targets, responsibilities, milestones, and deliverables (tuned to business goals). Manage the change project, rigorously. Monitor performance, looking to usage and use, pre- and post-change. Manage risks.

5. Consistently Communicate

Mobilize stakeholder support and use different communication channels. Vision, content, progress, and results must be consistently communicated. Do not confuse leadership and democracy. Engrain change into management behaviors. "Walk the talk."

6. Deliver Tangible Results Fast

Change where there is a pressing need. Fast and sustainable results create trust. Set up the transformation in incremental steps periodically to deliver tangible value. Monitor the implementation and institutionalization of the change with a few measurements, such as use and usage.

7. Capitalize on Changes

Success motivates more changes. Show how new ways of working actually deliver better results. Anchor new behaviors within your organizational culture. Consolidate achieved results by updating organizational templates, such as budgeting. Ensure that changes are engrained to culture and periodically re-assessed. Results are sustainable only when they are delivered without management pressure.

We have introduced the concept of value-driven process improvement in order to focus processes—and their improvement—on the objectives they must achieve [4]. Processes are a means to an end and need to be lean, pragmatic, efficient, and effective—or they will ultimately fail, despite all the push one can imagine. We show with this chapter how value-driven process evolution is used for continuous adaptation of engineering and maintenance processes with the underlying goal of productivity improvement. Specifically, we show how adequate measurement is used as a precondition to define the right objectives and, later on, systematically follow through.

4.3 Performance Measurement

Change programs need performance measurement. A successful performance improvement project always starts with identifying business needs and then translates those into a transformation of the current state as defined by its products, people, and processes to a future state with improved performance. Performance improvement needs to look to value achieved today, and value improvement as is necessary for staying in business, or getting better. Performance improvement is thus framed by quantitative objectives. The progress in achieving these quantitative, performance improvement objectives must be closely monitored with adequate performance measurements.

We recommend using a goal-oriented, measurement approach, such as the *E4-measurement process* (Establish, Extract, Evaluate, Execute) [4]. Figure 4.2

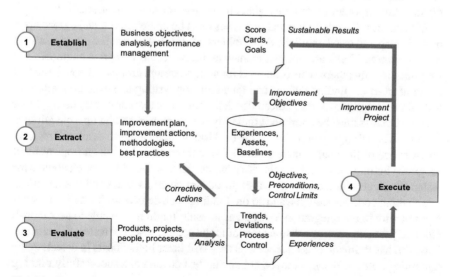

Fig. 4.2 Goal-oriented measurement ensures that process improvement is embedded in a closed-feedback loop

shows the interdependencies between the execution of a process, its definition, and the improvements. It shows how to apply value-driven performance measurement starting with business objectives (Establish), through executing the process and measuring results (Extract), evaluating results (Evaluate), and deriving and implementing concrete improvements (Execute). This E4-measurement process is well suited to implement value-driven process improvement because it starts with a breakdown of business-oriented objectives.

If the organization does not yet actively use process and performance measurements, some fast ramp-up is necessary in order to determine a measurement baseline. Improvements are only feasible if they are quantitatively tracked against such a baseline, which then serves as a yardstick on progress and a pointer for directions to take. Processes must be quantitatively judged whether they are good or bad, or whether they are better or worse than before. To make change sustainable, it is based on realistic improvement objectives. The interaction of objectives and feedback is obvious in day-to-day decision-making. Different groups typically work toward individually controlled targets that build up to business division-level goals and corporate goals.

Let us look at a specific example to understand these interdependencies better. A department or business division-level goal could be to improve maintainability within legacy systems, as it is strategically important for most software and IT companies. Design managers might break that down further to redesigning exactly those components that are at the edge of being maintainable. Product and project managers, on the other hand, face a trade-off with time to market and might emphasize incrementally adding functionality instead. Clearly, both need appropriate indicators to support their selection processes that define the way toward the needed quantitative targets related to these goals. Obviously, one of the key success criteria for process improvement is to understand the context and potentially hidden agendas within the organization, in order to find the right compromises or to weigh alternatives.

Objectives related to individual processes must be unambiguous and agreed upon by their respective stakeholders. Stakeholders are those who use the process or who benefit from it. These are not just management, but could comprise engineers and suppliers, among others. This is obvious for test and design groups. Although the first are reinforced for finding defects and thus focus on writing and executing effective test suites, design groups are dedicated to delivering code that can be executed without defects. Defects must be corrected efficiently which enables setting up a quantitative objective for a design group, that is, the backlog of faults it has to resolve. This may uncover one of the many inherent conflict situations embedded in an improvement program. Setting an overall target of reducing defects found by the customer, for instance, triggers immediate activities in design, such as improved coding rules, establishing code inspections, and so on. Finding such defects up front means better input quality to the integration test that, as a result, might not be able to accomplish efficiency targets, such as a distinct rate of faults per test case. For testers this change, however, has dramatic consequences, as they will incur higher costs in detecting the remaining defects. Besides maybe enhancing test coverage, a successfully running test case has little worth from a cost reduction perspective. Their own performance measurements have to change in order to achieve better customer quality, combined with higher efficiency.

4.4 Focus: Productivity Improvement

Productivity improvement is a major goal in industry due to growing global competition and the need to focus scarce resources on what really matters for value-creation. Most companies are forced to boost their productivity continuously, but are not satisfied with what they achieve. Admittedly, productivity programs are difficult to set up and hard to implement. We thus focus in this section on process improvement for better productivity. Let us work in the four steps that guarantee you will get a grip on productivity. This stepwise approach to productivity improvement, based on the E4-measurement process, can be summarized as follows:

1. Agree on objectives. The first step is to set a business-driven objective. This implies that you understand what you mean by productivity (establish).
2. Determine where you are. The next step is to determine where you are and what should be improved (extract).
3. Determine how to improve. Then you analyze in detail how you are doing, compare that with competitors, evaluate how specific industry best practices might help, and agree on concrete actions for productivity improvement (evaluate).
4. Implement improvements. On this basis, you will systematically improve and subsequently repeat the previous steps (execute).

How can software engineering productivity be effectively improved? Based upon an understanding of what is productivity (step 1) and where we are (step 2), it is a simple step to move forward and determine what must be changed. Figure 4.3 shows the different levers to improve productivity.

The first thing we realize is that, in order to improve productivity, it is wrong to simply talk about cost reductions. Often the one and only mechanism that is triggered, when it comes to R&D or IT productivity, is to reduce costs, which is done mostly by cutting out what does not matter at present or by outsourcing. Both have detrimental effects on overall enterprise performance and long-term stability. Reducing investments in new products will create short-term yields, but will equally reduce market attractiveness. Productivity improvement means to look to both numerator and denominator.

Improving productivity starts always on the output side and reflects whether you are truly delivering value to your customers—inside and outside the company.

Do you sufficiently manage product content and roadmaps? Are the business case and needs of your customers understood and considered in the product portfolio? Do

- Effectiveness: Doing the right things (i.e., sales, market share, value, focus)
- Value creation (right products and features, improve customer business case, nonfunctional requirements, customer satisfaction)
- Innovation (business model, products, services, and support)
- Quality improvement
- Cycle time reduction
- Variant reduction, product-line engineering (PLE), roadmap management
- Product/Service lifecycle management
- Portfolio management

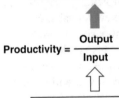

$$\text{Productivity} = \frac{\text{Output}}{\text{Input}}$$

- Efficiency: Doing things right (e.g., processes, "good enough" strategy, sourcing)
- Improve engineering cost structure
- Employee motivation, workspace attractiveness
- Balance of localization and globalization
- Reduce cost of rework, cost of non-quality
- Business process reengineering
- Improve engineering maturity, discipline, management, competences
- Optimize make vs. by vs. reuse strategy
- Master technology, tools, architecture

Fig. 4.3 Levers for productivity improvement

you have too many variants for different markets and waste effort on customization that is not paid for? Which of your products have the highest market share and market growth? Analyze and manage your portfolio to ensure that scarce resources are spent on critical portfolio elements (i.e., cash cows for today's cash flow and stars for new technologies). Reduce the number of versions and rather spend more time on strategic management together with your product managers, marketers, and sales people. Are you doing the right thing?

> Note that cost reduction, along with doing the wrong things, will reduce expenses but will not improve performance!

We recommend that each product manager maintains for his major products a roadmap document with the product strategy and the functional and technical features and dependencies planned in the releases for the coming years [3]. Managing and maintaining roadmaps and the portfolio as a mix of resources, projects, and services is the focus of each product manager who wants to improve value. With moving targets, the sales department has no guidance on how to influence clients, and engineering will decide on its own which technologies to implement with what resources.

When it comes to his own portfolio, the product manager has to show leadership and ensure dependable plans and decisions that are effectively executed. Apply adequate risk management techniques to make your portfolio and commitments dependable. Projects may need more resources, suppliers could deliver late, or technology will not work as expected. As mitigation, platform components used by several products might use resource buffers, whereas application development applies time boxing. If there is a change in committed milestones or content within your portfolio, it must be approved first by the core team and secondly, where necessary, by the respective business unit's management, and then documented and communicated with rationales.

After having addressed the output side, look to the input side. It is about efficiency, but certainly not only about the cost of labor, although this matters most in software engineering. Evaluate for what you are spending which effort. Embark on a rigorous activity-based accounting to determine which processes consume effort and how much they contribute to value-creation. Look to your rework along the entire product lifecycle. Rework is not only created with changing requirements, insufficient variant management, or defect corrections. Rework also comes from insufficient processes and lack of automation. Investigate which of your processes need more guidance or management control. Focus on the cost of non-quality, because it typically is a huge share in software development and maintenance. If test consumes 40 % of resources, this is the process to look into, because test results in no value-creation. Are there techniques that could improve quality during design and development and thus reduce test overheads? How much of your test is redundant? How do you determine what to test and how much to test? Rarely do companies have rules to find out what is good enough and then build this notion around a business case.

Starting in the 1980s, several studies have been performed to understand what impacts on the productivity of a software or IT project. The general finding by researchers like C. Jones or F. Brooks shows that there are productivity factors that can be controlled (i.e., process-related and accidental) and factors that cannot be controlled (i.e., product-related and essential) [1, 5]. Jones found that product-related and process-related factors account for approximately the same amount—roughly one-third—of productivity variance.

Often hardware productivity improvement is used as benchmark to raise demands on the software side. Admittedly hardware productivity had been exploding over several decades—but this was above that which any other industry ever experienced. The anomaly is not that software progress is so slow, but that computer hardware progress is so fast. No other technology since civilization began has seen a seven orders of magnitude price–performance gain in just 50 years. In hardly any technology can one choose to blend the gains from improved performance and reduced costs. We cannot expect to see two-fold productivity gains every two years in other engineering fields. But we should strive to improve software productivity continuously. By applying this basic insight, we identified two basic approaches for improving productivity in software projects, namely [4]:

- Reduce accidental barriers (e.g., improve engineering and management discipline, processes and tools; apply standards—from cradle to grave—languages, templates, IDEs, and so on; design to quality, change, cost, and so on; introduce lean and agile concepts such as smaller teams, components, iterations, and so on).
- Control essential barriers (e.g., understand what are the real needs and implement those in the product; do not implement each single change request; evaluate carefully the customer's business case behind a requested feature and do not implement where there is no clear business case; improve domain understanding; use suitable modeling languages to achieve a "unified" understanding; develop self-generating and self-updating software; reuse components).

4.5   Case Study: Productivity Improvement

To better explicate the basics, we introduce a brief case study on productivity improvement [4]. Figure 4.4 shows how a productivity improvement project was launched and implemented in a globally leading IT company which we supported in their process transformation. Our starting point is the business objective to reduce the cost of engineering by 20%. We do not discuss the story behind it, as it might identify the client. Needless to say, senior management immediately suggested outsourcing parts of the development process to India. Our proposal was to first look into what drives productivity before embarking on a mechanism which in fact might not create the hoped for benefits. Outsourcing is such an example. It is often demanded because

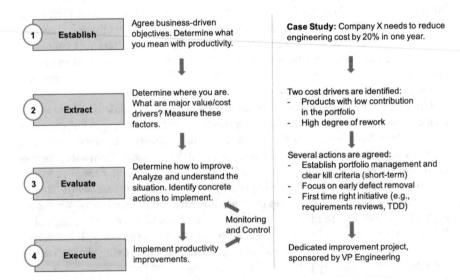

Fig. 4.4 Case study: Implementing productivity improvement

it looks attractive. However, what is missed in this thinking is the long learning curve of two years until tangible results are achieved, and the relatively low—compared to expectations—savings potential of 15–20 % if executed well [4].

In that company, we found two major cost drivers, the first of which was an *overly high amount of small customization projects that did not create much value*. Some had been started simply because sales claimed that they would otherwise lose that market. A sound business case and delivering according to the intended value proposition however was missing. A second observation was a *high cost of non-quality created by finding defects too late*. We proposed and evaluated a set of potential improvements, where we agreed on three concrete actions after careful analysis of cost, impacts, duration, and feasibility in the specific context of our client. The first was to install portfolio management with a clear decision-making and execution process. This meant that all projects and products were screened based on their contribution and strategic adherence. Within six months, we could remove projects with an effort contribution of over 20 % compared to overall engineering cost, but this was just a one-time effect. We had to move further in a second step.

We therefore also embarked on early defect removal and a dedicated "first time right" initiative in engineering. Unexpectedly, this latter initiative got very good buy-in from engineering because they realized that many changes, and thus rework, were introduced from outside. Controlling it and having clear criteria regarding which changes to implement based on portfolio management decision-making was a strong support to focus on value-creation in engineering, rather than defect corrections. Some concrete actions show how we achieved early defect removal and first time right.

A key change was to establish a strong requirements-management process with reviews of requirements and their changes by a defined expert group of product managers, systems engineers, testers, and the project manager. Requirements without the customer business case and clear internal business forecast were not accepted and had to pass a monthly steering board under the lead of the business unit vice president. Test-driven development (TDD) was installed to ensure that requirements were consistently broken down to the design specifications and final code. We used TDD specifically to create unit test cases that could be reused with each iteration where code was changed and redelivered. This caused a significant reduction of defects found by integration and system test and therefore helped after some 10–12 months to gradually reduce these late testing activities.

Another action was to use automatic, code analysis tools that would be used by engineers before delivering their code complete milestones in the current increment. Although it took a while to tailor and adjust the screening rules to the most relevant defects, it helped to give ownership of defect removal to designers, rather than testers. These combined changes helped in delivering work products right the first time along the development process, and thus to improve efficiency.

4.6 Conclusion

Based on empirical results, this chapter portrayed how to set up and drive a value-oriented improvement program based on concrete business goals and development challenges and how to deliver tangible value. We showed that often the reason for failures in implementing process improvement is that objectives are unclear or overly abstract (e.g., "Reduce cycle time by 20 %") and as a consequence the entire project is handled adhoc with no concrete benefits.

The notion of value-driven process improvement has been introduced to underline the need to start with clear business objectives and from these derive a specific and tailored approach toward achieving engineering excellence.

With a case study from a global leading IT company, we demonstrated the concrete impacts on cost and quality over a long timeline. Our starting point is the business objective to reduce the cost of engineering by 20 %. Needless to say, senior management immediately suggested outsourcing parts of development to India. Our proposal was to first look into what drives productivity before embarking on a mechanism that in fact might not create the hoped-for benefits. Outsourcing is such an example. It is often demanded because it looks attractive. However, what is missed in this thinking is the long learning curve of two years until tangible results are achieved, and the relatively low—compared to expectations—savings potential of 15–20 % if executed well. In that company, we found two major cost drivers, the first of which was an overly high amount of small customization projects that did not create much value. Some had been started simply because sales claimed that they would otherwise lose that market. What was missing, however, was a sound business case and valuation that could prove this statement. A second observation was a high cost of non-quality created by finding defects too late. We proposed and evaluated a set of potential improvements, where we agreed on three concrete actions after careful analysis of cost, impacts, duration, and feasibility with the specific contact of our client. The first was to install portfolio management with a clear decision making and execution process. This meant that all projects and products were screened based on their contribution and strategic adherence. Within six months, we could remove projects with an effort contribution of over 20 % compared to overall engineering cost. But this was just a one-time effect.

Improvement programs will fail without strong leadership. Leadership and management buy-in will only happen if there is a clear alignment with business objectives. Theoretic improvement paradigms and isolated so-called process improvement programs driven from somewhere in the middle of the organization fail. Performance improvement needs continuous effort and must be professionally implemented. There is no silver bullet, despite all the promises by tool vendors and framework junkies. Broad experience in engineering and product lifecycle management helps in selecting the right actions with the most value in a certain environment. Clear objectives, a value-driven process evolution program, and excellent change management are key to introducing sustainable and tangible performance improvement.

Acknowledgments Some parts of the article appeared first in Ebert and Dumke: Software Measurement [4]. Copyrights: Springer, Heidelberg, New York, 2007/2016. Used with permission. We recommend reading respective portions of the book as an extension of the quantitative concepts mentioned in this chapter.

References

1. Brooks, F.: No silver bullet essence and accidents of software engineering. IEEE Comput. **20**(4), 10–19 (1987)
2. Crosby, P.B.: Quality Is Free: The Art of Making Quality Certain. Mentor (1980)
3. Ebert, C.: Software product management. CROSSTALK J. Def. Softw. Eng. **22**(1), 15–19 (2009)
4. Ebert, C., Dumke, R.: Software Measurement. Springer, New York (2007) (fully revised edition (2016))
5. Jones, C.: Estimating Software Costs 2nd Edition. McGraw-Hill (2007)
6. Saint-Exupery, A.D.: The little prince. http://www.generationterrorists.com/quotes/the_little_ prince.html (2015)

Chapter 5
Are We Ready for Disruptive Improvement?

Andreas Rösel

Abstract In the IT industry, the continuous improvement approach as an established way for process management is doomed to fail at critical points. In particular, we consider the aspect of dealing with disruptive business changes requiring a disruptive process improvement response. This chapter is based on the experience of a significant disruption in a large IT company. First, we consider how easy it is to continue on an improvement path that, in such a context, leads to failure. We then explore the alternative non-continuous responses required to avoid failure. We look at elements that can help an organization to be better prepared for disruptive improvements, including experiences with the introduction and impact of Design Thinking and Agile Development.

5.1 Introduction

The continuous improvement approach is a well-established way for process management in the IT industry. We discuss how disruptive change challenges us to leave this comfort zone or fail. We describe the defining attributes of disruptive changes where this failure is likely and explain how easy it is to go down that path. Then we focus on what differentiates an appropriate, disruptive process improvement response that is required to design, document, and establish the processes within the organizational units for their new context. In Sect. 5.2, we provide information about the context of observing disruptive process improvement in a large IT company. In Sect. 5.3, we consider the definition of disruptive innovation and then contrast our definition of disruptive process improvement with continuous process improvement. By means of an example of process improvement metrics, we illustrate the dramatic difference between a continuous and a disruptive improvement response. In Sect. 5.4, we give some negative examples in the form of tactics that help to avoid inappropriate disruptive improvement. In Sect. 5.5, we share experiences from a disruptive innovation in a large IT company and how non-continuous steps are required to avoid failure.

A. Rösel (✉)
SAP SE, Hasso-Plattner-Ring 7, 69190 Walldorf, Germany
e-mail: andreas.roesel@sap.com

© Springer International Publishing Switzerland 2016   77
M. Kuhrmann et al. (eds.), *Managing Software Process Evolution*,
DOI 10.1007/978-3-319-31545-4_5

In Sects. 5.6 and 5.7, we look at elements that can help an organization to be better prepared for disruptive improvements, and we share some experiences with the introduction and impact of Design Thinking and Agile Development in Sect. 5.8. In the conclusion in Sect. 5.9, we consider what we learned from reflecting on the experiences with disruptive process improvements and an outlook on readiness for disruptions. Finally, in Sect. 5.10, we include pointers to information on Design-Thinking and on the topic of Intrapreneurship, where companies are encouraging individuals and groups to adopt an entrepreneurial approach within their company to improve their readiness for disruption.

5.2   Background and Context

Improvement in a business context is a well-established approach and is necessary to manage complexity and to increase efficiency and improve performance overall. Further, there is no doubt that improvement is effective when it is aligned with the organization's strategy. When we look at improvement activities as a response to strategy, then the most dynamic situation will be the improvement response to a disruption in the strategy. Our consideration of appropriate "disruptive" improvement responses should be of interest to anyone working in or with a company where strategic disruptions occur.

In the following, we focus on the process improvement perspective in the context of disruptive improvements. Processes describe our way of working as a company, as a department, or as a team. Looking at process improvement in this generic view means that improving how we are working will or should involve improving our processes. The particular context of the main experience referred to here is a large IT company. The example is enhanced by the author's extensive experience working as Transformation and Process Consultant with companies developing software as a vital part of their core business.

5.3   Disruptive Versus Continuous Improvement

First, we consider the definition of disruptive innovation and then contrast our definition of disruptive process improvement with continuous process improvement.

A disruptive technology or innovation helps create a new market and value network, and thereby eventually disrupts an existing market and value network. The term is used in business and technology literature to describe innovations that improve a product or service in ways that the market does not expect [6]. Christensen expanded his earlier model of disruption, which is explained in the book *The Innovator's Dilemma* [5], an acclaimed bestseller, but also critically questioned, for example, by Dvorak [8] and Cohen [7].

Table 5.1 Characteristics of disruptive and continuous improvement

Disruptive	Continuous
Radical	Incremental
Breakthrough	Sustaining
Risky	Lower risk

In the context of this chapter, we use the term "disruptive improvement" to discuss aspects of process improvement that are not continuous. The differences are illustrated in Table 5.1 in terms of the contrasting attributes of disruptive versus continuous process improvement. Some quality practitioners distinguish between *continuous* and *continual* improvement as follows [9]. Continual improvement is a broader term to refer to the general processes of improvement and encompassing "discontinuous" improvements—that is, many different approaches, covering different areas. Continuous improvement is a subset of continual improvement, with a more specific focus on linear, incremental improvement within an existing process.

The introduction of disruptive innovation would be a trigger for such disruptive process improvement, and, applying the attributes listed above, we can state more generally that any radical breakthrough or risky change in a company's strategy would be a trigger. The difference between responding to a disruptive context change with either continuous or disruptive process improvement is illustrated in Fig. 5.1. Along the y-axis we see the amount of change. The strategy disruption curve shows how the defined IT strategy was disrupted with a very significant change in the middle of the year. The dotted curve shows the number of improvements released to implement the process aspects of the defined strategy for that year. Up to the middle of the year, the curve shows the accumulated actual improvements released; from then on, it shows the planned releases based on the improvement plan according to the original strategy. The solid response curve is in line with the dotted one up to the middle of the year, then it shows how the number of process improvements released changes dramatically in response to the disruptive change.

The curves illustrate the difference between a disruptive improvement response and a continuous improvement response. Although it is an illustration, we found these types of curves as a result of plotting the data of actual process improvement responses. Note that both improvement responses are continual in that the improvement does not stop. Yet, although the continuous improvement keeps the focus on linear incremental improvement, it is the disruptive process improvement response that shows a correlation to the disruptive trigger. Next, we focus on the disruptive end of the spectrum of change and the associated disruptive process improvement.

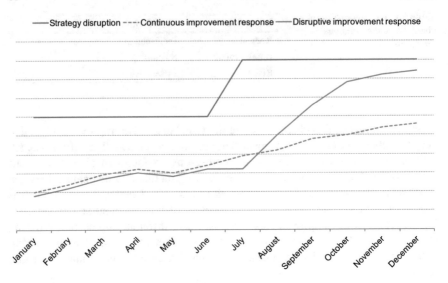

Fig. 5.1 Disruptive versus continuous process improvement response

5.4 How to Ignore Strategy Disruption and Ensure Continuous Improvement Failure

Here we play the devil's advocate in the scenario where a strategy disruption has occurred and the process improvement organization and process improvement experts continue the main work and efforts along the established continuous improvement path. Our approach is to give some negative guidelines as to how a valid strategy disruption may be ignored from a process improvement perspective. Indeed, this would avoid the appropriate disruptive improvement response and work against the company. For general examples of how and why change triggers are being ignored, see the literature on the topic of change and resistance to change, e.g., those by John P. Kotter relevant to urgent disruptive change [13, 14].

So let us take a reverse look. Table 5.2 summarizes some ways to ignore strategy disruption, based on my experiences as a process consultant with a number of organizations. Practitioners should be able to recognize one or the other tactic having been applied, whether consciously or unwittingly, in a company they know.

For the car manufacturer VW, the original Beetle was a winning model. It was produced in essentially the same shape for nearly three decades. Continuous improvement was a strong point of VW and appreciated by the buyers. In fact, the continuous improvement was so successful that none of the numerous prototypes for a new model to succeed the Beetle made it to production. Finally, the competition of new generation cars became so oppressive that the very existence of VW was threatened [4]. The strategy disruption of the Golf innovation saved the day, but it is an example where the switch away from continuous improvement came almost too late.

Table 5.2 Tactics to avoid appropriate disruptive improvement

Category	Tactics
Too slippery to be caught	Stick to your long-term continuous improvement plan:
	• Use silos and departmental firewalls to avoid direct involvement in changes of strategy and process.
	• Prove the value of continuing step-by-step improvements using your improvement metrics.
	• Don't change long-term continuous plans and process-release cycles. Use yearly plans with limited releases.
Too heavy to be moved	Cast your processes in concrete:
	• Aim for documentation of all process details and variants as you have always done.
	• Ensure you have a fine-grained structure with hundreds of roles.
	• Raise risks to standards and audits as reasons why your processes must remain as they are.
Too cushioned to be hurt	Built-in shock-absorbers:
	• Separate the process organization from operations to avoid or reduce the impact of operational issues and goals.
	• Empower people to stop progress if a resource or some input from a stakeholder is missing.
	• Slow down new processes by insisting on iterating the process flow with all involved to handcraft a fully consistent version before the first publication.

5.5 Accepting Strategy Disruption and Responding with Disruptive Process Improvement

Major technology trends in IT include Cloud, Mobile, and Big Data [10, 19]. Cloud, from an IT perspective, is about savings through virtualization, convenience through Infrastructure as a Service, and flexibility through a hybrid model. Mobile includes Mobile Workspaces, Mobile Device Management, and integration of the mobile access into the core workflows. Big Data, where more and more companies are looking at volumes in terabytes and petabytes, requires new approaches regarding management, analysis, and distribution. The users and usage of big data are dramatically increasing and demand processing that is magnitudes faster.

In this context, the strategy disruption of our company was the decision to set up SAP HANA Enterprise Cloud with the objectives [20]:

• Accelerate the transition to the real-time enterprise through cloud computing.
• Analyze vast amounts of data instantaneously for critical business insights.
• Transform operations to enable real-time business.

In the middle of 2013, a new unit was established to deliver these benefits not only to external customers, but also, beginning with the early versions, to our own organization, true to the commitment SAP-runs-SAP. Here we are not looking at the technology innovation supporting this move (In-Memory Database, Mobile device integration technology, etc.), rather, we are focusing on the process improvement response—in particular, by the IT Process Office.

The members of the Global IT Process Office could have applied many of the tactics listed in Table 5.2 to avoid changing to a disruptive improvement mode. For example, the Process Office itself was not part of the new organization, so the tactics of the, category "Too cushioned to get hurt" were tempting. Similarly, the tactics from the category "Stick to your long-term continuous improvement plan" could have been employed as the process consulting resources were committed for the remainder of the year to agreed improvement plans and release cycles of process descriptions. Instead, the disruptive strategy trigger was answered with a disruptive improvement response. Examples of tactics and associated results are shown in the following list. The interested reader will find and recognize respective counter-tactics from Table 5.2.

Tactic 1 (Define an improvement plan and process-release cycles in line with the strategy disruption.) This tactic aims to produce the following results:

- Weekly process deliveries in the hot phase
- Defined and released a first version of the Process Value Chain for the new organization within six weeks

Tactic 2 (Utilize relevant standards and audits as reasons to drive process definition and adoption.) This tactic aims to produce the following results:

- Close collaboration with the security team and readiness for external audit within three months
- Passed the Service Organization Control compliance audits (SOC1 & SOC2 Type I) with no exceptions

Tactic 3 (Simplify) This tactic aims to produce the following results:

- A switch to a simpler process documentation was accelerated so it could be applied in this fitting context.
- Processes were published at "80 % readiness." This proved useful in early projects and provided valuable feedback.
- Process, operational, and audit issues were tracked in one tool.

Tactic 4 (Closely work as process consultants and team with the new organization.) This tactic aims to produce the following results:

- Ensured that clearly assigned process responsibilities were part of the set-up
- Process consultants worked in tandem with process managers and became recognized go-to people, for example, for integration aspects

The mind-set for change is surely one important factor influencing our readiness for disruptive improvement. It may be coincidental, but the members of the process office have been trained, and several have also been very active, in applying Design Thinking principles as well as Agile development methods. In the following, we consider why and how these approaches may foster disruptive improvement.

5.6   Design Thinking

Design Thinking is a method for innovation that brings together the creative aspects of the brain with the analytical aspects of the brain. There are typically six steps in a full design-thinking cycle:

1. Understand, where you define the problem by "finding the right question"
2. Observe, where you explore the problem space with a mind as value-free and neutral as possible and where you try to develop a sense of empathy for the user in order to understand the personal, organizational, and functional dimensions of the challenge
3. Define Point of View, where you make a first design decision by condensing all information down to one topic and one user to focus on
4. Ideate, where you explore the solution space and generate as many ideas as possible to serve the previously identified needs
5. Prototype, where you develop a prototypical implementation of the idea combining, expanding, and refining the most powerful ideas
6. Test, where you seek feedback from a diverse group of people, including your end users, to gain new insights

The process involves more than executing the steps in a linear manner. It requires an open culture that is focused on the end-user and the flexibility to loop through the steps as required. One significant contributor to making the connection from design thinking to IT product development is Hasso Plattner, one of the founders of SAP. He established a collaboration with the Institute of Design at Stanford and extended the work on Design Thinking with the HPI (Hasso Plattner Institute) in Potsdam [11]. He is a strong advocate of the application of Design Thinking in IT and, with this, had a large impact on the processes in SAP. In its application at this large IT company, it has been proposed as a unique engagement experience and mind-set of combining business thinking with design thinking, thus generating ideas that will lead to value for customers and their stakeholders by:

- Rethinking existing problems to unlock spaces for innovation and creative solutions
- Visualizing the impact of disruptive technology as it relates to the business in focus
- Leveraging a proven approach that has been used with other companies to help them create game-changing value for their customers

In the activities stated above, we can see the link to disruptive improvement already in the terms used, including game-changing, innovation space, and disruptive.

The steps of Design Thinking are typically applied in order to explore new angles and perspectives or tricky problems to unearth underlying desires and needs: prioritize new ideas, create road maps, and build persuasive business cases; create high-fidelity visualizations as a tangible artifact that represents the generated ideas, and how they may be implemented. Several tools can be used in the course of a design-thinking exercise and include customer-journey mapping, graphical facilitation/sketching, art-of-the-possible visualizations, and rapid prototyping. For examples of using Design Thinking in the IT context, see customer success stories on an open community Web site [21]. Although SAP is helping their customers in applying Design Thinking, it is also fostering the Design Thinking culture and applying this approach in its own IT organization. There are workshops on Design Thinking, coaches to support design thinking in internal IT projects, and also rooms with equipment to facilitate these activities. How radical the shift away from a linear approach is may be illustrated by a provocative statement found on the wall of a Design Thinking room: "Fail early and often!" This goes far beyond the old, but nevertheless most useful, prototyping advice: "Build one to throw away" [3].

5.6.1 Fail Early

Individuals and teams are challenged to seek ways to fail as early as possible. According to the Design Thinking philosophy, the decision on success or failure comes from the end-customer. Getting feedback from customers on ideas and possible solution directions extremely early is a must. With such a mind shift, it is possible to get feedback in less than a day, even hours or minutes—rather than in weeks. So, an idea that may have looked like a good one could go, without Design Thinking, through a cycle of design, implement, test, and then, during validation, receive the feedback from the majority of end-users that it is not acceptable. In this case, significant effort and weeks, even months, may have been invested. With Design Thinking, the idea would have received the fail-feedback much earlier, thus avoiding wasting time and effort on a solution approach leading nowhere.

5.6.2 Fail Often

Individuals and teams are challenged to look for ways to fail multiple times, on purpose. Failing is good, and failing often is even better? This seems to contradict our striving for efficiency and the high quality of our work. It is success that we seek and strive for. This provocation to fail on purpose is about helping teams and individuals to break out of limiting frameworks that govern and constrict our thinking even without our being aware of it. Indeed, Design Thinking contributes to the successful end-result in that the end-customer receives an overall, very satisfying solution and, for this contribution, Design Thinking needs to open up the solution space to include more and, it is hoped, more satisfying solutions. This large solution space needs to be explored with end-user feedback to ensure that valuable opportunities for the customer are not missed. Having customer feedback that several or even many solution options have failed is an indicator that a large solution space is being explored with the end-user.

For an example of what "Fail early and fail often" means in practice, we consider some aspects of a recent Design Thinking activity of Global IT and business for improving the internal flow of financial information. The Design Thinking team included a variety of stakeholders with roles such as business end-user, process manager, user-interface expert, architect, developer, and coach. The focus was on providing a mobile dashboard solution. In Table 5.3, we look at activities during one of the cycles through the Design Thinking steps.

We consider where the "Fail early and fail often" advice is applied in this example. In the *Observe* step, the initial feedback on "what was expected as a solution" failed the validation check with another set of end-users. This showed that the preconceived solution space for this project was too limited. Additional feedback activities identified the highly ranked requirement for a broader and more mobile provision of key information. At the same time, the information needed to be presented in a more role-relevant manner. In the *Ideate* step, a number of options were explored using simple, user-interface prototyping and direct feedback in the design team. Several options were rejected in the discussion of the Design Thinking team including the members representing the end-users. In the *Test* step, where the early prototype

Table 5.3 Example of one cycle through the *Design Thinking* steps

Understand	Define the problem by "finding the right question"	What financial dashboard information helps me to get an overview of financial key figures in [area] for making decisions in my role as [role name]?
Observe	Explore the problem space Develop a sense of empathy for the user	Existing feedback was validated and an additional pain-point survey was conducted to get more reliable feedback from potential end-users
Define point of view	Make a preliminary design decision focus on one topic and one user	The team described a persona, Laura, representing a typical end-user including her work context, personal preferences, expectations, and so on
Ideate	Explore the solution space generate many ideas to serve the identified needs	Solution options for Laura's needs were developed using whiteboard and mini-sticky-notes to simulate key fields and interaction scenarios, as well as the look and feel of various mobile device sizes
Prototype	Develop a prototypical implementation of the idea	A cardboard and paper prototype of the financial dashboard was built showing variants of content fields and possible interactions by sliding in various paper "screens" in response to "clicks"
Test	Seek feedback from a diverse group of people, including your end-users to gain new insights	The Laura prototype was played through in two variants with end-users, as well as random colleagues by a pair of Design Thinking team members. The user interaction and reactions were observed regarding value of information provided, ease of use, and overall fit for purpose

was used to execute the proposed solution options with different types of end-users as well as other people, an additional need became apparent in that the application should also support direct initiation of key actions.

It is not unusual that during the phases and iteration cycles of an IT project the requirements and implementation diverge from the initial envisaged and requested solution. The contribution of Design Thinking in this case was to achieve a clarification in a dramatically shorter timeframe. Here, well-intended solution proposals were identified, as off-target and previously hidden requirements and unimagined solution options were identified, early on and very quickly. One can imagine the much higher impact when Design Thinking is applied to visualize the effects of a disruptive technology such as HANA and Big Data for a specific business context.

Design Thinking is a technique that can be applied to look systematically for solutions outside the linear, continuous-improvement approach. It can be used to identify disruptive ideas or to come up with ideas for applying a disruptive technology in a certain business context. In either case, it is a tool to address systematically a wider scope of possibilities, accelerate improvement, and reach a disruptive impact. These aspects of Design Thinking clearly fit with the requirements of an accelerated and disruptive response, as discussed for disruptive process improvement.

5.7 Agile Development

Now let us turn to Agile development, another major influencer. Agile Development refers here to Agile Software Development as the flexible and light-weight development approach in contrast to the more linear and heavy-weight waterfall methods. The movement for Agile Development has a long history, and its key elements are summarized in the Agile Manifesto, the 12 principles [2] and Practices [1]. For more details on the element of Agile Development, see also Chap. 2.

How might the exposure to Agile Development and an associated mind-set foster readiness for disruptive improvement? Let us look where change and disruption are considered in the fundamental elements of Agile Development. In the Agile Manifesto, one of the four statements is, "We have come to value responding to change over following a plan." In addition, two of the twelve agile principles refer to change and adaption: "Welcome changing requirements, even late in the project" and "Regular adaptation to changing circumstances." This emphasizes how Agile Development relies on a mind-set to accept and respond to change and, in particular, significant change. Another aspect of the mind-set for change is customer focus. Keeping the focus on the customer and customer needs during a disruption increases the likelihood of recognizing and reacting to changing requirements. Note that, with a disruptive change, it may mean that "the customer" is also changing to a different person or organization and the requirements then come from a different source.

In our context of a large IT company, the topic of Agile Development has been introduced and established over a period of more than 10 years. The development organization is now working largely in agile teams applying the Scrum approach.

Company-wide standard trainings include Agile development and Scrum topics, from introduction to advanced, and internal coaches in these areas to support ongoing training and practice. In addition, communities of practice have been established for topics including Lean and Agile Community and Scrum Master. In the internal IT department, where we observed the topic of disruptive process improvement, Agile Development is the standard approach for all Business Analytics projects, and for other IT projects, Agile Development is applied in accordance with the size and context of the project.

We established the link between Agile Development and disruptive improvements via the principles of readiness for change and customer focus. In the following chapter, we now look at overall readiness for disruptive improvement.

5.8 Readiness for Disruptive Improvement

A disruptive innovation is likely to require a disruptive process improvement response. How ready can we be? Here we consider how the Agile Methods and Design Thinking relate to our observed case of disruptive process improvement.

Members of the IT process team were trained in Agile Methods as well as in Design Thinking. In addition, they were exposed to the operational practice of Agile Development and Design Thinking in the projects of their organization. Design Thinking fosters a readiness for innovation, change in scope, and a focus on the customer that helps to let go of previous solution approaches when needed. Agile Development also fosters a readiness for change and radical change in alignment with changing requirements. Let us have a closer look at the tactics in the chapter "Accepting Strategy Disruption and Responding with Disruptive Process Improvement" (Sect. 5.5) to examine which of the Agile Principles [2] and Design Thinking aspects (Sect. 5.6) apply.

The tactic, "Define an improvement plan and process-release cycles in line with the strategy disruption," employed frequent deliveries, thus following Agile Principle 1 *customer satisfaction by rapid delivery* and Agile Principle 3 *deliver frequently*. The decision to adopt such a fast-paced delivery schedule in an environment where a transition is still in progress also fits with the Design Thinking advice to rather fail early and often, in that an approximate solution with imperfections is deemed acceptable, and in fact desirable, as its use provides early and repeated feedback on what is really required. The next tactic, "Utilize relevant standards and audits as reasons to drive process definition and adoption," focused on audit readiness as a high-impact requirement. The very tight engagement with security colleagues as key stakeholders for this business aspect followed Agile Principle 4 *close, daily cooperation between business people and developers*. One can also see a relation to the Design Thinking aspect of early and close engagement of relevant stakeholder groups. The tactic "Simplify", resulting in simplified process representation and tooling, clearly maps to the Agile Principle 10 *simplicity*. The final tactic in Sect. 5.5 is "Closely work as process consultants and team with the new organization;" this again fits with Agile Principle 4 *close, daily cooperation between business people and developers.*

From this systematic examination of our sample case of process improvement, we can conclude that Agile Methods and Design Thinking have the right fit to support readiness for an appropriate disruptive improvement response to a disruptive change. This matches our experience that the training and exposure to these approaches helped to increase the overall readiness for a disruptive change response in the individual members and the IT process team as a whole.

Taking an active part in a disruptive process improvement response means taking higher risks (see Table 5.1). Fast changes, big changes, new stakeholders, and unstable requirements have to be dealt with as consequences of such a decision. Taking on higher risks potentially to achieve higher business value requires an entrepreneurial attitude. In the context of large organizations, there is a particular challenge to respond to disruptive change. The size and the number of departments and people affected can increase the inertia and therefore increase the likelihood of following a continuous path as a default response. Large organizations recognize the need to have more people act in an entrepreneurial way, so that the organization is able to respond appropriately to disruptive change. This is also relevant for SAP, where the concept of "Intrapreneurs" is fostered in the form of intrapreneur bootcamps and competitions. In addition, greenhouses for testing new business models are provided, as well as connections with ventures outside the organization. In the section Further Reading, we provide some links to additional information on this topic related to readiness for disruption.

We covered some aspects of readiness for disruptive improvement. We do not claim, however, that the aspects covered are the most vital ones. We considered Agile Methods and Design Thinking and touched on Intrapreneurship because, based on our observation and knowledge of the situation, they were deemed most relevant in the context of our main example. Let us briefly look at candidates for additional aspects that could be considered to increase readiness for disruptive improvement. One candidate could be Elements of Organizational Change Management that help prepare for disruptive change and how to introduce this preparation into the organization. Another candidate would be recognizing and managing manageable parts of disruptions earlier. For this last candidate, one example could be that, for a certain company, buying and merging with another company was a very significant strategy disruption requiring an appropriate disruptive improvement response. The buying company may recognize that this is a type of disruption that, although it was a first historic event for them, now has a higher likelihood for reoccurrence. So, it may make sense to build up competences specific to such disruptive triggers that will increase their readiness.

For our sample case, we found that Agile Methods and Design Thinking have the right fit to support readiness for an appropriate disruptive improvement response to a disruptive change. Further, we considered the relation of Intrapreneurship. We can recommend that readers consider if and how these approaches can help in the context of their work to increase the readiness to respond to strategy disruptions with appropriate disruptive improvement responses. We finished with an outlook on additional approaches that could be helpful to manage readiness and disruption.

5.9   Conclusion

We conclude with some essential lessons learned and a view to readiness for disruptions. We presented an example of how an appropriate, disruptive process improvement response in a large IT company produced successful results where a continuous response would have surely led to failure. One lesson for us was not to take this for granted. To accept the radical change as a challenge and respond this way, required groups and individuals taking risks and not succumbing to the temptation of staying in the comfort zone of continuity. Although continually improving is a good thing, we must not get stuck in the "continuous" trap but must be ready for disruptive improvement. We also learned that we can foster such readiness individually, but that, at the company level, more is required. From the example of a large IT organization, we can see that elements such as Design Thinking and Agile Development can, and perhaps should, be fostered more consciously also with respect to process development, to increase the responsiveness to disruptions and the ability to adopt an appropriate disruptive improvement approach.

5.10   Further Reading

For some of the aspects discussed in this chapter, this section provides additional references and information.

The distinction between disruptive and continuous process improvement introduced at the beginning focused on the appropriate disruptive-innovative response required to match a disruptive innovative trigger. We referred to [6] for radical change and disruptive triggers. The aspect of the radicalness of the process-reengineering activity itself as a topic is discussed in [12]. In his publication, William J. Kettinger considers the radicalness of the process-change project and provides a framework for assessing and considering the radicalness. Although techniques and tools have changed somewhat over the years, this work on business process change provides guidelines for evaluating the radicalness of change and a framework that could provide valuable insights for the interested reader. As a further aspect [18] considers how the processes for software/IT have attributes of software and what should be learned from this regarding the way we (should) approach the activities of process definition, process documentation, and process management. It deals with the question: "What can we learn from the software process with respect to the process of (software) process improvement?" Continuing with this thought, the applicability of Agile Development (see also Sect. 5.7) for the process improvement and disruptive process improvement, in particular, are conclusions to consider.

To further gather insights on the topic of Design Thinking discussed in Section six, the interested reader will find in [15] information from original inspirations such as Bauhaus, the development of d.school at Stanford University, and applications in multiple contexts. The major part of the books is devoted to accounts and experiences of Design Thinking in research and education, industry, and across the globe.

Additional information on the topic of Intrapreneurship (see Sect. 5.8 Readiness for disruptive improvement) is found in [16]. Here, Howard W. Oden provides details on Intrapreneurship in the context of steering a corporate culture towards increased readiness for innovation. The currency of this topic is apparent in [17], which looks to answer the very direct question: "What the heck is an 'intrapreneur'?".

Acknowledgments With great pleasure, I thank all colleagues from the SAP IT Process team that inspired this chapter by taking up the challenge to respond to a disruptive change with a disruptive process improvement response. Such a response does not always happen, and, when it happens, it does not always work. It was great to learn together from this challenge.

References

1. Agile Alliance: Guide to agile practices. http://guide.agilealliance.org (2001)
2. Beck, K., Beedle, M., van Bennekum, A., Cockburn, A., Cunningham, W., Fowler, M., Grenning, J., Highsmith, J., Hunt, A., Jeffries, R., Kern, J., Marick, B., Martin, R.C., Mellor, S., Schwaber, K., Sutherland, J., Thomas, D.: Manifesto for agile software development. http://agilemanifesto.org (2001)
3. Brooks, F.P.: The Mythical Man-Month. Addison Wesley, Boston (1975)
4. Cartecc.com: VW-history. http://www.kfz-tech.de/Engl/Hersteller/VW/VW3.htm (2013)
5. Christensen, C.M.: The Innovator's Dilemma: When New Technologies Cause Great Firms To Fail. Harvard Business School Press, Boston (1997)
6. Christensen, C.M.: Disruptive innovation. In: Soegaard, M., Dam, R.F. (eds.) The Encyclopedia of Human-Computer Interaction, 2 edn. The Interaction Design Foundation, Aarhus (2014)
7. Cohen, J.: Not disruptive, and proud of it. http://blog.asmartbear.com/not-disruptive.html (2010)
8. Dvorak, J.C.: The myth of disruptive technology. http://www.pcmag.com/article2/0,2817, 1628049,00.asp (2004)
9. for AS Quality: Continuous improvement. http://asq.org/learn-about-quality/continuous-improvement/overview/overview.html (2015)
10. Gartner Inc.: Gartner identifies the top 10 strategic technology trends for 2014. http://www.gartner.com/newsroom/id/2603623 (2013)
11. Hasso-Plattner-Institut, Universität Potsdam: HPI school of design thinking. http://hpi.de/school-of-design-thinking.html?L=1 (2014)
12. Kettinger, W.J., Teng, J.T.C., Guha, S.: Business process change: a study of methodologies, techniques, and tools. MIS Q. **21**(1), 55–98 (1997)
13. Kotter, J.P.: Leading Change. Harvard Business Press, Watertown (1996)
14. Kotter, J.P.: A Sense of Urgency. Harvard Business Press, Watertown (2008)
15. Meinel, C., Weinberg, U., Krohn, T.: Design Thinking Live. Murmann Publishers, Hamburg (2015)
16. Oden, H.W.: Managing Corporate Culture, Innovation, and Intrapreneurship. Praeger, Westport (1997)

17. Odenwald, T.: What the heck is an 'intrapreneur'? http://scn.sap.com/community/business-trends/blog/2014/06/20/what-the-heck-is-an-intrapreneur (2014)
18. Osterweil, L.J.: Software processes are software too. In: Proceedings of the International Conference on Software Engineering, pp. 2–13. IEEE, Washington, DC, USA (1987)
19. Praxmarer, L.: Die zehn wichtigsten IT-Trends (the ten most important it-trends). http://www.computerwoche.de/a/die-zehn-wichtigsten-it-trends,2551615 (2014)
20. SAP: SAP HANA Enterprise Cloud – the power of real-time business and simplicity of the cloud. http://global.sap.com/campaigns/2013_Hana_Enterprise_Cloud (2013)
21. SAP Community Network: Design thinking with SAP. http://scn.sap.com/community/design-thinking (2014)

Chapter 6
Trials and Tribulations of the Global Software Engineering Process: Evolving with Your Organisation

Oisín Cawley

Abstract This chapter will provide the reader with a firsthand account of the trials and tribulations of working in and managing a Global Software Engineering (GSE) function. By describing the move from a distributed collection of self-sufficient manufacturing plants with locally managed software engineering resources, to a GSE function as a shared service, the focus will be on how the management of that group had to fundamentally change in order to satisfy the complex projects and customer base which resulted. In parallel it will discuss the effect of regulation on the software engineering management process. Tracing the introduction of financial systems regulations, it will discuss the issues this brought to the GSE process and how they were successfully overcomed. These topics will be augmented by research that the author has carried out into regulated software development.

6.1 Introduction

The term Global Software Engineering (GSE) is fairly well understood within both industry and academia, but the devil is in the detail. Companies or Information Technology (IT) departments do not develop efficient software engineering functions at a global level overnight. Typically, these companies will be large organisations with offices in multiple countries and/or geographical regions, and are therefore subject to the well documented effects of separation (geographical, temporal, and cultural). However, such companies often come from humble beginnings, and through various forms of growth (organically or through mergers and acquisitions), evolve into organisations which necessarily must function differently. It follows, therefore, that the business processes which have been in place at the beginning must change or evolve in tandem with the organisation's growth. The Software Engineering function is one of those key processes, and it is not immune to these changes.

O. Cawley (✉)
Department of Computing, Institute of Technology Carlow, Kilkenny Road, Carlow, Ireland
e-mail: oisin.cawley@itcarlow.ie

© Springer International Publishing Switzerland 2016
M. Kuhrmann et al. (eds.), *Managing Software Process Evolution*,
DOI 10.1007/978-3-319-31545-4_6

This evolution can cause a lot of organisational pain as the work load increases and diversifies. The need for additional resources and personnel usually requires a change to team structures, reporting lines and perhaps job descriptions in order to support the business on a more global scale. As competition in the market place increases, cost pressures often make companies look at outsourcing options. This alone can be a major challenge, but combined with the effect of having to adhere to newly created regulatory controls raises the bar significantly.

The author's experiences bears witness to a lot of what has been mentioned above, having spent 17 years working on software projects, large and small, in both small and multi-national companies. In addition, his research into the effects regulatory controls have on the software engineering function, contributes an expert insight on the topic.

6.2 Background and Context

Managing a team of highly skilled individuals, who are located in different countries, often in different time zones, to successfully deliver a software project on time and within budget can be a difficult task [7]. Table 6.1 from [2] provides an overview of the key software development process difficulties which can be encountered due to the effects of the different dimensions of "distance."

Often, such a GSE function exists as a virtual shared service for the entire organisation [16]. This can help to eliminate resource duplication, and maintain some semblance of development standards. It can however introduce a bottleneck within the organisation, as each business unit vies for priority on the software development queue [12]. This raises an interesting question. Then how should projects be prioritised? In a global organisation, who really controls the GSE resources?

6.2.1 Positioning the GSE Function

Before looking at the area of control in more detail, let us first draw a distinction, in broad terms, between two types of organisations who may employ such a GSE function. Group one are companies whose primary business is to sell software. They may produce the software in a number of ways, in-house, outsourced or a combination of the two. The in-house approach can also be implemented in two forms; collocated, where the software engineers sit together in the same place, or global, where they are geographically spread-out. Such companies may also have some form of support agreement that they sell with the software, but their focus is/should be on selling high quality software. The higher the quality, the lower the failure rate and consequent need for costly maintenance.

Table 6.1 An overview of the framework of issues in Global Software Engineering

Process	Dimension		
	Temporal distance	Geographical distance	Socio-cultural distance
Communication	Reduced opportunities for synchronous communications, introducing delayed feedback. Improved record of communications	Potential for closer proximity to market, and utilization of remote skilled workforces. Increased cost and logistics of holding face to face meetings	Potential for stimulating innovation and sharing best practice, but also for misunderstandings
Coordination	With appropriate division of work, coordination needs can be minimized. However, coordination costs typically increaser with distance	Increase in size and skills of labor pool can offer more flexible coordination planning. Reduced informal contact can lead to reduced trust and a lack of critical task awareness	Potential for learning and access to richer skill set. Inconsistency in work practices can impinge on effective coordination, as can reduced cooperation through misunderstandings
Control	Time zone effectiveness can be utilized for gaining efficient 24x7 working. Management of project artifacts may be subject to delays	Difficult to convey vision and strategy. Communication channels often leave an audit trail, but can be threatened at key times	Perceived threat from training low-cost 'rivals'. Different perceptions of authority/hierarchy can undermine morale. Managers must adapt to local regulations

Group two are those companies where the software they develop is merely a tool to support the company's business objectives (whatever they may be). We do not underestimate the importance of the software, however, for these companies the focus is on selling something else, and software is a supporting/enabling mechanism. Such companies may also take an in-house, outsourced or combination approach. This is an important distinction between the two groupings, as it positions the GSE function relative to the business objectives. It is also important because the software often plays a critical role in one or more business processes. For example, delivering inventory to a manufacturing line in a just-in-time fashion requires the order management, warehouse management and purchasing management departments to function in a coherent manner. Any issues encountered in the supporting systems have the potential to stop everything.

The two groupings here are sometimes referred to as Packaged versus IS (information systems) teams. Packaged teams normally produce an end product. This product is packaged up and sold commercially. IS teams are generally considered to be working internally to support corporate objectives. Carmel and Sawyer [8] state that the differences between IS and Packaged software teams include cost pressures versus time-to-market pressures, and bureaucratic versus entrepreneurial cultural milieus.

There are, of course, companies who do not fit within either of these broad groups, such as charities and other not for profit organisations. Such organisations tend to have different objectives and work ethea, for example, volunteer employees, and so some aspects of this chapter may not be so relevant in their cases.

6.2.2 The GSE Problem

Managing a GSE process brings new challenges. Let us consider, for example, the maintenance phase of a typical software development lifecycle (SDLC) of a company from group two. When a production issue occurs (let's say the order management system above loses a customer order, and so that particular order never makes it onto the production schedule), it must be acted on immediately. It becomes an "all hands on deck" situation because the business process is suffering. In these situations you need personnel who are qualified and trained to troubleshoot the issue. Once the issue is identified, for example, a corrupt index in the database, you need the appropriate personnel (often different to the people who did the trouble-shooting) to fix the issue. You may have these resources on site and under your control, and so issues can be reacted to rapidly. But things are quite different within a global setting. No longer are your resources local, perhaps not even in your geographical region, and in addition they more than likely report to a different manager. It is clear that the process to resolve issues cannot be managed the same in both organisational structures.

6.2.3 Regulation

According to [6], regulations are simply a form of social organisation: *"rules, principles, or conditions that govern procedure or behaviour"* [33]. But why do we have or need regulations? Fundamentally it is because we want to try and ensure a certain outcome. They provide a blueprint for how something should be done, and if we follow the rules we should end up with a good quality product or process. There are those, however, who argue that there is too much regulation and that not enough research has been done in assessing the adequacy of regulations in achieving their intended aims [6]. For example, regulations governing financial institutions, such as the Basel II Accord [3] and the Sarbanes–Oxley Act [1], did not prevent the global banking crises of 2007.

Software Regulation In relation to software, regulations are becoming more and more prevalent due to software becoming so pervasive in society. We have come to rely on it more and more in our daily lives [18] and consequently, when it fails or is misused, the effects can be quite devastating. To counteract this risk, various authorities have introduced regulations which aim to govern how software is developed, secured and interacts with other systems. For example, the Enron scandal 2001, which resulted in the loss of over $11 Billion of investors' and employees stocks and pensions, was due to fraudulent financial reporting [4]. In Panama, 21 patients died from overdoses of radiation during cancer treatment as a result of software failure combined with software misuse [5]. FDA analysis of 3,140 medical device recalls between 1992 and 1998 found that 242 (over 7 %) were attributable to software [20]. Significantly, of the 23 recalls in 2007 of what the FDA classify as life-threatening, 3 of them involved faulty software [23]. Consequently, regulations have been imposed to help reduce the possibility of such events recurring.

Publicly listed American companies are now subject to the Sarbanes–Oxley Act (SOX) of 2002 [1] to help ensure the accuracy of the data coming from financial systems. Medical device manufacturers are subject to a raft of regulations such as the United States Quality Systems Regulations 21 CFR part 820 [21] or the European Medical Device Directive [19]. These diverse sources of regulations are increasing as software continues to push boundaries, be misused and get embedded in ways which were not envisioned before.

6.2.4   The G-SC Case Study

To examine these aspects in detail we will look at the transformation of G-SC, a global leader in supply chain business process management. From an IT perspective, the company moved from a collection of around 30 international self-sufficient facilities, to a centralised, shared services IT model which included a globally distributed software development team with members located in the United States, Europe and Asia. This transformation was in fact an evolution of a company which grew organically initially and then through acquisitions and mergers. We will examine it from a process evolution perspective where we will also see how external influences, in particular from regulatory bodies, helped to shape that evolution.

6.3   Process Evolution

The structure of an organisation is crucial to its success. While it is important to design an appropriate structure in the early days of an organisation, it needs to be continuously appraised, *"A company needs to continuously revisit and challenge its answers to the who-what-how questions in order to remain flexible and ready to adjust its strategy..."* [30]. However, there is a level of foresight or design beyond which you cannot go with any certainty. Slack and Lewis [29] tell us *"...many environmental and operational variables are unknown in advance (and in some cases, unknowable)"* and therefore it is imperative to periodically review your situation. Thomas Friedman writes in his book 'The World Is Flat' that *"the best companies stay healthy by getting regular chest x-rays"* [22].

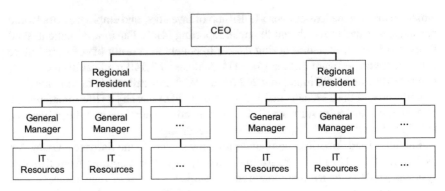

Fig. 6.1 G-SC initial management structure

Hand in hand with structure goes the way in which an organisation operates. Job descriptions are specified, roles are assigned, levels of authorisation are conferred, operating procedures defined and so on. These processes are overlaid on the management structure and are typically closely adhered to. But the world does not stay still, and so successful organisations are the ones most able to adapt to the changing environment in which they find themselves.[1]

Different environments can sustain totally different management structures and it is difficult to know precisely what will and will not work well. But experience shows that change is inevitable. New Chief Executive Officers (CEO) favour different management structures, new Chief Information Officers (CIO) favour certain technologies or development methodologies. Sometimes change is forced through, sometimes the status quo is required before introducing change. For example, when IBM bought Lotus Development in 1995, in the biggest corporate software take over up to that time, the contrast in work styles, dress codes, management hierarchy, etc., was stark, and a large risk to the entire project. IBM was very careful not to march in and take over, but gradually integrated the workforces and technologies over time (resistance is futile).

6.3.1 The G-SC Evolution

G-SC focused on high technology industries and as such was heavily invested in bespoke systems development. Consequently, they had built up a substantial IT workforce which included a large number of software engineering professionals. The initial global management structure is depicted in Fig. 6.1 and shows a typical structure for a disparate collection of self-sufficient solution centres (focus here on IT resources).

---

[1] I borrow the phrase from a quote about the evolution of species often attributed to Charles Darwin. There is some debate about whether Darwin actually said or wrote these exact words.

The individual General Managers (GM) had a lot of autonomy and full control over all local IT resources which allowed them build up a strong reputation in the local market for excellent customer service and rapid response times. Typically each solution centre had an IT manager with support, business analysis and software development expertise. This provided them with everything a good software engineering function needs.

The software engineering function within G-SC could be classified as residing somewhere between packaged and IS groups. Carmel and Sawyer [8] believe that *"...packaged software firms function in an environment of intense time-to-market pressure relative to IS development efforts"*. However, G-SC (clearly not a Packaged type organisation) was expected to have new business processes operational within the timelines governed by the customer (often packaged software firms) who in turn operated to their own specific market-driven product release schedules or seasonal consumer activities. Thus, having full control of local resources meant they could respond to these demands by reassigning resources, reprioritising projects or a combination of the two.

6.3.2   Sharing the Service

G-SC went through a merger and a subsequent acquisition which brought large-scale changes to the organisation. Along with a change in the business strategy, for example building global business teams to service global customers, the company introduced the role of CIO. The intention was clear, look for ways to gain efficiencies in the IT systems and personnel. This meant some form of integration from both perspectives, not a task to be underestimated [14]. From a globalisation perspective, in order to achieve integration, some level of standardisation is required, but, according to [8] and as we found out, the effort for standardisation of packaged teams pales in comparison to the scale of obstacles that a global IS function has to deal with.

By grouping all IT resources under the CIO, the new organisational structure looked like Fig. 6.2. Beneath the CIO, all IT resources were sub grouped into broad areas with further sub groupings for more specialised functions like software development. The immediate and involuntary effect of this reorganisation is that the new "Global" software development group becomes a bottleneck to the organisation since every solution centre vies for the finite resources (as indicated by the direct lines). But this reorganisation was in response to the new business strategy, to present the company as a unified, focused and globally serving service organisation.

It is worth noting that aligning the business and ICT strategies is a never ending cycle. *"(IT alignment) is complex, multifaceted and never completely achieved. It is about continuing to move in the right direction and being better aligned than competitors. This may not be attainable for many enterprises because enterprise goals change too quickly, but it is nevertheless a worthwhile ambition because there is real concern about the value of IT investment"* [26]. The CIO in this case has responsibility for ensuring that alignment.

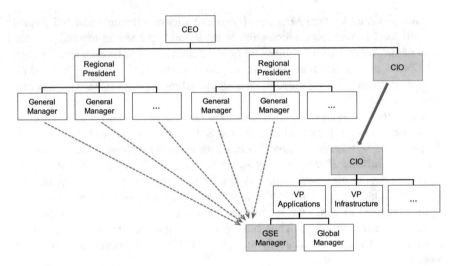

Fig. 6.2 The new G-SC management structure

6.4   Some Growing Pains

Operating as a shared service means that the group gets software project requests from all corners of the organization. In a global context that means that internal customers can be physically located anywhere and also that different business managers and indeed regional presidents are vying with each other for development resources. Many times this led to conflict and internal management escalations in order to secure resources. Sometimes these conflicts required resources to be sourced through expensive external consultants. Resourcing a project by this means has the benefit of a quick solution but also tends to incur a large amount of technical debt (see Chap. 15).

6.4.1   Project Prioritisation

One of the most problematic areas with this new structure was around the scheduling and prioritisation of software projects. With a finite number of GSE resources, and disparate business units needing work done, how do you decide on the order in which projects will be scheduled? Each manager can equally claim that their project is critical. To remediate this, a project review board (PRB) was instigated which consisted of a business representative from each solution centre attending a weekly conference call and helping set the priorities of development projects for the region. Key IT personnel who could advise from a technical perspective also attended these calls (Fig. 6.3). It is important to say that the business representatives had to have the authority to speak on behalf of their centres, which is why it was crucial that the respective General Manager appointed them to the PRB. Overall this worked

Fig. 6.3 The software review board structure

quite well but it still proved difficult to get consensus on prioritisation when multiple centres were under pressure to deliver projects within the same timelines.

Educating the internal business community was therefore also required and was performed by means of global email communications and solution centre visits. It is also worth noting that having management located in Ireland (a "Bridge") did help alleviate some of the temporal distance issues, since normal working days overlapped between Asia and Ireland and also the US and Ireland [31].

6.4.2 Personnel Management

From a software personnel management point of view, a number of issues arose. As the manager of a new GSE function, you inherit a lot of resources spread out across the globe. Personal unfamiliarity, time zone differences, cultural differences, varying levels of expertise all make for a very dynamic environment. Some people are better than others at adjusting to such a new working environment. Many people see this as a threat to their position, status, or very job, and so the management approach requires some significant adjustment.

The primary objective should be to get the group familiar with each other and comfortable working together. A key manifestation to overcome in the team is one of fear [10]. Temporal issues are extremely difficult to eradicate completely, but implementing processes around working arrangements can assist. For example, at times European developers worked the equivalent of US times to keep a project on track. Due to an asymmetry in knowledge and skills it took a long time before a more "follow the sun" approach could be implemented. Issue resolution was on average longer when dealing in the distributed environment but specific escalation paths were introduced in order to expedite special cases.

A source of much frustration for the software developers was getting in touch with someone at a remote site. This was typically to help with things like clarifying user requirements, user-testing functionality or carrying out a local installation. The PRB process, however, ensured that each site had a representative who could help get such situations resolved swiftly.

Building a team ethos through regular communication, sharing knowledge, cross-site projects, site visits and perseverance are some of the tools in the manager's toolbox for making this work. Building relationships with remote groups and aligning with other functions to deliver a coherent service are also things that need to be undertaken. For example, within a distributed organisation you will typically find local technical support personnel who act as the first line of support for local system issues. These people need to be considered part of the GSE process and should be an integral part of any system deployment, with knowledge transfer sessions and supporting documentation made available. Coordinating such handover processes needs careful consideration [10].

6.4.3 Seeing the Wood Despite the Trees

Following any organisational transformation it is easy to point out the hardships endured and the failures which occurred. But being part of a multi-national, multi-cultural, cross-functional team of skilled professionals is a fascinating, educational and often exhilarating experience. Fundamentally people are the same. They have similar concerns, ambitions, dependencies, and fears. But once things settle down and they start seeing global projects, of which they played a part, being deployed successfully, it generates a sense of satisfaction and belonging to something bigger, that they otherwise would not have been exposed to.

In this sense, whole teams of people evolve in their roles as the organisation evolves. People start to think outside their own box. They start to ask questions about the possible usefulness of a particular local process or project to the wider organisation. They see opportunities to share what they do but also the potential of using what other people do. For example, in G-SC a production manager may come up with an idea on how to better organise a certain manufacturing process but which requires a specific piece of functionality to be developed. The global software engineer/business analyst who examines this request starts to see how this might also work in other manufacturing sites around the world. By a slight extension/modification to the original requirements a globally reusable component is developed and made available to anyone who wants it.

It is imperative to recognise these successes [28]. People like to see that what they are doing is contributing to the success of the larger team. It helps to build or simply maintain employee motivation. It helps build confidence in the new process.

6.4.4 Regulating the Software Process

Software regulations typically expect an organisation to have a published software development process which clearly shows how the concerns of the regulator are addressed. In addition, the organisation will have to prove that they are following this approved process through some form of record keeping and usually an external audit. Interestingly there is much debate about the suitability of the more modern software development methodologies such as agile or lean in such regulated domains [13]. For more information on agile and lean approaches to Software Engineering, see Chap. 2 and Chap. 3.

Due to differing concerns between domains, different software development regulations have been created and consequently affect the development processes differently. The SOX regulations, for example, were designed to ensure accurate financial reporting. Very different concerns, however, are at the heart of regulations pertaining to safety-critical domains such as Aviation, Nuclear, or Medical Devices. In such domains the obvious concern is for human safety, and the regulations are designed to minimize to an acceptable level any related risk. To be SOX compliant you are expected to demonstrate that the software has been adequately tested. However, safety-critical regulations put a much heavier emphasis on this and expect thorough verification and validation of the software [20]. This level of detail, as required by the international standards such as IEC 62304 [25] for Medical Devices software life cycle processes, and ISO 13485 [24] for Medical Devices quality management systems, is far more onerous, and compliance must be demonstrated right throughout the entire software development lifecycle.

6.4.4.1   Regulatory Effects on the GSE Function

The SDLC within a regulated area is reflective of a number of key influences. My prior research [11] categorises these influences into 4 groups (Fig. 6.4). Within the model, the arrows emanating from the Regulations box are shown leading to the other three categories, indicating that compliance with the regulations must be addressed within multiple levels and contexts.

The organisation component influences the software development process by defining development tasks and delegating roles (such as developers and testers), responsibilities (such as project management and software validation), and authority (such as approvals). The regulatory context will influence the organisation's ethos

Fig. 6.4 Categories of influences on the software development lifecycle within a regulated context

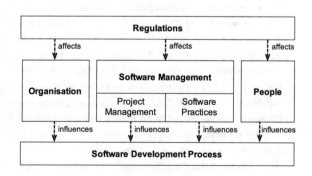

in terms of ensuring the quality of the software, the workforce's attitude to risk management, and their sense of responsibility.

The software management component (of tasks, resources and schedules) naturally influences the SDLC since it will be within these competencies, capabilities and situational contexts that the SDLC will need to be framed. For example, the technical nature of the product will automatically dictate the type of skills required and the type of development environment needed. The availability or lack or availability of these resources will shape the resulting SDLC [27]. Different people and organisations approach project management of software development differently. A company which sees the software as being strategically important may, therefore, also be more supportive of pursuing software process improvement initiatives.

The effect of regulatory compliance is very notable at a personnel level as it is precisely the human activities that are being governed. When moving from an unregulated into a regulated environment, unless the work processes are already fulfilling the regulations (experience suggests that this is unlikely), there is a need for peoples' daily activities to change. For example, both SOX and the Medical Devices regulations look for some level of independence in certain key areas. SOX looks for segregation of duties when it comes to code deployment or even access to a production system, while Medical Devices regulations expect independence between developers and validation engineers. The typical approaches to activities such as communication and knowledge transfer, where important ad hoc conversations go undocumented, or an approval is given verbally, are no longer acceptable. When people are accustomed to operating in an environment where issues can be fixed "on the spot," these tighter controls can be very frustrating for both the technical employee as well as for the person awaiting resolution.

6.4.4.2   G-SC under SOX Regulations

In 2002, the SOX regulations were passed into law in the United States. A critical element of those regulations refers to the ITGCs (Information Technology General Controls) which are intended to ensure: that financial data is stored securely, that only the relevant people have access to certain systems and functionality, and also that any software/modifications developed which could affect the financial data are developed within a robust and documented software development process.

It was therefore imperative that, within the G-SC environment, management were confident that each developer, regardless of location, adhered to the internal processes which were aligned with the expectations of SOX. A single set of "Global" processes/controls was rolled out to all developers and support members and proved instrumental in moving toward a cross-regional function. However, it added an extra overhead to management, who then spent a substantial amount of time ensuring that all team members, especially external contractors, were following the processes and maintaining the necessary documentation.

In addition, the regulatory requirement for segregation of duties is worth noting. For example, a software developer should not have full access to a live production system. Prior to being regulated, the G-SC developers were given such access by default. This was in order for them to perform technical tasks such as code deployment and resolving production issues. To mitigate the regulatory concerns, the database administrators were trained up in how to perform the deployments and where necessary supervised by the software expert. For trouble shooting production issues, the software engineers were given temporary administrator access, a record kept of when and why it was granted, and access revoked upon issue resolution. These records would subsequently be reviewed during the annual SOX audit.

6.5 Conclusion

As a company changes over its lifetime, for whatever reason, it must modify its business processes accordingly. The software engineering function which supports these processes must therefore be amenable to change also. The larger the company, the more disruptive the change but perhaps the more necessary it is.

Contemporary businesses are under huge pressure from competitors. In particular smaller companies must fight hard to win business from larger companies. Large companies are often looking for ways to reduce their costs in order to remain competitive. From a software engineering perspective, both small and large companies are looking at having some of their software developed at remote locations. Small companies are looking to outsource to low cost economies, while large companies are looking to "virtualise" their distributed software engineers into a globally shared service. In both cases, this new GSE function cannot work the same way as before. The process must change to support the business.

In addition, regulatory controls which are becoming more pervasive within the software engineering function, introduce additional complexities to the smooth delivery of the GSE service. The effects are felt right throughout the SDLC, and are magnified when the context is a global organisation.

With change comes challenge and opportunity. The challenges are not insurmountable and the opportunities reveal themselves as you evolve. We need to overcome the first to exploit the second.

6.6 Further Reading

The GSE topic has undergone quite a lot of academic research in the last number of years. The seminal work by Erran Carmel "Global software teams: collaborating across borders and time zones" [7], is a must read for those wishing to delve in to the subject. A research team based in the University of Limerick, Ireland have spent the last 10 years researching the theme, and have developed a global teaming best practice model. Some useful papers include: [9, 17, 32]. Readers are also encouraged to peruse their website at http://www.lero.ie/publications.

As introduced in this chapter, there has been a large growth in the number of industries which are becoming subject to software regulation, for security, criticality, safety, or quality reasons. This is still an area which requires further examination. The question remains as to how the current GSE research is relevant in these regulated contexts. Some introductory readings include: [6, 15].

References

1. 107th Congress: Sarbanes-Oxley Act of 2002. Technical report. Enrolled Bill: H.R. 3763, Congress of the United State of America (2002)
2. Ågerfalk, P.J., Fitzgerald, B., Holmström, H., Lings, B., Lundell, B., Conchúir, E.Ó.: A framework for considering opportunities and threats in distributed software development. In: Proceedings of the International Workshop on Distributed Software Development, pp. 47–61. Austrian Computer Society (2005)
3. Bank for international settlements: Basel II: international convergence of capital measurement and capital standards: a revised framework. http://www.bis.org/publ/bcbs107.htm (2004)
4. BBC: enron scandal at a glance. http://news.bbc.co.uk/2/hi/business/1780075.stm (2002)
5. Borrás, C.: Overexposure of radiation therapy patients in panama: problem recognition and follow-up measures. Pan Am. J. Public Health 20(2–3), 173–187 (2006)
6. Campbell, M.: Regulations. IEEE Potentials 23(2), 14–15 (2004)
7. Carmel, E.: Global Software Teams: Collaborating Across Borders and Time Zones. Prentice Hall, Upper Saddle River (1999)
8. Carmel, E., Sawyer, S.: Packaged software development teams: what makes them different? Inf. Technol. People 11(1), 7–19 (1998)
9. Casey, V., Richardson, I.: Practical experience of virtual team software development. In: Proceedings of the EuroSPI 2004 Industrial Proceedings. Trondheim (2004). http://ulir.ul.ie/handle/10344/2149
10. Casey, V., Richardson, I.: Virtual teams: understanding the impact of fear. Softw. Process.: Improv. Pr. 13(6), 511–526 (2008)
11. Cawley, O.: The application of a lean software development methodology within the regulated domain of medical device software. Ph.D. thesis, University of Limerick (Computer Science and Information Systems) (2013)
12. Cawley, O., Richardson, I.: Lessons in global software development – local to global transition within a regulated environment. In: European Systems and Software Process Improvement and Innovation (2010)
13. Cawley, O., Wang, X., Richardson, I.: Lean/agile software development methodologies in regulated environments - state of the art. In: Abrahamsson, P., Oza, N. (eds.) Lean Enterprise Software and Systems. Lecture Notes in Business Information Processing, vol. 65, pp. 31–36. Springer, Heidelberg (2010)
14. Cawley, O., Wang, X., Richardson, I.: Regulated software development - an onerous transformation. In: Weber, J., Perseil, I. (eds.) Foundations of Health Information Engineering and Systems. Lecture Notes in Computer Science, vol. 7789, pp. 72–86. Springer, Heidelberg (2013)
15. Cawley, O., Richardson, I., Wang, X., Kuhrmann, M.: A conceptual framework for lean regulated software development. In: Proceedings of the 2015 International Conference on Software and System Process, pp. 167–168. ACM, New York, USA (2015)
16. DeLone, W., Espinosa, J., Lee, G., Carmel, E.: Bridging global boundaries for is project success. In: Proceedings of the 38th Annual Hawaii International Conference on System Sciences, p. 48 ff. IEEE Computer Society, Washington, DC (2005)

17. Deshpande, S., Beecham, S., Richardson, I.: Global software development coordination strate-gies - a vendor perspective. In: Kotlarsky, J., Willcocks, L., Oshri, I. (eds.) New Studies in Global IT and Business Service Outsourcing. Lecture Notes in Business Information Process-ing, vol. 91, pp. 153–174. Springer, Heidelberg (2011)
18. Duranton, M., Black-Schaffer, D., De Bosschere, K., Maebe, J.: The hipeac vision for advanced computing in horizon 2020 (2013)
19. European Union: Medical Device Directive 2007/47/EC of the European Parliament and of the council. Official Journal of the European Union (2007)
20. FDA: General Principles of Software Validation; Final Guidance for Industry and FDA Staff. FDA Standard, U.S. Food and Drug Administration – Center for Devices and Radiological Health (2002)
21. FDA: Code of Federal Regulations 21 CFR Part 820 - Quality System Regulation. FDA Standard Part 820, U.S. Food and Drug Administration (2015)
22. Friedman, T.L.: The World Is Flat: A Brief History of the Twenty-First Century. Holtzbrinck Publishers (2005)
23. IEEE Reliability Society: Annual technical report 2008. Transactions on Reliability 57(3), 398–425 (2008)
24. ISO: Medical devices – quality management systems – requirements for regulatory purposes. International Standard ISO 13485:2003, International Organisation for Standardisation (2003)
25. ISO/TC 210: Medical device software – software lifecycle processes. International Standard IEC 62304:2006, International Standards Organization (2006)
26. IT Governance Institute: Board briefing on it governance. Available from http://www.isaca.org/Knowledge-Center/Research/ResearchDeliverables/Pages/Board-Briefing-on-IT-Governance-2nd-Edition.aspx (2003)
27. Kettunen, P., Laanti, M.: How to steer an embedded software project: Tactics for selecting the software process model. Information and Software Technology 47(9), 587–608 (2005)
28. Kotter, J.P.: Leading change: why transformation efforts fail. Harvard Business Review 73 (1995)
29. Lewis, M., Slack, N.: Operations Strategy. Prentice Hall, Upper Saddle River (2002)
30. Markides, C.C.: A dynamic view of strategy. Sloan Manag. Rev. 40(3), 55–63 (1999)
31. Richardson, I., Avram, G., Deshpande, S., Casey, V.: Having a foot on each shore - bridging global software development in the case of smes. In: Proceedings of the International Confer-ence on Global Software Engineering, pp. 13–22. IEEE, Washington, DC (2008)
32. Richardson, I., Casey, V., Mccaffery, F., Burton, J., Beecham, S.: A process framework for global software engineering teams. Inf. Softw. Technol. 54(11), 1175–1191 (2012)
33. The Free Dictionary: regulations. http://www.thefreedictionary.com/regulate (2015)

Chapter 7
The Route to Software Process Improvement in Small- and Medium-Sized Enterprises

Mary-Luz Sánchez-Gordón, Ricardo Colomo-Palacios, Antonio de Amescua Seco and Rory V. O'Connor

Abstract The software development industry is dominated by a myriad of small- and medium-sized enterprises (SMEs). The main goal of this chapter is to provide a characterization of SMEs based on previous studies. It also includes an overview of a number of software process models and software process improvement (SPI) models, which are aimed at assisting SMEs in improving the way they develop software. Furthermore, this chapter discusses the extent of SPI approaches published in the literature as a way to understand the particular context and some of the major challenges faced. From there, we propose an approach to integrate software process practices. This proposal is based on the results of our study on this topic carried out in small software companies. It is focused on what small organizations could actually do, more than on what they are currently practicing.

7.1 Introduction

In the current global economy more and more based on knowledge, software is key. Hence, countries need the capacity to adopt, adapt, and develop relevant software [131]. According to the *Organization for Economic Co-operation and Development* (OECD), small- and medium-sized enterprises (SMEs) constitute the dominant form

M.-L. Sánchez-Gordón (✉) · A. de Amescua Seco
Universidad Carlos III de Madrid, Av. Universidad 30, Leganés,
CP 28911, Madrid, Spain
e-mail: mary_sanchezg@hotmail.com

A. de Amescua Seco
e-mail: amescua@inf.uc3m.Es

R. Colomo-Palacios
Department of Computer Science,
Østfold University College, BRA Veien 4, 1783, Halden, Norway
e-mail: ricardo.colomo@hiof.No

R.V. O'Connor
Dublin City University, Glasnevin, Dublin 9, Ireland
e-mail: rory.oconnor@dcu.ie

© Springer International Publishing Switzerland 2016
M. Kuhrmann et al. (eds.), *Managing Software Process Evolution*,
DOI 10.1007/978-3-319-31545-4_7

of business organization in all countries worldwide, accounting for over 95 % and up to 99 % of the business population depending on the country [91]. In most developing and transition economies, the sector is dominated by small and young enterprises. Local software expertise is in a stronger position to understand local needs and, as a consequence, to develop relevant and innovative applications and content [131]. Therefore, it is of particular importance to ensure that this sector can support the public and private sectors' local needs [131]. Moreover, this sector is able to generate skilled jobs and foreign exchange earnings through the export of products and services produced at a distance [130, 131].

However, the implementation of controls and structures to properly manage their software development activities is necessary. This constitutes a major challenge. In this sense, a common way to achieve process management software development is through the introduction of a software process [88]. Although such management is recognized as important to business success, some studies (e.g., [9, 23, 26]) suggest that SMEs do not adopt a proactive and highly prioritized approach to software process improvement (SPI).

The aim of this chapter is to provide a characterization of SMEs based on previous studies and to give an overview of existing SPI initiatives. From there, we propose an approach to integrate software process practices based on the results of our study about this topic, carried out in very small software companies.

7.2 Background and Context

The term SME refers to a category of company that is essentially not a large organization. There is no globally accepted uniform definition of SMEs. The term SME covers a wide range of definitions and measures, varying from country to country and among the sources reporting SME statistics. Some of the commonly used criteria are the number of employees, total net assets, sales and investment level. However, the most common definitional basis used is employment, and here again, there is variation in defining the upper and lower size limit of an SME. Despite this variance, a large number of sources define an SME to have a cut-off range of 0–250 employees [8]. For instance, the European definition of SME [29] states:

> *The category of micro-, small-, and medium-sized enterprises (SMEs) is made up of enterprises which employ fewer than 250 persons and which have an annual turnover not exceeding 50 million euro, and/or an annual balance sheet total not exceeding 43 million euro.*

There are two further classifications within the SME category: small and micro enterprises. A small enterprise is defined as employing:

> *fewer than 50 persons and whose annual turnover does not exceed 10 million euro [...]*

and a micro enterprise is defined as employing:

> *fewer than 10 persons and whose annual turnover does not exceed 2 million euro [...]*

7.2.1 Software SMEs

Although an international classification exists for computer software and services, little international official data is available outside Europe and North America. In Europe, Eurostat uses the General Industrial Classification of Economic Activities within the European Communities (NACE Rev.2) that identifies computer software and related computer services as a subcategory:

- Division 62: computer programming, consultancy, and related activities
- Division 63: information service activities

In 2010, according to Eurostat [30], 99.8 % of enterprises in this sector were medium-sized (<250 employees). Small enterprises (<50 employees) make up at least 98.8 % and micro (<10 employees) are 94 %. In this sector, micro enterprises employed more than 30.74 % of people and made up 24 % of turnover. Similar scenarios occur in many other countries, especially in Brazil and Canada [52].

Likewise, the definition of "small" and "very small" enterprises is challengingly ambiguous, as there is no commonly accepted definition of the terms. For instance, Laryd and Orci [56] have proposed a classification of *Very Small Entities* (VSEs). In this classification, three different sizes constitute VSEs: the extra extra small (XXS), which are companies that had less than 3 employees; the extra small (XS), which are companies that had between 3 and 16 employees; and small (S), which are companies that had between 16 and 50 employees. According to Sánchez-Gordón [115], VSE includes small software development departments and small projects within larger organizations, which employs less than 25 people. In this study, we used a paper published by the Centre for Software Process Technologies [68] to help define the size of small organizations. This last definition has been accepted by the *International Organization for Standardization* (ISO) due to the crucial role played by VSEs in the software industry [44].

Besides the number of employees, McFall et al. [68] realized that the priorities and concerns for organizations with fewer than 20 employees are different from those of larger organizations. Not all the software companies are the same and vary according to factors including size, market sector, time in business, management style, product range, and geographical location [88]. Richardson and von Wangen-heim [109] stated that these companies often require different approaches because of specific business models and goals, resource availability (financial and human), process and management capability, organizational differences, among other things. Clarke and O'Connor [24] defined this as the situational context which includes eight classification factors: personnel, requirements, application, technology, organization, operation, management, and business.

Although the Software SME sector has been examined by researchers in terms of the number and proportion of individual organizations that qualify as SMEs, due to the rich variety of software development settings, the implementation of a set of practices for software development may be quite different from one setting to another [43]. One clear example is the startup phenomenon, there is no unique definition in literature on what constitutes a startup [93]. However, high uncertainty and rapid evolution are the two key characteristics for startups, which better differentiate them from more established companies [38].

7.2.2 Software Process in SMEs

The software process involves all the stages and activities that are followed by an organization to develop a software product [147]. Sommerville [123] states that a development process should be updated, improved, and maintained in order to meet current business and customer requirements. Thus, a software process model is an abstracted description of a software development process [102, 123] and it is prescriptive [123] since it indicates how software should be developed.

According to Pressman [102], there are three major general categories of software process models, namely: *waterfall*, *incremental*, and *evolutionary*. Furthermore, there are also specialized process models such as component-based and test-driven. Nevertheless, Boehm and Turner [13] outlined that there are two major software process categories: *agile* and *plan-driven*, which have been considered traditionally as opponents: On one hand, agile methods are based on iterative and incremental development using short development cycles [13]. The most important priority of agile methods is to keep the customer satisfied with early and continuous delivery of software functionality. Although agile software development methods have caught the attention of software engineers and researchers worldwide, scientific research still remains quite scarce [1]. On the other hand, the traditional software development world, characterized by the engineering and process improvement advocates, includes plan-driven methods that focus on the quality of the software artifacts and the predictability of the processes [13].

In practice, software development is beset with many challenges and constraints [43]. Although there are multiple approaches for organizing the software development process and multiple factors influencing the software development process [24], SMEs can have a low software development process priority [9], since they are focused on the product quality and delivery time rather than in the process quality [11]. Software SMEs report that they adopt a mix-and-match philosophy to their software development process, mixing aspects of different prescribed software development approaches in order to fulfill their needs within their constraints [25]. In other words, these companies do not use a software process model in a "textbook" fashion [26, 138, 140], preferring instead either to drop elements of their chosen model or, develop something proprietary best suited to their specific needs. Likewise, software engineering work practices are chosen opportunistically, adapted and configured to provide value under the constrains imposed by their context [93, 138]. In fact, organizations are adopting multiple methodologies on projects and choosing to follow a hybrid approach to software development [129, 138].

There is evidence that the majority of small, especially very small software organizations, are not adopting existing standards as they perceive them as being orientated toward large organizations and studies have shown that small firms' negative perceptions of process model standards are primarily driven by negative views of cost, documentation and bureaucracy [52]. Small companies generally need external assistance in order to adopt and implement standards [54]. As a result, in 2010, the ISO published the ISO/IEC 29110 standard, which addresses specifically the software lifecycle needs of VSEs, and it is still under development. Its adoption has been sometimes difficult, sometimes easier, but it is still incipient [76] and its impact on literature is also plain [77]. Therefore, it is an emerging standard and has work to be done yet.

The existence of a software process does not guarantee that software will be delivered on time, that it will meet the customer's needs, or that it will exhibit the technical characteristics that will lead to long-term quality characteristics [102]. Thus, the process itself can be assessed to ensure that it meets a set of basic process criteria that have been proved to be essential for a successful software engineering practice. For this reason, over the past years different approaches to software process assessment and improvement for the SME context have emerged.

7.2.3 Software Process Improvement in SMEs

While other industries have agreed in sets of best practices, to date, the software industry does not have universally accepted practices. The low adoption of best practices, as indicated from several previous surveys (e.g., [20, 26, 54, 68, 84]), suggests that process improvement should be a high priority for many software SMEs. These surveys have also established that many SMEs are interested in improving their software processes.

There exists a broad variety of *Software Process Improvement* (SPI) approaches. The most prominent due to their acceptance rates among large organizations are the ISO 9000 and ISO/IEC 15504 standards, and the Capability Maturity Model (CMM) and Capability Maturity Model Integration (CMMI) of the Software Engineering Institute (SEI). However, they are not being widely adopted and their influence in the software industry therefore remains more at a theoretical than at a practical level [26]. Schweigert et al. [121] have also not found a commonly accepted agile maturity model.

Despite significant investments in SPI that these large organizations have done, they still face problems in their implementation [81, 82]. Although SMEs adapt and use these models to initiate their improvement efforts, in many cases the efforts have not led to the expected improvements and failure rates are high. In spite of their importance, in general it has been observed that the successful implementation of these models is not possible in the context of SMEs [44], as they are not capable of dealing with the requirements and bear with the costs associated to the implementation of these SPI initiatives [46, 124, 142]. Moreover, there are significant differences in their awareness of quality issues and in the resources available [39]. Therefore, SPI initiatives in SMEs should be implemented using another approach to deal with their particular needs. On one hand, Kautz [46] and Mishra and Mishra [71] identified that CMM, ISO/IEC 90003:2004, TickIT, Bootstrap, and IDEAL models were not considered to be necessary or appropriate in SMEs contexts. On the other hand, Garcia et al. [34] state that SMEs are increasing the use of CMMI in number year by year but they did not show evidence to support it.

Nevertheless, the Software Engineering community has shown an ever-increasing interest in tackling SPI in SMEs [96], but it is still a problem scarcely studied in the world. Notable international initiatives are *European Systems and Software* (ESSI) promoted by the European Union, which have promoted the SPIRE project (Software Process Improvement in Regions of Europe), the MoProSoft model in Mexico, the MPS.BR project in Brazil, the SIMEP-SW in Colombia, the COMPETISOFT model in Latin America and ITMark, among others. However, none of them have been widely accepted or implemented, this has motivated the academia and the software industry to work together to study the components needed to improve the quality of their products and services, as well as the process performance.

Accordingly, many researchers are focusing their attention on adapting and using SPI approaches and how to guide and prioritize the SPI efforts in SMEs [96]. This means that often researchers consider small organizations together with medium enterprises, not differentiating their specific characteristics [109]. Therefore, this can affect research approaches and results. Due to limited in scale and resources, small software companies find software process improvement a major challenge [64].

Regarding the most prominent models, novel assessment methods tailored to the context of SMEs have been developed, such as an adaptation of the IDEAL model [96], *Rapid Assessment for Process Improvement for Software Development* (RAPID), *Software Process Improvement Initiation* (SPINI), and *Método de Avaliação de Processo de Software* (MARES). Regarding CMM, MESOPYME with objectives similar to those of the IDEAL model, and for CMMI, EPA which is an example of an ARC class-C compliant method and its expansion ADEPT. Finally, the approach presented in [128] and the *Agile Framework for Small Projects* (AFSP; [57]) are derived from Boehm and Turner's Agility/Discipline assessment.

In summary, taking into account studies and efforts in the area of SPI for small organizations [11, 25, 48, 54, 120, 126], it is evident that there is a need to find mechanisms that allow them to incorporate process improvement into their daily work, taking into account their business model, situational factors, limited resources, and cost and time constraints which are specific to their environment.

The systematic review carried out by Valtierra et al. [135] present a list of the most frequently improved processes: project planning, requirements management, configuration management process, and risk management. However, some organizations focus on processes such as requirements development, verification, project monitoring and control, and process and product quality assurance. Additionally, Pino et al. [96] in their systematic review included the documentation process as one of these processes.

7.3 Research Methodology

According to [114], in order to achieve an overview of the state of the question, a research must be carried out following the guideline on *Systematic Literature Reviews* (SLRs) by Kitchenham and Charters [47]. An SLR is defined as a methodical way to synthesize existing work in a manner that is fair and accurate. An SLR is a means of identifying, evaluating, and interpreting all available research relevant to a definite topic.

7.3.1 Motivation and Objectives

The literature presents a lack of studies on the whole view about the best known SPI methods, models and frameworks in SMEs. At the present time, there is limited documented and published research work regarding SPI in SMEs [54, 96, 135]. Therefore, this study will facilitate the understanding of the current status of research in this topic and outline further research. Finally, it will assist practitioners in the realization of the different approaches.

7.3.2 Research Method

This study has been undertaken as a SLR based on the Kitchenham and Charters' guidelines [47]. This section describes the steps carried out in this SLR.

7.3.2.1 Planning

The goal of this study is to develop an overview of the current status of the more SPI-identified approaches of the scientific literature on SMEs. After reviewing the literature on SLR for similar research objectives, it can be identified that there is no previously published search on the topic. We used a primary set of publications and manually searched for the SPI approaches and its references. This initial review reflected 40 SPI approaches to be explored in this study. For this primary search, we refer to the authors and publications summarized in Table 7.1, which later on also serve as control values.

Table 7.1 Key contributions of primary search

References	Title
[54]	The Application of International Software Engineering Standards in Very Small Entities
[71]	Software Process Improvement in SMEs: A Comparative View
[96]	Software Process Improvement in Small and Medium Software Enterprises: a systematic review
[125]	An Extended Systematic Review of Software Process Improvement in Small and Medium Web Companies
[135]	Characterization of Software Processes Improvement Needs in SMEs

Then, an SLR protocol was adapted to describe the plan for the review. The protocol includes research background, research questions, search strategy, study selection criteria and procedures, data extraction, and data synthesis strategies to ensure that the study is undertaken as planned and reduce the possibility of researcher bias. Next, the implementation of each step followed is briefly described.

7.3.2.2   Research Questions

The research question is threefold:

1. What is the impact of the SPI approaches in the scientific literature?
2. What has the evolution of the SPI approaches been?
3. Which research trends are revealed from the systematic review of the SPI approaches?

The keywords used to find an answer to the research questions were the name of SPI approach (e.g., MoProSoft, IDEAL, CMMI), which were taken from the pre-defined list (Sect. 7.3.2.1): `software process improvement`, `software process`, `sme`, and `small company`. Sometimes, it was necessary to include the name of the standard on which it is based in order to limit the search. For instance, the resulting search strings were:

- MOPROSOFT, (IDEAL) **and** (CMMI) **and** (software process)
- (CMMI) **and** (software process) **and** (sme **or** small company)

The results expected at the end of the systematic review were, among others, to discover what surveys exist as well as to identify the implications of each SPI approach in scientific literature. Authors also expected to see which applied researches had been carried out on the topic, as well as which trends are revealed from the performance of the systematic review.

Table 7.2 Inclusion (I) and exclusion (E) criteria

Kind	Criteria
I	Studies written in English or Spanish language
I	Studies explicitly related to each SPI approach
I	Studies in the SME context
E	Studies that are not written in the specified languages
E	Studies that are not relevant to the topic
E	Studies out of the SME context

7.3.2.3   Search Strategy and Search Process

Having the search strings to conduct the review the selected sources were: IEEE Xplore, ACM Digital Library, ScienceDirect, Wiley Online Library, and Springer Link. The search process included: first, the search string was selected; then a selected source was chosen and each search string was applied. Once the search results were obtained, a list of relevant studies was made based on titles, abstracts, conclusions, references, and keywords. Having the single result sets available, all results were combined and used as basis for the data analysis.

When there was doubt about its relevance, the reference was included leaving open the possibility of discarding the paper during the second phase when the full texts of the papers were studied. Sometimes, further studies were identified and included due to its relevance. After that, each full article was retrieved, read and analyzed to verify its inclusion or exclusion (Table 7.2) and the reason for that was properly documented. A test–retest approach and reevaluation of a random sample of the primary studies was made. Finally, the primary studies were identified.

7.3.2.4   Data Extraction

The data extracted from each paper was documented in a spreadsheet and kept in a reference manager. In addition, mind maps of the features of each initiative were made in order to understand the relations between them. After identification of the papers, the following data was extracted:

1. Source (journal or conference),
2. Title,
3. Authors,
4. Publication Year,
5. Relevance (defined during further analysis),
6. SPI approach features, and
7. Comments of the research, including which questions were solved.

Table 7.3 Inclusion (I) and exclusion (E) criteria

Source	Papers
Wiley Online Library	315
ScienceDirect	474
ACM Digital Library	209
IEEE Digital Library	152
SpringerLink	675
Number of potential papers	1825
Selected by abstract	297
Selected by full text (without duplicates)	90

7.3.3   Data Synthesis and Results

The searches for this SLR were conducted from December 2014 to January 2015. A total number of 1,825 studies were found from all sources based on the search strings defined. 90 primary studies were selected based on the in-/exclusion criteria. Table 7.3 presents the results of the search and the source of the documents. The results of the review are discussed in the following subsections.

7.3.3.1   Impact of the SPI Approaches in the Scientific Literature

Regarding the first research question, the 90 papers studied included one novel standard, 13 of the most recognized models and methods, five well-known frameworks and two techniques which were Pisko and its extension, LAPPI (Table 7.4). It is worth mentioning that ASPE/MSC and Adept also have been extended (ASPE/MSC, ASPEI/MSC and Adept, Automotive/Adept). They are distributed as follows: frameworks (40 %), models/methods (33 %), standards (20 %) and techniques (7 %). In the light of this, we can see that a lot of effort has been put into developing frameworks and models/methods. As Table 7.5 shows, the frameworks arosed since 2005. In this segment, it is worth noting that 50 % of the publications in 2007 are about MPS.BR.

Table 7.4 Papers by type

Type	SPI approaches	Papers	
		#	%
Standard	ISO/IEC 29110*	18	20
Model/Method	OWPL, MARES, EPA, Adept**, Impact, Mesopyme, ASPE/MSC***, iFlap, Processus, SPM, RAPID, XPMM Model, Agile SPI	30	33
Framework	MoProSoft, COMPETISOFT, MPS.BR, ITMark, Tutelkan	36	40
Technique	Pisko – LAPPI	6	7

* Includes UP-VSE model, ** include Automotive/Adept, and *** include ASPEI/MSC

Table 7.5 Papers by year

Type	1997	2000	2001	2002	2003	2004	2005	2006	2007	2008	2009	2010	2011	2012	2013	2014
Framework							2	2	7	2	5	7	3	4	1	3
Model/Method	1	1	4	3		2	2	4	2	4	2	1	1	1	2	
Standard										1		5	1	2	3	6
Technique				1	1	1		1	1						1	

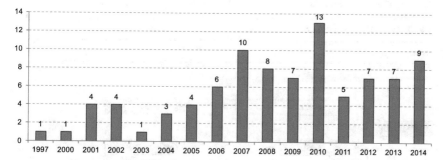

Fig. 7.1 Number of publications per year

In 2010, an important fact to take into account is the emergence of the ISO/IEC 29110 standard reflected in 38 % of the papers published on that year.

Figure 7.1 shows that 80 % of the articles were published from 2006 and the remainder (20 %) was published in the previous seven years. This seems to mean that there is an increasing interest in this field.

It is also important to remark that we have found scarce publications in some of the most cited models/methods: Impact (1), Mesopyme (1), Processus (2), SPM (2), XPMM (2) and RAPID (3). There is no hard evidence of their evolution after 2006. Adept (2) and ASPE/MSC (2) are in a similar situation after 2009. Likewise, EPA has 5 publications, but its last one was in 2009. Agile SPI has one paper published in 2010, which was taken from references found in the COMPETISOFT model. In consequence, there are 10 SPI approaches that demonstrate actual work in progress (Table 7.6). They make up for the 70 % of total.

7.3.3.2 Evolution of the SPI Approaches

The process of gradual, increasing change and development has resulted in a progression of SPI approaches including techniques, methods/models, frameworks, and integration of approaches. Thus, the ISO launched the ISO/IEC 29110 in 2010 in order to benefit the SPI in SMEs. Figures 7.2 and 7.3 show the 21 SPI approaches (Table 7.4) and their relations—bearing in mind UP-VSE model is taken as part of

Table 7.6 Current SPI approaches

SPI Approach	Type	2006	2007	2008	2009	2010	2011	2012	2013	2014	Total
ITMARK	Framework								1		1
iFlap	Method			1					1		2
Tutelkan	Framework					1	1				2
OWPL	Method			1				1	1		3
MARES	Method	2					1				3
Pisko-LAPPI	Technique		1	1					1		3
MoProSoft	Framework		1	1		1		2	1	1	7
COMPETISOFT	Framework		1	1	4	3	2	1			12
MPS.BR	Framework	2	5		1	2		1		1	12
ISO/IEC 29110	Standard			1		5	1	2	3	6	18
Total											63

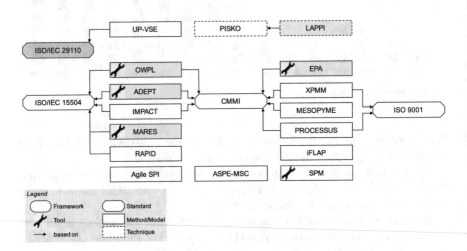

Fig. 7.2 Relations between models/methods, techniques, and standards

the ISO/IEC 29110 standard. These relations were identified during this review. The CMMI, ISO/IEC 15504, ISO/IEC 12207, and ISO 9001 standards have been the major foundation on which most of the models and methods have been developed.

Figure 7.2 shows that EPA, XPMM, MESOPYME, OWPL, PROCESSUS, IMPACT, and ADEPT are based on CMMI. However, some of them are also based on others standards. Therefore, XPMM and PROCESSUS are based on ISO 9001, and IMPACT, ADEPT, and OWPL on ISO/IEC 15504. Likewise, RAPID and MARES are based on ISO/IEC 15504. Furthermore, there are models based on other ones, like SPM which is based on QFD/SPI model focused on the House of Quality or ASPE/MSC that is tailored out of existing approaches, these standards are adapted and simplified either by incorporating a matrix (as in SPM model) or process guides (as in ASPE-MSC). The same applies to iFlap that is based on the inductive method.

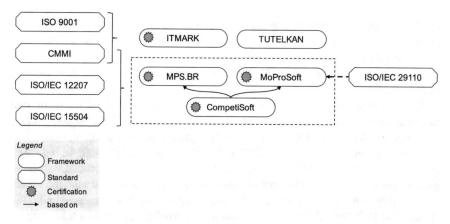

Fig. 7.3 Relations between frameworks and standards

Finally, UP-VSE is a software process model based on the Unified Process, which implements the requirements engineering practices of ISO/IEC 29110-5-1-1. Therefore, UP-VSE has been taken as papers of the standard in order to illustrate how ISO/IEC 29110 arises in this context. Moreover, agile methodologies such as XP or Scrum also have inspired new approaches, such as the XPMM model or Agile SPI. The latter is less known but was studied for COMPETISOFT in order to develop its process improvement model. Finally, LAPPI is an evolution of the PISKO technique. The LAPPI technique provides an easy to use, lightweight tool for process modeling and improvement target identification. Therefore, it is useful in the diagnosing phase of SPI.

Figure 7.3 depicts the frameworks and their relations with the standards CMMI, ISO/IEC 15504, ISO/IEC 12207, ISO 9001, and ISO/IEC 29110. CMMI, ISO/IEC 15504, ISO/IEC 12207 have a major influence on MoProSoft, MPS.BR, and COMPETISOFT. In turn, the last one is based on the top two. CMMI also provides the basis for Tutelkan, which incorporates ISO 9001 and ITMARK that in turn encompass EFQM and ISO/IEC 27001. Each framework has its own reference and assessment model, and approaches to their implementation that includes automated tools. Consequently, almost all of them have mechanisms for their certification. However, Tutelkan is a framework that does not provide certification. It allows SMEs to become aware of their level of compliance with international standards, since each reusable asset contains information about the specific CMMI practices, ISO 9001 clauses and COMPETISOFT activities that it conforms to. On the other hand, MoProSoft has been selected by the authors of the ISO/IEC 29110 standard in order to quickly achieve initial products. This standard aims to address the difficulties of SMEs by developing profiles and by providing guidance for conformance with ISO/IEC software engineering standards. This framework attempts to ease the use of ISO/IEC 12207 processes and ISO 9001, and reduce the conformance obligations by providing VSE profiles. The ISO/IEC 29110 standard has a series of Deployment Packages (DPs) and Implementation Guides that have been developed to define guidelines and explain in more detail the processes defined in the ISO/IEC 29110 profiles. Although a DP is not a process reference model, packages are designed such that a VSE can implement its content without having to implement the complete framework. A DP also includes mapping to other standards or models, such as the CMMI.

Regarding the adoption of the 10 SPI approaches outlined in Table 7.6, by the end of 2013, after 10 years, the MPS-SW of MPS.BR surpassed the 500 assessments in companies located in Brazil's five regions, mostly including micro, small, and medium-sized enterprises. The LAPPI technique has evolved through 42 industrial cases conducted during 1999–2011 in 31 different companies. The official website of Itmark[1] point out a list of 155 certified companies in 17 countries around the world. Accordingly to NYCE,[2] more than 400 organizations have been assessed under the standard NMX-I-059/02-NYCE, best known as MoProSoft, and there are 11 certified companies under basic profile of the ISO/IEC 29110 standard. The selected papers about COMPETISOFT describe some case studies and 5 certified companies in Peru.

In 2008, OWPL reported an experience concerned to 93 evaluations of 86 different organizations in 3 countries (Wallonia, Quebec and France). Finally, the selected papers about MARES, Tutelkan, iFlap show quiet few case studies carried out in order to validate their proposal.

7.3.3.3   Research Trends

In this section, we describe the main research trends of the SPI in SMEs revealed from this SLR. In relation to the number of publications, Fig. 7.4 shows that lately there is an increasing interest on the ISO/IEC 29110 standard which overcomes the other types of initiatives (models/methods, techniques, and frameworks). Nevertheless, the initiatives have given experience and knowledge in the field of SPI so its usefulness extends to practitioners and researchers. In fact, the distribution of publications on SPI initiatives (Fig. 7.5) also shows that MPS.BR, MoProSoft and COMPETISOFT correspond to more than 50 % of the papers, which is in accordance with the aforementioned adoption data. The SPI approaches have evolved through the collaborations among academy and software industry during 1997–2014 in different kinds of SME around the world. However, the SPI initiatives are primarily located in Europe and America where the strength of local government support for these initiatives has been in large. It also has been a key factor affecting their dissemination. In addition, the development of mechanisms such as automated tools or deployment packages to facilitate the implementation of the initiatives is important and necessary to achieve their adoption among SMEs.

---

[1] Available from: http://it-mark.eu.

[2] Available from: http://www.nyce.org.mx/moprosoft.

Fig. 7.4 Number of publications by type per year

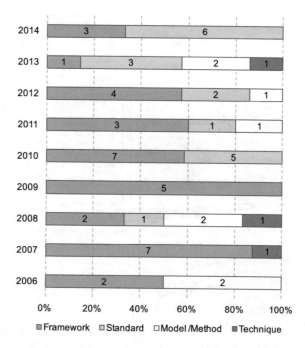

Fig. 7.5 Distribution of publications by software process improvement initiative

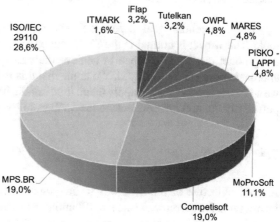

7.3.3.4 Limitations of Current Research

Regarding the search string, we attempted to collect all the strings that were representative of the SPI approaches identified and the three research questions. Based on the results obtained, the search strings were refined on several occasions in order to maximize the selection of papers related to the SLR. Then, we ensured that the studies with which we were familiar were in the results.

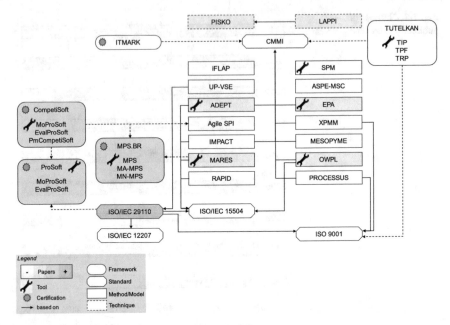

Fig. 7.6 Relations between software process improvement initiatives and the standards: CMMI, ISO/IEC 12207, ISO/IEC 15504, ISO 9001, and ISO/IEC 29110

Another potential weak aspect is that there are very few papers related to this topic. This aspect is normal in the SME context, where the tendency is to maximize the product quality as a mean to achieve the best quality in use. Therefore, SPI approaches are rarely deployed. We argue that this is not the best way to work and we advocate another way to apply them: first, establish what they actually do or could potentially do; and later on, ensure the SME stability and address an SPI initiative.

7.4 Conclusions

A main objective of the SLR was to investigate specific SPI initiatives. We have investigated the current evidence of SPI initiatives in the context of SMEs. Due to our inclusion/exclusion criteria, the number of relevant studies found was small but the overall search process was very comprehensive, and following the protocol defined performed it. As a result, 90 papers were chosen and a total of 21 SPI approaches were studied from these papers, although only 63 are pertinent for this SLR. The rest of the papers are about less known and consequently less used initiatives. A full list of papers is shown in Sect. 7.6.

Regarding the categories in which the SPI approaches can be divided, we found 5 frameworks, 13 models/methods, 2 techniques, and 1 standard (see Fig. 7.6). Many of the publications are focused on frameworks (40 % out of the total) but the ISO/IEC 29110 has lately received a lot of attention (20 %). However, the current work is revealed by 3 methods/models (iFlap, OWPL and MARES), 5 frameworks

(MoProSoft, COMPETISOFT, MPS.BR, ITMark, Tutelkan) and the ISO/IEC 29110 standard. However, the MoProSoft, COMPETISOFT, and MPS.BR work with their own reference and assessment models and offer their own certifications. Although two techniques were found in this topic, they refer only to one approach because LAPPI extends Pisko.

There is quite few information about the results of the above SPI initiatives in terms of case studies, lessons learned, and number of certified SMEs. Therefore, it is difficult to determine the actual scope of such initiatives and their success. That means that more dissemination and support is necessary. These factors strongly influence the number and the period in which the adoption appears: very few contributions were found before 2006. Consequently, a growing increase appears in the last 10 years. In addition, we have found novel approaches, such as ArSPI model, which by its nature could become more relevant in the coming years.

It is worth mentioning that most of the SPI initiatives are based on CMMI, ISO/IEC 12207, ISO/IEC 15504 and ISO 9001 standards (Fig. 7.6), the relations between them and the framework are displayed in Fig. 7.3. Additionally, there is a strong tendency for use of the ISO/IEC 29110 standard for instance UP-VSE model is based on it.

Considering the rich variety of software development settings, the route to SPI in SMEs depends on the amount of resources, effort, and objectives of each one. On one hand the ease of use (automated tools), lightweight and low cost are important features. On the other hand the support of local governments and international institutions such as ISO is an important part of the key.

7.5 Further Reading

This paper discusses SPI methods, models and frameworks for SMEs from a comparative perspective. The most related work has been developed by Mishra and Mishra [70, 71], who reviewed and compared various SPI methodologies on different significant attributes supported by various studies. Additionally, there are four systematic literature reviews (SLRs) on this topic: three of them [54, 96, 135] identified the SPI approaches but did not focus on understand their evolution, and the last one [125] is focused on web companies.

This book chapter extends previous work in a substantial way because we are considering a measure of the impact of publications by means of a systematic literature review of each SPI-identified approach (method, model, and framework) from previous reviews. Therefore, a rigorous and up-to-date literature review with the latest related references has been included.

Recommended literature for further information about this topic is available in the proceedings from conference series such as *International Conference on Software and System Process* (ICSSP; [42]), *European System & Software Process Improvement and Innovation* (EuroSPI; [10, 67]) and *International SPICE Conference* (SPICE; [72, 146]) as valuable information resources for researchers. Furthermore, recommended literature for additional information about ISO/IEC 29110 is available: http://29110.org and there is a Public Site of the ISO Working Group

Mandated to Develop ISO/IEC 29110 Standards and Guides for Very Small Entities involved in the Development or Maintenance of Systems and/or Software References. Recommended literature for further information about MoProSoft: http://www.nyce. org.mx/moprosoft and recommended further reading regarding ArSPI is available from [49, 50].

7.6 List of SLR Papers

This section gives an overview of the reviewed papers and provides a classification. Furthermore, the acronyms and abbreviations used in this chapter are explained (Tables 7.7 and 7.8).

Table 7.7 Summary and classification of the papers of the systematic literature review

Type	Initiative	References
Framework	COMPETISOFT	[27, 28, 60, 61, 90, 92, 97–101, 139]
	ITmark	[55]
	MoProSoft	[7, 35–37, 78, 110, 136]
	MPS.BR	[12, 21, 31, 32, 45, 73–75, 111, 112, 116–118, 143]
	Tutelkan	[132, 133]
Model/Method	Adept	[63, 65]
	ASPE/MSC	[40, 142]
	EPA	[58, 59, 66, 144, 145]
	iFlap	[94, 95]
	IMPACT	[122]
	MARES	[6, 140, 141, 148]
	MESOPYME	[16]
	OWPL	[22, 39, 149]
	PROCESSUS	[41, 113]
	RAPID	[17–19]
	SPM	[107, 108]
	XPMM	[33, 79, 80]
Standard	ISO/IEC 29110	[5, 14, 15, 51–53, 62, 69, 83, 85–87, 89, 104–106, 127, 137]
References	LAPPI	[103]
	PISKO	[2–4, 119, 134]

Table 7.8 Current SPI approaches

Abbreviation	Name
Prosoft	Programme for the Development of the Software Industry (Programa para el Desarrollo de la Industria del Software)
↪ MoProSoft	Process Model for the Software Industry (Modelo de Procesos para la Industria de Software)
↪ EvalProSoft	Process Assessment Method for Software Industry (Método de Evaluación de Procesos para la Industria del Software)
MPS.BR	Brazilian Software Process Improvement (Melhoria de Processos do Software Brasileiro)
↪ MA-MPS	MPS Assessment Method (Método de Avaliação para Melhoria de Processo de Software)
↪ MN-MPS	MPS Business Model (Modelo de Negócio para Melhoria de Processo de Software)
SIMEP-SW	Colombian Software Development Process Improvement System (Sistema Integral para el Mejoramiento de los procesos de Desarrollo de Software en Colombia)
COMPETISOFT	Process Improvement for Promoting Iberoamerican Software Small and Medium Enterprises Competitiveness
RAPID	Rapid Assessments for Process Improvement for software Development
MARES	Methodology for Software Process Assessment (Método de Avaliação de Processo de Software)
EPA	Express Process Appraisal
AFSP	Agile Framework for Small Projects
OWPL	Walloon Observatory for Software Practices (Observatoire Wallon des Pratiques Logicielles)
ASPE/MSC	Approach for Software Process Establishment in Micro and Small Companies
ASPEI/MSC	Approach for Software Process Establishment and Improvement in Micro and Small Companies
iFlap	Improvement Framework Utilizing Lightweight Assessment and Planning
SPM	Software Process Matrix
XPMM	eXtreme Programming Maturity Model
Agile SPI	Agile Software Process Improvement
Tutelkan	
↪ TIP	Tutelkan Implementation Process
↪ TPF	Tutelkan Process Framework
↪ TRP	Tutelkan Reference Process
LAPPI	Light-weight Technique to Practical Process Modeling and Improvement Target Identification
Automotive-adept	Lightweight assessment method for the automotive software industry
UP-VSE	Unified Process for Very Small Entities
ArSPI	Artifact-based Software Process Improvement & Management

References

1. Abrahamsson, P., Oza, N., Siponen, M.T.: Agile software development methods: a comparative review. In: Dingsøyr, T., Dybå, T., Moe, N.B. (eds.) Agile Software Development, pp. 31–59. Springer, Heidelberg (2010)
2. Ahonen, J.J., Forsell, M., Taskinen, S.K.: A modest but practical software process modeling technique for software process improvement. Softw. Process Improv. Pract. 7(1), 33–44 (2002)
3. Ahonen, J., Junttila, T.: A case study on quality-affecting problems in software engineering projects. In: Proceedings of the International Conference on Software: Science. Technology and Engineering, pp. 145–153. IEEE, Washington (2003)
4. Ahonen, J.J., Junttila, T., Sakkinen, M.: Impacts of the organizational model on testing: three industrial cases. empir. softw. eng. 9(4), 275–296 (2004)
5. Alvarez, J.J., Hurtado, J.A.: Implementing the software requirements engineering practices of the ISO 29110-5-1-1 standard with the unified process. In: Proceedings of the Computing Colombian Conference, pp. 175–183. IEEE, Washington (2014)
6. Anacleto, A., Von Wangenheim, G., Salviano, C., Savi, R.: A method for process assessment in small software companies. In: Proceedings of the International SPICE Conference on Process Assessment and Improvement, pp. 69–76. ICSOFT, Portugal (2004)
7. Ariza, P., Pineres, M., Santiago, L., Mercado, N., De la Hoz, A.: Implementation of moprosoft level I and II in software development companies in the colombian caribbean, a commitment to the software product quality region. In: Proceedings of the Central America and Panama Convention, pp. 1–5. IEEE, Washington (2014)
8. Ayyagari, M., Beck, T., Demirgüc, A.: Small and medium enterprises across the globe: a new database. Policy Research Working Papers. The World Bank, Washington (2003). URL http://elibrary.worldbank.org/doi/book/10.1596/1813-9450-3127
9. Baddoo, N., Hall, T.: De-motivators for software process improvement: an analysis of practitioners' views. J. Syst. Softw. 66(1), 23–33 (2003)
10. Barafort, B., O'Connor, R.V., Messnarz, R. (eds.): Systems, Software and Services Process Improvement. Communications in Computer and Information Science, vol. 425. Springer, Heidelberg (2014)
11. Basri, S., O'Connor, R.V.: Understanding the perception of very small software companies towards the adoption of process standards. In: Riel, A., O'Connor, R.V., Tichkiewitch, S., Messnarz, R. (eds.) Systems, Software and Services Process Improvement, Communications in Computer and Information Science, vol. 99, pp. 153–164. Springer, Heidelberg (2010)
12. Boas, G., da Rocha, A., Pecegueiro do Amaral, M.: An approach to implement software process improvement in small and mid sized organizations. In: Proceedings of the International Conference on the Quality of Information and Communications Technology, pp. 447–452. IEEE, Washington (2010)
13. Boehm, B., Turner, R.: Balancing Agility and Discipline: A Guide for the Perplexed. Addison-Wesley, Boston (2003)
14. Boucher, Q., Perrouin, G., Deprez, J.C., Heymans, P.: Towards configurable ISO/IEC 29110-compliant software development processes for very small entities. In: Winkler, D., O'Connor, R.V., Messnarz, R. (eds.) Systems, Software and Services Process Improvement, Communications in Computer and Information Science, vol. 301, pp. 169–180. Springer, Heidelberg (2012)
15. Buchalcevova, A.: Software process improvement in small companies as a path to enterprise architecture. In: Pooley, R., Coady, J., Schneider, C., Linger, H., Barry, C., Lang, M. (eds.) Information Systems Development, pp. 243–253. Springer, Heidelberg (2013)
16. Calvo-Manzano Villalón, J.A., Gonzalo Cuevas, A., San Feliu Gilabert, T., de Amescua Seco, A., García Sánchez, L., Cota, M.P.: Experiences in the application of software process improvement in SME's. Softw. Qual J 10(3), 261–273 (2002)
17. Cater-Steel, A.: Process improvement in four small software companies. In: Proceedings of the Australian Software Engineering Conference, pp. 262–272. IEEE, Washington (2001)

18. Cater-Steel, A.: Low-rigour, rapid software process assessments for small software development firms. In: Proceedings of the Australian Software Engineering Conference, pp. 368–377. IEEE, Washington (2004)
19. Cater-Steel, A., Toleman, M., Rout, T.: Process improvement for small firms: an evaluation of the RAPID assessment-based method. Inf. Softw. Technol. **48**(5), 323–334 (2006)
20. Cater-Steel, A.P.: COTS developers lead best practice adoption. In: Proceedings of the Conference on Software Engineering, pp. 23–30. Los Alamitos (2000)
21. Chaves Weber, K., Ramalho de Araujo, E., Scaler, D., Pereira de Andrade, E., Cavalcanti da Rocha, A., Montoni, M.: MPS model-based software acquisition process improvement in brazil. In: Proceedings of the International Conference on the Quality of Information and Communications Technology, pp. 110–122. IEEE, Washington (2007)
22. Cholez, H., Girard, F.: Maturity assessment and process improvement for information security management in small and medium enterprises. J. Softw. Evolut. Process **26**(5), 496–503 (2013)
23. Clarke, P., O'Connor, R.V.: The influence of SPI on business success in software SMEs: an empirical study. J. Syst. Softw. **85**(10), 2356–2367 (2012)
24. Clarke, P., O'Connor, R.V.: The situational factors that affect the software development process: towards a comprehensive reference framework. Inf. Softw. Technol. **54**(5), 433–447 (2012)
25. Clarke, P., O'Connor, R.V.: An empirical examination of the extent of software process improvement in software SMEs. J. Softw. Evolut. Process **25**(9), 981–998 (2013)
26. Coleman, G., O'Connor, R.: Investigating software process in practice: a grounded theory perspective. J. Syst. Softw. **81**(5), 772–784 (2008)
27. Cruz, P., Villarroel, R., Mancilla, F., Visconti, M.: A software testing process for the reference model of competisoft. In: Proceedings of the International Conference of the Chilean Computer Science Society, pp. 51–59. IEEE, Washington (2010)
28. Davila, A., Basurto, C., Flores, L., Arisaca, R., Manrique, R., Sánchez, J., de Paula Pessôa, M.: The peruvian component of Competisoft project: Lesson learned from academic perspective. In: Proceedings of the Conferencia Latinoamericana En Informatica, pp. 1–7. IEEE, Washington (2012)
29. European Commission: The new SME definition. Enterprise and industry publications. Office for Official Publications of the European Communities, Luxembourg (2005)
30. Eurostat: Annual enterprise statistics by size class for special aggregates of activities (nace rev. 2). Available from: http://epp.eurostat.ec.europa.eu/statistics_explained/index.php (2014)
31. Ferreira, A., Santos, G., Cerqueira, R., Montoni, M., Barreto, A., Barreto, A., Rocha, A.: Applying ISO 9001:2000, MPS.BR and CMMI to achieve software process maturity: BI informatica's pathway. In: Proceedings of the International Conference on Software Engineering, pp. 642–651. IEEE, Washington (2007)
32. Ferreira, A.I.F., Santos, G., Cerqueira, R., Montoni, M., Barreto, A., Rocha, A.R., Figueiredo, S., Barreto, A., Filho, R.C.S., Lupo, P., Cerdeiral, C.: Taba workstation: Supporting software process improvement initiatives based on software standards and maturity models. In: Richardson, I., Runeson, P., Messnarz, R. (eds.) Software Process Improvement, Lecture Notes in Computer Science, vol. 4257, pp. 207–218. Springer, Heidelberg (2006)
33. Fontana, R.M., Meyer Jr., V., Reinehr, S., Malucelli, A.: Progressive outcomes: a framework for maturing in agile software development. J. Syst. Softw. **102**, 88–108 (2015)
34. Garcia, I., Pacheco, C., A Calvo, J.: Quantitative project management in small and medium-sized software enterprises. Latin America Trans., IEEE (Revista IEEE America Latina) **12**(3), 508–513 (2014)
35. Garcia, I., Pacheco, C., Cruz, D.: Adopting an RIA-based tool for supporting assessment, implementation and learning in software process improvement under the NMX-I-059/02-NYCE-2005 standard in small software enterprises. In: Proceedings of the ACIS International Conference on Software Engineering Research, Management and Applications, pp. 29–35. IEEE, Washington (2010)

36. Garcia, I., Pacheco, C., Cruz, D., Calvo-Manzano, J.A.: Implementing the modeling-based approach for supporting the software process assessment in SPI Initiatives Inside a Small Software Company. In: Lee., R. (ed.) Software Engineering Research, Management and Applications, Studies in Computational Intelligence, vol. 377, pp. 1–13. Springer, Heidelberg (2012)

37. Garcia, I.A., Calvo-Manzano, J.A., Pacheco, C.L., Perez, C.A.: Software engineering education for a graduate course: a web-based tool for conducting process improvement initiatives with local industry collaboration. Comput. Appl. Eng. Educ. **23**(1), 117–136 (2013)

38. Giardino, C., Unterkalmsteiner, M., Paternoster, N., Gorschek, T., Abrahamsson, P.: What do we know about software development in startups? IEEE Softw. **31**(5), 28–32 (2014)

39. Habra, N., Alexandre, S., Desharnais, J.M., Laporte, C.Y., Renault, A.: Initiating software process improvement in very small enterprises: experience with a light assessment tool. Inf. Softw. Technol. **50**(7–8), 763–771 (2008)

40. Hauck, J.C.R., Wangenheim, C.G.v., Souza, R.H.d., Thiry, M.: Process reference guides— support for improving software processes in alignment with reference models and standards. In: O'Connor, R.V., Baddoo, N., Smolander, K., Messnarz, R. (eds.) Software Process Improvement, Communications in Computer and Information Science, vol. 16, pp. 70–81. Springer, Heidelberg (2008)

41. Horvat, R.V., Rozman, I., Györkös, J.: Managing the complexity of SPI in small companies. Softw. Process Improv. Pract. **5**(1), 45–54 (2000)

42. Jeffery, R., Raffo, D., Armbrust, O., Huang, L. (eds.): Proceedings of International Conference on Software and System Process (ICSSP). IEEE, New Jersey (2012)

43. Jeners, S., Clarke, P., O'Connor, R.V., Buglione, L., Lepmets, M.: Harmonizing software development processes with software development settings—a systematic approach. Systems. Software and Services Process Improvement, pp. 167–178. Springer, Heidelberg (2013)

44. JTC 1, SC 7: Software engineering – lifecycle profiles for very small entities (VSEs) part 5-1-1: Management and engineering guide: Generic profile group: Basic profile. International Standard ISO/IEC TR 29110-5-1-2:2011(E), International Organization for Standardization, Geneva (2011)

45. Kalinowski, M., Weber, K., Franco, N., Barroso, E., Duarte, V., Zanetti, D., Santos, G.: Results of 10 years of software process improvement in Brazil based on the MPS-SW model. In: Proceedings of the International Conference on the Quality of Information and Communications Technology, pp. 28–37. IEEE, Washington (2014)

46. Kautz, K.: Software process improvement in very small enterprises—does it pay? Softw. Process Improv. Pract. **4**(4), 209–226 (1998)

47. Kitchenham, B., Charters, S.: Guidelines for performing systematic literature reviews in software engineering. Technical report EBSE-2007-01, Keele University, Staffordshire (2007)

48. Kroeger, T.A., Davidson, N.J., Cook, S.C.: Understanding the characteristics of quality for software engineering processes: a grounded theory investigation. Inf. Softw. Technol. **56**(2), 252–271 (2014)

49. Kuhrmann, M., Beecham, S.: Artifact-based software process improvement and management: a method proposal. In: Proceedings of the International Conference on Software and System Process, pp. 119–123. ACM, New York (2014)

50. Kuhrmann, M., Méndez Fernández, D.: From pragmatic to systematic software process improvement: an evaluated approach. IET Softw. **9**(6), 157–165 (2015)

51. Laporte, C., O'Connor, R.: Systems and software engineering standards for very small entities: implementation and initial results. In: Proceedings of the International Conference on Quality of Information and Communications Technology, pp. 38–47. IEEE, Washington (2014)

52. Laporte, C.Y., Alexandre, S., O'Connor, R.V.: A software engineering lifecycle standard for very small enterprises. In: O'Connor, R.V., Baddoo, N., Smolander, K., Messnarz, R. (eds.) Software Process Improvement, Communications in Computer and Information Science, vol. 16, pp. 129–141. Springer, Heidelberg (2008)

53. Laporte, C.Y., O'Connor, R.V.: A systems process lifecycle standard for very small entities: Development and pilot trials. In: Barafort, B., O'Connor, R.V., Poth, A., Messnarz, R. (eds.) Systems, Software and Services Process Improvement, Communications in Computer and Information Science, vol. 425, pp. 13–24. Springer, Heidelberg (2014)

54. Laporte, C.Y., Renault, A., Alexandre, S.: The application of international software engineering standards in very small enterprises. In: Oktaba, H., Piattini, M. (eds.) Software Process Improvement for Small and Medium Enterprises Techniques and Case Studies, pp. 42–70. Information Science Reference, Hershey, New York (2008)
55. Larrucea, X., Santamaria, I.: An industrial assessment for a multimodel framework. J. Softw. Evolut. Process **26**(9), 837–845 (2014)
56. Laryd, A., Orci, T.: Dynamic CMM for small organizations. In: Proceedings of the Argentine Symposium on Software Engineering (2000). URL http://www.uml.org.cn/cmm/pdf/1116/laryd00dynamic.pdf
57. Lee, S., Yong, H.S.: Agile software development framework in a small project environment. J. Inf. Process. Syst. **9**(1), 69–88 (2013)
58. Lester, N., Wilkie, F., McFall, D., Ware, M.: Evaluating the internal consistency of the base questions in the express process appraisal. In: Proceedings of the EUROMICRO Conference on Software Engineering and Advanced Applications, pp. 289–296. IEEE, Washington (2007)
59. Lester, N.G., Wilkie, F.G., McFall, D., Ware, M.P.: Investigating the role of CMMI with expanding company size for small- to medium-sized enterprises. J. Softw. Maint. Evolut. Res. Pract. **22**(1), 17–31 (2010)
60. Luzuriaga, J.M., Martínez, R., Cechich, A.: Setting SPI practices in Latin America: an exploratory case study in the justice area. In: Proceedings of the International Conference on Theory and Practice of Electronic Governance, pp. 172–177. ACM, New York (2008)
61. Martínez-Ruiz, T., Pino, F.J., León-Pavón, E., García, F., Piattini, M.: Supporting the process assessment through a flexible software environment. In: Cordeiro, J., Shishkov, B., Ranchordas, A., Helfert, M. (eds.) Software and Data Technologies,Communications in Computer and Information Science, vol. 47, pp. 187–199. Springer, Heidelberg (2009)
62. Mas, A., Lluis Mesquida, A.: Software project management in small and very small entities. In: Proceedings of the Iberian Conference on Information Systems and Technologies, pp. 1–6. IEEE, Washington (2013)
63. Mc Caffery, F., Richardson, I., Moller, P.: Automotive-adept: a lightweight assessment method for the automotive software industry. Softw. Process Improv. Pract. **13**(4), 345–353 (2008)
64. Mc Caffery, F., Taylor, P.S., Coleman, G.: Adept: a unified assessment method for small software companies. IEEE Softw. **24**(1), 24–31 (2007)
65. McCaffery, F., Coleman, G.: Lightweight SPI assessments: what is the real cost? Softw. Process Improv. Pract. **14**(5), 271–278 (2009)
66. McCaffery, F., McFall, D., Wilkie, F.G.: Improving the express process appraisal method. In: Bomarius, F., Komi-Sirviö, S. (eds.) Proceedings of the International Conference on Product-Focused Software Process Improvement, Lecture Notes in Computer Science, vol. 3547, pp. 286–298. Springer, Heidelberg (2005)
67. McCaffery, F., O'Connor, R.V., Messnarz, R. (eds.): Systems, Software and Services Process Improvement, Communications in Computer and Information Science, vol. 364. Springer, Heidelberg (2013)
68. McFall, D., Wilkie, F.G., McCaffery, F., Lester, N., Sterritt, R.: Software processes and process improvement in Northern Ireland. In: Proceedings of the International Conference of Software and Systems Engineering and their Applications, pp. 1–10. Paris (2003)
69. Mesquida, A.L., Mas, A.: A project management improvement program according to ISO/IEC 29110 and PMBOK. J. Softw. Evolut. Process **26**(9), 846–854 (2014)
70. Mishra, D., Mishra, A.: Software process improvement methodologies for small and medium enterprises. In: Proceedings of the International Conference on Product-Focused Software Process Improvement. Lecture Notes in Computer Science, vol. 5089, pp. 273–288. Springer, Heidelberg (2008)
71. Mishra, D., Mishra, A.: Software process improvement in SMEs: a comparative view. Comput. Sci. Inf. Syst. **6**(1), 111–140 (2009)
72. Mitasiunas, A., Rout, T., O'Connor, R.V., Dorling, A. (eds.): Software Process Improvement and Capability Determination, Communications in Computer and Information Science, vol. 477. Springer, Heidelberg (2014)

73. Montoni, M., Santos, G., Rocha, A., Weber, K., de Araujo, E.: MPS model and TABA workstation: Implementing software process improvement initiatives in small settings. In: Proceedings of the International Workshop on Software Quality, p. 4 ff. IEEE, Washington (2007)
74. Montoni, M., Santos, G., Rocha, A.R., Figueiredo, S., Cabral, R., Barcellos, R., Barreto, A., Soares, A., Cerdeiral, C., Lupo, P.: Taba workstation: Supporting software process deployment based on CMMI and MR-MPS.BR. In: Münch, J., Vierimaa, M. (eds.) Proceedings of the International Conference on Product-Focused Software Process Improvement. Lecture Notes in Computer Science, vol. 4034, pp. 249–262. Springer, Heidelberg (2006)
75. Montoni, M.A., Rocha, A.R., Weber, K.C.: MPS.BR: a successful program for software process improvement in Brazil. Softw. Process Improv. Pract. **14**(5), 289–300 (2009)
76. Moreno, E., Sánchez-Gordón, M.L., Colomo-Palacios, R.: ISO/IEC 29110: current overview of the standard. Revista de Procesos y Métricas (RPM) **10**(2), 24–40 (2013)
77. Moreno-Campos, E., Sánchez-Gordón, M.L., Colomo-Palacios, R.: Amescua Seco, A.: Towards measuring the impact of the ISO/IEC 29110 standard: a systematic review. In: Proceedings of European System and Software Process Improvement and Innovation Conference. Communications in Computer and Information Science, vol. 425, pp. 1–12. Springer, Heidelberg, Luxembourg (2014)
78. Ñaupac, V., Arisaca, R., Dávila, A.: Software process improvement and certification of a small company using the NTP 291 100 (MoProSoft). In: Dieste, O., Jedlitschka, A., Juristo., N. (eds.) Proceedings of the International Conference on Product-Focused Software Process Improvement, Lecture Notes in Computer Science, vol. 7343, pp. 32–43. Springer, Heidelberg (2012)
79. Nawrocki, J., Walter, B., Wojciechowski, A.: Toward maturity model for extreme programming. In: Proceedings of the Euromicro Conference, pp. 233–239. IEEE, Washington (2001)
80. Nawrocki, J.R., Jasiński, M., Walter, B., Wojciechowski, A.: Combining extreme programming with ISO 9000. In: Shafazand, H., Tjoa, A.M. (eds.) EurAsia-ICT 2002: Information and Communication Technology. Lecture Notes in Computer Science, vol. 2510, pp. 786–794. Springer, Heidelberg (2002)
81. Niazi, M.: Software process improvement: a road to success. In: Münch, J., Vierimaa, M. (eds.) Proceedings of the International Conference on Product-Focused Software Process Improvement. Lecture Notes in Computer Science, vol. 4034, pp. 395–401. Springer, Heidelberg (2006)
82. Niazi, M.: An exploratory study of software process improvement implementation risks. J. Softw. Evolut. Process **24**(8), 877–894 (2012)
83. O'Connor, R.V.: Early stage adoption of ISO/IEC 29110 software project management practices: A case study. In: Mitasiunas, A., Rout, T., O'Connor, R.V., Dorling, A. (eds.) Software Process Improvement and Capability Determination. Communications in Computer and Information Science, vol. 477, pp. 226–237. Springer, Heidelberg (2014)
84. O'Connor, R.V., Coleman, G.: An investigation of barriers to the adoption of software process best practice models. In: Proceedings of the Australasian Conference on Information Systems, pp. 780–789 (2007)
85. O'Connor, R.V., Laporte, C.Y.: Towards the provision of assistance for very small entities in deploying software lifecycle standards. In: Proceedings of the International Conference on Product-Focused Software Process Improvement, pp. 4–7. ACM, New York (2010)
86. O'Connor, R.V., Laporte, C.Y.: Deploying lifecycle profiles for very small entities: An early stage industry view. In: O'Connor, R.V., Rout, T., McCaffery, F., Dorling, A. (eds.) Software Process Improvement and Capability Determination. Communications in Computer and Information Science, vol. 155, pp. 227–230. Springer, Heidelberg (2011)
87. O'Connor, R.V., Laporte, C.Y.: Software project management in very small entities with ISO/IEC 29110. In: Winkler, D., O'Connor, R.V., Messnarz, R. (eds.) Systems, Software and Services Process Improvement. Communications in Computer and Information Science, vol. 301, pp. 330–341. Springer, Heidelberg (2012)
88. O'Connor, R.V., Laporte, C.Y.: An innovative approach to the development of an international software process lifecycle standard for very small entities. Int. J. Inf. Technol. Syst. Approach **7**(1), 1–22 (2014)

89. O'Connor, R.V., Sanders, M.: Lessons from a pilot implementation of ISO/IEC 29110 in a group of very small irish companies. In: Woronowicz, T., Rout, T., O'Connor, R.V., Dorling, A. (eds.) Software Process Improvement and Capability Determination, Communications in Computer and Information Science, vol. 349, pp. 243–246. Springer, Heidelberg (2013)

90. Oktaba, H., Garcia, F., Piattini, M., Ruiz, F., Pino, F., Alquicira, C.: Software process improvement: the competisoft project. Computer **40**(10), 21–28 (2007)

91. SME and Entrepreneurship Outlook 2005. OECD Publishing, Paris (2005)

92. Osorio Martinez, Z., Irrazabal, E., Garzas, J.: Toward improving agile mantema: measurement, control and evaluation of maintenance projects in SME's. In: Proceedings of the Iberian Conference on Information Systems and Technologies, pp. 1–6. IEEE, Washington (2011)

93. Paternoster, N., Giardino, C., Unterkalmsteiner, M., Gorschek, T., Abrahamsson, P.: Software development in startup companies: a systematic mapping study. Inf. Softw. Technol. **56**(10), 1200–1218 (2014)

94. Pernstå l, J., Gorschek, T., Feldt, R., Florén, D.: Software process improvement in interdepartmental development of software-intensive automotive systems—a case study. In: Heidrich, J., Oivo, M., Jedlitschka, A., Baldassarre, M.T. (eds.) Proceedings of the International Conference on Product-Focused Software Process Improvement. Lecture Notes in Computer Science, vol. 7983, pp. 93–107. Springer, Heidelberg (2013)

95. Pettersson, F., Ivarsson, M., Gorschek, T., Öhman, P.: A practitioner's guide to light weight software process assessment and improvement planning. J. Syst. Softw. **81**(6), 972–995 (2008)

96. Pino, F.J., García, F., Piattini, M.: Software process improvement in small and medium software enterprises: a systematic review. Softw. Qual. Control J. **16**(2), 237–261 (2008)

97. Pino, F.J., García, F., Piattini, M.: An integrated framework to guide software process improvement in small organizations. In: O'Connor, R.V., Baddoo, N., Gallego, J.C., Muslera, R.R., Smolander, K., Messnarz, R. (eds.) Software Process Improvement. Communications in Computer and Information Science, vol. 42, pp. 213–224. Springer, Heidelberg (2009)

98. Pino, F.J., Garcia, F., Piattini, M.: Key processes to start software process improvement in small companies. In: Proceedings of the ACM Symposium on Applied Computing, pp. 509–516. ACM, New York (2009)

99. Pino, F.J., Pardo, C., García, F., Piattini, M.: Assessment methodology for software process improvement in small organizations. Inf. Softw. Technol. **52**(10), 1044–1061 (2010)

100. Pino, F.J., Pedreira, O., García, F., Luaces, M.R., Piattini, M.: Using scrum to guide the execution of software process improvement in small organizations. J. Syst. Softw. **83**(10), 1662–1677 (2010)

101. Pino, F.J., Ruiz, F., García, F., Piattini, M.: A software maintenance methodology for small organizations: Agile_MANTEMA. J. Softw. Evolut. Process **24**(8), 851–876 (2011)

102. Pressman, R.: Software Engineering: A Practitioner's Approach, 7th edn. McGraw-Hill Science, New York (2009)

103. Raninen, A., Ahonen, J.J., Sihvonen, H.M., Savolainen, P., Beecham, S.: LAPPI: a lightweight technique to practical process modeling and improvement target identification. J. Softw. Evolut. Process **25**(9), 915–933 (2013)

104. Ribaud, V., Saliou, P.: Process assessment issues of the ISO/IEC 29110 emerging standard. In: Proceedings of the International Conference on Product-Focused Software Process Improvement, pp. 24–27. ACM, New York (2010)

105. Ribaud, V., Saliou, P., Laporte, C.: Experience management for very small entities: Improving the copy-paste model. In: Proceedings of the International Conference on Software Engineering Advances, pp. 311–318. IEEE, Washington (2010)

106. Ribaud, V., Saliou, P., O'Connor, R.V., Laporte, C.Y.: Software engineering support activities for very small entities. In: Riel, A., O'Connor, R., Tichkiewitch, S., Messnarz, R. (eds.) Systems, Software and Services Process Improvement. Communications in Computer and Information Science, vol. 99, pp. 165–176. Springer, Heidelberg (2010)

107. Richardson, I.: SPI models: what characteristics are required for small software development companies? Softw. Qual. J. **10**(2), 101–114 (2002)

108. Richardson, I., Ryan, K.: Software process improvements in a very small company. Softw. Qual. Prof. **3**(2), 23–35 (2001)
109. Richardson, I., von Wangenheim, G.C.: Why are small software organizations different? IEEE Softw. **24**(1), 18–22 (2007)
110. Rios, B., Vargas, M., Espinoza, J., Peralta, M.: Experiences on the implementation of MoProSoft and assessment of processes under the NMX-I-059/02-NYCE-2005 standard in a small software development enterprise. In: Proceedings of the Mexican International Conference on Computer Science, pp. 323–328. IEEE, Washington (2008)
111. da Rocha, A., Montoni, M., Weber, K., de Araujo, E.: A nationwide program for software process improvement in Brazil. In: Proceedings of the International Conference on the Quality of Information and Communications Technology, pp. 167–176. IEEE, Washington (2007)
112. Rocha, A.R., Montoni, M., Santos, G., Mafra, S., Figueiredo, S., Albuquerque, A., Mian, P.: Reference model for software process improvement: A brazilian experience. In: Richardson, I., Abrahamsson, P., Messnarz, R. (eds.) Software Process Improvement. Lecture Notes in Computer Science, vol. 3792, pp. 130–141. Springer, Heidelberg (2005)
113. Rozman, I., Horvat, R.V., Györkös, J., Hericòko, M.: PROCESSUS—integration of SEI CMM and ISO quality models. Softw. Qual. J. **6**(1), 37–63 (1997)
114. Sánchez-Gordón, M.L., Colomo-Palacios, R., Amescua, A.: Towards measuring the impact of the spi manifesto: a systematic review. In: Proceedings of European System and Software Process Improvement and Innovation Conference, pp. 100–110. DELTA, Dundalk Institute of Technology, Ireland (2013)
115. Sánchez-Gordón, M.L., O'Connor, R.V., Colomo-Palacios, R.: Evaluating vses viewpoint and sentiment towards the ISO/IEC 29110 standard: a two country grounded theory study. In: Rout, T., O'Connor, R., Dorling, A. (eds.) Proceedings of the SPICE Conference, Communications in Computer and Information Science, vol. 526. Springer, Heidelberg (2015)
116. Santos, G., Kalinowski, M., Rocha, A., Travassos, G., Weber, K., Antonioni, J.: MPS.BR: A tale of software process improvement and performance results in the Brazilian software industry. In: Proceedings of the International Conference on the Quality of Information and Communications Technology, pp. 412–417. IEEE, Washington (2010)
117. Santos, G., Kalinowski, M., Rocha, A., Travassos, G., Weber, K., Antonioni, J.: MPS.BR program and MPS model: Main results, benefits and beneficiaries of software process improvement in Brazil. In: Proceedings of the International Conference on the Quality of Information and Communications Technology, pp. 137–142. IEEE, Washington (2012)
118. Santos, G., Montoni, M., Vasconcellos, J., Figueiredo, S., Cabral, R., Cerdeiral, C., Katsurayama, A., Lupo, P., Zanetti, D., Rocha, A.: Implementing software process improvement initiatives in small and medium-size enterprises in brazil. In: Proceedings of the International Conference on the Quality of Information and Communications Technology, pp. 187–198. IEEE, Washington (2007)
119. Savolainen, P., Sihvonen, H.M., Ahonen, J.J.: SPI with lightweight software process modeling in a small software company. In: Abrahamsson, P., Baddoo, N., Margaria, T., Messnarz, R. (eds.) Software Process Improvement. Lecture Notes in Computer Science, vol. 4764, pp. 71–81. Springer, Heidelberg (2007)
120. Schoeffel, P., Benitti, F.B.V.: Factors of influence in software process improvement: a comparative survey between micro and small enterprises (MSE) and medium and large enterprises (MLE). IEEE Latin America Trans. **10**(2), 1634–1643 (2012)
121. Schweigert, T., Nevalainen, R., Vohwinkel, D., Korsaa, M., Biro, M.: Agile maturity model: oxymoron or the next level of understanding. In: Mas, A., Mesquida, A., Rout, T., O'Connor, R.V., Dorling, A. (eds.) Software Process Improvement and Capability Determination. Communications in Computer and Information Science, vol. 290, pp. 289–294. Springer, Heidelberg (2012)
122. Scott, L., Jeffery, R., Carvalho, L., D'Ambra, J., Rutherford, P.: Practical software process improvement—the IMPACT project. In: Proceedings of the Australian Software Engineering Conference, pp. 182–189. IEEE, Washington (2001)
123. Sommerville, I.: Software Engineering, 9 edn. Addison-Wesley, Boston (2010)

124. Staples, M., Niazi, M., Jeffery, R., Abrahams, A., Byatt, P., Murphy, R.: An exploratory study of why organizations do not adopt CMMI. J. Syst. Softw. **80**(6), 883–895 (2007)
125. Sulayman, M., Mendes, E.: An extended systematic review of software process improvement in small and medium web companies. In: Proceedings of the Conference on Evaluation and Assessment in Software Engineering, pp. 134–143. IET, London (2011)
126. Sulayman, M., Urquhart, C., Mendes, E., Seidel, S.: Software process improvement success factors for small and medium web companies: a qualitative study. Inf. Softw. Technol. **54**(5), 479–500 (2012)
127. Takeuchi, M., Kohtake, N., Shirasaka, S., Koishi, Y., Shioya, K.: Report on an assessment experience based on ISO/IEC 29110. J. Softw. Evolut. Process **26**(3), 306–312 (2014)
128. Taylor, P.S., Greer, D., Sage, P., Coleman, G., McDaid, K., Lawthers, I., Corr, R.: Applying an agility/discipline assessment for a small software organisation. In: Proceedings of the International Conference on Product-Focused Software Process Improvement. Lecture Notes in Computer Science, vol. 4034, pp. 290–304. Springer, Heidelberg (2006)
129. Theocharis, G., Kuhrmann, M., Münch, J., Diebold, P.: Is water-scrum-fall reality? on the use of agile and traditional development practices. In: Proceedings of the International Conference on Product-Focused Software Process Improvement. Lecture Notes in Computer Science, vol. 9459, pp. 149–166. Springer, Heidelberg (2015)
130. Tigre, P.B., Marques, F.S. (eds.): Desafíos y oportunidades de la industria del software en América Latina, primera edn. Mayol Ediciones S.A, Colombia (2009)
131. UNCTAD: Information economy report 2012: the software industry and developing countries. Technical report, United Nations Publications, New York (2012)
132. Valdés, G., Astudillo, H., Visconti, M., López, C.: The tutelkan SPI framework for smallsettings: A methodology transfer vehicle. In: Riel, A., O'Connor, R., Tichkiewitch, S. Messnarz, R. (eds.) Systems, Software and Services Process Improvement. Communications in Computer and Information Science, vol. 99, pp. 142–152. Springer, Heidelberg (2010)
133. Valdés, G., Visconti, M., Astudillo, H.: The tutelkan reference process: A reusable process model for enabling SPI in small settings. In: O'Connor, R.V., Pries-Heje, J., Messnarz, R. (eds.) Systems, Software and Service Process Improvement, Communications in Computer and Information Science, vol. 172, pp. 179–190. Springer, Heidelberg (2011)
134. Valtanen, A., Ahonen, J.J.: Big improvements with small changes: improving the processes of a small software company. In: Jedlitschka, A., Salo, O. (eds.) Proceedings of the International Conference on Product-Focused Software Process Improvement, Lecture Notes in Computer Science, vol. 5089, pp. 258–272. Springer, Heidelberg (2008)
135. Valtierra, C., Munoz, M., Mejia, J.: Characterization of software processes improvement needs in SMEs. In: Proceedings of the International Conference on Mechatronics. Electronics and Automotive Engineering, pp. 223–228. IEEE, Washington (2013)
136. Vargas, E., Oktaba, H., Guardati, S., Laureano, A.: Agents, case-based reasoning and their relation to the mexican software process (MoProSoft). In: Proceedings of the International Computer Software and Applications Conference, vol. 2, pp. 326–334. IEEE, Washington (2007)
137. Varkoi, T.: Process assessment in very small entities—an ISO/IEC 29110 based method. In: Proceedings of the International Conference on the Quality of Information and Communications Technology, pp. 436–440. IEEE, Washington (2010)
138. Vijayasarathy, L., Butler, C.: Choice of software development methodologies—do project, team and organizational characteristics matter? IEEE Softw. (99), 1ff. (2015)
139. Villarroel, R., Gómez, Y., Gajardo, R., Rodríguez, O.: Implementation of an improvement cycle using the competisoft methodological framework and the tutelkan platform. In: Proceedings of the International Conference of the Chilean Computer Science Society, pp. 97–104. IEEE, Washington (2009)
140. von Wangenheim, C.G., Anacleto, A., Salviano, C.: Helping small companies assess software processes. IEEE Softw. **23**(1), 91–98 (2006)
141. von Wangenheim, C.G., Varkoi, T., Salviano, C.F.: Standard based software process assessments in small companies. Softw. Process Improv. Pract. **11**(3), 329–335 (2006)

142. Wangenheim, C.G.v., Weber, S., Hauck, J.C.R., Trentin, G.: Experiences on establishing software processes in small companies. Inf. Softw. Technol. **48**(9), 890–900 (2006)

143. Weber, K.C., Araújo, E.E.R., Rocha, A.R.C.d., Machado, C.A.F., Scalet, D., Salviano, C.F.: Brazilian software process reference model and assessment method. In: Yolum, P., Güngör, T., Gürgen, F., Özturan, C. (eds.) Computer and Information Sciences. Lecture Notes in Computer Science, vol. 3733, pp. 402–411. Springer, Heidelberg (2005)

144. Wilkie, F.G., Mc Caffery, F., McFall, D., Lester, N., Wilkinson, E.: A low-overhead method for software process appraisal. Softw. Process Improv. Pract. **12**(4), 339–349 (2007)

145. Wilkie, F.G., McFall, D., McCaffery, F.: An evaluation of CMMI process areas for small-to medium-sized software development organisations. Softw. Process Improv. Pract. **10**(2), 189–201 (2005)

146. Woronowicz, T., Rout, T., O'Connor, R.V., Dorling, A. (eds.): Software Process Improvement and Capability Determination, Communications in Computer and Information Science, vol. 349. Springer, Heidelberg (2013)

147. Zahran, S.: Software Process Improvement-Practical Guidelines for Business Success. Addison Wesley, Boston (1998)

148. Zarour, M., Abran, A., Desharnais, J.M.: Evaluation of software process assessment methods – case study. In: O'Connor, R.V., Rout, T., McCaffery, F., Dorling, A. (eds.) Software Process Improvement and Capability Determination, Communications in Computer and Information Science, vol. 155, pp. 42–51. Springer, Heidelberg (2011)

149. Zarour, M., Desharnais, J.M., Alarifi, A., Habra, N., Cassiers, G., Robaeys, A.: Gained experience by making intervention to improve software process in very small organizations. In: Mas, A., Mesquida, A., Rout, T., O'Connor, R.V., Dorling, A. (eds.) Software Process Improvement and Capability Determination, Communications in Computer and Information Science, vol. 290, pp. 51–61. Springer, Heidelberg (2012)

Chapter 8
Managing Software Process Evolution for Spacecraft from a Customer's Perspective

Christian R. Prause, Markus Bibus, Carsten Dietrich and Wolfgang Jobi

Abstract The Space Administration of the German Aerospace Center designs and implements the German space program. While project management rests with the agency, suppliers are contracted for building devices and their software. As opposed to many other domains, a spacecraft is a unique device with uncommon and custom-built peripherals. Its software is specifically developed for a single mission only and often controls critical functionality. A small coding error can mean the loss of the spacecraft and mission failure. For this reason, customer and supplier closely collaborate on the field of software quality. We report from a customer's perspective on how we manage software quality and ensure that suppliers evolve their processes: We contribute to standards, tailor quality, and process requirements to establish them in projects, and engage in cross-company product quality collaboration.

8.1 Introduction

The DLR is the national aeronautics and space research center of the Federal Republic of Germany. In addition to its own research, the DLR's Space Administration branch has been given responsibility for the planning and implementation of the national space program. It acts as customer and project manager during the making of hardware and software that it needs for executing its missions. The actual work of making is outsourced to external contractors.

The space sector is peculiar with respect to the fact that many spacecraft are one of the kind devices with uncommon and custom-built hardware and software. Scientific missions have no insurance; a second unit is never built. If the mission goal is not

C.R. Prause (✉) · M. Bibus · C. Dietrich · W. Jobi
Deutsches Zentrum für Luft- und Raumfahrt, DLR - Space Administration,
Königswinterer Straße, 522-524, 53227 Bonn, Germany
e-mail: christian.prause@dlr.de

M. Bibus
e-mail: markus.bibus@dlr.de

C. Dietrich
e-mail: carsten.dietrich@dlr.de

© Springer International Publishing Switzerland 2016
M. Kuhrmann et al. (eds.), *Managing Software Process Evolution*,
DOI 10.1007/978-3-319-31545-4_8

reached, for whatever reason, there is *no second chance*. Preparing a single mission and subsequent production of the spacecraft can take decades. Additionally, dependability requirements are very high because servicing hardware in flight is impractical to nearly impossible. Free-flying devices have to stay intact for decades under harsh environmental conditions. Software can potentially be updated in flight but whoever worked on 15-year-old software knows the troubles of maintaining aging software in a fast-paced technology field. Moreover, software often controls critical functionality. A single software failure can mean the loss of a spacecraft and its mission, for example, Ariane Flight 501 [11] or Mars Climate Orbiter [34]. Additionally, due to limited contact times with ground stations, uploading new software versions can take days. Therefore, higher efforts in avoiding software problems are justified [26, 28].

Project cost and time are nonetheless key topics: In the early 1990s, the NASA (United States' National Aeronautics and Space Administration) started its "Faster, Better, Cheaper" initiative; capping maximum project cost, reducing bureaucracy, and therefore enabling more parallel projects. The program put a high cost pressure on projects. Software became more important as a sponge for complexity, as "band-aid" for hardware design compromises [12, 28] and as a possibility to save on hardware and missions costs [36]. However, when several such light-weight missions failed, it became clear that it was necessary to reconcile speed with quality control [28]. In Germany, the Space Administration reacted to similar experiences [1] by significantly increasing its dedication to and efforts in hardware and software quality assurance activities [33]. Since that time, the product assurance department of the Space Administration is responsible for quality management in all major national space projects.

The agency's view on product assurance is dominated by the need for high quality and dependable products that result from novel and extreme technical challenges (Fig. 8.1), and the ever-new organizational contexts with the Space Administration's role as a customer without own making responsibilities but with a wide range of suppliers: Quality has to be—right from the start—built into the products that are provided by suppliers with highly diverse quality capabilities. Therefore, the suppliers' processes and their evolution are in the center of attention. Major challenges are, for example:

- Harmonize development processes at international level and across organizations
- Standardize tailoring to achieve consistent results and reduce subjective effects
- Check that software and software processes conform to applicable requirements
- Deal with suppliers' resistance to adapt their development processes
- Improve product assurance by exploring and introducing new methods and tools
- Evolve software processes to ultimately assure the quality of procured products.

This chapter describes the work of the Space Administration's software product assurance: Sect. 8.2 provides the context and background of this chapter. Section 8.3 introduces the ECSS system of standards, which is a joint effort of European space agencies and industries to harmonize their work. Section 8.4 explains how these standards are turned into a national catalog of quality and process requirements. Section 8.5 details the process of generating project-specific requirements from this

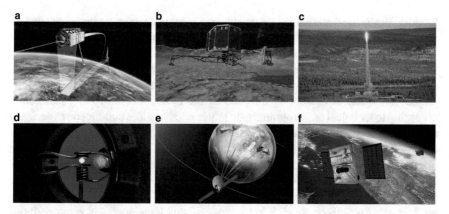

Fig. 8.1 a Radar twin satellites TerraSAR-X and TanDEM-X. *Source* DLR, CC-BY 3.0. **b** Philae touching down on Churyumov–Gerasimenko. *Source* DLR, CC-BY 3.0. **c** Rocket launch in the TEXUS Zero-G program in Kiruna. *Source* DLR, CC-BY 3.0. **d** Melting of materials without a container on board the ISS. *Source* DLR, CC-BY 3.0. **e** Laser communication terminal for inter-satellite and ground links. *Source* DLR. **f** TET-1 from FIREBIRD mission for detecting forest fires. *Source* DLR, CC-BY 3.0

national catalog through a standardized tailoring process. Section 8.6 outlines the responsibilities assumed by the DLR software product assurance during project execution including performance records, reviews, and technical visits. Section 8.7 gives an experience report on how a single process improvement was made possible against the initial resistance of suppliers. Finally, Sect. 8.8 concludes this chapter.

8.2   Background and Context

The DLR is Germany's space agency.[1] It consists mainly of distributed institutes that do research and development in the sectors of transportation, energy, flight, security, and spaceflight. DLR's Space Administration branch manages the German space program in the name of the federal government. It commissions devices (e.g., spacecraft) for its missions from a diverse range of suppliers including industrial and academic partners. It invites tenders, awards contracts for projects, supervises them afterward, and promotes innovative ideas in research and industry. As opposed to consumer products, devices are usually custom-built, expensive, and one-of-a-kind devices with high technical risk. Continuous customer, i.e., DLR, involvement in the process of making is therefore necessary. The role of the DLR Space Administration's

---

[1] *Note* ESA—the European Space Agency—is an international organization with currently 22 member states including Germany. DLR and ESA collaborate closely, and ESA committees include DLR representatives. Yet, they are separate organizations, both doing their own missions, having their own research divisions and mission operations, and procuring externally built devices.

Product Assurance department is to accompany technical processes in order to ensure product quality and successful completion of the project.

Product assurance is one of three primary project functions (the others being *project management* and *engineering*). It is a management discipline assuming the customers' viewpoint on product quality within the seller's organization. It supports project management in steering the product life cycle, and controlling production according to technical and programmatic requirements, while building on experience and lessons learned. Software product assurance disciplines include quality assurance with subordinate quality control, safety and dependability assurance, project planning, (independent) validation and verification, testing and evaluation, configuration management, and software measurement. Its functions are to observe, witness tests, analyze, and recommend, but not to develop or test, manage people, or set product requirements. Instead, it has organizational, budgetary, and product developmental independence meaning that it reports to highest management only, has its own budget, and does not expend labor to help building a product [6, 10, 32].

Customer product assurance mirrors the sellers' own product assurance function, acting as reviewer of contractors and technology providers ranging from large companies to small enterprises, research institutes, and universities. With respect to this, the function of product assurance is comparable to NASA's *Software Assurance Technology Center* (SATC; [3]). It assesses organizations and how they perform development activities in order to obtain software products that are fit for use and built in accordance with applicable project requirements [22]. For making sure that improvement (or evolution) of processes happens, enforcement is often necessary. This chapter makes a cross section through the several pillars of enforcement like relevant standards, contractual agreements, and active supervision (e.g., milestone reviews). It describes the managing of supplier software process evolution from a customer's perspective and through customer initiative.

Many organizations are usually cooperating in the production of a space device. They are bound by legal contracts in the roles of customer and suppliers which in turn act as customers to their lower tier suppliers. While the ECSS standards have no legal standing by themselves, they are made applicable by invoking them in the business agreements [15]. They provide a collection of what we call *process requirements* here (another term would be *software standards*). These are not to be confused with product requirements that describe what the product should do.

8.3 The ECSS Standards

Space technology is an extremely complex working field. In Europe, development and manufacturing of space systems is influenced by the cooperation of space agencies and industry since the beginning. One challenge of this work is the coordination of the use of compatible materials and implementation of compatible interfaces to reach quality and reliability as needed.

ESA developed *PSS* (*Procedures, Standards and Specifications*) standards to be applied in their projects for this purpose. Their use in projects of national European space agencies and industry had to be negotiated individually because national agencies developed standards individually and applied them to their projects. Rising demands made this approach more and more ineffective. Back in 1988, it was realized that there was the need of counteracting this trend [24].

In 1993 the European Cooperation for Space Standardization (ECSS) was founded to harmonize the requirements of existing standards for space projects and to develop and maintain a single, coherent set of standards for hardware, software, information management, and activities to be used in European space projects. The purpose of these standards is to continually improve the quality, reliability, functional integrity, and compatibility of all project elements.

The ECSS standards documents contain sets of requirements. Each requirement is verifiable, has a unique identification to allow full traceability and verification of compliance, and is supported by a minimal description necessary to understand its context. The documents themselves follow a systematic naming approach [15]:

ECSS-[branch]-[type]-[major][-minor][version]

where

Branch	One of the following values: P or S (ECSS system), M (management), E (engineering), U (sustainability), or Q (product assurance)
Type	The type is either ST (standard) or HB (handbook), which provides non-mandatory background information and reading help for a corresponding standard
Major	A two-digit number to identify the domain of the standard within its branch, e.g., *software engineering* (E-40) or *risk management* (M-80)
Minor	An optional two-digit number specifying a specialized substandard of a main standard, e.g., *ASIC and FPGA development* of the *Electrical, electronic and electromechanical components* domain (Q-60–02)
Version	A single letter from 'A' onwards for counting the major releases of the standards system (issue C at the moment)

The ECSS standards first and foremost focus on what has to be accomplished rather than on how to organize and perform the work. Interpretive help and details can, instead, often be found in the corresponding handbooks. This approach allows different producers and customers to apply established processes where effective as long as they remain within the fundamental constraints, and to improve and evolve processes gradually [15].

8.3.1 ECSS Policy, Members, and Organization

The ECSS policy is to develop and maintain an integrated and coherent set of management, engineering, product assurance, and space sustainability standards. The

Fig. 8.2 The ECSS
organizational structure [21]

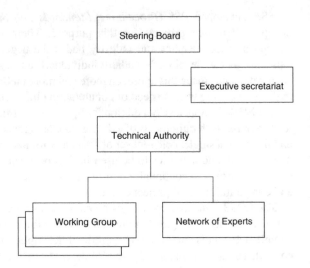

objectives of ECSS are to increase quality, reduce risks, improve competitiveness, enhance safety and reliability, improve collaboration, and to develop and disseminate fresh knowledge. Principles supporting these objectives are, for instance, to seek harmonization with international standards by contributing to and ingesting from, e.g., ISO, CEN, and to continuously improve on the basis of user feedback. The standards are made freely available[2] to promote their wider usage [38].

The members of the ECSS are from European space sector (industry and space agencies) and associated organizations. They are differentiated between full members, associated members, and observers. Full members are those who actively participate in production, maintenance, and use of ECSS standards, like ESA, DLR, several national agencies (from France, Italy, the Netherlands, Norway, and UK), and Eurospace as representative of industry. Being an associated member (like Canada) indicates the desire to participate in production of ECSS standards and their limited application. Observers are those who desire to be formally informed about changes and be able to provide input in case of a need for an update or new standard. For instance, observers are the European Defence Agency or EUMETSAT.

The ECSS is organized in several bodies which also represent working levels (see Fig. 8.2). The top level is the ECSS *Steering Board* which defines ECSS objectives, policy, strategy, and endorses the yearly work plan. The *Technical Authority* implements the objectives, policy, and strategy defined by the steering board. It is also responsible for setup, approval, implementation, and monitoring of the work plan endorsed by the steering board. The elaboration of new and the maintenance of existing ECSS standards has to be performed by the *Working Groups* according to the work plan. Both Technical Authority and Working Groups are supported by the *Executive secretariat*, which enforces drafting rules, provides administrative support, and ensures promotion and interface with other standard development organizations. The lowest level is a *Network of Experts* representing document and discipline focal

---

[2]Visit http://www.ecss.nl/ for online access to the standards.

points, which give support to the Technical Authority and Executive secretariat in specific tasks [24].

8.3.2   Production and Maintenance of ECSS Standards

The development and update of ECSS standards are iterative processes (see also Fig. 8.3). A new standard is initiated by ECSS members sending a document called *New Work Item Proposal* (NWIP) to the Technical Authority, respectively, Executive secretariat. The proposal describes the envisioned content and scope of the standard, a justification for it, initial inputs, designated activities and milestones for Working Groups, necessary resources (e.g., composition of Working Group in terms of member organizations, manpower, and required meetings), and what the desired output is. It is then provided to ECSS members for public review to identify the need of extensions of the work item, and to recruit volunteer representatives from interested organizations. After the new work item is approved, the Technical Authority appoints the representatives to the Working Group, which then starts its work [21].

When the Working Group has prepared a draft version of the new standard, it undergoes a public review for comments. It is provided to all member organizations of the ECSS for this. All comments received are discussed by the Working Group and a first decision about their implementation is taken. The decisions are then communicated to the originators of the work item for agreement. Where no consensus can be reached, a final decision is taken by the Technical Authority. After this, the new ECSS standard is finalized [21].

If the need for an update of an existing ECSS Standards is identified, a formal *Change Request* is submitted to the ECSS secretariat. The next steps then are as

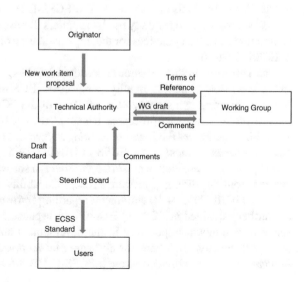

Fig. 8.3 Preparing new standard: information flow [14]

described above, starting with the preparation of a NWIP. If the Change Request highlighted problems without getting concrete on how to solve them, the Technical Authority calls for a special Working Group, a *Task Force*, to generate the NWIPs [21]. Through this process, European space projects have continuously returned feedback, corrections, and proposals to the ECSS standards and made the system extensive, efficient, and stable. The ECSS continues to be evolved and improved, also including the feedback processes themselves [38].

8.3.3 Software Standards in the ECSS System

Software pervades any space program and its product tree. For a concise overview of software development based on ECSS, see [29]. Apart from many general ECSS standards that are relevant to software development in space projects (e.g., configuration and information management [19]), there are several standards and handbooks specifically addressing software development.

The principles and requirements applicable to space software engineering are defined in ECSS-E-ST-40 (Space engineering—Software). Its first version appeared in 1999 as a specific adaptation of ISO/IEC 12207 to replace ESA's proprietary standard PSS-05-0 [29]. The current version takes the existing ISO 9000 family of documents into account and is in line with EN 50128 (railway applications) and DO-178 (airborne systems and equipment). It addresses development and use of software for manned and unmanned spacecraft, launchers, payloads, experiments and associated ground equipment and facilities, and services implemented by software. Covered aspects are software system engineering, requirements and architecture, design and implementation, validation, verification, delivery and acceptance, operation, maintenance and management. It also applies to nondeliverable software which affects the quality of products and services. The ECSS-E-HB-40A *Software Engineering Handbook* was created for daily use by suppliers. It provides advice, interpretations, elaborations, and best practices for the implementation of the requirements specified in ECSS-E-ST-40.

The software product assurance standard ECSS-Q-ST-80C [18] complements ECSS-E-ST-40C from the quality perspective. ECSS-Q-ST-80C interfaces with space engineering and management branches of the ECSS, and explains how they relate to product assurance processes. It is supplemented by five handbooks: ECSS-Q-HB-80-01A addresses the *Reuse of Existing Software*. The two volumes *Framework* and *Assessor Instrument* of the ECSS-Q-HB-80-02A *Software Process Assessment and Improvement* are known as *SPiCE for Space*, a software process maturity model derived from the SPiCE (Software Process Capability dEtermination) framework based on ISO/IEC 15504. Requirements regarding *Software Dependability and Safety* are further explained in ECSS-Q-HB-80-03A because dependability and safety are issues of paramount importance in the development and operations of space systems [20]. Finally, guidelines for *Software Metrication Programme Definition and Implementation* are provided through ECSS-Q-HB-80-04A.

Recently, the ECSS started to work on a handbook for agile development to live up to the growing interest in methodologies like Scrum and Extreme Programming. A respective standard is not yet planned due to a lack of consensus among partners regarding potential conflicts with established standards. Exactly this tension between agile and plan-driven development is further addressed in Chap. 2, where Diebold and Zehler also treat two approaches (evolutionary and revolutionary) for adding agility to plan-based processes.

8.4 Pre-Tailoring in the German National Space Program

Fig. 8.4a depicts different levels at which standardization can occur: international, regional, national, and company. International standards are usually rather specific in their scope. As opposed to this, the standardization process requires a very long time until consensus among diverse partners is found. On the other extreme are company-level standards. These in-house standards are the result of quickly made decisions among much more homogeneous parties, and they often cover a broader scope. Ideally, the different levels of standards are complementary, i.e., lower level standards only add details to a common, shared, higher level standard. In reality, however, the situation is not perfect. Standards at different levels overlap, and worse, sometimes contradict one another [24].

The reasons can be found, for example, in history (national space endeavors pre-date ESA), in corporate and national culture, in the different agencies' policies, or in different national interests. Likewise, German space industry differs from other

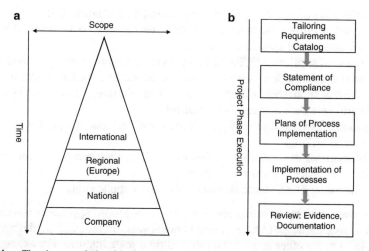

Fig. 8.4 a Time/scope relationship for different levels of standardization [24]. **b** Development process adaptation in project

European countries' space industry, and DLR differs from ESA. For example, conduction of advanced static analysis is a national requirement not found in ECSS.

So-called *pre-tailoring* is therefore regarded as necessary. It breaks the complex systems of standards down to national needs. These national needs are based on Germany's space strategy and cover also general project boundaries like environmental conditions, functionality, mission lifetime, and experiences from other projects. The standards considered for the pre-tailoring are national laws and standards, ECSS, ISO, military and NASA standards as well as requirements raised by the Russian space agency. The challenge of pre-tailoring is to identify requirements which are necessary for Germany's space projects but not contradicting rules and laws of other nations or organizations, which are partners. As an example, consider a project in which DLR delivers a payload for a satellite built by ESA: The industry contracted to manufacture the payload has not only to fulfill the requirements of DLR but also the ones from ESA. Due to the fact that Germany is no launch authority itself, the requirements of different launch authorities like Arianespace or NASA have to be considered, too.

8.4.1   Outline of the Pre-Tailoring Process

With *pre-tailoring* we denote a process that takes regional standards (ECSS) to turn them into a lower level but broader national catalog of requirements. The process is basically analogous to other tailoring processes as the 7-step process described in ECSS-S-ST-00C [15]. Of course, this tailoring is not yet aimed at a single project but at the virtual set of projects from the national space program. The steps are

1. Identification of possible types of projects and their characteristics.
2. Analysis of project characteristics with respect to cost, risk, technical drivers, critical issues, and specific constraints.
3. Selection of applicable ECSS standards as basis for pre-tailoring; standards referenced as applicable by selected standards become themselves selected.
4. Selection of applicable ECSS requirements from the selected standards by making a decision for each contained requirement.
5. Addition of new requirements specific to the national space program where ECSS is deemed lacking.
6. Harmonization of applicable requirements with respect to coherence and consistency of the overall set of requirements.
7. Documenting ECSS standards and requirements applicability.

On the one hand, by selecting requirements from several applicable standards at regional level, the scope of the resulting national standard broadens (as described for Fig. 8.4a). On the other hand, flexibility and time scale improve. For example, the ECSS is not yet harmonized with space standards from USA, Russia, or China [24]. On national level, however, consensus on integration can be reached easier.

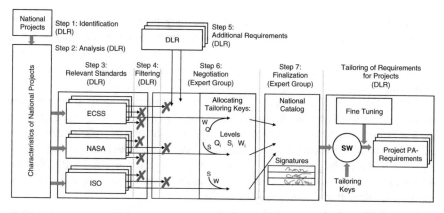

Fig. 8.5 Pre-tailoring, the national catalog, and computer-aided single-source tailoring

8.4.2 Pre-Tailoring Process Details

This section details the outline of the pre-tailoring process for the German national program (see also Fig. 8.5). Step 1 of pre-tailoring (in analogy to ECSS-S-ST-00C [15] tailoring) is to extract distinguishing characteristics from projects of the national space program. Relying on long experience, we selected several characteristics that distinguish projects in the national program. Such characteristics are, for example, the *Space Flight Type*, i.e., what kind of spacecraft, or *Utilization*, e.g., if the device is a free-flying satellite or used inside or outside of manned platforms like ISS or the space shuttle. In Step 2, these characteristics are complemented with refinement analyses regarding cost, risk, technical drivers, etc. Characteristics plus refinements form the dimensions of a nominal scale vector space. Any project can later be described as vector p consisting of these basic characterizations:

$$p \in C = C_{\{Sft,Lt,U,O,Mr,Sr,Fa\}} \times R_{\{L,B,C,Tr,Rp\}} \tag{8.1}$$

Step 3 of the pre-tailoring is to identify the relevant standards for software quality. First and foremost, this is the ECSS software product assurance standard [18] and parts of its complementary software engineering standard [17]. However, also requirements from other standards are integrated, for instance, configuration management (from [19]) or nonconformance reporting (from [16]).

In Step 4, every requirement is checked for its applicability to the national space program. For example, several requirements regarding software maintenance (ECSS-Q-ST-80C [18]; Sect. 6.3.8) were excluded because operations are out of scope of the space administration's product assurance.

Step 5 allows to add additional requirements to the catalog that are not yet considered by ECSS. For example, NASA and Roskosmos standards are necessary for ISS missions as these organizations are the safety authorities there. This step also allows to include novel processes not yet reflected in other standards (Sect. 8.7).

After the requirements have been gathered, they must be checked for internal coherence and consistency. Furthermore, it is necessary for later tailoring (Sect. 8.5) to discriminate more and less demanding process requirements. For this purpose, one or more requirement level tags are assigned to each requirement. Requirements imposed on software-specific processes are classified with one of four levels $w \in W_? = \{W_1, W_2, W_3, W_4\}$. The more rigorous requirement levels always include the all requirements of more light-weight levels: $W_1 \supseteq W_2 \supseteq W_3 \supseteq W_4$. The lower the level's number, the more demanding or expensive the process requirement is. For example, requiring the conduction of *Independent Software Verification and Validation* (ISVV) by a third party is at level W_1. It results in very high cost for the supplier. As opposed to this, software configuration management (W_4) is considered basic engineering rigor that should always be done.

In addition to software-specific process requirements, the software process is also influenced by cross-domain requirements from generic quality management and safety. They are classified analogously according to four Q levels, e.g., having a nonconformance control system in place is at Q_4. For safety, three S levels are defined, e.g., requiring conduction of software safety analysis is at S_3.

This sixth step is very work intensive and requires deep knowledge of the various requirements in order to assess their benefits, costs, effects, and cross-relations. It is therefore addressed by a work group of experts (Sect. 8.4.3).

Finally, as Step 7, the results of the requirements work group are documented in the product assurance requirements catalog [27]. They are additionally stored in a database used for automated tailoring (see Sect. 8.5).

8.4.3 Details for Step 6: Pre-Tailoring Expert Group

Every few years, the pre-tailoring expert group is convened to update the requirements catalog. It officially consists of one representative of every major stakeholder in the national program, i.e., from space administration and national industry. These formal representatives commonly have a *Head of Quality*-role or equivalent in their organization, and are supported by their domain/software expert. The expert group's input is an initial set of process requirements (partly from the previous version of the catalog) and its output is the national catalog. It enables

- to cope with the large amount of work associated with updating the catalog,
- to gather the necessary amount of practice and experience in one place, and
- to attain far-reaching justification and prominence for the resulting catalog.

Work starts by assigning so-called *field captains* to thematic subsets of the requirements, e.g., software product assurance, engineering management, or configuration management. The field captains then write a short review for each of their requirements. They see the item's ID, source, title, descriptive text, and requirement level tags ($W_?$, $S_?$). Additionally, they take into account aspects like cross-relations (duplications, contradictions, ...) or practical impact. They can propose a new title or text, write a review comment, and propose a resolution of *accept, reject* or *modify* (*accept* means that the requirement should be included in the catalog, *reject* the opposite, and *modify* that first it should be changed in the specified way).

Next, all experts provide a comment and cast one vote on the proposed resolution, which can also be *accept, reject,* or *modify.* If all experts accept, the resolution is accepted. If at least one expert rejects the resolution or requests modification, the field captain has to make a proposal how to proceed. The proposal consists of an explanatory comment and a revised requirement text. All other experts again vote on the requirement using *accept* or *reject* as answers. If the majority accepts the modified requirement, it is included in the catalog. Otherwise, the requirement remains in conflict state until the decision is finally made in a round table discussion.

The expert group meets physically once when it constitutes and once it finishes. For the weeks in-between, work is supported by a web-based tool specifically developed for this purpose. It lets contributors view a list of all requirements along with key facts like if there is a controversy about resolution or if it is included in the catalog. The software furthermore tracks open points, allows contributors to write their reviews, cast their votes, and view details of the entailing discussions. Finally, it documents decisions and maintains the database with the catalog of requirements. The catalog is additionally printed as book and signed off [27] by all representatives to confirm its symbolic value.

8.4.4 Lessons Learned

Pre-tailoring enables a gradual, smooth, and careful while steady transition from traditional processes toward the ECSS standards. Over the years, the percentage of ECSS requirements reflected in the national catalog has constantly risen, reaching 43 % in 2008, 57 % in 2010, and 63 % in 2012. However, it also shows that national needs still differ from European ones.

The catalog also forms an agreed baseline for the national space industry. As the major players get their votes in the expert group, where they can veto against unreasonable process requirements, it gets more difficult for them to argue against those requirements later in the projects. Interestingly, only very few requirements are actually rejected through the expert group.

Pre-tailoring provides a consensual, objective, mission-independent balancing of benefits and costs of requirements because contents of the catalog are discussed decoupled from actual missions. It ensures that the selection of requirements in the scope of projects is not based on the personal preferences of the person who tailors the process requirements for the project, but is instead based on a systematic, repeatable, and standardized process. Decisions are made against the specific background and needs of the German space program.

In contrast to the ECSS, where DLR is only one partner, influence at national level as the leading customer is unevenly greater. It is much better possible to position and later realize software process improvements through requirements. We will come back to this later in the experience report in Sect. 8.7. The small group of experts allows faster decision making when meeting every few years, and is more open to try out not-yet widespread technologies.

The ECSS system is yet to be harmonized with the standards of the traditional space-faring nations like USA or Russia. But because Germany does not have its own launch capacities or sites, it needs freedom to choose its partners; and it therefore needs to implement foreign standards at national level.

Maintaining the catalog is a costly endeavor that should not be underestimated. Working through several standards each with hundreds of requirements takes its time. And the work needs to be repeated every few years in order to keep up with changes in the still developing ECSS standards system. Besides the discipline and endurance that are necessary anyways, the expert group is an important ingredient to dealing with the efforts. The web-based content management reduces the amount of required co-location time. It enables several people with densely filled appointment calendars to still collaborate.

8.5   Tailoring the Requirements for a Project

The ECSS is a system of coherent standards that supports a wide range of diverse space projects. In its original form, it might therefore not yet suit the individual project very much. This can result in reduced project performance in terms of technical performance, life cycle cost-effectiveness, or timeliness of deliveries [15], and is therefore considered as a major project risk (cf. [31]). In order to reduce this risk, tailoring is "the act of adjusting the definition and/or particularizing the terms of a general description to derive a description applicable to an alternate (less general) environment" [25]. *Tailoring* means fitting requirements placed on the process to the specifics of individual projects [15].

The basis for tailoring is the national catalog of product assurance requirements, as mentioned in Sect. 8.4. Three functions

$$f_W : C \rightarrow W_? \tag{8.2}$$

$$f_Q : C \rightarrow Q_? \tag{8.3}$$

$$f_S : C \rightarrow S_? \tag{8.4}$$

process the project vector $p \in C$ in order to obtain the applicable requirement levels. The requirement levels then select or deselect the individual requirements, resulting in the set of requirements applicable to the software development process. This tailoring is, for the most part, automated through the software tool *QMExpert Tailoring*.

8.5.1 The QMExpert Tailoring Tool

Tailoring the software process requirements for a new project begins with collecting the basic characteristics and analyses for the vector $p \in C$, where

$$C = C_{Sft} \times C_{Lt} \times C_U \times C_O \times C_{Mr} \times C_{Sr} \times C_{Fa} \times R_L \times R_B \times R_C \times R_{Tr} \times R_{Rp}$$
(8.5)

The basic characteristic dimensions and their values are summarized in Table 8.1.

Figure 8.6 shows the first input screen. The characteristics and their possible values are further explained at the bottom of the screen to ease the selection of the correct value: For example, the *Lander Spacecraft* in the *Space Flight Type* dimension is "designed to reach the surface of a planet and survive long enough to telemeter data back to Earth. ESA's Rosetta spacecraft [...] comprises a large orbiter, [...] and a small lander. Each of these carries a large complement of scientific experiments designed to complete the most detailed study of a comet ever attempted" [27].

The next step is to refine the choice of basic characteristics entered on the first screen according to analyses regarding the characteristics shown in Table 8.2. Here, for example, the *Technology Risk* value *low* means that for "the realisation of the product proven technology that are state of the art are available and can be applied" [27]. As shown in Fig. 8.7, the selections made here directly lead to the applicable requirement levels for $W_?$, $Q_?$, and $S_?$.

Table 8.1 QMExpert tailoring tool dimensions and values

	Name	Values
C_{Sft}	Space flight type	Robotic Maintenance System, Orbiter Spacecraft, Flyby Spacecraft, Lander Spacecraft, Rover Spacecraft, Application Satellite, Manned Flight, Military Spacecraft, Scientific Observatory Spacecraft
C_{Lt}	Launcher type	Expendable, Manned Reusable, Unmanned Reusable, Unmanned nonreusable Automated Transfer
C_U	Utilization	Free-Flyer, ISS internal, ISS external, Manned Launch Vehicle
C_O	Objective	Spacecraft, Payload
C_{Mr}	Maintainability requirements	Generic, Advanced, Complete
C_{Sr}	Safety requirements	Generic, Advanced, Complete
C_{Fa}	Flight authority	ESA, NASA, Roscosmos

Table 8.2 QMExpert tailoring tool project characteristics

	Name	Values
R_L	Lifetime	>7 years, 2–7 years, < 2 years
R_B	Budget	>50 M EUR, 25–50 M EUR, 10–25 M EUR, < 10 M EUR
R_C	Complexity	High, Low
R_{Tr}	Technology risk	High, Low
R_{Rp}	Risk policy	High, Low

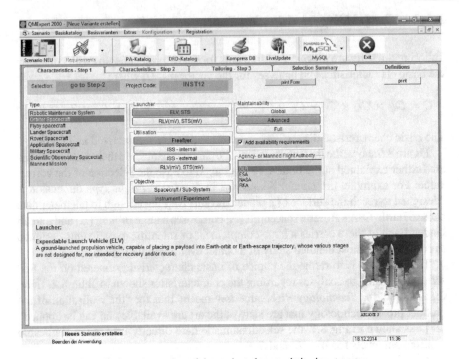

Fig. 8.6 Starting tailoring: screenshot of the project characteristics input screen

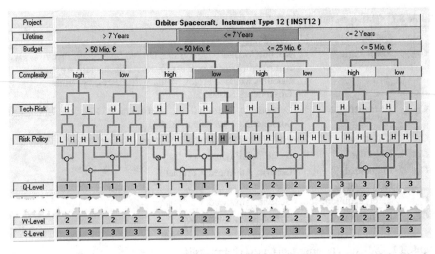

Fig. 8.7 Screenshot of adjusting tailoring parameters and resulting requirement levels $W_?$, $Q_?$, and $S_?$

After that, the tailoring tool picks the requirements for inclusion in the product assurance requirements document. As described before, all requirements in the catalog were tagged during pre-tailoring with one or more requirement level tags. For example, the requirement that a hardware–software interaction analysis should be conducted is tagged with S_2 and W_3. It means that the requirement is included if the safety level is $s \leq 2$ or if the software level is $w \leq 3$, which is all applications that are safety critical or which have important software parts.

Next, the user is presented with a preview of the requirements, and an overview of which ones were selected and deselected. For fine-tuning, he can select additional requirements, or deselect requirements that he wants to be removed. The tailoring tool also ensures consistency by making sure that all requirements are included which are not themselves selected but which are referenced from other requirements. Finally, the tool exports into a Word document for further processing (e.g., including in contractual documents). Front matters, table of contents, abbreviation lists, chapters, and the like are generated automatically.

8.5.2 Lessons Learned

Tailoring is necessary for fitting coherent but generic standards to the specificities of a project. However, the national catalog contains hundreds of requirements applicable to software development. Manually tailoring them would be a huge effort, influenced subjectively by the tailoring product assurance manager's perceptions and emotions, and difficult to validate against corporate rules.

Our semi-automated tailoring process based on the QMExpert Tailoring tool is without frills but sophisticated. It is straight forward enough to be practicable. A single person can tailor a complete product assurance requirements document for a project in a short time. While manual intervention is still needed in several phases of the process, the tool significantly reduces the efforts for tailoring. Manual adjustments can be summarized in a report for validation by higher-ups.

Through the years, the tool has aged technically—it relies on dated libraries and technologies—but the process it supports and its contents have matured. A lot of tacit knowledge and experience went into the requirement level classifications, contributing to the quality of the tailoring results. Of course, much effort has been invested in the catalog data itself.

8.6 Cross-Company Product Quality Management

Unless a customer accepts any project result and quality, customer and supplier will seek *visibility* in order to mitigate the high risks of, for instance, untested technologies, large sums of money, or loss of life. Possible ways to achieve visibility are

- to negotiate contracts with intermediate products and partial payments, and
- to increase customer involvement in the development process [10].

8.6.1 Customer Product Assurance

Regarding intermediate products, space projects are executed in a series of *phases* cf. [29]. Each of the phases includes end milestones in the form of project reviews, the outcome of which determine payments and readiness of the project to move forward to the next phase. These reviews are the main interaction points between customer and supplier. Regarding customer involvement, the three primary project functions (project management, engineering, and product assurance) are present on the customer side as interfaces to their supplier counter-parts.

All three functions take their roles in ensuring the desired outcome of the development project: Project management is typically interested in getting the project out the door, thinking that engineers will take care of its quality. Engineers, however, are too concerned with getting the product to work that they will not see risks and potential weaknesses. The role of product assurance is that of a devil's advocate in a constructive and non-confrontational way. Product assurance benevolently probes the software product's contents. It has organizational and budgetary independence, and helps shaping but not building the product [10].

In the Space Administration, the product assurance department assumes the role of customer-side quality assurance for the procurement of space devices. It interacts with the supplier-side product quality functions, and primarily with quality improvement function in order to trigger improvements in the suppliers' development processes where necessary. Yet, the interaction between customer and supplier is not a one-way street: feedback, experiences, and knowledge generated from project execution is used to improve product quality management on the customer's side (Fig. 8.8). The toolbox of processes, methods, and tools for product assurance is continuously evolved. As a member of the ECSS standardization body, knowledge generated in the national program is forwarded further upstream and may eventually find its way into the ECSS standards system.

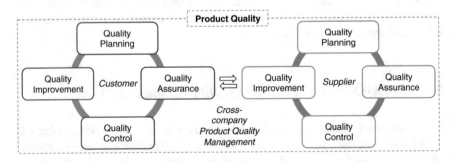

Fig. 8.8 Cross-company product quality assurance

8.6.2 The Implementation Process

Members of the customer product assurance are involved in project activities from the beginning. Software process requirements tailored from the national catalog (Sect. 8.5) are included in the contract as part of the work description. It is the foundation of product assurance work and defines objectives, policies, and rules for design, development, procurement, integration, and testing processes.

As part of the contractual negotiations, the supplier states his compliance to the prescribed development process requirements (see also Fig. 8.4b). The *statement of compliance* is a matrix indicating for each requirement the compliance status: either *fully compliant, partially compliant, non-compliant,* or *not applicable.* Unless a supplier declares full compliance with a requirement, the deviation and its reasons have to be explained in a commentary column of the matrix, and have to be accepted by the customer.

During the project, the supplier adapts its processes in order to comply with the requirements. For example, there is the general requirement of having established product assurance functions. While project management and engineering are commonly present on the suppliers' side, product assurance might be missing. Donaldson and Siegel [10] recommend to seriously question the maturity of such a supplier and its capability to ensure product delivery. In the national space program, however, the diverse small enterprises, universities, and research institutes often miss product assurance but still have to be involved for various reasons like promoting research and lack of alternatives. So one of the first process improvements is to establish product assurance.

As the requirements only prescribe what should be achieved but not how, the actual implementation is documented in respective plans, e.g., a Software Product Assurance Plan. The plans are reviewed at milestones for the customer to agree to their implementation. They serve to improve the visibility of the supplier's work, and are proofs of the implementation of requested processes. Besides milestone reviews, the customer's product assurance attends progress meetings, and looks out for deviations and defines the actions necessary to reach compliance. While most work is based on documents, the customer retains the right to visit a supplier's facilities any time and to perform inspections of work products.

In case a nonconformance is detected, product assurance participates in a *Nonconformance Review Board*, where further measures like root cause analysis, modification measures, and verifications are discussed and agreed upon. Typically, the supplier is capable of handling this by applying his quality management processes. If, however, the deviation's root cause is found to be in the supplier's processes, the deficiency is to be eliminated in the frame of process improvements.

8.6.3 Lessons Learned

The statement of compliance simplifies communication between customer and supplier by clearly summarizing the agreed-upon baseline of product assurance measures. It is part of the contract and often a major point of discussions and negotiations. Originally, suppliers only created plans in reaction to the requirements. This allowed them to more easily stretch requirement interpretations, and to better hide non-compliances. Through the statement of compliance, contradictions come up clearly and early in the project, reducing the risks of discovering them late.

Negotiating a statement of compliance that is accepted by both parties can be work intensive. Once agreed, however, it restates commitment of supplier project management to the development requirements. It is particularly valuable if a dispute arises during the project.

Attention should be paid to the understandability of comments in the statement of compliance because some projects last for many years. A change in personnel can mean that comments written too briefly may no longer be understood and cause new, unnecessary discussions. To reduce interpretive freedom and to avoid comments that negate a seeming compliance, we decided that comments (even explanatory ones) are not allowed for "fully compliant" responses.

8.7 Experience Report: Introducing Advanced Static Analysis

This section provides an experience report of how advanced static analysis was introduced in the German national space program. Static analysis is a widely used technology for detecting potential problems in software by analyzing human-readable or binary code without executing it. The ECSS prefers testing over static analysis for validation. But analysis is still recommended for verifying source code robustness and finding errors that are difficult to detect at runtime [17, 22]. The capabilities and complexity of static analysis techniques vary greatly from simple source code pattern analysis to formal methods including *abstract interpretation* [8].

In contrast to simpler analysis methods, tools based on abstract interpretation can prove the absence of several runtime errors (e.g., division by zero, arithmetic under- and overflows). Such a tool is also called *sound* [13]. One of the first commercially available tools capable of analyzing large code bases was Polyspace.[3] Compared to common simpler static analyzers, it is expensive with regard to financial cost and efforts. Annual license costs are tens of thousands of Euros plus one-time costs and initial trainings, and even on modern hardware analyses can run for hours.

---

[3] Available from: http://de.mathworks.com/products/polyspace/.

8.7.1   Polyspace Pilot Project

As a first step, a pilot project was set up. The purpose was to try out the capabilities of Polyspace, test if it will hold its promises, get a feeling for its handling, estimate if it is worth the cost, and generally build up expertise. The idea was to also try out, if Polyspace would fit into a toolbox for conducting software inspections as customer; metaphorically speaking, if it could be the software analogy to a magnifying glass a hardware customer uses when attending a *key inspection point* meeting.

For the pilot project, a Polyspace server was set up. One of the space projects that were just finishing volunteered to make available its satellite's flight software source code, which was about 22,000 lines of code. The software had passed all other validation and verification activities and was ready to be delivered. Next, it was imported into the Polyspace tool.

Polyspace decides for each line of code if the line is guaranteed to not contain the specified runtime errors (green), if the line will definitely cause a runtime error (red), dead code (gray), or if a decision could not be made (orange). The vendor forecast that in software of this maturity, Polyspace would still find about one runtime error per 1,000 lines of code. This forecast was met exactly. Consequently, several function-critical errors in the flight software could be fixed that might otherwise have caused serious troubles.

Yet, one drop of bitterness are the orange lines and computation time. The number of orange lines can be traded off against analysis computation time by adjusting the *precision* level. In our experience from other projects, rarely more than 20 % of lines are marked orange. This percentage and even lower values are also reported by other researchers [5]. Still, the undecided orange lines can cause non-negligible additional effort; in particular, as finding the root cause for a false positive (reported, but actually no error) located elsewhere in the code may require a thorough analysis.

Making rough estimates from the data provided in Emanuelsson and Nilsson [13], and Brat and Klemm [5], one can expect in 60,000 lines of fresh code: 40 error reports from tools like Coverity or Klocwork (both *unsound*), 9,000 orange lines from Polyspace, and 1,200,000 reports from FlexeLint (unsound) tool, which, however, can be tweaked down to 1,000 reports without thorough analysis. This means two things: First, unless one is willing to risk false negatives, i.e., missing out on certain errors, checking all suspect reports means a lot of work. So one better starts early. Second, a supplier may prefer to use an unsound tool in order to reduce the effort needed for checking suspects. The liability implications of knowing about potential errors (orange code) but not acting on them are, at best, unclear. But if the supplier did not know about the problems because he used an unsound tool, he can still plead research risks in case of an accident due to a software problem.

The pilot project showed that sound analysis is worth it because several critical errors were found in thoroughly tested code. However, it is not suitable for a quick inspection because major efforts are associated with importing the code into Polyspace, running the analyses, and checking orange code.

8.7.2 Toward Wider Adoption

The implication of the pilot project is that in order to reap the rewards of sound analysis, major efforts have to be invested in executing it. These efforts are beyond the capacity of customer software product assurance. Instead, industry should perform the analyses themselves. Only the reports were to be delivered for review. They serve as evidence that the analysis was executed, and allow to detect irregularities.

However, use of verification tools to demonstrate software quality is not explicitly specified in ECSS standards. Further, depending on the supplier, different tools are used. At the time we wanted to field Polyspace analysis processes, three projects were moving to their next phase. This meant that contracts (including software process requirements) were re-negotiated. Although the times were favorable, it turned out that introducing Polyspace was not simple. Separate and tiring negotiations for each project were necessary to place sound analysis. The space sector is conservative and dismissive toward changes to established processes. A common saying is "Only fly what has flown before!" The need for changing established processes and the costs associated with Polyspace (monetary license prices, and in terms of effort and legal risks) made it no surprise that industry would not easily agree. This holds true, in particular, if a process requirement is seemingly only imposed on a single project. But implementing a change from top-down through the ECSS standards seemed infeasible because consensus on multinational level would take many years and was further improbable to pass the respective committees without success stories.

In this situation, the convening of the pre-tailoring expert group offered the opportunity to implant the change on national scope. The invited top-level quality managers could be convinced of the net benefits of the sound static analysis, and without a concrete project in the background, the associated costs were too far away. In the end, the national catalog was extended correspondingly with a requirement regarding the proof of absence of several types of runtime errors. From there it gets tailored into requirements whenever a project moves to the next phase, and has nation-wide legitimation.

Meanwhile, sound static analysis is rather widely employed by suppliers. Even without being forced by a requirement, major suppliers have started procuring it for their other projects. However, every now and then, discussions still arise about sound static analysis during project execution. For example, if a supplier or one of its divisions are for their first time confronted with the need to provide the required report for a review. A supplier can then be pointed to the statement of compliance they signed (Sect. 8.6.2). If represented in the expert group, they can additionally be referred to the signing of the catalog by their head of quality (Sect. 8.4.3).

8.7.3 Lessons Learned

Conducting a pilot project first was important to learn that static analysis is a valuable addition to testing but also that it is not suitable as a tool for on-site inspections by the customer. Instead, the verification itself has to be executed by the supplier according to contractual requirements. Evidence is provided in form of a report.

Strong rejection was a real problem initially. It was not practically feasible to overcome this rejection. This achievement was made possible only by establishing and exploiting the right management tools (pre-tailoring, expert group, and statement of compliance). Today, sound static analysis is broadly accepted by suppliers who worked with it. Only every now and then there is a new supplier or branch that has not worked with it. For these cases, the right management tools are in place.

The experience report provided here is only one example of a software process improvement. Further technologies are continuously researched and evaluated, and, if considered fitting, introduced into the national program.

8.8 Conclusion

In this chapter we presented software process evolution from the viewpoint of a customer. Our goal is to assure the quality of a product that is developed for a single purpose: to assume critical functions in a spaceflight mission. To reach our goal, we set the frame for development: We manage software process evolution through requirements from a strategic perspective, not how evolution is actually implemented by the providers organizationally. At that strategic level, we

- seek harmonization with ECSS and other standards,
- ensure implementation of process requirements at suppliers, and
- generate and disseminate knowledge to continuously advance processes.

However, it is difficult to harmonize and improve the processes in a sector with unequal histories and objectives, and diverse players. We revisited several levels at which the strategic frames for process evolution are defined, starting at the level of

- international and regional standards, moving on to the
- national catalog of the German space program, and further to the
- tailoring of process requirements at project-level, and the
- quality improvement efforts through cross-company quality management.

Taking the example of advanced static analysis, we described typical problems that can be encountered. It shows how the management tools at different implementation levels can be used to trigger process evolutions.

Many (if not all) organizations try to improve their processes by themselves. This, of course, is very important. However, they might have a different focus on what is important to optimize with priority. In a small market where products cannot be bought off-the-shelf but where products are unique specimen specifically developed for the customer, close collaboration between customer and supplier is necessary. Given visibility and trust, both sides profit from cross-company quality management.

8.9   Further Reading

Quality, software processes, and their improvement are an all-pervading topic in the knowledge areas of software engineering [4]. Our work[4] is distinguished from others through the fact that we describe how we address the evolution of software development processes toward higher quality from a customer's point of view. On the one hand, countless publications focus on organizations' work on improving their own software processes, e.g., [23, 26]. Doing so, indeed, is very important. On the other hand, much effort has been put into standards and maturity levels as a means of giving customers ways to assess the capability of suppliers. For instance, see ISO/IEC 15504 or CMMI [7, 30]. Furthermore, Rosenberg and Gallo [37] describe software product assurance at the NASA. However, not much has been published on the daily work of product assurance as a customer, and how software, tools, and methods improve this work.

In the space domain, tailoring of requirements to software development processes is omnipresent for aligning customer quality expectations with development effectiveness and efficiency [38]. Most ECSS standards already include a tailoring notice that explicitly encourages tailoring the standard. The ECSS-S-ST-00C further explains a formal tailoring approach based on the *ECSS Applicable Requirements Matrix*. It advocates putting all requirements with their identifiers in a table, and marking them as either applicable without change, applicable with modification, not applicable, and newly generated [15]. An adaptation of this approach is to include all requirements in their original form, and then record any changes or deletions after the original text, which, of course, can lead to very long documents. Currently, the ECSS is working on a more complex standard for the tailoring of ECSS standards.

ECSS-E-ST-40C and ECSS-Q-ST-80C are "self-tailoring." It means that both standards' annexes provide a table that lists for each requirement if it should be included in software with a certain criticality from A (most critical) to D (least critical). To determine the criticality category of each software item, a safety and dependability analysis and a hardware–software interaction analysis are conducted. The severity of the consequences of possible failures determine the criticality level.

A software tool for tailoring the ECSS-E-ST-40 Issue B is provided by the ESA. The wizard-style tool first takes the user through a questionnaire containing single-choice questions in several areas, e.g., project characteristics (novelty, complexity, expected lifetime, use of commercial off-the-shelf items, ...), stakeholders (who is the customer, supplier, maintainer, user, ...), risks (e.g., long-term use, tricky design), verification, and so on. It then outputs a table that proposes for each requirement in the standard whether it should be included or not. Döler et al. [9] presented a web-based tool capable of tailoring several standards including ECSS-E-ST-40B, ECSS-Q-ST-80B, DIN EN 50128 (railway applications), internal standards, and RTCA/DO-178B (airborne systems). Again characteristics like technical domain, software type, and operational complexity are queried using 17 nonredundant single-choice questions. The tailoring rules are based on comparisons with other standards and long-term

---

[4]An earlier version of this chapter was published as [35].

experience from working in space projects. However, both tools seem to be no longer actively maintained. Rumor has it that the tedious maintenance of the requirements and rule database might have been too costly.

Armbrust et al. [2] address product quality through scoping, i.e., what to include in a process and what not. Their approach is similar in that it characterizes space projects using criteria like mission type, complexity, or criticality that then result in adapted processes. Their view complements ours as it is technical and supplier-oriented: For example, cooperation with ESA triggered process evolution on their side.

Kalus and Kuhrmann [31] present a systematic literature review of criteria for software process tailoring. They identified 49 tailoring criteria, such as team size, project budget, project duration, the degree of technology knowledge, the availability of commercial off-the-shelf products, tool infrastructure, legal aspects, or the domain.

In Chap. 10, the authors describe an assembly-based method of process evolution. A focus of their work is the enactability and assurance of the enactment of activities imposed through regulatory needs or our requirements. With the same goal, Chap. 11 explains how to adapt case management techniques to deal with problems that stem from trying to achieve flexibility and compliance at the same time.

Chapter 13 addresses the co-evolution of development processes and model-driven engineering. They research the implied consequences for costs and success of process tailoring. This happens against the background of the importance of customization and optimization for staying efficient and dealing with arising new challenges.

References

1. Abbott, A.: Battery fault ends X-ray satellite mission. Nature **399**, 93ff (1999)
2. Armbrust, O., Katahira, M., Miyamoto, Y., Münch, J., Nakao, H., Ocampo, A.: Scoping software process models—initial concepts and experience from defining space standards. Making Globally Distributed Software Development a Success Story. Lecture Notes in Computer Science, pp. 160–172. Springer, Berlin (2008)
3. Basili, V.R., McGarry, F.E., Pajerski, R., Zelkowitz, M.V.: Lessons learned from 25 years of process improvement: the rise and fall of the nasa software engineering laboratory. In: Proceedings of the International Conference on Software Engineering, pp. 69–79. ACM, New York, NY (2002)
4. Bourque, P., Fairley, R.E. (eds.): SWEBOK V3.0—Guide to the Software Engineering Body of Knowledge. IEEE Computer Society, Washington (2014)
5. Brat, G., Klemm, R.: Static analysis of the mars exploration rover flight software. In: Proceedings of the First International Space Mission Challenges for Information Technology, pp. 321–326 (2003)
6. Card, D.N.: Software product assurance: measurement and control. Inf. Softw. Technol. **30**(6), 322–330 (1988)
7. CMMI Product Team: CMMI for development, version 1.3 (2010)
8. Cousot, P., Cousot, R.: Abstract interpretation: A unified lattice model for static analysis of programs by construction or approximation of fixpoints. In: Proceedings of the ACM Symposium on Principles of Programming Languages, pp. 238–252. ACM, New York (1977)

9. Döler, N., Herrmann, A., Tapper, U., Hempel, R.: Ecss application in dlr space projects—experiences and suggestions for enhancement. Presentation slides from the ECSS Developer Day at ESTEC (Noordwijk) (2005)
10. Donaldson, S.E., Siegel, S.G.: Successful Software Development, 2nd edn. Prentice-Hall, Upper Saddle River (2001)
11. Dowson, M.: The ariane 5 software failure. ACM SIGSOFT Softw. Eng. Notes **22**(2), 84 (1997)
12. Dvorak, D.L.: Nasa study on flight software complexity: Final report. NASA (2007)
13. Emanuelsson, P., Nielsson, U.: A comparative study of industrial static analysis tools. Electron. Notes Theor. Comput. Sci. **217**, 5–21 (2008)
14. ECSS Secretariat (publ.): ECSS—standardization objectives, policies and organization. ECSS Standard ECSS-P-00A, European Cooperation for Space Standardization (2000)
15. ECSS Secretariat (publ.): ECSS system—description, implementation and general requirements. ECSS Standard ECSS-S-ST-00C, European Cooperation for Space Standardization (2008)
16. ECSS Secretariat (publ.): Space product assurance—product assurance management. ECSS Standard ECSS-Q-ST-10C, European Cooperation for Space Standardization (2008)
17. ECSS Secretariat (publ.): Space engineering—software. ECSS Standard ECSS-E-ST-40C, European Cooperation for Space Standardization (2009)
18. ECSS Secretariat (publ.): Space product assurance—software product assurance. ECSS Standard ECSS-Q-ST-80C, European Cooperation for Space Standardization (2009)
19. ECSS Secretariat (publ.): Space project management—configuration and information management. ECSS Standard ECSS-M-ST-40C, European Cooperation for Space Standardization (2009)
20. ECSS Secretariat (publ.): Space product assurance—software dependability and safety. ECSS Standard ECSS-Q-HB-80-03A, European Cooperation for Space Standardization (2012)
21. ECSS Secretariat (publ.): ECSS—standardization objectives, policies and organization. ECSS Standard ECSS-P-00C, European Cooperation for Space Standardization (2013)
22. ECSS Secretariat (publ.): Space engineering—software engineering handbook. ECSS Standard ECSS-E-HB-40A, European Cooperation for Space Standardization (2013)
23. Falessi, D., Shaw, M., Mullen, K.: Achieving and maintaining CMMI maturity level 5 in a small organization. IEEE Softw. **31**(5), 80–86 (2014)
24. Gammal, Y.E., Kriedte, W.: ECSS—an initiative to develop a single set of european space standards. In: Proceedings of Product Assurance Symposium and Software Product Assurance Workshop, pp. 43–50. ESA (1996)
25. Ginsberg, M.P., Quinn, L.: Process tailoring and the software capability maturity model. Technical Report CMU/SEI-94-TR-024, Carnegie Mellon University, Software Engineering Institute (1995)
26. Holzmann, G.J.: Mars code. Commun. ACM **57**(2), 64–73 (2014)
27. Jobi, W.: Tailoring catalogue: product assurance & safety requirements for dlr space projects. Technical report, Deutsches Zentrum für Luft- und Raumfahrt (2012)
28. Johnson, C.W.: The natural history of bugs: Using formal methods to analyse software related failures in space missions. FM 2005: Formal Methods. Lecture Notes in Computer Science, pp. 9–25. Springer, Berlin (2005)
29. Jones, M., Gomez, E., Matineo, A., Mortensen, U.K.: Introducing ECSS software-engineering standards within ESA. ESA Bull. **111**, 132–139 (2002)
30. JTC 1 SC 7: Information technology—process assessment—part 1: Concepts and vocabulary. International Standard ISO/IEC 15504-1:2012, International Organization for Standardization (2012)
31. Kalus, G., Kuhrmann, M.: Criteria for software process tailoring: A systematic review. In: Proceedings of the International Conference on Software and System Process, pp. 171–180. ACM, New York (2013)
32. Ley, W.: Management von Raumfahrtprojekten. Handbuch der Raumfahrttechnik, 4th edn, pp. 715–764. Carl Hanser Verlag, Germany (2011)
33. Marsiske, H.A.: Wendepunkt Mars. http://www.heise.de/tp/artikel/6/6775/1.html (2000)

34. Oberg, J.: Why the mars probe went off course. IEEE Spec. **36**(12), 34–39 (1999)
35. Prause, C., Bibus, M., Dietrich, C., Jobi, W.: Tailoring process requirements for software product assurance. In: Proceedings of the International Conference on Software and System Process, pp. 67–71. ACM, New York (2015)
36. Rechtin, E.: Remarks on reducing space science mission costs. In: Proceedings of the Workshop: Reducing the Costs of Space Science Research Missions, p. 23ff. National Academy Press, Washington (1997)
37. Rosenberg, L.H., Albert M. Gallo, J.: Software quality assurance engineering at nasa. In: Proceedings of the IEEE Aerospace Conference, vol. 5, pp. 5:2569–5:2575. IEEE, Washington (2002)
38. Schiller, D., Heinemann, J.: ECSS—20 years of collaboration for european spaceflight. DLR Newsl. Countdown **24**, 32–35 (2014)

Chapter 9
Modeling Software Processes Using BPMN: When and When Not?

Marlon Dumas and Dietmar Pfahl

Abstract Software process models capture structural and behavioral properties of software development activities, supporting the elicitation, analysis, simulation, and improvement of software development processes. Various approaches for the modeling and model-driven analysis of software development processes have been proposed but little progress has been made regarding standardization. With increasing demands regarding flexibility and adaptability of development processes, the constant evolution of development methods and tools, and the trend toward continuous product deployment, better support for process engineers in terms of universally applicable modeling notations as well as simulation and enactment mechanisms has become more desirable than ever. In contrast to software process modeling, the discipline of business process modeling has attained a greater level of consensus and standardization, leading most notably to the Business Process Model and Notation (BPMN). The success of BPMN as a standard business process modeling notation has made scholars ponder whether BPMN could also be used for modeling software development processes. This chapter analyzes this question by eliciting fundamental assumptions made in BPMN about the nature of business process models, which ultimately determine which aspects of the process are included in the model and which aspects are either left out or treated as ancillary.

9.1 Introduction

Software process models capture structural and behavioral properties of software development activities within dedicated organizations as well as in open source development settings. Such models support the elicitation, analysis, simulation, and improvement of software development processes. Various approaches for model-

M. Dumas · D. Pfahl (✉)
Institute of Computer Science, University of Tartu,
J Liivi 2, 50409 Tartu, Estonia
e-mail: marlon.dumas@ut.ee

D. Pfahl
e-mail: dietmar.pfahl@ut.ee

© Springer International Publishing Switzerland 2016
M. Kuhrmann et al. (eds.), *Managing Software Process Evolution*,
DOI 10.1007/978-3-319-31545-4_9

ing software development processes have been proposed in the past three decades [1, 8, 17] but little progress has been made regarding standardization to the extent that universally accepted software process modeling paradigms and associated notations remain elusive [20]. With increasing demands regarding flexibility and adaptability of development processes, the constant evolution of development methods and tools, and the trend towards continuous product deployment, better support for process engineers in terms of universally applicable modeling notations as well as simulation and enactment mechanisms has become more desirable than ever.

In contrast to software development processes, the discipline of business process modeling has attained a greater level of consensus and standardization, leading most notably to the *Business Process Model and Notation* (BPMN; [21]), a standard supported by dozens of commercial tools and used by thousands of practitioners across a wide range of industry verticals [14]. Empirical studies have shown that this success is due to the perception by adopters that BPMN strikes a suitable tradeoff between instrumentality (usefulness and performance of BPMN for process modeling) and ease-of-use (complexity of creating BPMN models) [24, 25].

The success of BPMN as a standard business process modeling notation has made scholars ponder whether BPMN could also be used for modeling software processes [5, 23]. This chapter analyzes this question by eliciting fundamental assumptions made in BPMN about the nature of business process models, which ultimately determine which aspects of the process are included in the model and which aspects are either left out or treated as ancillary. We highlight in particular that BPMN relies on three fundamental assumptions that affect its scope of applicability

1. A process consists of a set of isolated process instances (also called cases) that interact with each other in very limited ways.
2. A case is a sequence of activities that transform objects associated to the case, along the way from a start state to an end state (possibly among multiple possible end states).
3. Each atomic activity (also called a task) is an atomic unit of work performed by a single actor.

These assumptions fit well with certain classes of processes, including common business processes such as lead-to-quote, order-to-cash, or claim-to-resolution; but the same does not necessarily hold for software development processes.

Based on the identified assumptions, this chapter attempts to answer the question of when can BPMN be suitable for software process modeling and when not. The chapter starts by introducing the BPMN notation and basic concepts of software process modeling in Sect. 9.2. Using illustrative examples, this chapter then presents classes of processes that can be conveniently represented with BPMN, as well as classes of processes that cannot be conveniently or fully represented with BPMN in Sect. 9.3. These observations are followed by a brief discussion on the applicability of BPMN to model common software development processes in Sect. 9.4 and, finally, suggestions for further reading Sect. 9.5.

9.2   Background and Context

This section provides a brief introduction to BPMN and presents some basic concepts of software process modeling, as embodied in the *Multi-View Process modeling Language* (MVP-L). The section also introduces a working example that is used in the rest of the chapter to illustrate the scope and limitations of BPMN.

9.2.1   Business Process Modeling in BPMN

A BPMN process model is a graph consisting of three types of nodes: *events* (represented as circles), *activities* (represented as rectangles) and *gateways* (represented as diamonds). Events denote things that happen at a particular point in time. Activities denote work that needs to be performed. Gateways serve to route the flow of control along the branches of the process model. Nodes are connected by means of directed edges called *sequence flows*. A sequence flow basically says that the flow of control can pass from the source node to the target node. An illustrative example of a lending process—specifically the "loan application handling" portion thereof—is shown in Fig. 9.1. This model contains a single start event (leftmost element), an intermediate event where a revised loan application is received, and two end events (rightmost elements). These two end events correspond to two different ways of completing the process. The remaining elements are activities and gateways.

There are three basic types of gateways in BPMN:

1. XOR gateways (represented by an 'X'),
2. AND gateways (represented by a '+'), and
3. OR gateways (represented by an 'O').

A gateway is said to be a *split* gateway if it has multiple outgoing flows, or a *join* gateway if it has multiple incoming flows. It may happen that a gateway is both a split and a join gateway. If we put together the distinction between the three types of gateways (XOR, AND, and OR) and the distinction between split and join gateways,

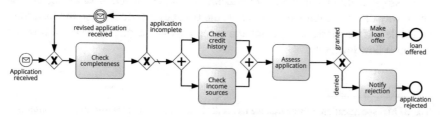

Fig. 9.1 Loan application process model

we obtain six different types of basic gateways[1]: XOR-split, XOR-join, AND-split, AND-join, OR-split, and OR-join.

- An XOR-split is a decision point where the flow of control is passed to exactly one of the outgoing flows of the XOR-split. The choice between outgoing flows is based on the evaluation of conditions attached to the gateway and/or to its flows. For example, Fig. 9.1 has two XOR-split gateways: one after task "Check completeness" and another after task "Assess application." In the case of the first of these XOR-split gateways, one of the outgoing flows is labeled with the condition "application incomplete," while the other outgoing flow is the default flow, denoted by a stripe through the flow. The default flow is taken if the condition(s) attached to the other conditional flow(s) is/are not fulfilled—in this example the default flow is taken if the application is complete. An XOR-join on the other hand merges two incoming branches into a single one. Figure 9.1 features an XOR-join just before task "Check completeness" which merges two incoming paths.
- An AND-split forks out one thread of execution into two or more parallel threads. For example, Fig. 9.1 has an AND-split that starts two threads in parallel corresponding to a credit check and an income source check. These two threads join in an AND-join just before task "Assess application." The AND-join is a synchronization point—it waits for both threads to complete.
- The OR-split (which we do not exemplify) is a hybrid between the XOR-split and the AND-split, allowing a split into *any* number of outgoing flows instead of *one* (XOR-split) or *all* (AND-split). Similarly, the OR-join is a hybrid between an XOR-join and an AND-join, synchronizing all active flows (but not those that are "inactive").

Another type of split gateway in BPMN is the *event-based exclusive gateway*. This latter gateway is similar to the XOR-split (which is also called data-based exclusive gateway in BPMN). However, instead of the choice between outgoing flows being determined by conditions (which are evaluated based on data), the choice is determined by the occurrence of one of multiple events. An event-based exclusive gateway is designated using a star symbol. Figure 9.2 features an event-based exclusive gateway. When the execution of the process arrives at this point (in other words, when a token arrives to this gateway), the execution of the thread stops until either the message event or the timer event occur. Whichever occurs first will determine which way the execution will proceed. If the timer event occurs first, the loan offer is canceled. If the message signaling the acceptance of the offer is received first, the execution flow proceeds.

---

[1]The BPMN specification uses alternative terms [21]: XOR-splits are *exclusive decision gateways*, XOR-joins are *exclusive merge gateways*, OR-splits are *inclusive decision gateways*, OR-joins are *inclusive merge gateways*, AND-splits are *parallel forking gateways* and AND-joins are *parallel joining gateways*. Here, we adopt a simpler and more uniform terminology covering those aspects required to understand the chapter easily, even for readers without in-depth knowledge of the BPMN specification.

Fig. 9.2 Loan offer process
model

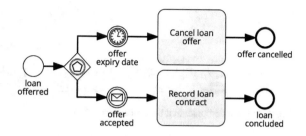

The above examples illustrate that BPMN supports several types of events, with different types of triggers. In particular, Fig. 9.2 includes plain events (the start event and the end events, which have no triggers) as well as an event with a message trigger and an event with a timer trigger. Other types of events in BPMN include *conditional events*, triggered when their associated conditions become true, and error events, triggered when an associated error type occurs. The latter type of events can also be used to capture exception handling in the style of "try-catch" blocks in modern programming languages. The range of event types in BPMN is very rich. There are more than 60 types of events, classified according to their position in the process model (start, end, intermediate, interrupting and non-interrupting boundary events) and their triggers (13 different types of triggers).

The process models shown above are "flat," meaning that all the activities in the model correspond to atomic units of work—also called *atomic tasks* in BPMN. BPMN also supports activities that correspond to the execution of entire *sub-processes*. Figure 9.3 shows a top-level BPMN model of the lending process. It consists of three subprocesses: the first two correspond to the processes shown in Figs. 9.1 and 9.2. Subprocesses are visually distinguishable from atomic tasks thanks to the '+' marker.

In addition to the '+' marker to denote a subprocess, BPMN offers other markers to capture repetition of a given activity (be it an atomic task or a subprocess). Specifically, two markers are provided for this purposes: the sequential repetition marker and the parallel multi-instance repetition marker. The sequential repetition marker indicates that multiple instances of a given task or subprocess need to be executed, one time after another. It is an alternative to capturing sequential repetition via a cycle in the process model as in Fig. 9.1. Meanwhile, the multi-instance repetition marker indicates that a given task or subprocess needs to be executed multiple times and that these executions occur in parallel. For example, Fig. 9.4 shows a subprocess "Perform disbursement" with a multi-instance marker, indicating that the various loan disbursements are executed in parallel. The annotation attached to this sub-

Fig. 9.3 Top-level transportation process model (with subprocesses)

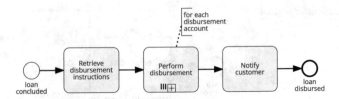

Fig. 9.4 Loan disbursement subprocess model

process tells us that the disbursement is made once for each account nominated by the customer.

The BPMN constructs introduced above allow us to capture tasks, events and their ordering. This aspect of business process modeling is generally known as the *control-flow* modeling perspective [16]. BPMN also allows us to capture data objects consumed and produced by tasks and events in a process (the so-called *data perspective*), as well as resource classes (e.g., roles) responsible for the execution of tasks in the process (the *organizational* or *resource* perspective). For example, Fig. 9.5 shows the same loan application process as in Fig. 9.1, now with input and output data objects as well as roles, represented as lanes that divide the tasks of the process according to the role of their performer. This latter process model contains two lanes corresponding to the "Loan applications handler" responsible for the initial processing of the loan application, and "Credit officer" responsible for the later parts of the

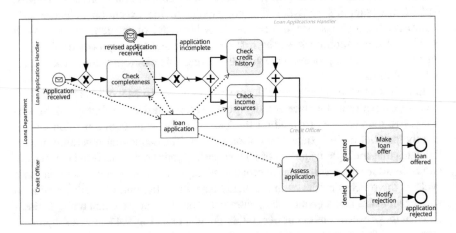

Fig. 9.5 Loan application subprocess with data objects and lanes

process. The process model also shows which tasks or events read from or modify the "loan application" data object—represented by a rectangle with a folded corner.

9.2.2 Software Process Modeling with MVP-L

In the following, we describe a typical work-test-rework-retest cycle with the help of a rigorous software process modeling language: *Multi-View Process modeling Language* (MVP-L). MVP-L was developed in the 1980s at the University of Maryland [28]. Subsequent development was conducted at the University of Kaiserslautern, Germany. The main focus of MVP-L is on modeling "in-the-large". It is assumed that the ability to understand, guide, and support the interaction between processes is more beneficial than the complete automation of low-level process steps [3]. In addition to the textual representation of MVP-L, a graphical representation is defined for MVP-L in order to facilitate understanding [4]. The main elements that are used in MVP-L for the description of process models are processes, products, resources, and quality attributes, as well as their instantiation in project plans [3]. A process model is actually a type description that captures the properties common to a class of processes. For easy adaptation of process models to different project contexts, the process models are structured using the concepts of a process model-interface and a process model-body.

MVP-L by Example As an example, a process model "Coding" (Fig. 9.6) could describe a class of processes that require an input of the product type User_Story which must produce an output of the product type Code and which must be executed by a resource of the type Programmers. These product and resource model declarations are part of the interface of the process model Coding. The actual implementation of the process model is "hidden" in the body of the process model.

Processes, products, and resources can be used for modeling the basic elements of a software project. Attributes can be used for defining specific properties of these three basic elements. More detailed descriptions and examples of these constructs can be found in the MVP-L language report [3] and in [20]. The instantiation of a process model allows operationalizing the process model and creating a concrete project plan, which can then be used for project analysis or execution. The notion of a project state is the basis for the enactment model in MVP-L [3]. A project state is defined as the set of all attribute values, i.e., all attributes of all objects instantiated

Fig. 9.6 Example of process model "Coding"

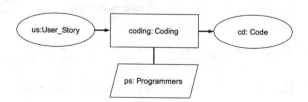

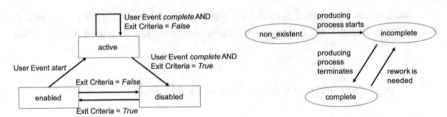

Fig. 9.7 State transition models for processes (*left*) and products (*right*), adapted from [20]

within a project plan. Thus, the project state provides valuable information about the status of the projects at any given time. The project state has two dimensions which are synchronized, i.e., process state and product state. The values of attributes of the different states of a process can be represented in a state transition model (left hand side of Fig. 9.7). Starting in the `disabled` state, processes may only get enabled when the entry criteria are true. An `enabled` process may get active when it is triggered by a user with the `start` invocation. As long as the exit criteria are not fulfilled and the user does not trigger the user invocation `complete`, the process will remain in the `active` state. When the exit criteria are fulfilled and the user invocation `complete` is triggered, then the process gets `disabled`. Additionally, for each project state, the state of the associated work products is represented as `non_existent`, `incomplete`, or `complete` (right hand side of Fig. 9.7). At the beginning, the product does not exist. When the producing process starts, the product state changes to incomplete. Finally, when the producing process terminates,

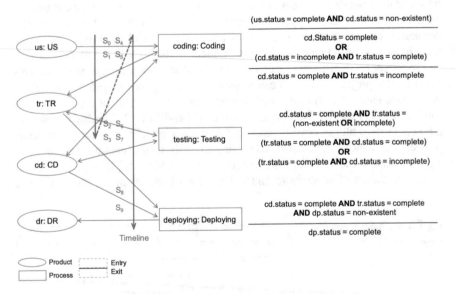

Fig. 9.8 Exemplary process in MVP-L graphical representation

the product state turns to complete. When rework is needed, several iterations between the product states complete and incomplete are possible.

Modeling a Project in MVP-L Figure 9.8 shows a simple example of a project illustrating the notion of the project state as well as the capabilities of MVP-L in implementing a constraint-oriented control-flow using entry and exit criteria. The exemplary process consists of three process instances, namely, coding, testing, and deploying. In this example, the process is not strictly sequential but allows for rework loops. There are four work products that constitute the product flow within this process. An arrow from a product to a process indicates that a product is consumed by this process. An arrow pointing from a process to a product indicates that a product is produced by this process. A bidirectional arrow indicates that a product is produced and consumed, i.e., a product can be modified (or enhanced). Control of the process flow is realized implicitly via pre- and post-conditions of the process. Since the process is not strictly sequential, all subprocesses consume more than one work product and two subprocesses produce (or modify) more than one work product, the entry and exit conditions can become complex. In the right column of Fig. 9.8, entry and exit criteria for our example process are specified. For subprocess Coding the entry and exit conditions are defined as follows:

Entry Criterion 1:	The input work product us (of type User_Story, US) is complete *AND* the output work product cd (of type Code, CD) is non-existent.
Entry Criterion 2:	The input work product cd is incomplete *AND* the input work product tr (of type Test_Report, TR) is complete
Exit Criterion 1:	(*corresponding to entry criterion 1*) The output work product cd is complete.
Exit Criterion 2:	(*corresponding to entry criterion 2*) The output work product cd is complete *AND* the output work product tr is incomplete (i.e., the code has to undergo another round of testing)

For subprocess Testing the entry and exit conditions are defined as follows:

Entry Criterion:	The input work product cd is complete *AND* the input work product tr is either non-existent OR incomplete.
Exit Criterion 1:	The output work products cd and tr are both complete (i.e., all tests passed and no further rework needed).
Exit Criterion 2:	The output work product tr is complete and the output work product cd is incomplete (i.e., rework of the code is required, due to bug fixing)

For subprocess Deploying the entry and exit conditions are defined as follows:

Entry Criterion:	The input work products cd and tr are both complete *AND* the output work product dr (of type Deployment_Report, DR) is non-existent.
Exit Criterion:	The output work product dr is complete.

State	Product				Process		
	us	cd	tr	dr	coding	testing	deploying
S_0	complete	non-exist	non-exist	non-exist	*enabled*	disabled	disabled
S_1	complete	*incomplete*	non-exist	non-exist	**active**	disabled	disabled
S_2	complete	complete	non-exist	non-exist	disabled	*enabled*	disabled
S_3	complete	complete	incomplete	non-exist	disabled	**active**	disabled
S_4	complete	*incomplete*	complete	non-exist	*enabled*	disabled	disabled
S_5	complete	*incomplete*	complete	non-exist	**active**	disabled	disabled
S_6	complete	complete	*incomplete*	non-exist	disabled	*enabled*	disabled
S_7	complete	complete	*incomplete*	non-exist	disabled	**active**	disabled
S_8	complete	complete	complete	non-exist	disabled	disabled	*enabled*
S_9	complete	complete	complete	*incomplete*	disabled	disabled	**active**
...	...	...	...	...	...	...	...

start(coding)
complete(coding)
start(testing)
complete(testing)
start(coding)
complete(coding)
start(testing)
complete(testing)
start(deploying)
...

Fig. 9.9 Example state table for a coding-testing-(re)coding-(re)testing cycle with subsequent deployment

Finally, between the columns *Products* and *Processes* in Fig. 9.8, project states are represented that correspond to the enactment scenario provided in the state (transition) table (Fig. 9.9). The state table provides a sequence of project plan execution states:

- Starting in project state S_0, we assume that the user story us is already complete and other products are non-existent. Since the user story is complete, the process instance coding can be enabled (entry criterion 1 is fulfilled). The process instance is initiated with the invocation start(coding) and state S_1 is reached.
- In state S_1, the coding process instance is active and the code document cd is being produced and is therefore in the state incomplete. Upon completion of cd, complete(coding) triggers another project state change.
- In state S_2, the code document is complete, and thus exit criterion 1 for coding is fulfilled and the coding process instance gets disabled.
- Now, the entry conditions for the testing process are fulfilled, state S_3 can be achieved (start(testing)), and the testing process instance becomes active. The active testing process instance creates the test report and therefore the test report is incomplete. All other process instances are disabled. Upon completion of the test report and the specification of the status of the tested code (i.e., either all tests passed and its state is unchanged complete, or defects were detected and its state is reset to incomplete), either exit criterion 1 or 2 is fulfilled, and complete(testing) is triggered.
- We assume that defects were detected, i.e., the code status is reset to incomplete, and state S_4 is reached.
- Now entry criterion 2 for the coding process is fulfilled, process instance coding is enabled and state S_5 can be entered (start(coding)).
- Upon completion (rework) of the code (complete(coding)), the test report status is set to incomplete as a new round of testing is required to check the correctness of the reworked code, and S_6 is reached.

- In S_6, the process instance coding is disabled and the testing is enabled. Invoking `start(testing)` brings us to state S_7 in which process instance testing is in state `active`.
- At completion of the (enhanced) test report we notice that no issues were found and therefore a change of the code status is not required. By invoking `complete(testing)` we reach state S_8. Now process instance testing is disabled and since its entry criterion is fulfilled, process instance deploying is enabled. Invoking `start(deploying)` changes its state to `active` and the state of output product deployment report changes from `non-existent` to `incomplete`.

9.3 BPMN for Software Process Modeling

In this section, we sketch a line between software processes or aspects thereof that can be captured straightforwardly using BPMN (the "good" aspects), those that cannot be captured due to inherent limitations of BPMN (the "bad"), and those that can be captured with a workaround and under some circumstances (the "ugly").

9.3.1 The Good

BPMN is in general suitable when it comes to capturing sequential relations between activities, whereby the completion of an activity enables other activities. For example, it is rather straightforward to capture in BPMN the control-flow relations shown in Fig. 9.9. The corresponding BPMN process model is given in Fig. 9.10.

More generally, it has been shown that BPMN-like languages are comparable in terms of control-flow expressiveness to a well-known class of Petri nets known as free-choice workflow nets [10, 13]. At the same time, BPMN is armed with special types of gateways that allow one to capture complex synchronization conditions. In particular, the OR-join (inclusive) synchronization gateway alluded to in Sect. 9.2.1,

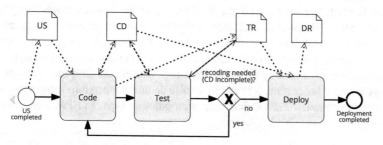

Fig. 9.10 Simple BPMN process model of code-test cycle with subsequent deployment

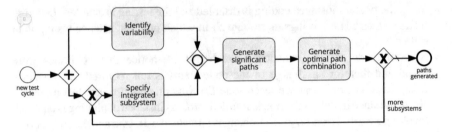

Fig. 9.11 Process for integration testing in software product lines (according to [27])

allows us to capture points in a process where the execution must wait for all "active" incoming threads to complete before proceeding.

9.3.1.1 Modeling Control Flows

Figure 9.11 shows a fragment of a process for integration testing in software product lines introduced in [27]. This process proceeds as follows. When the AND-split at the start of this process fires, both tasks Identify variability and Specify integrated subsystems are enabled. These tasks may be performed in any order. At this stage, the OR-join will wait for both tasks to complete before putting a token in its outgoing flow. Subsequently, tasks Generate significant paths and Generate optimal path combinations are performed (in this order). Assuming that the condition more subsystems holds true (i.e., more subsystems need to be integrated), the flow of control will come back to task Specify integrated subsystems. Eventually, this task will be performed, leading to a token being placed in one of the incoming flows of the OR-join. Note that in this second iteration, task Identify variability has not been enabled, i.e., this latter task is executed only once per execution of the process. Hence, at this point in the execution, the OR-join has a token coming from Specify integrated subsystems while no token is expected to arrive from Identify variability. Under these conditions, the OR-join will fire and enable task Generate significant paths. In other words, the OR-join does not "block" the execution unnecessarily: If a token arrives to one of its incoming flows, and no tokens are expected to arrive to its other flows, the OR-join immediately fires. This is in contrast with the AND-join, which will always wait for a token to arrive to every one of its incoming flows before firing. Without the OR-join construct, capturing the above process models would require detours such as duplicating fragments of the process model. The OR-join and other gateway types in BPMN (event-based gateway, complex gateways) are arguably a distinguishing feature of BPMN when compared to software process modeling notations.

9.3.1.2   Modeling Events and Messages

Another distinguishing feature of BPMN is its richness of event types, which range from the timer and message events exemplified in Sect. 9.2.1, to conditional events, escalation events, compensation events and error events as mentioned in Sect. 9.2.1. Given the wide range of events produced, and consumed by modern software development environments, the richness of the event type spectrum supported by BPMN is an attractive feature vis-a-vis of software process modeling.

9.3.1.3   Modeling Executable Processes

Last but not least, one of the strengths of BPMN is its ability to modeling processes for different purposes and at different levels of detail. We have focused above on capturing processes for the purpose of documentation and analysis. However, BPMN is designed to also support the enactment of business processes via so-called *executable BPMN* models. The executable subset of BPMN defines a number of *properties* that can be associated to processes, tasks, events and flows in order to specify the execution behavior to the level of detail required by a *Business Process Management System* (BPMS). For example, in executable BPMN, one can associate rules to the flows coming out of XOR-split or OR-split gateways, which can be interpreted by a BPMS. It is also possible to bind a task in a process to an external (Web) service (so-called *service tasks*) or to a *script* in a programming language (so-called *script tasks*). Finally, it is possible to define the schema of objects manipulated by a process as well as mapping rules to link the data objects manipulated by the process to the data required as input or provided as output by each individual task in the process. A range of BPMSs nowadays support the enactment of BPMN process models, ranging from sophisticated commercial solutions such as IBM Business Process Manager, Oracle Business Process Management Suite, or Bizagi BPM Studio, to Open Source alternatives such as Bonita BPM and Camunda BPM Platform. The sophistication of executable BPMN and of its supporting BPMSs is one of its strengths, especially when compared to the lesser support for process enactment found in the field of software process modeling.

9.3.2   The Bad

BPMN has some inherent limitations that hinder capturing software processes. This section describes the limitations.

9.3.2.1 Modeling Resources

While being relatively rich along the control-flow perspective, BPMN is rather limited along the resource perspective. As shown in Fig. 9.5, it is possible in BPMN to allocate tasks to *roles* via lanes. It is also possible to capture business processes that involve multiple independent entities, such as for example multiple companies in a business-to-business processes (e.g., a contractor and a sub-contractor) via so-called *pools* that communicate via *message flows*. However, one clear limitation of BPMN along the resource perspective is its inability to capture the fact that a given task is performed jointly by multiple resources (e.g., human actors) with different roles, e.g., an analyst and a developer. Indeed, a task in BPMN must belong to exactly one lane.

9.3.2.2 Modeling Data

Similarly, BPMN is rather limited along the data perspective. Along this latter perspective, BPMN primarily relies on the concept of *data object* (cf. Figs. 9.5 and 9.10), meaning a logical unit of data that can be read by or created or modified by a task or an event. It also supports a concept of *data store* that can be used to capture for example a database or document management system that is read by or modified by a task or event. However, data objects in BPMN do not have a notion of *state*. It is thus not possible to state that object cd in Fig. 9.10 should be in state complete when task Test is started as indicated in Fig. 9.9.

In comparison, Unified Modeling Language (UML) activity diagrams—a language that otherwise shares several features with BPMN at a semantic level—does provide the ability to designate the state in which a data object should be when it is consumed or produced by an activity in a process [12]. It also supports the ability to designate that a given activity in a process involves multiple performers with different roles.

9.3.2.3 Modeling "The Whole"

A third and perhaps more fundamental limitation of BPMN that may hamper its use for software process modeling is its inherent focus on business processes consisting of *isolated cases*. As many other process modeling notations, a BPMN model captures a process that consists of *instances* or *cases*. For example, a case of the loan application process in Fig. 9.1 is created every time a new loan application is received. Meanwhile, a case of the code-test process in Fig. 9.10 is created for every object us in a completed state. These cases are executed independently without any interaction between them besides the fact that they may share the same resources, e.g., multiple cases of the loan application process share the same loan applications handler or the same credit officer.

The *isolated case* assumption is generally a convenient abstraction. The modeler can focus on describing one case of the process in isolation, without worrying about possible interactions. On the other hand, this assumption hampers the inability for modelers to capture inter-case dependencies, which occur in software processes. Consider example the business process given in Fig. 9.10 but in a situation where a system consists of two types of components A and B, and the testing phase of a component of type B needs to wait for all components of type A to have reached the state CD complete before proceeding with testing. The latter scenario cannot be captured in BPMN. It is possible in BPMN to model the fact that a process spawns multiple instances of a subprocess and waits for some or all of them to complete (as shown in Fig. 9.4), but it is not possible to model the fact that a case of a process must wait for a collection of cases of the same process (or of another process) to reach a certain state before continuing.

The *isolated case* assumption is lifted by a family of process definition languages known as object-centric or artifact-centric process models, such as FlexConnect [26] and Guard-Stage Milestone (GSM; [15]). In these languages, a process consists of a collection of *object types* or *artifact types*, each with its own lifecycle. These life-cycles may be inter-connected in different ways. In the case of GSM, the lifecyle of a given artifact goes through a set of stages, during which one or multiple tasks may be performed. A stage is opened when a given guard becomes true and is closed when a given *milestone* becomes true. Both guards and milestones may refer to the currently opened stage(s) of the same artifact, but also to stages of other artifacts (of the same type) or even to stages of artifacts of different types. In this way, we can model a system consisting of components with stages coding, testing, and deploying with a data attribute type (of A or B). We can then model that the testing phase of a component of type B must wait for all components of type A to complete their coding stage, before it can enter the testing stage.

9.3.3 The Ugly

BPMN does not provide a mechanism that would allow one to link the completion of one task to a condition on the data objects manipulated by the process. For example, coming back to the example in Fig. 9.10, it is not possible to capture in BPMN that the normal completion of task Test occurs whenever a condition on the Test Report (TR) object becomes true, such as TR.status=complete as captured in MVP-L in Fig. 9.8.

It is possible to attach events, and in particular *conditional events* to a task in BPMN in order to capture the fact that the task in question is interrupted when the condition becomes true. For example, Fig. 9.12 provides an alternative BPMN process model of the code-test cycle where interrupting conditional events are used to capture the fact that completion of the tasks in the process is dependent on the data objects cd, tr, and dr reaching the status complete. Interrupting events are

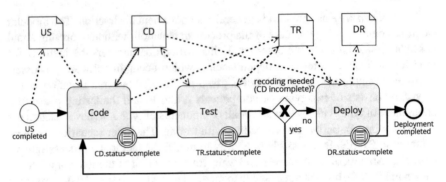

Fig. 9.12 An alternative BPMN process model of the code-test cycle with interrupting conditional events

attached to the boundaries of an activity to indicate that the occurrence of the event interrupts the task, and control is transferred to the outgoing flow of the boundary event.

While the process model in Fig. 9.12 does capture the fact that control should be transferred out of each task when the corresponding data object reaches the complete status, the tasks in this process complete abnormally. It is not possible to express in BPMN that the normal completion of a task is determined by a given condition becoming true. In other words, completion of a task in a BPMN process has to be explicitly signaled by the resource performing the task, and cannot be automatically determined based on the current state of the data objects in the process. We note that the latter assumption is also lifted by artifact-centric process modeling notations such as GSM, where completion of a stage in an artifact can be bound to a condition on the data attributes of the artifact.

9.4 Conclusion

We have illustrated that BPMN offers a rather rich spectrum of constructs to capture control-flow aspects of processes, which are applicable to software process modeling in particular. The richness of constructs in BPMN and its ability to support the specification of process models at different level of abstraction (from conceptual models down to executable ones), makes it attractive for the purpose of capturing software processes in the context of their automation. However, we have also identified weaknesses in BPMN along the data perspective and the resource perspective that affect its suitability for software process modeling. In particular, we have noted that the following inherent assumptions of BPMN hamper its use for software process modeling:

- The *isolated case* assumption of BPMN, which hinders on the ability to capture processes where there are complex dependencies between the lifecycle of different objects.
- The *explicit completion* assumption, meaning that completion of a task cannot be automatically determined based on the state of data objects in the process but instead is always explicitly determined by the resource performing the task.

Broadly speaking, these limitations hamper the use of BPMN for highly collaborative software processes, where for example different components of a system are developed—possibly in a distributed manner—by different teams, with complex synchronization inter-dependencies between the different types of components. We have suggested that artifact-centric process modeling languages such as GSM [15] lift the above two assumptions and, thus, could potentially be suitable in the context of software process modeling. Conducting a detailed suitability assessment of artifact-centric process modeling languages for software process modeling is thus an avenue for future work.

One area where the disciplines of business process modeling and software process modeling overlap and could potentially learn more from each other is that of *process variability modeling*. This latter problem has been widely studied in the field of software product lines, where it is necessary to model entire families of processes in order to produce, test, deploy, evolve, and manage multiple variants of a software product. A range of approaches to capture variability of software products and processes have been proposed and evaluated in the literature [2, 6, 19]. Separately, the business process modeling community has investigated the problem of modeling families of business processes via configurable or customizable process model, e.g., modeling an order-to-cash process in such a way that the resulting model can be customized for different types of products or services. This latter body of research has led to a range of extensions of BPMN and related process modeling languages aimed at capturing customizable process models and to support their customization [18, 29]. The potential synergies between these two bodies of research are evident and warrant closer attention [11].

9.5 Further Reading

There exists a wide range of literature describing software process modeling approaches and their application to software development processes as well as literature describing business process modeling approaches and their application to business processes. It is much harder to find literature on process modeling approaches that could be—or actually are—applied to both software development and business processes.

One such example is the work by Gruhn and colleagues. For example, in "Process Management in Practice Applying the FUNSOFT Net Approach to Large-Scale Processes" [9], Gruhn and Deiters present an approach to process management that has been applied to business and software processes. To enable cross-fertilization between both areas and the authors discuss lessons learned from the application of FUNSOFT Nets, a special version of colored Petri nets. While Gruhn et al.'s work is based on the well-known formalism of colored Petri-Nets, Lee Osterweil and his collaborators developed a completely new modeling approach, LittleJIL [22], originally used for modeling and analyzing software development processes, which has recently also been applied to modeling and analyzing business processes, for example medical processes such as chemotherapy processes [7].

Other chapters in this book describe and address the challenges of software process evolution (Chap. 13 in this volume), software process management (Chap. 10 in this volume), and software process evolution management (Chap. 8 in this volume). Once suitable ways have been found to apply enhanced business process notations to the context of software process modeling, we have hopes that the rich experience available in business process evolution, management, and especially enactment using BPMN could be transferred to the world of software process modeling.

Acknowledgments This work is supported by the institutional research grant IUT20-55 of the Estonian Research Council.

References

1. Bendraou, R., Jézéquel, J.M., Gervais, M.P., Blanc, X.: A comparison of six UML-based languages for software process modeling. IEEE Trans. Softw. Eng. **36**(5), 662–675 (2010)
2. Berger, T., She, S., Lotufo, R., Wasowski, A., Czarnecki, K.: A study of variability models and languages in the systems software domain. IEEE Trans. Softw. Eng. **39**(12), 1611–1640 (2013)
3. Böckers, A., Lott, C.M., Rombach, H.D., Verlage, M.: MVP-L language report version 2. Technical report Nr. 265/95, University of Kaiserslautern, Department of Computer Science (1995)
4. Bröckers, A., Differding, C., Hoisl, B., Kollnischko, F., Lott, C.M., Münch, J., Verlage, M., Vorwieger, S.: A graphical representation schema for the software process modeling language mvp-l. Technical report, University of Kaiserslautern (1995)
5. Campos, A.L.N., Oliveira, T.C.: Software processes with bpmn: an empirical analysis. In: Proceedings of the International Conference on Product-Focused Software Process Improvement. Lecture Notes in Computer Science, vol. 7983, pp. 338–341. Springer, Berlin, Heidelberg (2013)
6. Chen, L., Babar, M.: A systematic review of evaluation of variability management approaches in software product lines. Inf. Softw. Technol. **53**(4), 344–362 (2011)
7. Christov, S., Chen, B., Avrunin, G.S., Clarke, L.A., Osterweil, L.J., Brown, D., Cassells, L., Mertens, W.: Formally defining medical processes. Methods Inf. Med. **47**(5), 392–398 (2008)
8. Curtis, B., Kellner, M., Over, J.: Process modeling. Commun. ACM **35**(9), 75–90 (1992)
9. Deiters, W., Gruhn, V.: Process management in practice applying the funsoft net approach to large-scale processes. Autom. Softw. Eng. **5**(1), 7–25 (1998)
10. Dijkman, R.M., Dumas, M., Ouyang, C.: Semantics and analysis of business process models in bpmn. Inf. Softw. Technol. **50**(12), 1281–1294 (2008)
11. dos Santos Rocha, R., Fantinato, M.: The use of software product lines for business process management: a systematic literature review. Inf. Softw. Technol. **55**(8), 1355–1373 (2013)

12. Engels, G., Förster, A.F., Heckel, R., Thöne, S.: Process modeling using uml. In: Dumas, M., der Aalst, W.M.P.V., ter Hofstede, A. (eds.) Process-Aware Information Systems. Wiley, New York (2005)
13. Favre, C., Fahland, D., Völzer, H.: The relationship between workflow graphs and free-choice workflow nets. Inf. Syst. **47**, 197–219 (2015)
14. Harmon, P., Wolf, C.: Business Process Modeling Survey. BPTrends Associates (2011)
15. Hull, R., Damaggio, E., De Masellis, R., Fournier, F., Gupta, M., Heath, F.T., Hobson, S., Linehan, M.H., Maradugu, S., Nigam, A., Sukaviriya, P.N., Vaculín, R.: Business artifacts with guard-stage-milestone lifecycles: managing artifact interactions with conditions and events. In: Proceedings of the International Conference on Distributed Event-based System, pp. 51–62. ACM, New York, NY (2011)
16. Jablonski, S., Bussler, C.: Workflow Management: Modeling Concepts, Architecture and Implementation. International Thomson Computer Press, London (1996)
17. Kellner, M., Madachy, R., Raffo, D.: Software process simulation modeling: Why? what? how? J. Syst. Softw. **46**(2/3), 91–105 (1999)
18. La Rosa, M., van der Aalst, W.M.P., Dumas, M., Milani, F.: Business process variability modeling: A survey. BPM Center Report BPM-13-16, BPMcenter.org (2013)
19. Martínez-Ruiz, T., García, F., Piattini, M., Münch, J.: Modelling software process variability: an empirical study. IET Softw. **5**(2), 172–187 (2011)
20. Münch, J., Armbrust, O., Kowalczyk, M., Soto, M.: Software Process Definition and Management. Springer, Berlin, Heidelberg (2012)
21. OMG: Business process model and notation. OMG Standard BPMN 2.0, Object Management Group. http://www.omg.org/spec/BPMN/2.0/ (2011)
22. Osterweil, L.J.: Formalisms to support the definition of processes. J. Comput. Sci. Technol. **24**(2), 198–211 (2009)
23. Pillat, R.M., Oliveira, T.C., Fonseca, F.L.: Introducing software process tailoring to bpmn: Bpmnt. In: Proceedings of the International Conference on Software and System Process, pp. 58–62. IEEE Press, Piscataway, NJ (2012)
24. Recker, J.: Continued use of process modeling grammars: the impact of individual difference factors. Eur. J. Inf. Syst. **19**(1), 76–92 (2010)
25. Recker, J.: Opportunities and constraints: the current struggle with bpmn. Bus. Process Manag. J. **16**(1), 181–201 (2010)
26. Redding, G., Dumas, M., ter Hofstede, A.H.M., Iordachescu, A.: A flexible, object-centric approach for business process modelling. Serv. Oriented Comput. Appl. **4**(3), 191–201 (2010)
27. Reis, S., Metzger, A., Pohl, K.: Integration testing in software product line engineering: a model-based technique. In: Proceedings of the International Conference on Fundamental Approaches to Software Engineering. Lecture Notes in Computer Science, vol. 4422, pp. 321–335. Springer, Berlin Heidelberg (2007)
28. Rombach, H.: MVP-L: A Language for Process Modeling in-the-large. University of Maryland, College Park, MD (1991)
29. Valenca, G., Alves, C., Alves, V., Niu, N.: A systematic mapping study on business process variability. Int. J. Comput. Sci. Inf. Technol. **5**(1), 1–21 (2013)

Chapter 10
Software Processes Management by Method Engineering with MESP

Masud Fazal-Baqaie and Gregor Engels

Abstract Software process management (SPM) is seen as a key factor for the result-ing quality of software. Based on our experience in industrial process improvement projects, we see two major challenges to apply SPM effectively. Thereby, in our work, we focus on the method aspect of software development processes. First, methods have to be tailored consistently to projects by composing agile as well as plan-driven method building blocks. Second, methods have to be enactable to ensure that they are put into practice as intended. In this chapter, we present our assembly-based method engineering approach called Method Engineering with Method Services and Method Patterns (MESP) and explain how it tackles common SPM challenges. MESP fol-lows the service-oriented paradigm to create formally defined composition-based methods. The methods are created specifically for individual projects based on their characteristics. They are composed based on an extensible repository of formally defined method building blocks extracted from agile and plan-driven methods. With our novel notion of method patterns, we allow to restrict the solution space of method compositions to the desired ones. In addition, we provide tooling to define building blocks and to compose them to methods consistently and we support the correct enactment of methods with a workflow engine.

10.1 Introduction

As software systems become more widespread and more important, there is the ris-ing need to use mature development processes to create software systems. They are seen as a key factor for the resulting product or service quality. To acknowledge this trend, it is important for every organization to manage and evolve the use of the right software development processes. We thereby understand software devel-

M. Fazal-Baqaie (✉) · G. Engels
Database and Information Systems Research Group,
University of Paderborn, Zukunftsmeile 1, 33102 Paderborn, Germany
e-mail: masudf@uni-paderborn.de

G. Engels
e-mail: engels@uni-paderborn.de

© Springer International Publishing Switzerland 2016
M. Kuhrmann et al. (eds.), *Managing Software Process Evolution*,
DOI 10.1007/978-3-319-31545-4_10

opment processes to comprise project management aspects, organizational aspects, and methodological aspects. In our work, we focus on the method aspect of software development processes, that is what activities are carried out by which roles in what order using which input to produce which output.

Based on our experience in method improvement projects at companies of different scale,[1] we identified major challenges to effective software process management. Software development methods need to reflect project characteristics in order to avoid the drawbacks of one-size-fits-all approaches that are too unspecific and not effective enough [8]. This means that they should incorporate agile as well as plan-driven aspects [4], lessons learned, and best practices based on the project context [20]. They should be properly defined to avoid confusion and uncertainty and they should be enactable so that they can be carried out accordingly [18].

We developed the *Method Engineering with Method Services and Method Patterns* (MESP) approach that systematically supports software process management to mitigate the mentioned challenges [13]. In our approach, for each project a tailored software development method is created based on the project goal and the project characteristics. Methods are created by composing suitable method building blocks from a repository. Method building blocks are defined and stored in the repository upfront based on agile as well as plan-driven methods, lessons learned and best practices. Furthermore, MESP methods can be checked for consistency automatically based on their formal definition and they are enactable with tool support.

In this chapter, we first describe common SPM challenges and then explain the MESP approach and how it addresses these challenges. The chapter is structured as follows: we first provide background about common SPM challenges in Sect. 10.1. In Sect. 10.2, we provide an overview of MESP and introduce several roles that carry out tasks as part of MESP, where each role addresses specific SPM challenges. Based on this overview, we revisit each MESP role in the subsequent sections. Section 10.3 illustrates the tasks of the senior method engineer, who defines method building blocks. Section 10.4 investigates the tasks of the project method engineer, who composes methods. Section 10.5 then explains the enactment of MESP methods by the project team. Section 10.6 describes our tool support. Thereafter, we summarize the benefits of MESP for SPM in Sect. 10.7. We draw the conclusions in Sect. 10.8 and present further readings and the bibliography thereafter. In several method improvement projects carried out with industry, we observed that project-specific methods are required. One-size-fits-all approaches are too unspecific and to rigid, as described also by other authors [4, 7, 34], e.g., by not allowing to mix agile and plan-driven aspects. However, many organizations still struggle with creating their own situation-specific methods consistently and with following them properly.

The research field *Situational Method Engineering* (SME; [20]) explicitly addresses the creation of situation-specific software development methods, so-called situational methods. Based on the basic assumption that there is no one-size-fits-all method, SME is dedicated to engineering situation-specific software development

---

[1]Carried out within s-lab (Software Quality Lab of the University of Paderborn): http://s-lab.uni-paderborn.de.

methods from scratch or by adapting existing ones. Situation-specific here is understood as specific to the context of a certain project or organization, ensuring that the method is fitting to the business goals and that it is up-to-date. One field of SME is formed by so-called assembly-based approaches [5], which provide methods that are more specialized compared to the adaption of existing methods and which enable better reuse compared to the creation of methods from scratch. In assembly-based approaches, methods are composed based on a repository of reusable method building blocks.

Even though the first approaches have been proposed two decades ago, situational method engineering has still not received industrial acceptance and widespread adoption. The reason is, that existing approaches fail in providing adequate solutions for the fundamental requirements as stated in [34] and recently reconfirmed in [23]. A number of approaches address assembly-based method creation [5, 30, 33] or method enactment [3, 9], but apart from [6], not both. As [6] does not address the situation-specific creation of methods and their quality assurance explicitly, apart from MESP, no SME approach has been proposed that sufficiently addresses all aspects necessary to create situation-specific, consistent, and enactable methods. Thus, organizations still struggle with creating their own situation-specific methods consistently and with following them properly. Specifically, they face the following challenges that we focus on in this chapter:

Challenge 1—*Defining method content based on new trends, best practices, and lessons learned.* A major need of many organizations is to incorporate new trends, best practices and lessons learned by maintaining and updating the content of their methods, e.g., the used tasks, created and consumed work products, roles and the order of tasks. For example, they need to redefine a task in order to react to experienced challenges or they need to update the order of tasks used in all their methods due to regulatory needs. Often it is difficult to update the content of methods incrementally, as it is difficult to clearly scope the area to improve and to assess the implications for the unchanged parts [35]. As one example for the need of updated method content, in Chap. 1 in this volume, the authors explain that modern applications have evolved such that traditional methods are mostly unsuitable and need to be replaced.

Challenge 2—*Creating hybrid methods that integrate plan-driven and agile methods.* As agile methods become more and more popular, many organizations face the challenge to integrate agile principles into their rather plan-driven organizational methods [36], as fully adopting agile methods is not possible, because the context of the project or organization makes the use of plan-driven aspects necessary or at least beneficial [4]. Organizations struggle explicitly with the definition of hybrid methods that integrate content of these two seemingly incompatible directions. This challenge is explicitly addressed in Chap. 2 in this volume, where advantages and drawbacks of different ways to create a method with agile and plan-driven aspects are discussed.

Challenge 3—*Creating software development methods tailored to individual project goals and characteristics.* Many researchers and practitioners are convinced that there is no one-size-fits-all method and that the utility of methods depends on the context of their use. Cockburn, for example, calls aiming for an one-size-fits-all approach a common (method engineering) mistake [8]. While different researchers have proposed characteristics to be considered for method engineering, e.g., [2, 17], it remains a challenge to use them properly, as it is often unclear what characteristics allow the use of certain practices. It is also difficult for less-experienced people to derive a method systematically based on project goals and characteristics [22]. In Chap. 8, this challenge is illustrated by showing how it is addressed in the spaceflight domain.

Challenge 4—*Creating consistent software development methods.* Especially in small and medium-sized companies, the experience and expertize for software process management is often not broadly available. This is especially true when it comes to consistently defining software development methods with their activities, information flows and roles [24]. This leads sometimes to the use of ill-fitted methods or to an ad hoc management of the software development without a defined method. It also means that less-experienced process owners struggle with defining consistent software development methods [18]. In Chap. 13, this challenge is investigated based on the co-evolution of Model-driven Engineering (MDE) and the used methods. Here, changes in modeling languages and tool support of MDE require changes in the software development method and vice versa.

Challenge 5—*Enacting methods properly according to their definition.* One of the challenges of software process management is to ensure that how the work is actually carried out corresponds to the defined method [18]. If deviations are left undetected, software process management becomes ineffective. For example, gathering the lessons learned and tuning the method becomes very difficult, if it is not clear to everybody what the method is. Especially, in global software development projects it is challenging to maintain sufficient overview and to coordinate the tasks according to the defined method [25]. Another challenge then is to provide team members with guidance, especially, if the methods have evolved. Addressing this challenge, in Chap. 9, the authors investigate the suitability of the enactable workflow language BPMN as a notation for software development methods.

Our SME approach *Method Engineering with Method Services and Method Patterns* (MESP) tackles the described challenges by following the assembly-based method engineering idea [5]. It is designed to fill the gaps of other Situational Method Engineering approaches, by addressing the situation-specific, consistent composition of methods and their enactment.

10.2   Overview of MESP Roles and MESP Tasks

We provide an overview of our assembly-based method engineering approach that addresses the challenges presented in the previous section. In MESP, following the idea of "define once, use many times," methods are composed based on two types of preexisting method building blocks:

- *Method Services* reflect tasks with their associated work products and roles, while
- *Method Patterns* reflect meaningful patterns for the usage and order of method services.

MESP differentiates three different roles, where each role has different responsibilities and requires a different level of knowledge and experience. *Senior method engineers* are responsible for defining method building blocks, based on their own experience or information sources like method descriptions from literature and address Challenge 1. Instead of defining a project-specific method from scratch, *project method engineers* then can choose suitable method services and method patterns from these building blocks and compose them to a situational method for their respective project. With their tasks, they address Challenges 2–4. The *project team* follows the situational method to create the software in their project. They enact the composed method in a workflow engine that coordinates their activities and provides them with guidance on the pending tasks and thus ensures that they follow the method as prescribed. They thereby address Challenge 5. Figure 10.1 provides an overview of the roles, their tasks, and the SPM challenges they address.

In this chapter, we will use the terms *MESP roles*, *MESP tasks*, and *MESP work products* when we refer to the tasks, roles, and created outputs of the MESP approach

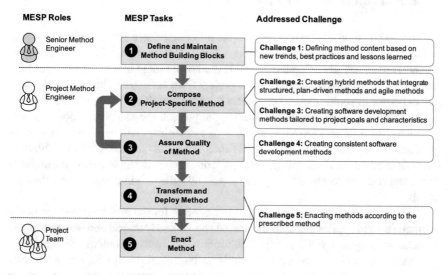

Fig. 10.1 Overview of the MESP approach

itself. In contrast, the "simple" terms *roles*, *tasks*, and *work products* are used to refer to the content of a method created with the MESP approach (i.e., a MESP work product).

10.2.1 Senior Method Engineer

The senior method engineer is responsible for defining and maintaining reusable and composable method building blocks (❶) for the method composition. Therefore, he derives these building blocks based on his experience and literature reflecting trends, best practices, and lessons learned, including agile and plan-driven methods.

The senior method engineer characterizes each building block such that less-experienced project method engineers can easily identify suitable method building blocks for their situational methods. The characterization includes the roles and work products referred to by method building blocks and so-called situational factors that express the suitability for certain project characteristics, for example, "small development team" or "low stakeholder participation." Beside method services and method patterns themselves, the senior method engineer also maintains the set of available situational factors, roles, and work products in a method repository.

The MESP role of the senior method engineer should be staffed by experienced practitioners and experts that are familiar with a wide range of methods and best practices.

10.2.2 Project Method Engineer

The project method engineer is responsible for composing a situational method with respect to a specific project (❷) based on the available method building blocks in the method repository. By using the available method building blocks, he does not have to create the situational method for the project from scratch and he can make use of the expertise of senior method engineers who created the building blocks. In order to compose a method that is suitable for the project, the project method engineer characterizes a project based on the sets of available situational factors and work products in the method repository. He then uses this characterization to identify suitable method services and method patterns. Doing that, he composes methods that comprise and combine both plan-driven and agile building blocks, based on the needs.

The project method engineer is also responsible for the quality assurance of the method (❸) and applies multiple automated checks that were realized with the Object Constraint Language (OCL; [28]). The tooling checks that methods are consistent, e.g., that no method service is missing and that there are no contradictions in the order of method services. In addition, it checks that the used method services and their order do not violate the method patterns used in the method. The MESP tasks of the project method engineer are carried out iteratively to allow for stepwise composition and quality assurance.

When the method assembly is finished, the project method engineer prepares the enactment of the method. He invokes a transformation into a BPEL4People [26] process model and the automatic deployment of the process model to the workflow engine (❹). In the workflow engine, he assigns individual project members to the roles used in the method and process model based on the staffing decisions of the project manager.

The MESP role of the project method engineer should be staffed by the person that is responsible for the course of actions and management of the resources in a project, e.g., the project manager himself.

10.2.3   Project Team

The project team has to enact the composed method (❺) and is supported by the workflow engine that enacts the process model transformed from the method. It ensures that the method is followed appropriately by assigning tasks to individuals according to their roles, by coordinating the order of these task assignments, and by displaying information about the current tasks to the project team. The MESP role of the project team is staffed by the project members.

10.3   The MESP Task of the Senior Method Engineer

In the previous section, we provided an overview of the different MESP roles and their tasks. In this section, we go into more detail and discuss how the senior method engineer creates method building blocks that are then used by project method engineers to compose methods. We first present the task characteristics by explaining the requirements and how they are implemented and then illustrate the task with examples thereafter.

10.3.1   Task Characteristics

The senior method engineer is responsible for defining reusable, maintainable building blocks that can be composed to methods and enacted later on. In order to enable him to accomplish his task, MESP has to fulfill several requirements. In the following, we present these requirements and briefly state how they are realized.

Requirement 1 Human-readable task descriptions have to be captured in order to give project members guidance on how to carry out tasks later during enactment. This is done by embedding task descriptions in method services.

Requirement 2 Structured meta information about these method services needs to be captured. This allows to abstract from the human-readable task description and thus eases finding method services to compose or update them. This is done by giving method services formal interface descriptions. The formal interfaces increase the maintainability of the method repository, because the identification of method services that should be updated or method services that are effected by updates becomes much easier.

Requirement 3 It has to be possible to break up big tasks into a composition of smaller method services so that method services are maintainable and easier to compose. MESP supports this by composite method services that instead of a textual description contain a formal process of composed method services.

Requirement 4 Methodological knowledge does not only comprise descriptions of tasks, but also more abstract patterns that for example describe that tasks of certain kind shall be carried out after tasks of another kind. These abstract structures cannot be captured in method services so other means are required. Thus, method patterns were introduced to MESP as a novel notion that is not supported by other SME approaches.

10.3.2 Define and Maintain Method Building Blocks

The MESP task of the senior method engineer is to define and maintain method building blocks. Based on methods that are growing in popularity, best practices, and lessons learned, a senior method engineer derives method services and method patterns that are composable with other existing services and patterns. We exemplify this by explaining how he derives method building blocks from agile and plan-driven methods described in literature. First, we illustrate the definition of method services. Thereafter, we explain what method patterns are and how they are derived. The composition of method services and method patterns by the project method engineer is then explained in the following Sect. 10.4.

10.3.2.1 Defining Method Services

As mentioned, we illustrate the case where method services shall be defined based on existing method descriptions. Table 10.1 exemplifies a method service derived from the task *Refine the Architecture* from the publicly available, plan-driven *OpenUP* method.[2] The information shown is required in order to allow the composition of situation-specific, consistent, and enactable methods. The upper part shows its name and description while the lower part shows the interface information of the method service.

---

[2] Available from: http://epf.eclipse.org/wikis/openup.

Table 10.1 Illustration of a method service derived from a task description of OpenUp

Method service	
Name	Refine the architecture
Content description	"This task builds upon the outlined architecture and makes concrete and unambiguous architectural decisions to support development. It takes into account any design and implementation work products that have been developed so far. In other words, the architecture evolves as the solution is designed and implemented, and the architecture documentation is updated to ..."
Method service interface	
Role	`Architect`
Input work products	`Architecture Notebook`
Output work products	`Architecture Notebook`
Situational factors	`Agility: Medium;` `System Criticality: Medium - High`
Categories	`Plan-Driven; Development; Design`

The Name and Content Description of the method service were directly taken over from the textual description of the task in *OpenUP*. As part of the Method Service Interface meta information the responsible Role "Architect" and Input Work Products as well as Output Work Products are referenced, here in both cases "Architecture Notebook." This information is usually easily determined, if not even stated explicitly in the information source.

Situational Factors, here "Agility: Medium" and "System Criticality: Medium–High," are used to define under which project characteristics the use of a method service is advisable. They are used later by the project method engineer to relate project characteristics to suitable building blocks.

Situational factors are often not stated in the information sources so that the senior method engineer has to derive them from the context and based on his knowledge and experience. For example, here the method service *Refine the Architecture* should be used in projects that are rather critical ("System Criticality: Medium–High"), but its use is advisable neither in projects that are very agile, where architectural decisions need to be updated frequently, nor in projects that are carried out completely sequentially without iterations or increments, where architectural decisions are taken upfront ("Agility: Medium"). Similarly, Categories are used to categorize method services based on origin, discipline, or typical phase. This information is often explicitly given or obvious.

Table 10.2 visualizes another method service that was defined based on the *Daily Scrum* of the agile *Scrum* method.[3] As shown it is described in a similar manner. However, the senior method engineer adjusted name, roles, and work products to

---

[3] Available from: http://www.scrumguides.org/scrum-guide.html.

Table 10.2 Illustration of a method service derived from the agile method Scrum

Method service	
Name	Hold standup meeting
Content description	"The Standup Meeting is a 15-min time-boxed event for the Development Team to synchronize activities and create a plan for the next 24 h. This is done by inspecting the work since the last Standup Meeting and forecasting the work that could be done before the next one. The Standup Meeting is held at the same time and place each day to reduce complexity. During the meeting, the Development Team members explain: …"
Method service interface	
Role	`Team lead`
Input work products	`Task List`
Output work products	`Task List`
Situational factors	`Agility: Medium - High;` `System Criticality: Low - High`
Categories	`Agile; Planning; Management`

keep the method service generic and compatible with other method services (from potentially other methods) in the method repository. Originally, the activity is called *Daily Scrum*, the whole "Development Team" is responsible to perform it, and the defined input and output artifacts are the "Work" done and remaining.

Beside defining atomic method services, the senior method engineer can also define composite method services. In this case, instead of a textual description, the method service contains a process that describes formally what method services are carried out in what order, similarly to how methods are described in MESP (see Sect. 10.4.2). In this case, the meta information can be mostly automatically derived from the referenced method services in the process, however, the senior method engineer needs to refine the situational factors manually.

10.3.2.2 Defining Method Patterns

Beside method services, the senior method engineer creates and maintains method patterns, for example, for the agile *Sprint Loop*. A *Sprint Loop* basically prescribes a repetitive process of fixed length, where planning activities are followed by implementation activities, which in turn are followed by reviewing activities.

Figure 10.2 shows a method pattern that describes an agile *Sprint Loop*. A method pattern consists of several so-called constrained scopes, where each constrained scope describes a constraint that needs to be fulfilled. Constraints are formulated with a small, specialized language that is part of the MESP metamodel. Constrained scopes in Fig. 10.2 are *Sprint Planning*, *Agile Construction*, and *Sprint Review*. Constrained scopes are connected by control flow, e.g., parallel or sequential flows, here an iteration loop.

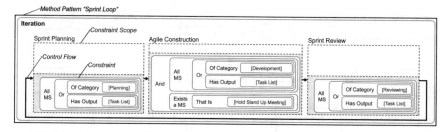

Fig. 10.2   A method pattern based on the Sprint loop from the Scrum method

The middle constrained scope *Agile Construction* requires that all method services placed inside are of Category "Development" or produce a "Task List" as an Output. Additionally, at least one method service has to be *Hold Standup Meeting*. The method services presented in Tables 10.1 and 10.2 would fulfill all these requirements and thus the constraint, if placed in this constrained scope.

Figure 10.3 shows a simplified pattern that was derived from the plan-driven *OpenUp* method in a similar manner. So again, like method services the method patterns form agile and plan-driven methods are modeled similarly.

The senior method engineer creates and stores method patterns alongside method service in the method repository. Method patterns can be combined and help the project method engineer later to create methods for his project that fulfill the chosen patterns. MESP supports a built-in language to describe constraints and automated means to check whether they are fulfilled during method composition.

Similar to method services, the method patterns possess interfaces with situational factors to ease the identification of useful patterns for specific project characteristics. For the presented patterns, the *Sprint Loop* has for example Agility: Medium-High assigned to it and the *OpenUp* phases Agility: Low-Medium. Patterns are often only implicitly described in methods. So the senior method engineer has to identify, extract, and model them explicitly.

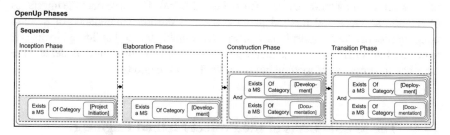

Fig. 10.3   A method pattern based on the phases of the OpenUp method

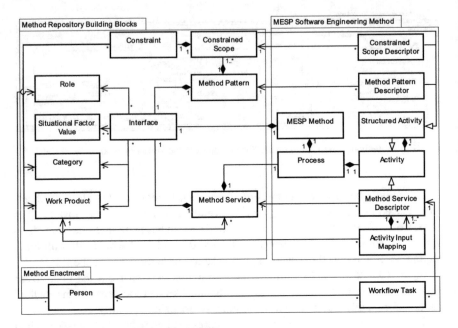

Fig. 10.4 The simplified metamodel of MESP

10.3.3   Metamodel Classes for the Senior Method Engineer

Figure 10.4 shows the simplified version of the implemented metamodel of MESP [13]. On the left, it shows the metamodel classes used by the senior method engineer. As shown, method services and method patterns reference work products, roles, situational factors, and categories. These elements are also created and maintained centrally by the senior method engineer. All elements in the method repository are part of the same interconnected model. This eases the maintenance of the method repository, as for example, changing a work product will be reflected in the interfaces of all referencing method services. Thus, the additional effort to model the interfaces of method services and method patterns pays of during maintenance of method building blocks. Also, algorithms to search for suitable method building blocks and to ensure the consistency of the method are also based on this shared model and the interface information of method building blocks and methods.

10.4   The MESP Tasks of the Project Method Engineer

In this section, we describe the MESP tasks of the project method engineer in more detail. He is responsible for composing methods that are then enacted later by the project team. We first present the task characteristics by explaining the requirements and how they are implemented and then illustrate the task with examples thereafter.

10.4.1   Task Characteristics

The project method engineer is responsible for defining consistent, enactable methods that are tailored to his project and that contains agile and plan-driven building blocks. In order to enable him to accomplish his tasks, MESP has to fulfill several requirements. In the following, we present these requirements and briefly state how they are realized.

Requirement 1 A method for a project needs to be derived based on its goals and characteristics, so that the method is tailored to the particular project. This is done by using the characterization of building blocks and methods stated in their interfaces.

Requirement 2 It has to be possible to integrate method patterns into the method, so that possible method compositions are restricted to the ones that implement the pattern correctly. This is implemented as part of our metamodel and our modeling and analysis tooling.

Requirement 3 A method has to formally describe the control flow (order of activities) as well as the data flow (data exchange between activities), so that it is unambiguous and can be enacted with a workflow engine later on. This is also implemented as part of our metamodel and our tooling.

Requirement 4 It has to be possible to invoke an automatic consistency check of the composed method, even for partial models, so that the project method engineer is supported in specifying correct methods and problems later during enactment are avoided. This is implemented as part of our tooling.

Requirement 5 It has to be possible to derive a process model for a workflow engine automatically from the method composition so that the enactment can be supported sufficiently. This is implemented as a transformation in our tooling.

10.4.2   Compose Project-Specific Method

The first MESP task of the senior method engineer is to compose a project-specific method. Based on the set of situational factors and work products defined in the method repository the project method engineer characterizes his project. He then identifies suitable method services and method patterns and composes them to a situational method.

The first step to compose a method suitable for a specific project is to characterize the project in terms of the project goal and the project situation. The project method engineer determines the project goal by defining which work products defined in the method repository have to be available at project start and which work products are to be delivered at the end of the project. For example, the project might start with an available "Requirements Specification" and might require the developed "Implementation" and "Integration Test Results" as resulting Output Work

Table 10.3 A project characterization as part of the interface of a situational method

Situational method interface	
Input work products	`Requirements Specification`
Output work products	`Implementation; Integration Test Results`
Situational factors	`Agility: Medium;` `Criticality: Medium`

`Products`. Beside this, the project method engineer determines the project situation in terms of situational factors, e.g., regarding "Agility" or "System Criticality." The project characterization is added to the `Interface` of the situational method to be created, as illustrated in Table 10.3 and is used to select suitable method services and method patterns in the following MESP tasks.

Next, the project method engineer can identify and compose suitable method services and method patterns based on the interface of the situational method. Composing the method solely using method services would not offer sufficient guidance to allow less-experienced project method engineers to compose a suitable method. Therefore, method patterns are used to restrict the potentially composable methods to meaningful ones. First, suitable method patterns are selected and combined, based on the situational method interface. For example, the method patterns that were introduced in Figs. 10.2 and 10.3 fit to the project situation depicted in Table 10.3. Suitable patterns can be combined to provide even more detailed guidance by restricting the number of composable methods even further. Figure 10.5 shows how the *OpenUp-Phases* pattern was combined with the *Sprint-Loop* pattern. Because of space constraints, the figure shows only the *Elaboration Phase* constrained scope.

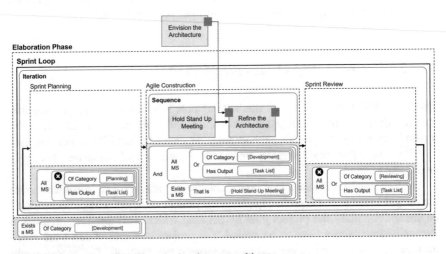

Fig. 10.5 A situational MESP method under composition

Third, after method patterns were selected and combined, suitable method services are identified based on the situational factors and now also the pattern constraints. For example, in the constrained scope *Agile Construction*, the constraint states that method services of `Category` "Development" and a "Hold Standup Meeting" method service are required. The method services *Refine the Architecture* (Table 10.1) and *Hold Standup Meeting* (Table 10.2) fit to the project characterization (Table 10.3) as well as the pattern constraints of the combined pattern and can therefore be added to the situational method, as depicted in Fig. 10.5.

By adding further method patterns and method services, the project method engineer composes the method step by step. To ensure the unambiguity and enactability, the specification of control and data flow is required. Therefore, in addition to method patterns and method services, the method is enhanced with structured activity elements to indicate the control flow, e.g., sequences, loops and (parallel) flows. To specify the flow of data of the method, each method service denotes, from where in the method it gets its input data. For example, the input mapping of the *Refine the Architecture* method service specifies that the input comes from a *Envision the Architecture* method service descriptor (outside the *Elaboration Phase*).

10.4.3 Assure Quality of Method

As the next MESP task, at any time during the composition the project method engineer can use the tooling to analyze the method for consistency as inconsistency threatens the enactability of the method later during the project. Our tooling detects metamodel-based inconsistencies, for example missing or removed method services that are referenced by the method. It also detects further inconsistencies based on consistency rules we formally modeled with the Object Constraint Language (OCL; [28]), for example, if a work product would be used as input of a method service, before it were produced. Additionally, the fulfillment of method pattern constraints is checked, so that for example the missing planning activity in the *Sprint Planning* constrained scope would be detected and reported to the user as denoted by the ✪ marks in Fig. 10.5.

10.4.4 Transform and Deploy Method

As his last MESP task, the project method engineer prepares the method such that it can be enacted with a workflow engine. He uses a transformation to automatically derive a process model from his consistently composed MESP method. The transformation creates equivalent control flow structures according to the MESP method. Every method service is transformed such that later during enactment proper workflow tasks are created and assigned to project team members. These tasks show the description, role, and work products from the method. After the transformation, the process model is deployed to a workflow server by the transformation component. Here, the project method engineer associates the members of his team with the roles used in the process model according to the resource planning of the project. Doing this, he ensures that later the right people are assigned the correct workflow tasks by the workflow engine.

10.4.5 Metamodel Classes for the Project Method Engineer

On the right of Fig. 10.4, the metamodel classes used by the project method engineer are shown. In a method, instead of using copies of method services from the repository, the used method services are referenced with so-called method service descriptors. Similarly, method pattern descriptors are used to reference the used method patterns. The data flow is specified with activity input mappings that indicate the source method service descriptors for required work products. Control flow is specified with specific sub meta classes of the depicted meta class structured activity, e.g., sequence, parallel flow, and iteration.

10.5 The MESP Tasks of the Project Team

In this section, we describe how the project team enacts the situational method that was composed by the project method engineer. We first present the task characteristics by explaining the requirements and how they are implemented and then illustrate the task with examples thereafter.

10.5.1 Task Characteristics

The project team is responsible for enacting the method as prescribed by the project method engineer using the workflow engine. In order to enable it to accomplish its task, MESP has to fulfill several requirements. In the following, we present these requirements and briefly state how they are realized.

Requirement 1 Workflow tasks need to be created in the order defined in the method and at the right point in time, which is when all the preceding workflow tasks are finished. This ensures that the team members know when they have to perform a certain activity. Especially composite method services need to be resolved properly, e.g., into a sequence of consecutive workflow tasks. This is taken care of by our transformation.

Requirement 2 The workflow tasks need to be assigned to people according to the roles assigned in the method. This is taken care of by the project method engineer and the human task interface of the workflow engine.

Requirement 3 The workflow tasks need to show the textual descriptions of the tasks from the method services so that the team members get guidance on what to do. Again, this is taken care of by our transformation.

Requirement 4 Input and output work products of workflow tasks need to be resolved and referenced correctly based on the method so that the assigned team member does not only see the type of work products, but the created workflow tasks themselves. This is also implemented as part of our transformation.

Requirement 5 The team should be shown information about the current state of enactment of the method and about the enactment history so that the team is provided with context for its actions. This is provided as part of our transformation and partly build in into the used workflow engine.

10.5.2 Enact Method

Using the workflow engine, the project team carries out its activities according to the underlying method. The workflow enactment support actually consists of two components: the workflow engine component itself hosts the deployed process model, while the human task management component manages the created workflow tasks and the interaction with team members. Thereby, workflows tasks basically represent runtime instances of method service descriptors in a method as they represent activities that a certain team member has to carry out in correspondence to what is defined by the situational method. Workflow tasks are created in the right order and at the right time, because for each method service descriptor in the MESP method a command to create and assign a workflow task (HumanTask Invocation) is created in the process model by the transformation from the method. This creates a workflow task when it is executed. For method service descriptors that reference composite method services the contained process is transformed. For example, a sequence of method service descriptors is transformed to a sequence of HumanTask Invocations.

Figure 10.6 shows a workflow task in the way it is presented to the team member. This particular workflow task is based on the method service *Refine the Architecture*.

Workflow tasks need to be assigned to the right people so that it is clear who should carry them out. Therefore, each workflow task contains a responsible role that is derived from the method service descriptor in the composed MESP method. The human task interface then shows this workflow task to all users logged in with the appropriate role. For example, the workflow task in Fig. 10.6 is assigned to team members with the role "Architect" according to the method service description in Table 10.1.

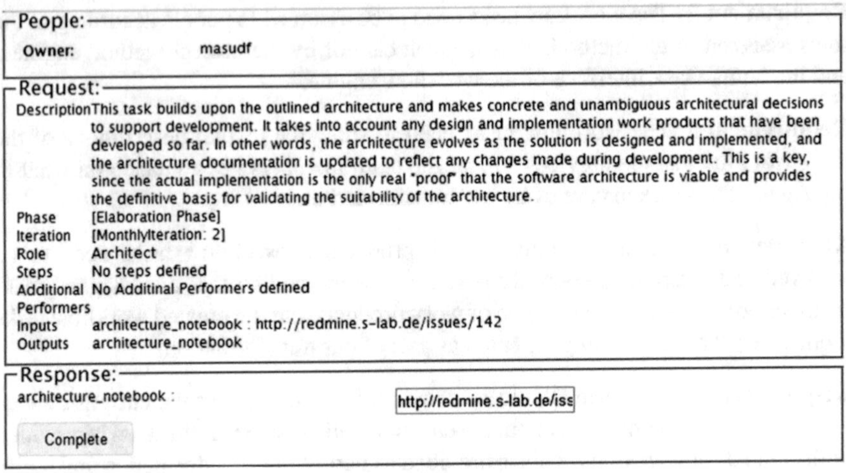

┌─**People:**──┐
│ **Owner:**   masudf   │
└──┘
┌─**Request:**───┐
│ DescriptionThis task builds upon the outlined architecture and makes concrete and unambiguous architectural decisions
│   to support development. It takes into account any design and implementation work products that have been
│   developed so far. In other words, the architecture evolves as the solution is designed and implemented, and
│   the architecture documentation is updated to reflect any changes made during development. This is a key,
│   since the actual implementation is the only real "proof" that the software architecture is viable and provides
│   the definitive basis for validating the suitability of the architecture.
│ Phase   [Elaboration Phase]
│ Iteration   [MonthlyIteration: 2]
│ Role   Architect
│ Steps   No steps defined
│ Additional   No Additinal Performers defined
│ Performers
│ Inputs   architecture_notebook : http://redmine.s-lab.de/issues/142
│ Outputs   architecture_notebook
└──┘
┌─**Response:**──┐
│ architecture_notebook :   ┌─────────────────────────────────┐
│   │ http://redmine.s-lab.de/iss   │
│   └─────────────────────────────────┘
│   ┌──────────────┐
│   │   Complete   │
│   └──────────────┘
└──┘

Fig. 10.6 A workflow task based on the method service "Refine the Architecture"

Especially important is that the description of the method service is shown to the team member as part of the workflow task in order to guide him in his activity. As shown in Fig. 10.6 the description is part of the workflow task description, because our transformation adds the descriptions as parameters to the HumanTask Invocations.

In order to be able to perform the workflow task, the team member needs to know which work products were created and should serve as an input. The team member also needs to give information on where the results of his work can be found. Our transformation ensures this and in our prototype this is handled by providing the URIs of the work products, e.g., from a ticket system or repository. Figure 10.6 illustrates this. Under the section "Inputs" it shows the URI of the input work product of this task and in the "Response" section the team member needs to give the location of his created (or updated) output work product.

Beside information about the actual workflow task itself our transformation ensures that workflow tasks also carry information on the execution state of the process model. Figure 10.6 shows for example that the workflow task is part of the *Elaboration Phase* and the second run of the iteration loop called "Monthly Iteration." In addition to this information, the workflow engine itself logs the execution events and offers means to investigate them.

10.6 Tool Support for MESP

Applying MESP would be infeasible without proper tool support. Thus, we implemented tooling that supports the presented MESP tasks. Figure 10.7 illustrates the components of our tool support. We created Eclipse-based tooling to carry out the

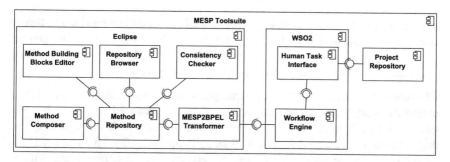

Fig. 10.7 An overview of the components of the MESP tool suite

MESP tasks ❶–❹ and use the WSO2 Business Process Server to enact the method within MESP task ❺ (cf. Fig. 10.1). Based on the formal metamodel described in Fig. 10.4, we offer an editor to model method building blocks (*Method Building Blocks Editor*) and to assemble MESP methods (*Method Composer*). We also implemented first algorithms into the method composer to relate suitable building blocks to project characteristics in order to support the search for suitable method building blocks. All model elements are stored in the *Method Repository*. On top of the metamodel, we implemented additional automated quality assurance mechanisms that uncover inconsistencies, e.g., contradictions or method pattern violations, in our *Consistency Checker*. In contrast to many other assembly-based method engineering approaches, e.g., [5, 30, 33], MESP provides workflow support. We created an automated transformation that transforms a MESP method into a standard BPEL4-People process model (MESP2BPEL Transformer; [26]) which is then executed with a workflow engine. We use the WSO2 Business Process Server as the basis for our workflow support. The BPEL4People process model derived from the MESP method is enacted within the *Workflow Engine*. This component creates workflow tasks according to the method service descriptors of the method (cf. Fig. 10.4) and protocols the process enactment. The *Human Task Interface* manages the workflow tasks by assigning them to team members and by transferring the results back to the BPEL4People process model. The results of performing workflow tasks are modeled as URIs to created or altered work products in an external *Project Repository*.

10.7   Benefits for Process Management

In this section, we revisit the described challenges for software process management of Sect. 10.1 and describe how they are addressed by MESP (Fig. 10.1):

Challenge 1: The senior method engineer addresses Challenge 1 by modifying the services and patterns that are offered for method creation (❶). Outdated practices are reflected, e.g., in removed method services and method patterns. Lessons learned are incorporated, e.g., by updating building blocks with that new insight. Trends and new best practices are reflected, e.g., in completely new building blocks. The formal definition of building blocks helps in maintaining the consistency when updating the method repository, for example, to identify composed methods with dangling references to removed method services and method patterns.

Challenge 2: In MESP, methods are composed based on building blocks. Hybrid methods that integrate content from structured, plan-driven methods and agile methods (Challenge 2) can be created by using building blocks from the repository that originate from both plan-driven as well as agile methods (❷). This is a particular strength of MESP as an assembly-based method engineering approach and with its notion of method patterns a particular strength of MESP alone [14].

Challenge 3: In MESP, software development methods are tailored to individual project goals and characteristics (❷). Projects are characterized among two dimensions: the project goal is characterized by the work products to be produced as the final result and the ones that are already available at project start. The project situation is based on situational factors determined by the project method engineer. Both directly influence what is denoted suitable by comparing the interfaces of method services and method patterns, as these are also characterized based on processed work products and/or situational factors.

Challenge 4: MESP knows two mechanisms to create consistent software development methods (❸). On the one hand, method building blocks and method compositions are formally defined with a metamodel. The formal description helps senior method engineers to create proper method services and method patterns and project method engineers to create proper methods. On the other hand, based on the metamodel, the consistency of software development methods is further formalized using the object constraint language (OCL). The formalization also includes the constraints imposed by method patterns. The MESP tooling can apply various automated checks at design time to notify about consistency violations. In addition, the tooling provides feedback that helps to mitigate consistency issues.

Challenge 5: MESP supports a project team in enacting the method properly as it is transformed into a BPEL4People process model (❹) and enacted with a workflow engine. The workflow engine then creates tasks for the project members according to the method and coordinates their activities, thus helping them to enact the method (❺) and reducing manual coordination effort. It also provides team members with the description and guidance on their tasks and shows them runtime information, e.g., the current iteration or the location, where input work products for their task are stored [15].

10.8 Conclusions

In this chapter, we explained how our approach Method Engineering with Method Services and Method Patterns (MESP) can help to overcome five typical challenges in the management of software development methods. We briefly introduced the challenges of (1) defining method content based on new trends, best practices, and lessons learned, (2) creating hybrid methods that integrate plan-driven and agile aspects, (3) tailoring methods to projects, (4) creating consistent methods, and (5) enacting methods. We then introduced the MESP approach, where experienced senior method engineers define a repository of reusable method building blocks called method services and method patterns. Project method engineers then select from the repository building blocks to assemble (potentially hybrid) methods specific to their projects. They use the provided tooling to check the consistency of these methods and deploy them to a workflow engine such that their project teams are supported in the enactment and coordination of the method.

We explained how the different aspects of the MESP approach help in overcoming specific challenges. New trends, best practices, and lessons learned (1) can be incorporated by updating the repository of building blocks. Hybrid methods can be created (2), because method services are described based on the same formal definition, irrespective of their plan-driven or agile origin. Additionally, method patterns support the project method engineer in mixing methodological ideas of different methods by restraining the solution space to desired combinations using method patterns. We explained that methods are tailored towards individual project goals and characteristics (3), because methods are assembled systematically based on a project characterization. The consistency of MESP methods (4) is ensured by the formal definition of building blocks and methods that reduces the risks to define faulty methods. In addition, the tooling offers formal analysis capabilities that detect inconsistencies and helps to mitigate them. The correct enactment of a method according to its definition (5) is supported by the workflow support of MESP that creates tasks for project members based on the current state of the method instance.

We are constantly improving our approach based on our industrial experience. We just upgraded the UI with an editor that is easier to use. In addition, we are continuously extending our method repository with method services and method patterns extracted from different sources.

10.9   Further Reading

MESP is a method engineering approach that follows a situational, assembly-based methodology and that supports the enactment of modeled methods. Further information about the MESP approach in particular and our research in the field of situational method engineering in general is available here[4] and here,[5] and on the websites of the authors.

Several *other chapters in this book* provide insight into topics that where discussed in this chapter. In Chap. 1 in this volume, the author explains that modern

---

[4]Available from: http://s-lab.uni-paderborn.de/ and [12].

[5]Available from: http://is.uni-paderborn.de/ and [11].

mobile and web applications have evolved in different ways such that traditional "high ceremony processes" are mostly unsuitable. This case illustrates an example for what we discussed as Challenge 1 in this chapter. In Chap. 2, the authors discuss the integration of agility into plan-based methods, a challenge that we discussed as Challenge 2 in this chapter. They discuss the advantages and drawbacks of different ways to achieve the integration. In Chap. 8, the authors share their experience of software development and software process management for spaceflight missions. They present an industrial example for the Challenge 3 that we discussed in this chapter, namely, assessing the project context and deriving process requirements that consequently need to be incorporated into the process of the software development method. In Chap. 13, the authors investigate the co-evolution of Model-driven Engineering (MDE) and the used software development processes. They identified that changes in the used languages and the provided tool support of MDE require changes in the software development process and vice versa, thus showing one example for Challenge 4, that is creating consistent software development processes. In Chap. 9 in this volume, the authors discuss the suitability of BPMN as a notation for software development methods. BPMN has the advantage that is widespread in the area of business process modeling and that it is enactable with a workflow engine (Challenge 5), but that is not known to be used for software development methods.

Related work comprises approaches to create methods that are designed to fulfill their purpose in the context of a specific situation (*situational method engineering*) and modeling languages for software development methods (*formal modeling of software development methods*).

As an introduction and to get a concise overview about the first research field *situational method engineering*, we recommend the paper [19] by Henderson-Sellers and Ralyté. For deeper understanding, we recommend the recently published book of Henderson-Sellers et al. [20] that provides a state-of-the art summery of the field published for example in the IFIP WG8.1 Working Conference Series [31, 32]. One field in situational method engineering are assembly-based approaches like MESP to create methods based on a repository of building blocks first proposed by Brinkkemper [5]. While several approaches were proposed in the past, e.g., [5, 30, 33] only few approaches address the challenges of SPM explicitly, such as [2, 37]. Especially, enactment support is offered only in very few cases, however mostly outdated and only one approach that was proposed recently by Cervera et al. [6]. This approach supports the creation of methods based on a method repository of method fragments and specifically focuses on deriving a suitable CASE environment for the method

Regarding the *formal modeling of software development methods*, we recommend as a general introduction to the topic the book [16] by González-Pérez and specifically the OMG standard Software and Systems Process Engineering Metamodel Specification (SPEM; [27]), that has his drawbacks [9], but is the most widespread metamodel to model software development methods. Still, current developments are mostly situated in academia, and it remains unclear whether and how proposals will be considered in the further development of SPEM [21]. One group of modeling approaches focuses on for later enactment. Here, Osterweil with his process programs is seen as one of the fathers of this idea [29]. His research lead to the Little-JIL language [38] that focuses on the coordination of tasks, while providing detailed descriptions of tasks is not in the scope of the language. In addition, the creation of situational methods is not explicitly supported. Bendraou et al. [3] and Ellner et al. [9, 10] propose extensions to SPEM, a language to model software development methods, to address its lack of executability. Both approaches offer a language to model methods from scratch, but no explicit support for situational method engineering is provided, which is one of our main goals. As part of the service-oriented integration framework ModelBus, Aldazabal et al. [1] developed components for the orchestration of arbitrary (web) services using BPEL. Their approach offers a component that transforms process models defined in SPEM into plain BPEL process models. As no further details are given, the focus seems to be on deriving the process flow from a SPEM model, so no guidance for the team members is directly derived. In addition, the creation of situational methods is not addressed.

References

1. Aldazabal, A., Baily, T., Nanclares, F., Sadovykh, A., Hein, C., Esser, M., Ritter, T.: Automated model driven development processes. In: Proceedings of the ECMDA Workshop on Model Driven Tool and Process Integration, pp. 43–54. IRB, Stuttgart (2008)
2. Bekkers, W., van de Weerd, I., Brinkkemper, S., Mahieu, A.: The influence of situational factors in software product management: an empirical study. In: Proceedings of the International Workshop on Software Product Management, pp. 41–48. IEEE, Washington, DC, USA (2008)
3. Bendraou, R., Combemale, B., Cregut, X., Gervais, M.P.: Definition of an executable SPEM 2.0. In: Proceedings of the Asia-Pacific Software Engineering Conference, pp. 390–397. IEEE, Los Alamitos, CA (2007)
4. Boehm, B.W., Turner, R.: Observations on balancing discipline and agility. In: Proceedings of the Conference on Agile Development, pp. 32–39. IEEE, Los Alamitos, CA (2003)
5. Brinkkemper, S.: Method engineering: engineering of information systems development methods and tools. Inf. Softw. Technol. **38**(4), 275–280 (1996)
6. Cervera, M., Albert, M., Torres, V., Pelechano, V.: Turning method engineering support into reality. In: Engineering Methods in the Service-Oriented Context. IFIP Advances in Information and Communication Technology, vol. 351, pp. 138–152. Springer, Berlin (2011)
7. Cockburn, A.: Selecting a project's methodology. IEEE Softw. **17**(4), 64–71 (2000)
8. Cockburn, A.: Agile Software Development. Addison-Wesley, Boston (2002)
9. Ellner, R., Al-Hilank, S., Drexler, J., Jung, M., Kips, D., Philippsen, M.: eSPEM – A SPEM extension for enactable behavior modeling. In: Modelling Foundations and Applications. Lecture Notes in Computer Science, vol. 6138, pp. 116–131. Springer, Berlin (2010)
10. Ellner, R., Al-Hilank, S., Jung, M., Kips, D., Philippsen, M.: An integrated tool chain for software process modeling and execution. In: Proceedings of the European Conference on Modelling Foundations and Applications, pp. 73–82. Technical University of Denmark (DTU), Copenhagen, Denmark (2011)
11. Engels, G.: TASQ project page. http://s-lab.uni-paderborn.de/s-lab-software-quality-lab/unsere-innovativen-projekte/aktuell/tasq.html (2011)
12. Fazal-Baqaie, M.: Situational method engineering research group. http://is.uni-paderborn.de/en/research-group/fg-engels/research/themen/situational-method-engineering.html (2015)
13. Fazal-Baqaie, M.: Project-specific software engineering methods: modularization, composition, enactment, and quality assurance. Ph.D. thesis, Paderborn University, Paderborn, Germany (to appear)

14. Fazal-Baqaie, M., Luckey, M., Engels, G.: Assembly-based method engineering with method patterns. In: Proceedings of the German Software Engineering Conference. Lecture Notes in Informatics, vol. 215, pp. 435–444. German Computer Society (GI e.V.) (2013)
15. Fazal-Baqaie, M., Gerth, C., Engels, G.: Breathing life into situational software engineering methods. In: Proceedings of the International Conference of Product Focused Software Development and Process Improvement. Lecture Notes in Computer Science, vol. 8892, pp. 281–284. Springer, Berlin (2014)
16. González-Pérez, C., Henderson-Sellers, B.: Metamodelling for Software Engineering. Wiley, Chichester (2008)
17. Harmsen, A.F.: Situational method engineering. Ph.D. thesis, University of Twente, Twente, Netherlands (1997)
18. Heijstek, W., Chaudron, M.R.V., Libing Qiu, Schouten, C.C.: A comparison of industrial process descriptions for global custom software development. In: Proceedings of the International Conference on Global Software Engineering, pp. 277–284. IEEE, Washington, DC, USA (2010)
19. Henderson-Sellers, B., Ralyté, J.: Situational method engineering: state-of-the-art review. J. Univers. Comput.Sci. 16(3), 424–478 (2010)
20. Henderson-Sellers, B., Ralyté, J., Ågerfalk, P.J., Rossi, M.: Situational Method Engineering. Springer, Berlin (2014)
21. Kuhrmann, M., Fernández, D.M., Steenweg, R.: Systematic software process development: where do we stand today? In: Proceedings of the International Conference on Software and System Process, pp. 166–170. ACM, New York, NY, USA (2013)
22. Kuhrmann, M., Linssen, O.: Vorgehensmodelle in Deutschland: Nutzung von 2006–2013 im überblick. GI WI-MAW Rundbrief 2015(39), 32–47 (2015)
23. Kuhrmann, M., Méndez Fernández, D., Tiessler, M.: A mapping study on the feasibility of method engineering. J. Softw.: Evol. Process 26(12), 1053–1073 (2014)
24. Martínez-Ruiz, T., Münch, J., García, F., Piattini, M.: Requirements and constructors for tailoring software processes: a systematic literature review. Softw. Qual. J. 20(1), 229–260 (2012)
25. Nguyen-Duc, A., Cruzes, D.S.: Coordination of software development teams across organizational boundary – an exploratory study. In: Proceedings of the International Conference on Global Software Engineering, pp. 216–225. IEEE, Washington, DC, USA (2013)
26. OASIS: Web Services – Human Task (WS-HumanTask) Specification Version 1.1 - Committee Draft 10 / Public Review Draft 04. http://www.oasis-open.org/committees/documents.php?wg_abbrev=bpel4people (2010)
27. OMG: Software and systems process engineering metamodel specification (SPEM) 2.0. Omg standard, Object Management Group (2008)
28. OMG: Object Constraint Language 2.4. Technical report, Object Management Group (2014)
29. Osterweil, L.J.: Software processes are software too. In: Proceedings of the International Conference on Software Engineering, pp. 2–13. IEEE, Washington, DC, USA (1987)
30. Ralyté, J., Rolland, C.: An assembly process model for method engineering. In: Proceedings of the International Conference on Advanced Information Systems Engineering. Lecture Notes in Computer Science, vol. 2068, pp. 267–283. Springer, Berlin (2001)
31. Ralyté, J., Brinkkemper, S., Henderson-Sellers, B. (eds.): Situational method engineering: fundamentals and experiences. In: Proceedings of the IFIP WG 8.1 Working Conference. IFIP Advances in Information and Communication Technology, vol. 244. Springer, Boston (2007)
32. Ralyté, J., Mirbel, I., Deneckère, R. (eds.): Engineering methods in the service-oriented context – 4th IFIP WG 8.1 Working Conference on Method Engineering. IFIP Advances in Information and Communication Technology, vol. 351. Springer, Berlin (2011)
33. Rolland, C.: Method engineering: towards methods as services. Softw. Process: Improv. Pract. 14(3), 143–164 (2009)
34. ter Hofstede, A.H.M., Verhoef, T.F.: On the feasibility of situational method engineering. Inf. Syst. 22(6–7), 401–422 (1997)
35. van de Weerd, I., Brinkkemper, S., Versendaal, J.: Concepts for incremental method evolution: empirical exploration and validation in requirements management. In: Advanced Information

Systems Engineering. Lecture Notes in Computer Science, vol. 4495, pp. 469–484. Springer, Berlin (2007)

36. Vijayasarathy, L., Butler, C.: Choice of software development methodologies - do project, team and organizational characteristics matter? IEEE Softw. **99**, 1ff (2015)

37. Vlaanderen, K., van de Weerd, I., Brinkkemper, S.: The online method engine: from process assessment to method execution. In: Engineering Methods in the Service-Oriented Context. IFIP Advances in Information and Communication Technology, vol. 351, pp. 108–122. Springer, Berlin (2011)

38. Wise, A., Cass, A.G., Lerner, B.S., McCall, E.K., Osterweil, L.J., Sutton, S.M.: Using Little-JIL to coordinate agents in software engineering. In: Proceedings of the International Conference on Automated Software Engineering, pp. 155–163. IEEE, Washington, DC, USA (2000)

Chapter 11
Adapting Case Management Techniques to Achieve Software Process Flexibility

Marian Benner-Wickner, Matthias Book and Volker Gruhn

Abstract Software processes have to be flexible in order to handle a wide range of software project types and complexities. Large companies that depend on custom-built software may therefore define different software processes in order to adapt to different recurring project contexts (e.g., hot-fix versus migration projects). However, the stakeholders do not always follow the intended "happy path"—not the least because any software project typically has to deal with a considerable amount of uncertainty. Following an agile process may not be possible due to a company's culture or policy restrictions (e.g., in the healthcare or financial domain) though. In this chapter, we present an approach to introduce more flexibility into software process models by adapting case management techniques to the domain of flexible software process management, in order to cope with key issues that come with software process evolution. Key functionalities of the approach have been implemented in a prototype and showcased to developers and architects via a live experiment. The feedback is promising as it shows that the approach helps to quickly identify context-specific actions and artifacts. This in turn reduces effort in structuring the daily work of software process stakeholders in an environment of evolving process elements specific to different kinds of projects, roles, and technologies.

11.1 Introduction

Most companies today rely on information systems for the execution of a wide range of mission-critical business processes. Digital enterprises whose core business entities are intangible data (e.g., in the finance sector), as well as traditional enterprises

M. Benner-Wickner (✉) · V. Gruhn
paluno - The Ruhr Institute for Software Technology, University of Duisburg-Essen,
Schützenbahn 70, 45127 Essen, Germany
e-mail: marian.benner-wickner@uni-due.de

V. Gruhn
e-mail: volker.gruhn@uni-due.de

M. Book
Deptartment of Computer Science, University of Iceland, Tæknigarður 208, Dunhagi 5,
107 Reykjavík, Iceland
e-mail: book@hi.is

© Springer International Publishing Switzerland 2016
M. Kuhrmann et al. (eds.), *Managing Software Process Evolution*,
DOI 10.1007/978-3-319-31545-4_11

who are operating with physical goods (e.g., in logistics or production), rely on complex information systems to manage their assets, to control processes, to make business decisions, to communicate with internal and external actors, and even to explore new business opportunities.

Information systems development, maintenance, and evolution in this context is shaped by a multitude of forces and conditions business strategies, existing infrastructures, available technologies, market influences, legal and regulatory frameworks, and so forth. These forces do not just shape what software is being developed, but also how it is developed: Software processes are influenced by and need to adapt to the business environment as much as the software systems do.

Many companies struggle with the adoption, implementation and evolution of a software process that is suitable for their particular systems in their particular business environment (see also Chap. 15 in this volume). At one end of the spectrum, heavy-weight, document-centric process models promise a clearly structured path to the intended project results that prescribes detailed procedures and artifacts that capture all aspects of the business domain—however, this completeness comes at the cost of high effort and low flexibility in the face of changing forces in the business environment. At the other end of the spectrum, agile process models promise ultimate flexibility, but at the expense of the predictability, guidance, and accountability that more structured models provide.

In addition, even within one organization, there will typically be different types of projects that require different approaches (see also Chap. 3 in this volume) [10]. Developing a mobile app for online banking from scratch, and customizing an SAP-based back-end component for credit transfers, pose quite different challenges that can neither be satisfactorily addressed by the same heavy-weight or the same agile software process. Yet, some frame conditions will be the same—whether developing a mobile app or a back-end component, banks will have to implement risk management and compliance regulations set forth by financial supervision authorities.

While several heavy-weight process models offer ways of tailoring their procedures, and agile process models are supposed to be adaptive by design, neither provides guidance on how to adapt a process to the specific business, technology and lifecycle contexts of a particular project in a particular domain, while ensuring that the relevant regulatory requirements are being adhered to [5].

In this chapter, we present an approach to resolve this dilemma, drawing on solutions for similar challenges that can be found in the business process management field. To be exact, we will adapt case management principles and techniques (Sect. 11.2.2) into the domain of flexible software processes. Since case management is a wide field of research with several techniques, we will focus on adapting the *agenda-driven case management approach* (adCM; [1]) in Sect. 11.3.

11.2   Background and Context

In business process management field, the concept of *case management* has gained prominence in recent years [9, 11]. While classical business process management approaches assume that business processes can be described precisely in all their inputs and outputs, actions and conditions, and that they can be executed exactly as specified, the case management approach recognizes that there are certain business activities that cannot be shoehorned into a precise process model: Even though such activities also have a core set of typical actions, there is no fixed execution sequence and no precise description of the produced and consumed information. Instead, such activities are characterized by a context in which they typically occur, the outcome they are expected to produce, and the steps that are recommended to be undertaken to achieve this. The concrete actions involved in executing each instance of such an activity (i.e., resolving a case) are then highly dependent on the characteristics of each individual case.

11.2.1   Drawing an Analogy

We consider software processes to be more similar to case management activities than to "strict" business processes of the traditional kind, and therefore propose to employ a similar approach to shaping them. This similarity can be observed in three characteristics of case management and software processes.

First of all, a *high level of interaction*: Resolving a case typically involves a number of stakeholders from different backgrounds, who all provide bits of information on different aspects of the case. Rather than fitting together like complementary pieces of a jigsaw puzzle, the information provided by these stakeholders may be contradictory, redundant, imprecise, or have gaps, requiring the case manager to interact with stakeholders in order to clarify, negotiate, resolve, and adapt the relevant information. A considerable amount of that information typically is expert knowledge, which needs to be understood both by the case manager and the stakeholders. The same is true in software engineering, where product owners, software architects, and developers need to work with a team of business experts and end users to elicit requirements, design the software, and resolve conflicting architecture and implementation decisions, etc.

Second, both successful case management and successful software development requires *procedural flexibility*: Case management is predicated on the observation that no two cases are alike, so the best way to resolve a case may differ depending on the circumstances, the availability of information, the behavior of stakeholders, unforeseen events, and so on. This is true for software engineering as well rarely are two projects exactly the same, even if they are in the same application domain: Existing system landscapes, legacy data structures and technologies, different business goals and strategies, and changing requirements all require flexibility in how to run a software project, and how to deal with changes along the way. This means that software development processes need to resemble flexible case management processes much more than fixed production processes.

Finally, both case management and software engineering require *initiative, creativity and innovation*: In an environment where no fixed paths can simply be followed to success, the stakeholders' ability to come up with individual solutions to a wide range of problems is key. Some of these solutions will be unique to a particular case or project situation, but some might turn into best practices if they are found to apply to more projects. For these cases, both case management and software engineering should provide mechanisms to recognize such best practices and establish recommendations based on them.

11.2.2 Case Management Principles

To understand the transfer of case management techniques to software process management, we will first introduce some basic concepts of techniques like agenda-driven case management.

McCauley et al. [9] describe case management as activities where *"the path of execution cannot be predefined. Human judgment is required in determining how to proceed, and the state of a case can be affected by external events"*. Case management techniques reflect the need for high flexibility in both the control-flow perspective as well as the data perspective. To achieve this, they make a paradigm switch from juggling a comprehensive process model to working with *manageable pieces of process knowledge*. These pieces are templates of activities and artifacts known to be useful when organizing the actor's work towards achieving a very specific project goal. Another main principle is the shift from a process-centric point of view to an *artifact-centric perspective*. It is vital to support the actor in every task related to artifacts, e.g., exploring, organizing, and evaluating data.

When adapting the principle of manageable pieces of knowledge to the domain of flexible software processes, we assume that there will be no imperative software model that can be applied to every software project (and no one would stick to it, anyway). So, in preparation of a project, *only vital actions or artifacts should be defined* as pieces of process knowledge, e.g., compliance-relevant milestones and respective checklists. During the project, these *pieces should be hot-plugged* to adapt to each very specific project situation, e.g., integrating a review cycle for software components that have been identified as risky by the architect. Conversely, it is also possible to remove design tasks and replace them with the review of a design that has already been done in a previous design project.

In the domain of flexible software processes, changing the focus to an artifact-centric perspective has one main implication: Driving a process by just "fueling" a strict core process model with input artifacts (e.g., requirements specifications) does not work. At the beginning of a process, most of the information is neither complete nor mature. There are far too many variables that can sidetrack the plan which are

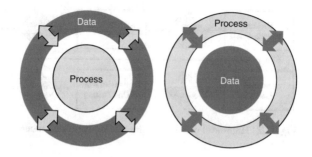

Fig. 11.1 Process- versus artifact-centric perspective (based on [11])

not specified, yet. So the software engineering artifacts cannot be seen as fuel of a process. Instead, the artifacts are in the focal position and the *process has to be justified towards the production of the artifacts* (Fig. 11.1). While the output artifacts usually remain stable, all actions are replaceable, which facilitates flexible software process management.

In the rest of this chapter, we will show in more detail how case management principles and techniques can be adapted for flexible software process models.

11.3   Agenda-Driven Software Process Management by Example

As introduced above, the main contribution of this chapter is the adaptation of case management principles for the domain of flexible software processes, resulting in an *agenda-driven software process management* (adSPM) approach.

In order to illustrate how the adapted approach works amid the real-world problems of flexible software process management, we will first introduce a genuine software process of a German bank. It reflects many issues of an evolving flexible software process, as it is quite new (i.e., not yet established throughout the company) and many activities are only relevant in a specific context. In the next step, we then discuss how such flexible software processes benefit from the pivotal case management principles in general. Inspired by these ideas, we will go into details of the agenda-driven software process management approach.

11.3.1   Example Process

Due to a future risk management compliance audit, the process described below was introduced into the bank's software development department. It explicitly aims at software process industrialization. Besides some generic high-level actions, it contains a *sophisticated set of artifacts* as well as distinct quality gates and corresponding

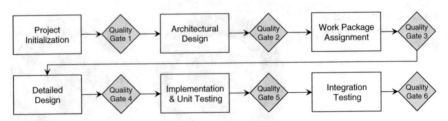

Fig. 11.2 High-level overview of the case study process model

checklists that satisfy the compliance policies. A high-level overview of the process is shown in Fig. 11.2. Each quality gate requires the delivery of up to eight different artifacts.

The process *documentation is dispersed* among three manuals and several technology-specific directions for action. One manual explains all artifacts; the other two manuals describe all process element definitions for design and implementation activities. All manuals are accessible via the bank's intranet.

In order to cope with flexibility due to project-specific peculiarities, *six different project types* are defined within the manuals. The process tailoring according to these project types is described by decision tables (see Table 11.1). They define which quality gate has to be passed in which project type: When realizing less risky project types like change requests, fewer quality gates have to be passed than in full-fledged implementation projects.

However, there are not only project-specific, but also technology-specific peculiarities. Hence all these definitions are further refined by *technology-specific instructions*, which introduce specific document templates. Examples are document templates for a design specification of enterprise resource planning (ERP) customizations or for test documentation of Java 2 Enterprise Edition (J2EE) web applications.

Overall, this process model seems to be both compliant and flexible. It reflects project-specific as well as technology-specific needs. However, in practice it turns out very *difficult for the actors to obtain the latest and right task definitions* for a given project. This is because the definitions are spread over multiple documents and

Table 11.1 Matrix for quality gate tailoring

Quality Gate #	Project type					
	Big	Medium	Maintenance	Conception	Infrastructure	Small
1	✓	✓		✓	✓	
2	✓				✓	
3	✓					
4	✓					
5	✓	✓	✓			✓
6	✓	✓	✓			✓

cannot be transformed into one process model fitting a given project context. The capability to present all necessary tasks for the current project type, technology and role is missing. As a result, the *compliance is actually at risk*, because important artifacts and tasks like code reviews for risky components may be left out.

11.3.2 Introducing Agenda-Driven Software Process Management

Agenda-driven case management, even though originally introduced for the insurance and medical domain, addresses most of the issues that the example process exhibits. It is a lightweight method with three basic concepts: an agenda, agenda templates and artifacts. In this section, we will explain how flexible software processes can benefit from adapting these concepts in general, and how they can be used in the example process.

In order to keep track of his project responsibilities, an actor needs an overview of different important process elements like quality gates, activities and artifacts. Due to the need for flexibility, the elements may have to be reorganized at any time. These requirements are covered by the pivotal element of agenda-driven case management: the *agenda*. It is a hierarchically structured list containing all entities that an actor considers important for the completion of his project responsibilities. It is ideally derived from a guideline for a certain project type, but the actor is free to (re-)organize the agenda according to the particularities of each project, and may even start with a blank agenda. Of course, with respect to the compliance policies in the example process, the agenda concept should also consider restrictive elements. For example, the process owner should be able to prescribe actions that are read-only, strictly in order and mandatory to pass. Using the agenda, the actor however still has the necessary flexibility to align his actions around the focal artifacts and quality gates.

Ensuring compliance by defining mandatory items is a need that can be covered by the adaptation of the second concept: the *agenda template*. Agenda templates are context-specific and originally designed to make best practices available to the actor. When adapting this concept to the management of flexible software processes, such best practices can be extended by obligatory agenda templates. They contain quality gates with corresponding actions, checklists and artifacts. They can be connected with business rules so that projects can only be closed if these items are marked as finished (in the given sequence).

When defining agenda templates, the degree of specificity can be chosen arbitrarily. Agenda templates may contain quality gates for a certain project type and omit technology-specific items. But they may also contain technology-specific artifacts by attaching appropriate *document* templates (not to be confused with the *agenda* templates introduced above) and notes containing tailoring information. Consider, for example, the design documentation of standard ERP software. Describing architectural decisions is feasible when dealing with custom software. However, since standard software usually has a predefined architecture, a chapter on architectural decisions may not be necessary in that case.

The need for attaching artifacts to agendas and agenda templates calls for the third key concept: the *workspace*. It is designed to hold almost any data that is necessary for carrying out the process, including regular files, web links and notes. Its structure is defined by the agenda, so the relationship between artifacts and agenda items is always clear. For the purpose of clarification and traceability, artifacts in the workspace can be associated with each other using well-defined semantics. For example, the overall architecture of an application can be associated with more detailed specifications using the binary relation "refined by." Moreover, the workspace allows *n*-ary relations for artifacts belonging together like a bag of detailed specifications for a given system.

After introducing the three main concepts individually, we will next illustrate how agendas, agenda templates and artifacts work together using the example of a software developer who is designated to perform a small change in one of the bank's J2EE applications, and has to carry out the process activities scheduled for this kind of project type:

The first step is instantiating one of the many existing agenda templates originally developed by the process owner (at template design-time). As described above, agenda templates are context-specific, so the right template can be chosen by the developer according to context parameters. In the example process, these parameters are the project type, the actor's role and the technology (see Fig. 11.3). In this example, the project type is a small project. This has been predefined by management before the developer had been assigned to his task. The technology (J2EE) was also predetermined by an architect at the time the software project was launched.

The software developer's second step is to fill the workspace with input artifacts (see Fig. 11.4 for an example workspace). Most of the contents originate from the agenda template, others are added or instantiated by the developer. Consider, for example, the root item of the agenda, which is the main task "Adding a read-access timestamp to ABC app." It is the instantiated root node of the template and has been named by the developer according to his task. It already contains a link to the

Fig. 11.3 Identifying project context parameters

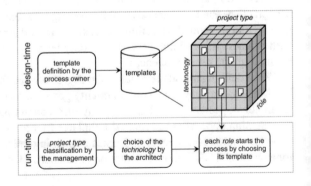

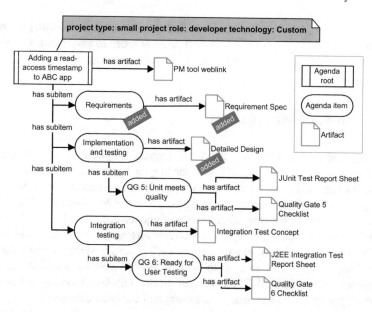

Fig. 11.4 Instantiated agenda template containing items specific to the context (small custom technology project, developer perspective)

project management tool as well as the two subordinate items "implementation & unit testing" and "integration testing." These items are the activities of the overall process that are relevant for the given context. The agenda item "requirements" and its artifact, however, have been added by the developer as he found they were important input artifacts for this task. The developer also added the detailed design specification supplemented by the new functionality to the "implementation and testing" agenda item. Initially, the item only contains a mandatory quality gate with an empty technology-specific test report sheet and a checklist that helps the developer to keep track of compliance policies associated with the task. With respect to these policies, it is necessary to fill the test report sheet with confirmations that all tests have been passed, in order to fulfill the quality gate.

After completing his task, the developer finishes the agenda items, closes the project and forwards the new status using the corporate project management tool. Since the templates contained agenda items relevant for compliance, the system checks compliance using business rules. For example, any quality gates in a closed project that have not been denoted as finished are detected and reported.

Given the discussion above, it is clear that agenda templates are the key support capability of adSPM. As a result, we will provide more details about how adSPM facilitates agenda template management in the following sections.

11.4 Template Management

In the original case management approach, agenda templates are mined automatically out of common agenda items in order to gain and improve knowledge of the treatment process. However, they can of course also be defined manually. Since mining of process knowledge is not a crucial use case in the domain of flexible software processes, supporting the manual definition of agenda templates is more important, especially when enforcing compliance policies through templates. In this section, we will first supplement the example agenda template introduced above with some further templates in order to give an idea of the necessity of intelligent template management within adSPM. Then, we will discuss challenges and opportunities of such management functions, using the example of the bank case study.

11.4.1 Example Templates

The case study only contains one example agenda template yet. To apply the case management approach to a broader range of situations, we need to introduce more templates for different situations. Since describing all combinations of the three possible template context dimensions (project type, role, and technology) would go far beyond the scope of this chapter, we will simplify the context by selecting the most distinct combinations. To do this, we first classify similar project types and then justify the selection of three distinct roles and two sample technologies.

Looking at the different project types in Table 1, big projects (PB) are noticeably different from the other project types as they include every single quality gate. We should therefore develop at least one example agenda template with that type. However, there are only few differences between mid-size, maintenance and small projects, so we will combine them into the class of small projects (PS). Integration projects are similar to conception projects as well, since there is no development effort. So we include them with the conception projects (PC).

In the original process, there are at least six roles more or less directly involved in the project. However, the main tasks are apportioned between the architect (RA) and the developer (RD). There is no distinct tester role necessary as unit and integration testing is done by "any other" developer, according to the process manuals.

When choosing the example technology, we use our experience from numerous discussions with the bank's actors to identify two types of technologies which

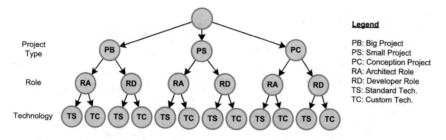

Fig. 11.5 Decision tree containing all combinations of the simplified context characteristics

Table 11.2 Decision table with the remaining combinations

Project type	PB				PS				PC			
Role	RA		RD		RA		RD		RA		RD	
Technology	TS	TC	TS	TC	TS	TC	TS	TC	TS	TC	TS	TC
Template	1	5	3	6			4	7	2			

have proven to be very different from each other, including a considerable need for distinct ways of documentation. These are standard software (TS), which is often closed source, and custom software (TC). Figure 11.5 shows the initial decision tree containing all 12 combinations of the project context characteristics.

We can now reduce these combinations further by excluding ineligible branches. For example, conception projects by definition do not include development tasks. Moreover, such projects do not yet contain technology-specific artifacts. As a result, we can strike out concept project combinations that involve developers and do not need to take care of the technology. Also, small projects do not have an architect since the design is already done or its change is negligible. Table 11.2 shows the remaining combinations using a decision table.

In collaboration with the example process owner, we elaborated the elements of the agenda templates for these variants, as depicted in Fig. 11.6. The templates seem to have many redundant elements at a first glance; especially the PM tool weblink is present in every template. Also, process phases and quality gates do not change with technology. However, most of the artifacts used in the late phases are connected to either Java (custom software) or SAP (standard software).

In collaboration with the example process owner, we elaborated the elements of the agenda templates for these variants, as depicted in Fig. 11.6. The templates seem to have many redundant elements at a first glance; especially the PM tool weblink is present in every template. Also, process phases and quality gates do not change with technology. However, most of the artifacts used in the late phases are connected to either Java (custom software) or SAP (standard software).

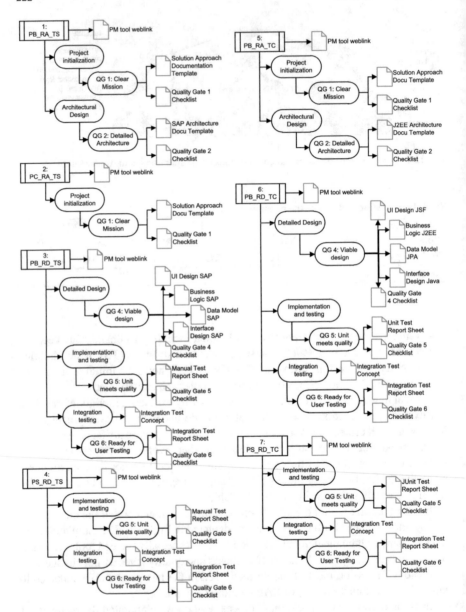

Fig. 11.6 Tree structure of selected agenda templates according to the given context (project type, role and technology)

Even though we already reduced the complexity twice by simplifying the context characteristics and selecting only the most distinct combinations, it is obvious that the management of these agenda templates is tedious and error-prone. To ease this, we will next introduce the adSPM template management functions.

11.4.2   Template Management Functions

The downside of allowing process flexibility is the effort required to manage a set of agenda templates. To alleviate this, support for template management is necessary. In this section, we discuss four main challenges for agenda template management we identified using the example of the process above: *redundancy, integrity, compliance* and *change*.

The previous section showed that the process owner has to manage several different agenda templates with partially overlapping content. When policies change, he needs to keep all of them consistent and up to date. Doing this by hand is error-prone because there are many technology-specific templates which differ just in a few artifacts, and quite a few project-specific templates only differing in the presence of one or two quality gates. In the traditional adCM approach, templates are just managed individually, without regard for any dependencies and redundancies between them.

But in the domain of flexible software processes and especially in the given case study, we claim that there are fewer variants and more compliance policies; so, agenda templates have much more artifacts and agenda items in common. So it is necessary to manage *redundancy within a set of templates*. To achieve this, we introduce a central template management tool using a graph model that is aware of common items within the templates. It serves as a single process model containing all quality gates, activities and artifacts necessary to drive the process considering each and any context characteristic. This way, the approach is capable of reducing technical debts due to process evolution (see Chap. 15 for detailed information about the connection between process evolution and technical debt).

Figure 11.7 shows the implementation of such a tool based on the example process. Its persistence layer manages a single graph structure joining all agenda templates introduced in Sect. 11.4.1. The graph nodes of context-specific elements are tagged using the three context parameters. Of course, such a joined graph is not human readable. We therefore implemented a filter mechanism facilitating a context-specific perspective in the style of an intuitive faceted search. If, for example, the process owner wants to review the current agenda template for J2EE conception projects, he adjusts both context filter parameters. The tool then shows a subgraph containing all template elements relevant for this context, without regard to the role. Since context parameters may be subject to change, they are customizable in an XML configuration file including all of their possible options.

However, template management is not all about managing redundancies. According to the example process, compliance policies require the *integrity* of the prescribed agenda and its artifacts. In this case there shall be no opportunity to change the intended agenda (besides ignoring the template and following one's own agenda). The implementation of this requirement is straightforward as it just requires a read-only flag in the agenda template data model, together with simple role/authorization management functions.

In addition, the process owner may sometimes not only want to ensure integrity, but also *compliance*. This means it needs to be ensured that agenda templates and

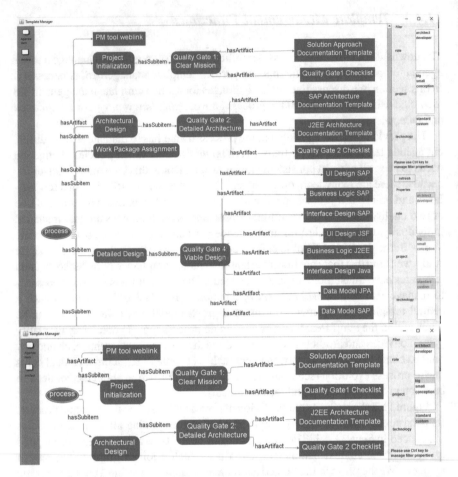

Fig. 11.7 The adSPM template management tool (overall template and PB_RD_TS perspective)

their elements are not ignored or bypassed, so template elements should be denotable as mandatory. Also, some agenda items may have to be executed and some artifacts may be required to be produced. As a result, the course of activities has to be checked for these mandatory elements. (However, the actor should still be free to supplement the template with his own items, in order to sustain creativity or incorporate actors' experience.)

A similar function is already provided in the adCM approach as it monitors the execution history in an event log and stores the final state of closed cases in a graph database. In the domain of flexible software processes, both the log and the final agenda state can be analyzed to measure compliance with the prescribed agenda template, e.g., using business rules. Therefore, an adSPM tool needs to provide an additional business rule management function. Our example implementation of the business rule management is designed as a web application following a responsive

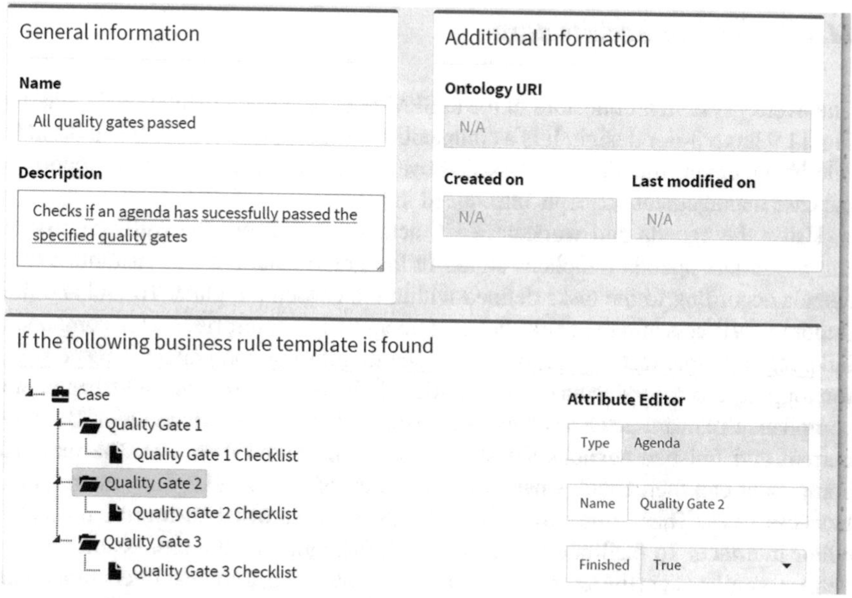

Fig. 11.8 Example of the business rule generator

web design [7]. Rules defined this way (see Fig. 11.8) are transcoded into a Resource
Description Framework Schema (RDFS) and stored within the graph database using
a REST API. In the graph database, the rules can be regularly checked against all case
instances by a built-in reasoner. Consider, for example, the rule depicted in Fig. 11.8.
It applies whenever the agenda contains the given pattern. That is, the agenda holds
three quality gates denoted as "finished", each containing the corresponding checklists.

Of course, the example implementation also contains a rule dashboard that gives
an overview whether or not the cases are compliant to all rules defined by the management interface.

Obviously, a key aspect of process flexibility is change. Keeping actors compliant therefore also means keeping them compliant according to *changing policies*.
However, ongoing projects are usually not subject to policy changes. As a result, the
agenda template management needs to be aware of different template versions. Since
we propose to store templates using a graph database, changes in a template graph
can be tagged with a version number. Whenever a finished agenda has to be checked
against a template, its version number is considered. The traceability of template
versions can be provided by the adSPM tool or a version control tool, depending on
organizational preferences.

11.4.3   System Architecture

The overall system architecture of the adSPM reference implementation depicted in Fig. 11.9 has a 3-tier design. It is a composition of the agenda template and business rule management functions discussed above, integrated with execution support for the case management concepts introduced in [2].

Using the agenda and workspace UI, actors carrying out the software process can instantiate agenda templates stored in the graph database and customize their agenda according to the tasks defined within the chosen template. To find and link important artifacts into the workspace, we integrated an enterprise search component indexing the organization's repositories. The monitoring component is responsible for logging the actors' course of activities. It is used to measure whether or not compliance-relevant activities have been executed in the prescribed order. Both the current and finished agendas are stored within the graph database. The reasoner component can then check whether the structure of the agendas fits preconfigured business rules. These rules are defined by the process owner using the dedicated editor interface. To facilitate agenda template instantiation, the process owner also defines templates via the template editor. For convenience, a context filter component provides a manageable view of the templates according to preconfigured context parameters.

To conclude, adapting case management concepts to the management of flexible software processes using the adSPM approach seems to be promising, because it promises a good trade-off between flexibility and control. On the one side, the agenda provides maximum flexibility to the actor; on the other side, agenda templates can integrate best practices, agreements on common procedures and compliance policies. However, it is challenging to manage templates that are subject to ongoing change, need to assure compliance policies, are free of redundancy, and cannot be manipulated. Whether or not the template management functions introduced above solve these problems in practice is subject to evaluation.

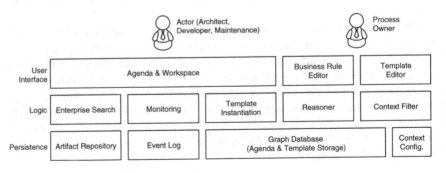

Fig. 11.9 Overview of adSPM system architecture

11.5 Case Study

The features of the adSPM tool have been evaluated in a demonstration experiment with several participants executing the bank's example process. In this section, we will first outline the design of the evaluation, followed by details of the results.

11.5.1 *Experiment Design*

Eleven stakeholders (five architects, five developers and one process owner who manages the processes and assesses the compliance of each project in the whole bank) were asked to answer a survey and execute a specific task in the adSPM problem domain.

Since the experience of a stakeholder will affect the need for support when driving/managing a process, we first asked the participants how they would describe their experience in their process role, in order to detect the expected bias when evaluating the approach's utility. In addition to this appraisal, we also asked the stakeholders to quantify the experience in terms of how many projects they work on each year.

In the next interview topic, we wanted to learn more about how the participants currently address compliance. We therefore asked the developers and architects how they organize their work in order to be compliant with the process manuals and use the latest technology-specific document templates. In addition, we asked the process owner about how he conducts the compliance audits.

In order to find out how developers and architects assess the effort they need to invest to be compliant, we asked them to roughly estimate the amount of time they spend to check the next process steps, for example. We also asked the process owner to estimate his efforts in managing the manuals and checking the compliance of each project. In order to estimate the overall impact, we also asked for the frequency of all these efforts (i.e., how often they occur per project).

After assessing the status quo, we proceeded to the experiment examining the utility of the adSPM template management tool. The experiment simulates a project situation where developers and architects have to figure out all process steps and artifacts relevant for their respective role in a randomly selected project type and technology. After a brief introduction on how to interact with the tool, the developers and architects had ten minutes to answer the following questions:

1. Which quality gates have to be passed?
2. Which questions have to be checked to pass each quality gate?
3. Which document templates have to be applied and filled out?

The evaluation of the business rule and the agenda template editor by the process owner was performed differently. Since managing and checking the process is a much more complicated step than just identifying relevant tasks, we only presented the user interface to him without conducting a simulation. However, we closed all interviews by requesting that participants judge the utility of the presented methods and tools compared to the status quo.

11.5.2 Evaluation Results

We will discuss the results starting with the answers from the developers and architects. Each year, these participants work on about three projects on average, but not more than six. Since the current process version is about one year old, this is also the absolute number of projects that are subject to the current manuals. Most of the architects and developers therefore are already somewhat experienced with the process, though they do not know it by heart yet. Considering this, we would expect that there is a need for process support.

When asked how they make sure that they always use the current document template version, 9 out of 10 participants referred to a custom document template menu in the word processor. They consistently reported that they are very content with that kind of support, though it is only relevant for creating new documents. However, the adSPM approach does not include a solution for keeping the form up to date in case document templates evolve.

When asked which actions they take or which kinds of resources they rely on in order to be compliant, most of the participants mentioned the project tracking tool (7 out of 10) and a process model handout (6 out of 10). But also workmates and handouts containing consolidated information about process specificities are important resources (5 each out of 10). 4 of 10 participants consider the intranet (wiki). However, most interestingly, only one participant considered the official process manuals to ensure being compliant with the process. Independent of the cause, we can conclude that keeping only these manuals up to date will immediately lead to compliance issues.

In the next question, we asked about the time spent on the actions discussed above, and how frequently this effort has to be invested for each project. Due to the fact that one half of the participants is mostly assigned to many small projects and the other half is mostly assigned to a few big projects, the estimated efforts ranged quite widely. Also, the participants may have different conceptions of which kind of actions have to be aggregated into the effort estimation. We therefore have to be very careful in interpreting the results, which vary from a recurring effort of 5 min to half of a day, resulting in 30 to 840 min of total effort for each project (see Table 11.3).

After asking about the effort of the status quo method, we proceeded to the experiment in which the participants had to identify all tasks and artifacts necessary for their role in a random project type with a random technology within 10 min. Seven participants answered the questions perfectly, however, one made a small mistake and two left out one of the three questions. Only half of the participants needed the full time to complete the experiment; on average, each experiment took less than 7 min.

Table 11.3 Time spent (in minutes) on identifying actions relevant to compliance and comparison of the efforts in the status quo versus in the experiment (#NV: the participant was unable to estimate, #NP: The participant did not pass the experiment)

	Participants										
	1	2	3	4	5	6	7	8	9	10	∅
Effort (status quo)	15	30	150	240	#NV	10	#NV	5	120	240	101.3
Frequency (status quo)	50	1	1	3.5	1	4	#NV	10	1	3.5	8.3
Total	750	30	150	840	#NV	40	#NV	50	120	840	352.5
Effort (experiment)	6.17	4.17	9.80	10.0	9.75	9.75	2.17	3.00	10.0	4.75	6.95
Total (1st calculation)	308.30	4.17	9.80	35.00	#NP	39.00	#NV	30.00	10.00	#NP	62.32
Total (2nd calculation)	308.30	4.17	–	–	–	39.00	–	30.00	–	–	95.37

To compare these results with the estimated efforts carefully, we excluded the two participants who did not complete the task (almost) correctly. We also decided to make two different calculations. The first ignores the differences between the very different effort estimations. The second calculation only considers the low efforts (5–30 min) as we believe these have been estimated using a conceptual basis that is closer to our definition. Table 11.3 shows the results using both calculations.

If we compare the status quo with the efforts during the experiment using the first total effort, it is reduced from 352.5 min on average to 62.32 min, which is less than a fifth. The second, probably less biased calculation is also promising as the effort is reduced to 95.37 min, which is less than a third.

In the last step of the interview, we asked the participants to evaluate the utility of the tool for finding compliance-relevant tasks and artifacts. On a rating scale from 1 (very high) to 5 (very low), two participants estimated a very high utility and the other eight participants estimated a high utility (i.e., 1.8 on average).

We also interviewed the process owner by asking similar questions concerning his role. Asked about both constructive and analytic actions he uses to ensure compliance, the process owner mentioned the process manuals first, despite the fact that they played no role for the vast majority of developers and architects. In contrast, the process owner did not mention the process model handouts as a compliance-supporting tool, even though they were used by several developers and architects. And although the process owner does use the project tracking tool to randomly check the project's compliance, he was not aware that this tool is an important resource for developers and architects. In summary, the resources prominently managed and updated by the process owner are not the same as those used by developers and architects.

We also asked the process owner to evaluate his effort for managing the process and analyzing the compliance. To him, managing the process does not seem to be a very time-consuming task, although he has to manage different redundant resources. Instead, analyzing the compliance is more expensive, since a few steps between exporting the data from the project tracking tool and importing it into the reporting application are not fully automated yet. According to the process owner, coaching the other roles in driving the process is one of the most time-consuming activities. We then showed the process owner our adSPM tool containing the agenda template editor for process management and the business rule management interface for compliance checking. Compared to his current approach and the corresponding efforts, he found it beneficial that irrelevant process elements can be filtered out. Moreover, he expects that the central definition of process elements will reduce redundancy. On the other side, he claims that such a tool has to be integrated well into the project management tool.

Just as with the developers and architects, we closed the interview by asking the process owner to estimate the utility of the new approach compared to the status quo on a rating scale. He judged that the business rule interface has the same utility as the status quo, arguing that it depends a lot on the data quality whether or not the business rules can decide on a given situation. However, he is convinced that it is much easier to define business rules than handling the current business intelligence application. Concerning the management of the process elements, this process owner estimates the utility of the status quo approach to be higher than the agenda template editor, since his current approach is straightforward and not too expensive.

Given the divergence between the expected and actual use of the compliance instruments in the status quo, we foresee compliance issues and would therefore argue for a central resource that is accessible by all roles.

11.6   Conclusion

Due to emerging technologies, regulatory frameworks and several other forces, not only information systems but also software processes need to adapt to business environment changes. Despite mature research efforts in both heavy-weight and agile software processes, companies today struggle with the adoption of these process models. This is because neither agile nor heavy-weight approaches can combine flexibility and compliance adequately. Especially in companies where the software process model depends on several project context parameters such as project type and technology, compliant development becomes a challenging task as each role has to be constantly up to date with its very specific rights and duties.

In this chapter, we presented an approach addressing this dilemma by adapting case management techniques to the domain of flexible software process management. Based on the foundation of case management principles such as an artifact-centric perspective, we have shown how the corresponding concepts (i.e., agenda templates, agendas and their workspaces) can help software process stakeholders in their daily work. For example, dedicated agenda template management components are designed to maintain and visualize the process. They address the vital challenges that stakeholders cope with in a real process: redundancy, integrity, compliance and change.

After conducting interviews with several different stakeholders we can conclude that the approach seems to be promising especially for stakeholders that carry out the process, like the software developers or architects. Results from a short experiment show that the effort spent by these roles on identifying compliance-related tasks and artifacts can be reduced by the presented approach. The participants stated that the main contribution of the adSPM approach is to enable any stakeholder to obtain a quick and current overview of his tasks with respect to compliance policies, best practices and state-of-the-art process steps. According to the approach, these elements are always kept up to date using a common overall agenda template definition managed by the process owner. However, beside this very specific perspective, each role also has the opportunity to broaden their view of the process steadily from flanking roles to the comprehensive big picture. We believe this is important since understanding areas of accountability is vital to proper interaction.

The support for managing flexible software processes can be enhanced by incorporating a distributed agenda template improvement capability into the adSPM approach. Since we suggest using a graph structure to store agendas and templates, it is very easy to compare agendas initialized from a template with their final state after the project is closed. Given this information from the history of several projects, parts of templates that are subject to frequent changes can be identified. They point to important issues in process management like concept drift [14] and enable measuring the process model fitness [3] compared to the real process carried out in the field.

11.7 Further Reading

The approach we presented here is inspired by work in two fields: agile software development and case management.

Münch et al. [10] give a comprehensive overview of software process definition and management in large-scale projects. While agile techniques such as Scrum, Extreme Programming (XP) or Kanban (as for instance discussed in [4]) at first glance seem to suitably answer the need for flexible software processes, they may be too "radical" for some application domains that are subject to compliance regulations mandating documented requirements, specifications and design decisions, but in which projects are too unique to justify the use of one tailored version of, e.g., the Rational Unified Process (RUP), the V-Model XT or other document-centric approaches. While approaches to support the enactment of such heavy-weight process models exist (such as the Process Enactment Tool Framework by Kuhrmann et al. [6]), implementing a heavy-weight process model is not just a matter of producing the appropriate documents, but also of ingraining the process in the organization's culture.

The challenges inherent in software process tailoring have been the subject of considerable discussion: In a survey spanning almost 20 years of process tailoring literature, Martínez-Ruiz et al. [8] found that "tailoring notations are not as mature as the industry requires." In another systematic literature review, Kalus and Kuhrmann confirmed in [5] that "the factors influencing the tailoring are well understood, however, the consequences of the criteria remain abstract and need to be interpreted on a project-per-project basis." The work of Xu and Ramesh [15], meanwhile, is an example for an attempt at suggesting some guidelines for process tailoring, based on empirical experience.

Meanwhile, case management techniques (as for instance described in [11]) seem to provide a suitable approach not just for the knowledge-intensive and clinical settings (e.g., in healthcare [8]) that they were originally intended for. While originally conceived in the business process management community [12] to deal with a level of process flexibility that traditional process mining tools could not cope with [13], it seems that case management's pragmatic combination of process guidance, expert knowledge, and artifact focus also makes it an interesting model for software development enabling a philosophy of "tamed agility" that retains the flexibility of agile approaches, but reconciles it with the compliance and planning requirements of large-scale software projects.

References

1. Benner, M., Book, M., Brückmann, T., Gruhn, V., Richter, T., Seyhan, S.: Managing and tracing the traversal of process clouds with templates, agendas and artifacts. In: Business Process Management, Lecture Notes in Computer Science, vol. 7481, pp. 188–193. Springer, Berlin (2012)
2. Benner-Wickner, M., Book, M., Brückmann, T., Gruhn, V.: Execution support for agenda-driven case management. In: ACM Symposium on Applied Computing, pp. 1371–1377. ACM, New York (2014)
3. Buijs, J.C.A.M., van Dongen, B.F., van der Aalst, W.M.P.: On the role of fitness, precision, generalization and simplicity in process discovery. In: On the Move to Meaningful Internet Systems: OTM 2012, Lecture Notes in Computer Science, vol. 7565, pp. 305–322. Springer, Heidelberg (2012)
4. Dingsøyr, T., Dybå, T., Moe, N.B.: Agile software development: current research and future directions. Springer, Berlin (2010)
5. Kalus, G., Kuhrmann, M.: Criteria for software process tailoring: a systematic review. In: Proceedings of the International Conference on Software and System Process, pp. 171–180. ACM, New York, (2013)
6. Kuhrmann, M., Kalus, G., Then, M.: The process enactment tool framework–transformation of software process models to prepare enactment. Sci. Comput. Program. **79**, 172–188 (2014)
7. Marcotte, E.: Responsive web design. In: Keith J., Cederholm D., Kissane, E., Marcotte, E., Walter, A., Wroblewski, L., Monteiro, M., McGrane, K. (eds.) A Book Apart. Book Apart, New York (2010–2012)
8. Martínez-Ruiz, T., Münch, J., García, F., Piattini, M.: Requirements and constructors for tailoring software processes: a systematic literature review. Softw. Qualit. J. **20**(1), 229–260 (2012)
9. McCauley, D.: Achieving Agility. In: Swenson, K.D. (ed.) Mastering the unpredictable, pp. 257–276. Meghan-Kiffer Press, Tampa (2010)
10. Münch, J., Armbrust, O., Kowalczyk, M., Soto, M.: Software process definition and management. In: The Fraunhofer IESE Series on Software and Systems Engineering. Springer, Berlin (2012) ISBN: 978-3-642-24290-8
11. Swenson, K.D. (ed.): Mastering the Unpredictable: How Adaptive Case Management will Revolutionize the Way that Knowledge Workers Get Things Done. Meghan-Kiffer Press, Tampa (2010)

12. van der Aalst, W.M.P.: Process Mining. Springer, Berlin (2011). ISBN: 978-3-642-19344-6
13. van der Aalst, W.M.P., Weske, M., Grünbauer, D.: Case handling: a new paradigm for business process support. Data Knowl. Eng. **53**(2), 129–162 (2005)
14. van der Aalst, W.M.P., Adriansyah, A., de Medeiros, A.K.A., Arcieri, F., Baier, T., Blickle, T., Bose, J.C., van den Brand, P., Brandtjen, R., Buijs, J., Burattin, A., Carmona, J., Castellanos, M., Claes, J., Cook, J., Costantini, N., Curbera, F., Damiani, E., de Leoni, M., Delias, P., van Dongen, B.F., Dumas, M., Dustdar, S., Fahland, D., Ferreira, D.R., Gaaloul, W., van Geffen, F., Goel, S., Günther, C., Guzzo, A., Harmon, P., ter Hofstede, A., Hoogland, J., Ingvaldsen, J.E., Kato, K., Kuhn, R., Kumar, A., Rosa, M.L., Maggi, F., Malerba, D., Mans, R.S., Manuel, A., McCreesh, M., Mello, P., Mendling, J., Montali, M., Motahari-Nezhad, H.R., zur Muehlen, M., Munoz-Gama, J., Pontieri, L., Ribeiro, J., Rozinat, A., Pérez, H.S., Pérez, R.S., Sepúlveda, M., Sinur, J., Soffer, P., Song, M., Sperduti, A., Stilo, G., Stoel, C., Swenson, K., Talamo, M., Tan, W., Turner, C., Vanthienen, J., Varvaressos, G., Verbeek, E., Verdonk, M., Vigo, R., Wang, J., Weber, B., Weidlich, M., Weijters, T., Wen, L., Westergaard, M., Wynn, M.: Process mining manifesto. In: Business Process Management Workshops, *Lecture Notes in Business Information Processing*, vol. 99, pp. 169–194. Springer, Berlin Heidelberg (2012)
15. Xu, P., Ramesh, B.: Using process tailoring to manage software development challenges. IT Prof. **10**(4), 39–45 (2008)

Chapter 12
A Researcher's Experiences in Supporting Industrial Software Process Improvement

Kai Petersen

Abstract Industry–academia collaboration in software engineering is essential for the relevance of research, as research may make important contributions to the improvement of software engineering. Thus, software engineering researchers are an asset in software process improvement. In this chapter, I present different experiences of being an embedded researcher in industry contributing to software process improvement. The process improvement works were focused on helping organizations to move from plan-driven processes to agile and lean processes. We will elaborate on the challenges, essential practices, and related benefits that were observed when working closely with industry in the role of embedded researchers. Supporting examples from different published cases form the basis for this experience report.

12.1 Introduction

Industry and academia have different interests. At the same time, industrial applications of research results are considered as highly important from an academic point of view to evaluate solutions to software engineering problems under realistic conditions. Multiple factors are important to consider to achieve realistic experiments [50], namely:

Tasks   The tasks should be realistic, for example in terms of scale.
People   People should represent practitioners well in terms of skills and
             experience.
Environments The environment should be realistic.

Similarly, Ivarsson and Gorschek [16] highlighted the importance of relevance in software engineering research, raising the need to conduct research in a realistic environment, thus challenging solutions with regard to their scalability. Furthermore, they highlighted the need to have subjects representative for the industry to perform tasks. Consequently, looking at software processes and the improvement thereof, it is

K. Petersen (✉)
Blekinge Institute of Technology, Valhallavägen, 37141 Karlskrona, Sweden
e-mail: kai.petersen@bth.se

© Springer International Publishing Switzerland 2016
M. Kuhrmann et al. (eds.), *Managing Software Process Evolution*,
DOI 10.1007/978-3-319-31545-4_12

essential to look at industrial processes. That is, it would be challenging to replicate industrial processes with a very high number of people involved, though tasks on team level (small agile team) are more likely to be replicated. As pointed out by Sjøberg, students in such a context may work in a company besides their studies, or have worked in a company before. Overall, the conclusion is that it is important to study software engineering processes and solutions in a realistic and industrial context. A large number of studies highlights the need for relevance of research for practice (see, for example, [14, 16, 36, 45]).

As researchers we would like to achieve this industrial relevance, thus we need collaborations the industry. As Runeson points out *"it takes two to tango"* [45]. That is, there is a need for industry to see the value in the collaboration with academia. Without seeing the value companies are not willing to invest time and money in the collaboration with academia. This may be the reason for the observation made by Lionel Briand in his key note at the *International Conference on Software Maintenance*, where he states that

> Though in essence an engineering discipline, software engineering research has always been struggling to demonstrate impact. This is reflected in part by the funding challenges that the discipline faces in many countries, the difficulties we have to attract industrial participants to our conferences, and the scarcity of papers reporting industrial case studies.[1]

The goal of this chapter is to explore the challenges, benefits, and practices that help in industry and academia collaboration to facilitate process improvement. In particular, the benefits in relation to the investments made by the companies are highlighted. As this chapter is an experience report, it reflects the author's view of what is important. Three types of support are discussed:

1. Helping the companies to assess their processes. A company could hire a consultant to asses their processes, or they could solely do this themselves, for example through a department responsible for process assessment and improvement. We argue that researchers can make a unique and valuable contribution in this activity (Sect. 12.3).
2. Supporting the company with "scientific knowledge" from research papers. Practitioners are often not aware of scientific publications (e.g., many will not be aware of scientific journals that also require a subscription to access their contents). Though, as relevant evidence is provided in these publication forums, researchers may serve as the "bridge" between academic literature and industry practice, making the findings accessible to industry (Sect. 12.4). This may simply be in the form of a report or presentation, or may contain more active involvement as well (see Point 3).
3. As a researcher, actively inducing a change to the company to help improving the processes. This type of support requires the researcher to actively induce changes to processes within the company, aiming to improve the situation at the company and at the same time scientifically capturing the lessons learned (Sect. 12.5).

---

[1] Available from: http://apsec2013.eng.chula.ac.th/keynotes/.

12.2   Background and Context

In recent years, the interest in systematically analyzing and improving the collaboration between industry and academia in software engineering has increased. This section discusses challenges and best practices as well as models of industry–academia collaboration.

12.2.1   Challenges and Best Practices

When working with industry a wide range of challenges occur. In a recent systematic review, we identified a total of 63 challenges that were reported in the literature [11], which were categorized into ten groups. Examples of frequently mentioned challenges were the differences in time horizons, the lack of relevance of research results hindering industry adoption, addressing validity concerns when working in a realistic environment, and the mismatch between industry and academia with respect to different time horizons as well as interests and objectives. Table 12.1 provides an overview of the most common challenges reported in the literature.

In order to address such challenges, a variety of best practices and success factors were presented in the literature [11]. Table 12.2 provides an overview of the success factors. Wohlin et al. [54] prioritized success factors with the help of industry practitioners. An actual prioritization is a valuable complement to the frequency of mentions in the literature, as these frequencies indicate the commonality of best practices used, but not their importance. Thus, Table 12.2 shows the rank of the common practices as reported by Wohlin et al. [54] for two countries (Sweden and Australia) based on prioritizations done by experts from industry and academia. The literature and the ranking show that management support, champions, and social skills as well as the ability to show benefits are essential. The practices relate to activities to take

Table 12.1 Frequently mentioned challenges in the literature (most common of those identified by Garousi et al. [11])

	Challenge	References
C_1	Differences in time horizons	[2, 3, 13, 18, 19, 45, 47, 48, 51]
C_2	Lack of industrial relevance	[5, 10, 14, 24, 27, 36, 39, 49]
C_3	Lack of resources from industrial and academia side	[3, 9, 13, 19, 25, 30, 42, 48]
C_4	Privacy concerns and limited access to data	[3, 7, 9, 15, 18, 25]
C_5	Different goals and interests	[13, 26, 45, 49, 51, 54]
C_6	Different perceptions of what are valuable solutions and technologies	[4, 15, 19, 26, 41, 53]
C_7	Different terminology and vocabulary	[10, 18, 19, 25, 31]

Table 12.2 Frequently mentioned success factors in the literature (cf. [11]).

	Success factors	References	Rank [54]
S_1	Provide workshops and seminars on a regular basis	[9, 14, 15, 24–27, 30, 45, 47–49, 51, 52, 54, 54]	
S_2	Ensure management commitment	[2, 7, 13, 15, 25, 25, 27, 27, 43, 45, 48, 49, 51, 52, 54]	$1_{S,A}$
S_3	Understand the real-world problems	[4, 9, 13–15, 18, 20, 24–27, 31, 49, 51, 52, 54]	
S_4	Work in an agile and incremental way	[2, 14, 15, 20, 24, 25, 27, 30, 36, 45, 47–49, 51, 54]	
S_5	As a researcher be co-located on-site	[7, 14, 15, 25, 30, 36, 41, 42, 45, 47, 52, 54]	
S_6	Assure the support of the right champion	[15, 18, 25, 26, 41, 43, 45, 48, 51, 52, 54]	$2_{S,A}$
S_7	Make benefits of research solutions explicit (impact)	[2, 3, 7, 9, 10, 14, 20, 41, 48, 49]	3_A
S_8	Assure the quality of the solution (scalable, sustainable, adaptable, simple, customizable)	[4, 10, 13, 20, 25, 25, 27, 39, 43]	
S_9	Improve communication and presentation skills	[9, 13, 18, 19, 24, 25, 43, 45, 47]	
S_{10}	Be willing to make long-term commitments	[9, 15, 19, 24, 30, 36, 48, 53]	
S_{11}	Make an effort to establish trust	[15, 20, 42, 43, 48, 51, 54]	
S_{12}	Improve university and research communities	[3, 19, 26, 30, 53, 54]	
S_{13}	Improve social skills	[15, 45, 49, 51, 52]	3_S
S_{14}	Work as a team between both partners	[9, 19, 20, 36, 51]	

S: Sweden, A: Australia

place in industry–academia collaboration. In order to achieve a successful collaboration, it is important to structure the process of collaboration and make informed decisions.

12.2.2 Industry and Academia Collaboration Processes

In the literature, we can find proposals for processes and activities to facilitate the collaboration between industry and academia in joint research projects. The technology transfer model [14] distinguishes the two perspectives of academia and industry, and emphasizes which activities are strongly tied to either perspective (Fig. 12.1). In the beginning of the collaboration, it is important to understand the problem to be solved (mapping to success factor S_3). The problem provides input to the solutions we should be looking for in the literature (state of the art). This provides input to

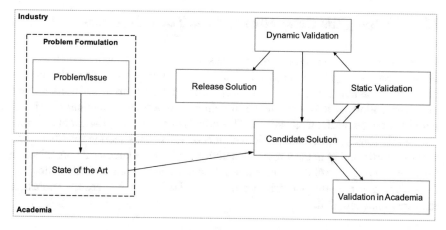

Fig. 12.1 Technology transfer model (according to [14])

jointly formulate a candidate solution solving the problem. It is recommended to test the solution before utilizing it in industry. That is, validation in academia (e.g., in the form of a controlled experiment or a case study in a student project) should be conducted before investing industry resources in testing the solution. This allows to learn and improve the candidate solution before trying it in the industry setting.

In the industrial context, two types of validation were recommended, namely static and dynamic validation. During static validation, the practitioners provide feedback on the solution, e.g., after a presentation, walk through, or trying out the solution on a small-scale example. During the dynamic validation, the solution is used in the live environment. The process is iterative in nature and lessons learned are incorporated in the candidate solution. When the solution is stable and deemed useful it is released. At that stage, the company ought to be able to use the solution without the support of the researcher.

Action research has been proposed as a means to collaborate between industry and academia [36]. Action research shares many similarities to the technology transfer model. Both approaches highlight the diagnosing (problem understanding) activity, and are iterative in nature. Another aspect that is crucial in action research is the participatory nature, where the researchers should be embedded in the organization sharing their experience and knowledge and introducing a change (e.g., a solution to improve the software processes).

The following sections provide the experiences of participating in the three types of support in process improvement highlighted in the introduction, namely (1) help the company to understand their context, processes, challenges, and where to improve, (2) support the company with "scientific knowledge" from research papers, and (3) as a researcher, actively inducing a change to the company.

12.3 Helping the Company to Assess Their Processes

Helping companies to assess their processes relates to the problem and issue identification step in Fig. 12.1. Large organizations are complex in terms of the number
of systems, the number of people involved in the development of software, and the
processes followed. It is a challenge to gain a common understanding of what is
working or not working well, and what the effects of process improvement activities
are. In this context researcher participation is of value. This section reports experiences of participating in the a research activity to support a large-scale organization
in understanding the effects of their shifts to an incremental process with agile practices from an originally plan-driven process. Table 12.3 summarizes the context of
the experience reported.

12.3.1 Challenges

In general, the challenges reported in Table 12.1 seem to be relevant to any industry–
academia collaboration.

In the reported case, the biggest challenge was to understand the context and needs.
In the company the employees often refered to concepts in the form of abbreviations,
which have to be mapped to general concepts (e.g., *Last System Version* (LSV) test
was an integration test). In particular, as PhD student, one has been mostly exposed to
terminology used in literature and often this terminology does not map to the practice.
For example, the term "unit test" may not map at all to its use in the literature [44].
Another challenge was to find acceptance of the findings if they are contradicting
with the conclusions drawn by the practitioners.

Table 12.3 Helping the company to assess their processes—case overview

Case attribute	Description
Company	Provider of solutions to enable large-scale Telecom operations
Goal of the company	Gain an understanding of the effect that their change to incremental and agile development had on their development performance
Research methods used	Industrial case study using triangulation (interviews, study of measurements, document analysis)
Researcher role	Industrial PhD student with full employee access (access card, PC, access to databases), parts of the salary paid by the company and the university
Related publications	The case study designs and results are reported in [32, 33, 35]

In the literature, another common threat was that resources were not available and there were concerns with regard to access to data. These challenges are relevant, though they were not hindering the research during the initial phase of the PhD studies (helping the company to analyze their processes and finding improvement areas), which can be explained by the best practices and the history of the collaboration with the company, which are reflected on in the next section.

12.3.2   Best Practices and Related Benefits

The following best-practices have been observed as beneficial:

- Strive and establish a long-term partnership
- Employment, co-location and access
- Consider an industrial PhD student as researcher
- Having champions and contact persons
- Communicate results
- Agree on privacy handling

Strive for and establish a long-term partnership   A key prerequisite for the collaboration and the access to people is an interest and commitment from the company. Given the complex nature of the recent shift to agile was interesting for the company to investigate as the effects were not well understood. Thus, the company was interested and made interviewees available in a timely fashion. A reason for the interest was also the long-term collaboration ongoing between the university and the company. Hence, trust has already been established. Thus, one ought to strive for long-term collaboration with companies as this eases collaboration and reduces many challenges commonly observed. In particular, a strategic partnership between companies and a research institution should be the goal.

Benefits   In total 33 interviews were conducted in the end. If the company would not have been interested in the investigation it would have been challenging to conduct a high number of interviews. In different cases where companies were not strongly interested, only a low number of interviewees or none could be obtained. With regard to the reported case, the resources provided by the company were beneficial from the academic perspective as a rich set of data and insights could be obtained, and at the same time the research was also interesting from an academic perspective. From the industrial perspective, this could be considered as a training and introduction to the company, as without being introduced and understanding the context the collaboration with the researcher becomes less useful. As the PhD funding was available for 5 years, it was important to efficiently introduce the researcher to the company; such a case study was a very good way of doing that. In particular, as a researcher one gets a good insight into the terminology used as well as a contact network.

Employment, co-location and access   Being an industrial PhD student with access and an office at the company was perceived as extremely useful. Early on I shared an office with three other PhD students, but very soon the company realized that it would be more beneficial to locate us in the departments and units where our work becomes most relevant. As my work was focused on process improvement, I was co-located in the office of the unit responsible for that (referred to as "Operational Improvement Unit"). During the whole PhD, I was spending three to four days of the week in the unit. This also involved regular discussions with colleagues, shared coffee breaks, and also social events held by the company (e.g., Christmas celebrations).

Benefits   The co-location and employment comes with several benefits. As a researcher, the understanding of the context is greatly improved; in particular, due to the co-location and ongoing discussions between members in the unit where I was located. Also, help was immediately available, e.g., in order to understand abbreviations, documentation, and so forth. The employment was beneficial during the interviews as the researcher is not perceived as external. For example, it was visible on the access cards whether one is an employee or a guest/consultant. Consequently, interviewees appeared very open to questions as they trusted the interviewer. The co-location also meant that one may pick up interesting discussions and needs from the company. This aids in understanding their challenges and thus facilitates the ability of the researchers to increase the practical relevance of their research. Access to the company's systems and documentation was also essential to understand terminology, access and prepare an analysis of measurements, etc. For example, in the study [33], we analyzed the fault-slip through measure [6] and the effect of the change from plan-driven to agile. The measure is powerful in determining the effectiveness of tests, defining where defects should have been found, and where they were actually found.

Consider an industrial PhD student as researcher   When being embedded in the company, there is a risk that the company may ask the researcher to act as a regular employee. Thus, it is essential that the company does not consider an industrial PhD student as an employee who does a PhD. Rather, the company benefits more if it considers the student a researcher. In the regulations for PhD students in Sweden, it is emphasized that the student shall spend 80 % of the PhD time on research and PhD courses, and 20 % on other activities (either teaching at the university or operational work in the industry). This assured that enough time was available for conducting the actual research, which includes time not immediately visible as productive time, such as studying research methodologies and designing the research, and the analysis of data. In particular, the analysis of the qualitative data in this case was time consuming.

Benefits   In order for companies to accept the researcher role the unique benefits a researcher may provide were as follows:

- *Providing an outsider's perspective*: The researcher is not involved in the day-to-day activities of the operations at the company. Thus, similar to a consultant the researcher is less influenced and biased by the current processes and views present in the company.

- *In-depth analysis and high rigor*: The researcher will follow a research methodology in order to assess the processes of the company. For example, this includes an emphasis on triangulation. In the case studies, we thus utilized multiple sources for information, and covered multiple roles in the process when interviewing. Rigor is of particular importance also for companies as the research is used as input for decision making.
- *Incorporation of insights from the scientific literature into the analysis*: Practitioners often do not have access to scientific publishers and libraries, thus limiting their ability to make use of the literature. Overall, the case study conclusions and the insights become richer and more valid when comparing and complementing them with findings from literature. From the point of view of understanding the processes retrospectively this aspect is important. For example, when investigating the advantages of agile development observed in the case (see case study results reported in [32]), it could be interesting to understand why some advantages reported in the literature are not observed, pointing to further potential for improvements. When looking for solutions, the scientific literature becomes even more important to not reinvent the wheel, and utilize the knowledge already obtained.
- *High quality of reporting*: Researchers are trained to package information in a readable format, e.g., writing different types of papers (short papers, experience reports, research studies in different forums such as journals and conferences). This training becomes useful when summarizing and presenting information in a concise manner, as was highlighted and appreciated in several occasions at the company.
- *Awareness of validity concerns (e.g., with respect to measurement data)*: As researchers we analyze the limitations of our findings with regard to validity threats. At the same time this analysis helps improve the collection of data. Furthermore, an awareness of the validity of measurements is important when giving recommendations to the companies. Overall, the consideration of validity with regard to scientific guidelines (e.g., by Runeson and Höst [46]) contributes to the correctness of the findings.

Having champions and contact persons   As a new researcher in the organization one would not know who to interview. This requires a good understanding of the processes and roles in the organization. Thus, the champion plays an essential role. The champion formulated which roles were available throughout the process, and the researcher articulated the need to have a good coverage of the roles to achieve an end-to-end understanding. Another role of the champion was to provide access to the people company, helping to communicate with interviewees in order to convince them to participate in the research activities. In particular, the e-mail to invite the practitioners for an interview was most likely to be accepted when the champion wrote the mail.

Benefits   In the context of process assessment, the champion was a prerequisite to be able to conduct the study with a high number of interviewees, who otherwise would have been unlikely to participate.

Communicate results As a means to communicate the results presentations were given (e.g., at development unit meetings). Furthermore, an internal Wiki page was created where all the results were summarized and links to research papers were provided.

Benefits In particular, persons working with process improvement looked at the summaries and full papers, and thus makes the progress of the research project and value added to the company explicit for the organization. In one example, a member of the process improvement group could utilize the information available to reflect on how the organization has changed 2 years after the studies have been conducted, indicating how the company has progressed further.

Agree on privacy handling Privacy concerns were handled on the project level (i.e., what we were allowed to publish) and the individual level (handling of the information collected from each individual).

- *Project level*: On the project level, a key agreement was that a paper needed to be approved by a responsible from the company. Thus, a contact person was provided by the company to check papers written for approval. In order to get the paper approved, a number of rules were formulated which allowed to report the findings in sufficient depth to make a valuable scientific contribution, but at the same time were acceptable to the companies. The main rules were to not mention any product names or organizational units. Furthermore, no absolute values ought to be reported, but rather only relative values. For example, when reporting different types of defects, not the absolute number of defects were stated, but the percentage of the total defects associated with different defect types.
- *Individual level*: Each individual interviewee was informed that they do not have to answer any questions they do not want to answer. Furthermore, data would only be presented in aggregated form, not being associated with an individual.

Benefits From a researcher's perspective, there was no hindrance in publishing the results of research studies. In most cases, it was also approved that we could name the company when following the above rules. In particular, when investigating and reporting on process improvements, it was also positive for the company to report that they are investigating and continuously working on improving their processes.

12.4 Support with Scientific Knowledge ("State of the Art")

This activity is reflected in the step of studying the state of the art as input for a candidate solution (Fig. 12.1). A wide range of results are available in the literature to support and conduct processes. This ranges from how to plan, conduct, and assess/measure improvements. The literature is published in scientific journals and conferences and thus often not easily accessible to practitioners. To make use of what is published in the literature in process improvement, it is helpful to involve a researcher to make the knowledge accessible in companies. The case related to the experiences reported in this section is summarized in Table 12.4.

Table 12.4 Support with scientific knowledge—case overview

Case attribute	Description
Company	Automotive company
Goal of the company	Gain input for analysis of their testing process with regard to improvement potentials to become more agile
Research methods used	Industrial case study to understand the problems and systematic literature review [23]
Researcher role	M.Sc. student embedded in the company in collaboration with senior researcher (supervisor)
Related publications	The study results are reported in [21]

12.4.1 Challenges

A vast amount of literature (such as empirical studies) exist on different topics of process improvement. The challenge is how to scope the literature study to decide what is most relevant for the company.

In particular, one has to decide to what degree do the findings match to the context of the company. From previous experience in the cases it was apparent that companies are less likely to accept results that do not share similarities with their contexts. For example, the automotive company (Table 12.4) was most interested in studies conducted in the automotive context, or at least in the context of embedded systems development.

Furthermore, a problem found at the company was often not isolated and covered a variety of areas when looking at process improvement. In the example of the company case, the challenges were not isolated to one activity of the test process. That is, from a problem perspective the company needed to focus on challenges in test planning, test design, test implementation, and assessment of testing outcomes. Challenges occurred even outside the testing process which are, for example, dependent on the requirements process. This makes the published literature reviews less useful as they may not have the specific problem focus required by industry; for example, they investigated a single solution (e.g., test-driven development [29]) or a very specific problem (e.g., how to choose regression test cases [8]).

12.4.2 Best Practices and Related Benefits

The following best-practices have been observed as beneficial:

- Focusing the literature search on the domain and problem perspective
- Utilizing value stream mapping to map the literature findings to the processes

Focusing the literature search on the domain and problem perspective Recently, as part of evidence-based software engineering, a more systematic way of finding and synthesizing findings from existing studies has been recommended (i.e., systematic literature reviews and mapping studies). Important activities in such studies are search, study inclusion and exclusion, data extraction, and synthesis. When working with a concrete problem from industry, we propose to scope the search for relevant research results from two perspectives, the domain perspective and the problem perspective. With regard to the domain perspective, we searched for automotive as well as embedded in combination with software. With regard to the problem perspective, we looked into solutions for test processes, hence focusing on the key words test, verification, and validation. In addition, we searched for requirements as this was an area largely affecting the testing in the company. As the company wanted to have an agile testing process, we also searched for embedded and automotive studies focusing on agile, Scrum, Extreme Programming, and Lean Software Development. In addition, it was important that the paper comprises an empirical evaluation in an industrial context.

Benefits The key benefit of focusing the search was to reduce the effort of analyzing the literature in order to provide timely feedback to the company. Conducting a full literature review on all problem areas would not have been feasible. In addition, the solutions are more trustworthy from the point of view of the practitioners when they were obtained from their domain. That is, a practitioner in the telecommunication domain would, for example, not consider the evidence from a different context as relevant. For example, one's experience at the company results from the Banking sector were presented, which was not considered as relevant by the practitioners. Having a background as a researcher plays a key role in designing such a literature study, as the researcher was aware of different approaches to conduct literature studies, such as how to search, select, and synthesize literature in a systematic way.

Utilizing value stream mapping to map the literature findings to the processes
In many projects focused on process assessment, we utilized value stream mapping as a tool for process assessment and improvement. Value stream mapping comprises of activities to assess a current process with regard to wastes, and provides a guide of how to identify and document improvements. The value stream mapping activities were complemented by utilizing the evidence obtained from the literature. Value stream mapping consists of the following steps [22]:

1. *Identify the current state process*: In this step, the current process is drawn highlighting activities and waiting times between activities. Waiting times are an indicator for inefficiencies, as are activities taking very long time. It is important to capture the end-to-end process to understand the whole, and thus avoiding suboptimization when seeking improvements.
2. *Waste identification and root-cause analysis*: The main wastes (i.e., everything that does not contribute value to the customer) are identified, such wastes include waiting times, extra processes, rework, and technical debt, etc. Thereafter, the most significant wastes are prioritized and the root causes for them are investigated. As far as possible, this should be complemented by measurements and documentation, which allow to triangulate information from what is said during the waste identification and root cause analysis.

3. *Creation of a future state process*: Based on the identified problems, potential solutions are identified and a new process is documented incorporating the solutions. Multiple ways are possible to do this, such as using the value stream notation, or using quantitative assessment of the impact of changes, such as using simulations [1]. In order to identify the potential changes, we found it useful to first locate where the root cause for a problem is in the process, which solution and literature source addresses the problem, and then where the problem is addressed in the future state process. Figure 12.2 (an outcome of the research conducted in [21]) shows a future state process with the improvements mapped to the activities (solution proposal SP1 to SP7), where solution proposals are mapped to process activities where they should be implemented. For example, the solution SP2 is suggested in [40] and mapped to a concrete activity. As is evident, the solution was from the area of automotive embedded systems, given the focusing of the investigation of the state of the art [40].

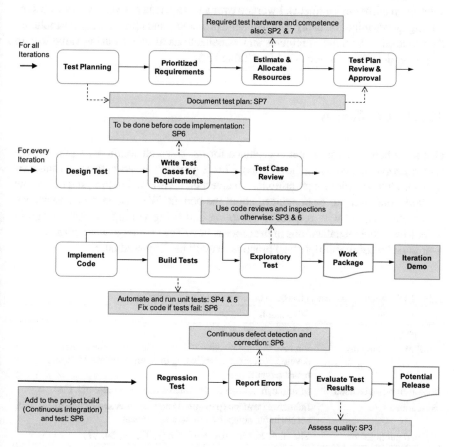

Fig. 12.2 Future state map example from [21] that provides solution proposals (SP) to improvements for specific activities

Benefits The existing evidence and its mapping to the root-causes helped to achieve traceability from problems to solutions. Furthermore, given the existing evaluations, a rational could be given for why an improvement may be considered a viable option. Value stream mapping helps in providing a framework to structure the assessment activity, making the focus on customer value explicit, and allowing to focus on the most significant wastes. Details on the use of value stream mapping can be found in [1, 22, 28], and are further discussed in the following section (Sect. 12.5).

12.5 Actively Induce a Change to the Company

Introducing a change in the company requires multiple activities presented in Fig. 12.1, namely proposing a candidate solution and conducting various validations of it, such as static validation (getting feedback) and dynamic validation (trying a solution in a live environment). I worked over a time period of over 5 years with supporting an organization using lean and agile principles and approaches, this included the proposal of lean measurements and visualizations as well as using value stream mapping, described in Sect. 12.4 (see Table 12.5).

12.5.1 Challenges

One key challenge was to get acceptance for the research solutions, a prerequisite for the people to start using the solution. This is generally referred to as resistance of change. Thus, in order for practitioners to invest their effort in learning and using new methods, they have to be convinced about the benefit. We experienced a resistance to change early on with respect to accepting and being willing to provide data in order to conduct visualizations of the process flow. The challenge was addressed and overcome by using multiple best practices as will be discussed later.

Table 12.5 Actively induce a change to the company—case overview

Case attribute	Description
Company	Telecom company
Goal of the company	Improve the organization to become lean in terms of their development process, including different lean processes and measurements
Research methods used	Multiple in industrial case studies and action research [36]
Researcher role	Industrial PostDoc (part-time) and thereafter senior researcher with access to the company, but no employment
Related publications	The study results are reported in [1, 17, 22, 34, 37]

Another challenge we faced was the risk of loosing a champion. The company was going through reorganizations, which also led to changes in the organizational unit where I as a researcher was located. Consequently, this also was connected to a change in champions when people were leaving the unit. Key champions also left the company, which makes it more challenging to follow up and reenter the organization with continuation-projects.

12.5.2   Best Practices and Related Benefits

The following best-practices have been observed as beneficial:

- Employment, co-location, and access
- Get involved in the regular work
- Educate and train people about research solutions
- Work in a team
- Work iteratively and incrementally
- Establish a steering group

Employment, co-location, and access   We highlighted earlier that co-location is a benefit when helping the company to assess their processes. When being actively involved in improvement activities this becomes even more important, as improvement activities require a continuous dialog and understanding of the situation. Furthermore, choices for specific improvements may also be affected by political considerations, which could only be understood when being more closely involved and present in the environment.

Benefit   The co-location was very beneficial and we believe was a key for improvement suggestions to be adopted, as the co-location allowed to connect to a network of people, gain champions (i.e., contributing to getting involved, see the next practice). An additional benefit of being co-located during the design and implementation of improvements was to learn about other challenges of the company, not directly related to the current research project. That is, the awareness of other challenges allows for the identification of further collaboration opportunities, which facilitates long-term collaboration.

Get involved in the regular work   During process improvement activities, the company had several tasks for the researcher to contribute. In particular, input and analysis of data related to process measurements (in particular measuring the flow of software development) was given on a monthly basis. The analysis was based on the methods developed earlier in collaboration with the company [17, 34, 37] to drive lean improvements. Given the regular interactions and preparations much communication was needed, in particular, with data providers and participants of meetings where the analyses conducted were reviewed. This allowed to become a part of the team that was responsible for the analysis, and also creating a network of people in different positions, including management. As mentioned earlier, it is important that the researcher still mainly stays in the role of a researcher, while active involvement in the company's activity is also important.

Benefit Given the good network and also the knowledge about the research spread in the network, the risk of a loosing a champion is reduced. For example, when a new person was taking the responsibility of the team analyzing the results, the person was already familiar with the researcher given the active involvement in the company. Furthermore, the contact network allowed to ask for help (e.g., in finding people that could provide input in interviews or focus groups).

Educate and train people about research solutions Training and educating people in the improvements proposed was important. As an example, slides and examples were created to show people how to interpret the process flow analysis proposed in [34]. We also provided lectures to the stakeholders presenting the training material. Furthermore, we utilized the train-the-trainer concepts. For example, in the studies related to value stream activities, the researchers took part in moderating and conducting the activity, and company representatives could observe to later on drive the activities themselves.

Benefit One key goal of research is to achieve mutual knowledge exchange. As researchers, we received very valuable feedback during training sessions. This includes feedback on the improvement solution itself, but also about how to communicate the solution in a better way. The practitioners may only adopt an approach that they find intuitive and simple to use (e.g., [20]), and training helped in facilitating a good understanding.

Work in a team Besides training and education, the work in a team is important. Working in a team refers to designing a solution together with the practitioners, continuously seeking input and also having design meetings for solutions was very valuable. Furthermore, practitioners were also present during trainings and facilitated workshops together with the researchers (e.g., in the context of the value stream mapping activity).

Benefit When both sides, industry and academia, influence how the solution should look like the commitment and engagement to implement the solution is increased. That is, the practitioners are also more willing to champion the solution itself within the company. We found this commitment essential for the solution to spread and become part of the practices used. For example, for the flow and bottleneck visualizations practitioners were strongly involved, and were over time driving for such visualizations to become part of the corporate dashboard. Or, value stream mapping has been used across multiple development sites with the help of a champion at the company. Another benefit of working in a team is that researchers and practitioners may complement each other well. Earlier, the researchers have more knowledge about the solution which they transfer though they will lack knowledge of the domain and also may not know people's interests and motivations in the company. This knowledge is available from the practitioners' side. Both, the knowledge about the solution and the knowledge about the company's context and people were important for a successful implementation of improvement solutions.

Overall, working in a team as well as being co-located and putting effort in training and education were important to address the challenge of accepting a solution as well as reducing the dependence on one particular champion.

Work iteratively and incrementally As with software development, getting it right the very first time is not likely. Finding solutions is an iterative process, and each iteration provides important lessons learned. In one case, we proposed a solution we were convinced about, and the solution failed. The solution was an elicitation instrument for measurement program planning, with one measurement program being related to lean and agile transformation. Directly after the sessions in which we recognized the failure, we analyzed the reason for the failure which led to a completely different approach to elicitation (see details in [38]). That is, in order to successfully utilize research solutions in industrial processes, we have to be willing to change and adapt. Thus, I utilized action research as a method, experiences on using action research can be found in [36].

Benefits In action research it is important to report the results of each iteration, as the reasoning for making changes in iterations provides an important learning from a research perspective, as it answers why a solution has been designed the way it was. Furthermore, working in iterations, starting small and then expanding and trying a solution for process improvement in different contexts facilitates generalizability. Though, this may not be possible in small organizations, while in the large organizations it was possible to study multiple teams and systems.

Establish a steering group Generally management support is important, and keeping them in the loop was essential. A good way of doing this is to establish a steering group where the researchers could present the results they achieved at the company on a regular basis (monthly or bi-monthly). As part of the steering group, senior management as well as champions should participate. Furthermore, depending on the need, people interested in the results were invited.

Benefits Having a steering group makes the progress and results transparent, which positively affects the long-term buy in from the company. The steering group is an additional opportunity to get feedback on an improvement solution and supports to plan the continuation of the research.

12.6 Conclusion

Industrial processes are complex and are hard to simulate in academic environments, e.g., student projects. Large organizations often develop products with hundreds of people involved. Thus, when conducting process improvement research it is important to conduct the research in realistic environments. In this chapter, experiences of collaborating with the industry to achieve success in software process improvement are presented. The experiences cover the different activities of industry–academia collaboration from problem analysis, how to utilize academic literature to analyze processes, and the development of improvement solutions.

Overall, it was helpful to have a long-term partnership with the company. Furthermore, employment and co-location was beneficial as it allowed to build a network and learn about the context of the company. As co-location is so effective in producing valuable results, I encourage companies to hire industrial PhD students. The researchers need to be supported by champions, and this chapter provides suggestions how to assure commitment from the company and champions, in particular communication of results, training, working in a team, and building a network was key.

Researchers are also encouraged to conduct investigations of how industry and academia can collaborate in a good way in the context of software engineering.

12.7 Further Reading

A comprehensive and synthesized list of challenges, best practices, and anti-patterns can be found in Garousi et al. [12]. The report by Garousi et al. is based on a systematic literature review aggregating existing works on industry–academia collaboration. Different concrete processes and guidelines have been proposed. The process proposed by Gorschek et al. [14] describes the process presented in Sect. 12.2 in further detail, and complements it by key lessons learned.

Other chapters in this book complement the findings presented in this chapter. As we propose to work iteratively, and also in an action research way, the work presented in Chap. 5 providing further experiences in disruptive process improvement. In order to find and suggest improvements as a researcher, engineering approaches presented in Chap. 10 are of value and may prove useful in value stream mapping activities suggested here.

References

1. Ali, N.B., Petersen, K., de França, B.B.N.: Evaluation of simulation-assisted value stream mapping for software product development: two industrial cases. Inf. Softw. Technol. **68**, 45–61 (2015)
2. Baldassarre, M.T., Caivano, D., Visaggio, G.: Empirical studies for innovation dissemination: ten years of experience. In: Proceedings of the International Conference on Evaluation and Assessment in Software Engineering, pp. 144–152. ACM, New York (2013)
3. Briand, L.C.: Useful software engineering research - leading a double-agent life. In: Proceedings of the IEEE International Conference on Software Maintenance, p. 2. IEEE, Washington, DC (2011)
4. Briand, L.C.: Embracing the engineering side of software engineering. IEEE Softw. **29**(4), 96 (2012)

5. Connor, A.M., Buchan, J., Petrova, K.: Bridging the research-practice gap in requirements engineering through effective teaching and peer learning. In: Proceedings of International Conference on Information Technology: New Generations, pp. 678–683 (2009)
6. Damm, L., Lundberg, L., Wohlin, C.: Faults-slip-through - a concept for measuring the efficiency of the test process. Softw. Process: Improv. Prac. 11(1), 47–59 (2006)
7. Eldh, S.: Some researcher considerations when conducting empirical studies in industry. In: Proceedings of the International Workshop on Conducting Empirical Studies in Industry, pp. 69–70. IEEE Press, Piscataway, NJ (2013)
8. Engström, E., Runeson, P., Skoglund, M.: A systematic review on regression test selection techniques. Inf. Softw. Technol. 52(1), 14–30 (2010)
9. Enoiu, E.P., Causevic, A.: Enablers and impediments for collaborative research in software testing: an empirical exploration. In: Proceedings of the International Workshop on Long-term Industrial Collaboration on Software Engineering, pp. 49–54. ACM, New York (2014)
10. Franch Gutiérrez, J., Ameller, D., Ayala Martínez, C.P., Cabot Sagrera, J.E.A.: Bridging the gap among academics and practitioners in non-functional requirements management: some reflections and proposals for the future. Modelling and Quality in Requirements Engineering, pp. 267–273. Verlagshaus Monsenstein und Vannerdat (2012)
11. Garousi, V., Petersen, K., Özkan, B.: Industry-academia collaborations in software engineering: A systematic literature review. Technical Report, Hacettepe University Software Engineering Research Group, HUSE-2015-01. https://drive.google.com/open?id=0B6dKdxaNjBENSWRwRlNJbExYUWc (2015)
12. Garousi, V., Petersen, K., Özkan, B.: Online slr repository for industry-academia collaborations in SE. http://goo.gl/gWrGrg (2015)
13. Glass, R.L., Hunt, A.: Software Conflict 2.0: The art and science of software engineering. developer.* Books (2006)
14. Gorschek, T., Garre, P., Larsson, S., Wohlin, C.: A model for technology transfer in practice. IEEE Softw. 23(6), 88–95 (2006)
15. Grünbacher, P., Rabiser, R.: Success factors for empirical studies in industry-academia collaboration: a reflection. In: Proceedings of the International Workshop on Conducting Empirical Studies in Industry, pp. 27–32. IEEE Press, Piscataway (2013)
16. Ivarsson, M., Gorschek, T.: A method for evaluating rigor and industrial relevance of technology evaluations. Empir. Softw. Eng. 16(3), 365–395 (2011)
17. Jabangwe, R., Petersen, K., Smite, D.: Visualization of defect inflow and resolution cycles: Before, during and after transfer. In: Proceedings of the Asia-Pacific Software Engineering Conference, pp. 289–298. IEEE Computer Society, Washington, DC (2013)
18. Jain, S., Babar, M.A., Fernandez, J.: Conducting empirical studies in industry: balancing rigor and relevance. In: Proceedings of the International Workshop on Conducting Empirical Studies in Industry, pp. 9–14. IEEE Press, Piscataway, NJ (2013)
19. Kaindl, H., Brinkkemper Jr., S., Bubenko, J.A., Farbey, B., Greenspan, S.J., Heitmeyer, C.L., do Prado Leite, J.C.S., Mead, N.R., Mylopoulos, J., Siddiqi, J.I.A.: Requirements engineering and technology transfer: obstacles, incentives and improvement agenda. Requir. Eng. 7(3), 113–123 (2002)
20. Kanso, A., Monette, D.: Foundations for long-term collaborative research. In: Proceedings of the International Workshop on Long-term Industrial Collaboration on Software Engineering, pp. 43–48. ACM, New York (2014)
21. Kasoju, A., Petersen, K., Mäntylä, M.: Analyzing an automotive testing process with evidence-based software engineering. Inf. Softw. Technol. 55(7), 1237–1259 (2013)
22. Khurum, M., Petersen, K., Gorschek, T.: Extending value stream mapping through waste definition beyond customer perspective. J. Softw.: Evol. Process 26(12), 1074–1105 (2014)
23. Kitchenham, B., Charters, S.: Guidelines for performing systematic literature reviews in software engineering. Joint Technical Report EBSE 2007-001, v. 2.3, Keele University and Durham University (2007)
24. Krishnan, P., Ross, K.J., Salas, P.A.P.: Industry academia collaboration: An experience report at a small university. In: Proceedings of the Conference on Software Engineering Education and Training, pp. 117–121. IEEE, Washington, DC (2009)

25. Martínez-Fernández, S., Marques, H.M.: Practical experiences in designing and conducting empirical studies in industry-academia collaboration. In: Proceedings of the International Workshop on Conducting Empirical Studies in Industry, pp. 15–20. ACM, New York (2014)
26. Misirli, A.T., Erdogmus, H., Juzgado, N.J., Dieste, O.: Topic selection in industry experiments. In: Proceedings of the International Workshop on Conducting Empirical Studies in Industry, pp. 25–30. ACM, New York (2014)
27. Morris, P., Masera, M., Wilikens, M.: Requirements engineering and industrial uptake. In: Proceedings of the International Conference on Requirements Engineering (Putting Requirements Engineering to Practice), pp. 130–137. IEEE, Washington, DC (1998)
28. Mujtaba, S., Feldt, R., Petersen, K.: Waste and lead time reduction in a software product customization process with value stream maps. In: Proceedings of the Australian Software Engineering Conference, pp. 139–148. IEEE Computer Society, Washington, DC (2010)
29. Munir, H., Moayyed, M., Petersen, K.: Considering rigor and relevance when evaluating test driven development: a systematic review. Inf. Softw. Technol. **56**(4), 375–394 (2014)
30. Osterweil, L.J., Ghezzi, C., Kramer, J., Wolf, A.L.: Determining the impact of software engineering research on practice. IEEE Comput. **41**(3), 39–49 (2008)
31. Petersen, K., Engström, E.: Finding relevant research solutions for practical problems: the serp taxonomy architecture. In: Proceedings of the International Workshop on Long-term Industrial Collaboration on Software Engineering, pp. 13–20. ACM, New York (2014)
32. Petersen, K., Wohlin, C.: A comparison of issues and advantages in agile and incremental development between state of the art and an industrial case. J. Syst. Softw. **82**(9), 1479–1490 (2009)
33. Petersen, K., Wohlin, C.: The effect of moving from a plan-driven to an incremental software development approach with agile practices - an industrial case study. Empir. Softw. Eng. **15**(6), 654–693 (2010)
34. Petersen, K., Wohlin, C.: Measuring the flow in lean software development. Softw.: Prac. Exp. **41**(9), 975–996 (2011)
35. Petersen, K., Wohlin, C., Baca, D.: The waterfall model in large-scale development. In: Proceedings of the International Conference on Product-Focused Software Process Improvement. Lecture Notes in Business Information Processing, vol. 32, pp. 386–400. Springer, Berlin (2009)
36. Petersen, K., Gencel, Ç., Asghari, N., Baca, D., Betz, S.: Action research as a model for industry-academia collaboration in the software engineering context. In: Proceedings of International Workshop on Long-term Industrial Collaboration on Software Engineering, pp. 55–62. ACM, New York (2014)
37. Petersen, K., Roos, P., Nyström, S., Runeson, P.: Early identification of bottlenecks in very large scale system of systems software development. J. Softw.: Evol. Process **26**(12), 1150–1171 (2014)
38. Petersen, K., Gencel, Ç., Asghari, N., Betz, S.: An elicitation instrument for operationalising gqm+strategies (GQM+S-EI). Empir. Softw. Eng. **20**(4), 968–1005 (2015)
39. Pfleeger, S.L.: Understanding and improving technology transfer in software engineering. J. Syst. Softw. **47**(2–3), 111–124 (1999)
40. Puschnig, A., Kolagari, R.T.: Requirements engineering in the development of innovative automotive embedded software systems. In: Proceedings of the IEEE International Conference on Requirements Engineering, pp. 328–333. IEEE, Washington, DC (2004)
41. Raschke, W., Zilli, M., Loinig, J., Weiss, R., Steger, C., Kreiner, C.: Embedding research in the industrial field: a case of a transition to a software product line. In: Proceedings of the International Workshop on Long-term Industrial Collaboration on Software Engineering, pp. 3–8. ACM, New York (2014)
42. Rombach, H.D., Achatz, R.: Research collaborations between academia and industry. In: Proceedings of the Workshop on the Future of Software Engineering, pp. 29–36. IEEE Computer Society Press, Washington, DC (2007)
43. Rombach, H.D., Ciolkowski, M., Jeffery, D.R., Laitenberger, O., McGarry, F.E., Shull, F.: Impact of research on practice in the field of inspections, reviews and walkthroughs: learning from successful industrial uses. ACM SIGSOFT Softw. Eng. Notes **33**(6), 26–35 (2008)

44. Runeson, P.: A survey of unit testing practices. IEEE Softw. **23**(4), 22–29 (2006)
45. Runeson, P.: It takes two to tango - an experience report on industry - academia collaboration. In: Proceedings of the IEEE International Conference on Software Testing, Verification and Validation, pp. 872–877. IEEE, Washington, DC (2012)
46. Runeson, P., Höst, M.: Guidelines for conducting and reporting case study research in software engineering. Empir. Softw. Eng. **14**(2), 131–164 (2009)
47. Runeson, P., Minör, S.: The 4+1 view model of industry-academia collaboration. In: Proceedings of the International Workshop on Long-term Industrial Collaboration on Software Engineering, pp. 21–24. ACM, New York (2014)
48. Runeson, P., Minör, S., Svenér, J.: Get the cogs in synch: time horizon aspects of industry-academia collaboration. In: Proceedings of the International Workshop on Long-term Industrial Collaboration on Software Engineering, pp. 25–28. ACM, New York (2014)
49. Sandberg, A., Pareto, L., Arts, T.: Agile collaborative research: action principles for industry-academia collaboration. IEEE Softw. **28**(4), 74–83 (2011)
50. Sjøberg, D.I.K., Anda, B., Arisholm, E., Dybå, T., Jørgensen, M., Karahasanovic, A., Koren, E.F., Vokác, M.: Conducting realistic experiments in software engineering. In: Proceedings of the International Symposium on Empirical Software Engineering, pp. 17–26. IEEE, Washington, DC (2002)
51. Wohlin, C.: Empirical software engineering research with industry: top 10 challenges. In: Proceedings of the International Workshop on Conducting Empirical Studies in Industry, pp. 43–46. IEEE Press, Piscataway, NJ (2013)
52. Wohlin, C.: Software engineering research under the lamppost. In: Proceedings of the International Joint Conference on Software Technologies, pp. IS–11. ICSOFT (2013)
53. Wohlin, C., Regnell, B.: Strategies for industrial relevance in software engineering education. J. Syst. Softw. **49**(2–3), 125–134 (1999)
54. Wohlin, C., Aurum, A., Angelis, L., Phillips, L., Dittrich, Y., Gorschek, T., Grahn, H., Henningsson, K., Kågström, S., Low, G., Rovegard, P., Tomaszewski, P., Toorn, C.V., Winter, J.: The success factors powering industry-academia collaboration. IEEE Softw. **29**(2), 67–73 (2012)

Chapter 13
Lessons Learned from Co-Evolution of Software Process and Model-Driven Engineering

Regina Hebig, Andreas I. Schmied and Ingo Weisemöller

Abstract Software companies need to cope with permanent changes in market. To stay competitive it is often inevitable to improve processes and adopt to new technologies. Indeed, it is well known that software processes and model-driven engineering (MDE) are subject to evolution. Simultaneously, it is known that MDE can affect process tailoring, which makes it possible that evolution in MDE triggers process evolution and vice versa. This can lead to undesired process changes and additional cost, when process adaptations constitute a need for further investments in MDE tooling. However, there is little knowledge so far whether this co-evolution exists and how it looks like. In this chapter, we present two industrial case studies on co-evolution of MDE and software process. Based on these case studies, we present an initial list of co-evolution drivers and observations made on co-evolution of software processes and MDE. Furthermore, we compile our lessons learned to directly help process managers dealing with co-evolution.

13.1 Introduction

Customization and optimization of software processes is important for companies to stay efficient and to be able to deal with arising new challenges. Tailoring of processes, e.g., by adapting activities, artifacts, and roles [19], is the first step in adjusting a process to the company's or project's needs. Furthermore, process standards evolve,

R. Hebig (✉)
Software Engineering Division, Chalmers University
of Technology & University of Gothenburg, Chalmersplatsen 4,
SE-412 96 Gothenburg, Sweden
e-mail: hebig@chalmers.se

A.I. Schmied
Capgemini Deutschland GmbH, Löffelstraße 46, 70597 Stuttgart, Germany
e-mail: andreas.schmied@capgemini.com

I. Weisemöller
Carmeq GmbH, Carnotstr. 4, 10587 Berlin, Germany
e-mail: ingo.weisemoeller@carmeq.com

© Springer International Publishing Switzerland 2016
M. Kuhrmann et al. (eds.), *Managing Software Process Evolution*,
DOI 10.1007/978-3-319-31545-4_13

as for example the V-Modell XT for which by now four major versions have been released. What the variation amongst several instances of a software process line actually looks like in practice is approached in [15], where the evolution of V-Modell XT variants is studied to identify what changes occur most. Thus, evolution of software processes is a well-known and desired phenomenon. In fact, the overview in [12] shows: it can be expected that underlying technologies and platforms have the potential to cause evolution of software processes, which need to accommodate the changes. One such technology is model-driven engineering (MDE) that targets at improving quality and efficiency of software development by introducing modeling languages in addition to source code. MDE aims to provide a higher level of abstraction which can be used to support communication and planning, but also for early quality assurance and code generation [5].

Similar to software processes, MDE is subject to evolution as well. Such evolution occurs to the used (modeling) language versions, but also to single automated steps, such as transformations or code generators [29]. As we found in our previous work, in practice, it is not seldom that MDE evolution goes even further and can affect the whole structure or combination of used languages, tools, and automated steps [8]. Hence, when using MDE, evolution needs to be expected. Nevertheless, there is a general awareness that software processes and MDE are not independent [9]. Those impact can be far reaching—even affecting the structure of phases or sprints as described in [16], or simply affect the roles [18]. In our previous survey, we found that—despite the awareness for this topic—there is still a big lack in the understanding of the interconnection of both, software process and MDE [7].

It attracted our attention that the aspects of software process that are related to MDE, such as roles, are also known subjects to software process evolution [15, 19]. Taking the points above: if there is (a) evolution in software processes, (b) evolution in MDE, and (c) a mutual influence between software processes (tailoring) and MDE, it is probable that, when MDE is used, the evolution of software process and MDE is interrelated, too. Therefore, we formulate the following working hypothesis:

Working Hypothesis (Co-Evolution). *There is a co-evolution of an applied software process and the used MDE.*

So far there is no knowledge how this co-evolution (if existent) looks like. For example, is the co-evolution working in both directions or is it single directed, i.e., propagating evolution only from the software process to the MDE, or only the other way around? If the process can be affected by co-evolution, what aspects of a process can be affected by this "tailoring on the fly"?

These questions are relevant, as answers can imply consequences for the *cost and success* of process tailoring. Imagine the MDE evolution could trigger unintended or even unnoticed process evolution. That would lead to the risk that the software process does not fit the intended tailoring anymore thus risking its success. A possible consequence is that specifications and standards regarding process quality cannot be met. Further, if software process evolution could lead to the need of MDE evolution, this might cause expensive changes on MDE tools, which would become an additional cost factor. Therefore, we are convinced that gaining more knowledge about co-evolution of software processes and MDE will lead to important insights for both, practitioners and researchers.

In this chapter, we approach the above-mentioned questions by presenting and investigating *two industrial case studies*. In the context of our previous work, we stared to capture evolution histories of the MDE approach of the two studied cases (together spanning 14 evolution steps). The case studies had been captured using semi-structured interviews. For this chapter, we re-approached the two case studies and systemically examined their MDE evolution histories. The goal of this examination was to identify (a) the evolution steps of the MDEs that had been triggered by preceding changes in the process, and (b) the evolution steps of the MDEs that had caused succeeding changes in the process. For each identified pair of MDE change and process change, we further investigate the situations between preceding and succeeding change. This way we learn about the "drivers" of co-evolution.

Altogether, we found eight cases of changes that triggered co-evolution: four MDE evolution steps that were followed by process changes, and four MDE evolution steps that had been caused by preceding process changes. This collection confirms our working hypothesis that co-evolution between software processes and MDE exists. Moreover, we retrieved three kinds of results: First, we identified *co-evolution drivers*, i.e., needs or additional burdens that arise as a result from evolution of software process or MDE and are absorbed by co-evolution. These drivers can also be improvement opportunities. Further, we made some *observations on co-evolution* of which we assume they will help researchers and practitioners better understand co-evolution of processes and MDE. Finally, we collected *lessons learned* that can directly help process managers.

This chapter is structured as follows: In Sect. 13.2, we give an overview about background and applied research method. Further, we present the two case studies in Sect. 13.3 and Sect. 13.4. Afterward we introduce the collected co-evolution drivers, observations, and lessons learned in Sect. 13.5 and discuss the results in Sect. 13.6. Finally, we conclude the chapter in Sect. 13.7 and provide a guide to related works in Sect. 13.8.

13.2 Background and Context

In this section, some background information is given. Further the investigation method applied to perform the research presented in this chapter is described.

Background Evolution is an inevitable aspect of software development, which affects processes and MDE as well. Software processes evolution mainly has two reasons: on the one hand, process standards evolve and, on the other hand, evolution might be applied within companies for reasons of software process improvement. The evolution of process standards happens frequently. For example, for the V-Modell XT[1] four major versions were published in the last 8 years.

---

[1] Available from: http://www.v-modell-xt.de/ (last accessed Jan. 10, 2016).

For MDE we know today that evolution in practice affects the whole *MDE setting*, i.e., the languages, tools, transformation, generators, and artifacts [8]. This evolution is partially triggered by developers, who aim at easing development, e.g., by introducing additional generators. Other reasons are changes in the priorities of a company, such as shifting focus from increasing automation to reducing total cost of ownership. It is estimated that structural evolution affects more than 25 % of all MDE settings [8].

There are good reasons to assume that the evolution of process and MDE might be coupled. As for instance discussed by Stahl et al. [26] and Kleppe et al. [14], model-driven techniques might be combined with arbitrary processes. That MDE and software processes are not independent can be seen on two symptoms in literature. First, there exist a multitude of processes or methodologies that have been developed specifically for MDE [2]. Second, proposals for using MDE in the context of standard processes often define changes regarding the process and restrictions to the applied MDE setting [7]. Based on such examples as well as on several empirical studies, it is today known that MDE can affect the roles in a process as well as process structure.

Whether this interrelation between the process and MDE also causes a co-evolution of both is investigated in this chapter.

Applied Investigation Method In the following, we describe how the case studies have been conducted. The initial collection of the case studies happened in the context of a previous study on evolution histories of MDE settings [8]. For this particular study, we used semi-structured interviews. The usual duration of an interview was one hour. For each case study, we performed an initial interview, followed by two rounds of feedback in the form of follow-up interviews. Due to the partially structured character of the interviews, we collected data on the structure of the MDE settings and their evolution. In doing so we also created models of the MDE settings. The partially unstructured character of the interviews enabled us to collect a lot information on motivations and triggers for changes, but also on opinions about advantages and improvement potentials of the captured development approaches.

For the extended investigation of the two case studies from AUTOSAR (with interviewees from Carmeq) and Capgemini, we got together as team of two former interviewees (one for each of the two case studies) and the former interviewer. This allowed us to extend the data set, relying on the formerly captured evolution steps of the MDE settings, with additional details about surrounding process changes. Further, we extended the Capgemini case study with data on the evolution of an MDE setting that is used by a second team when working in cooperation with the team of the initial case study.

As a result of the data collection, we gained a data set of 14 steps of MDE evolution, as well as about 18 pages (spanning more than 5000 words) of interview records and additional notes on process changes.

For the analysis of the data our first step was to identify cases of co-evolution between process and MDE settings. Therefore, we systematically analyzed all captured MDE evolution steps and investigated whether they have been triggered by a change in the process and whether they have been triggering changes in the process.

As a result we identified eight cases of co-evolution: five of them in the Capgemini case study and three co-evolution steps in the AUTOSAR case study. Of these eight cases, four represent MDE changes that triggered process changes, while the other four represent MDE changes that were triggered by process changes.

In order to learn about co-evolution drivers, we further analyzed the identified co-evolution steps. Therefore, we investigated the situations in between the respective initial evolution step and the evolution step that was triggered by the initial one. In fact, in some cases, three years or even more are between these two evolution steps, while in other cases the co-evolution happened nearly instantly. After capturing these situations, we systematically searched for commonalities and reasons that lead to the co-evolution. These reasons we summarized as initial list of co-evolution drivers.

13.3 Co-Evolution at Capgemini

The first case study was conducted in collaboration with Capgemini in Germany. Capgemini is a worldwide provider of consulting, technology, outsourcing services and local professional services. Present in over 40 countries with almost 140,000 employees, the Capgemini Group helps its clients transform in order to improve their performance and competitive positioning. The analyzed project was to build a novel product data management system for electronics/electrics components in the automotive industry. It was started from the beginning as an MDD project, to be future-proof with respect to its methodological basis and flexible to respond at a rapid pace to changes in the functional and nonfunctional requirements, which were meant to be generated to a large extent.

13.3.1 Introduction to Case Study

The business requirements were provided by the client's domain experts team and were translated by the Capgemini design team into an IT concept. The IT concept was represented as a UML model and had to be constructed by a well-educated team having technofunctional expertise. Having extended the UML base language with UML profiles, a wide range of project-specific metaphors led to a semantically rich model covering most of the functional and technical aspects necessary for further automated processing and code generation.

Once the IT concept phase of a release had been completed, the UML model was exported into a machine-readable XMI having all the tool-specific model features for being transformed back into valid UML. Using this UML model as its main input, several stages of generators and text templates produced a considerable amount of the code and configuration artifacts of the project. Both, server-side and client-side artifacts were created, ranging from scaffolding code necessary to fulfill architecture requirements to parametrized business logic fragments. The generated artifacts were strictly separated from their manually written complements and were coupled by means of an enhanced generation gap pattern.

A different frequency of "model-generate-code" cycles was applied, depending on the current phase of a project release. The overall tool chain was heavyweight with a long sequence of model validation and transformation steps involved. Hence, the typical length of iterations could vary to occupy several weeks during a specification phase, with occasional generation events to assure model quality, or only a few days during a development or bug fixing phase in crunch mode.

Besides the specification team of up to 20 people in a multinational team mix, a generator operator team with rotating duty was responsible to conduct the heavyweight validation and generation process, and to monitor any manual correction by the specification team. Due to a lack of constraining features in the chosen UML tool, manual intervention was necessary to assure a minimum cycle time and high quality of both model input and code output.

13.3.2 Observed Co-Evolution

In the following, we introduce the cases of co-evolution occurred in the Capgemini case study.

Capgemini MDE Change 1

Initially, the main part of the requirements specification was created within a traditional requirements engineering tool as a collection of textual requirements. This document was provided by the *requirements provider team* to the *design team*, which then used a UML modeling tool [23] for the design. In an evolution of the requirements provider team's MDE setting, this modeling tool was used to substitute the requirements engineering tool. A special detail of this new setting was that the two teams agreed upon specific "metaphors" to be used within the requirements (now expressed as UML diagrams) to ensure a clear communication of the intended semantics.

Resulting Situation This change in the MDE setting had two consequences. First, the requirements provider team was confronted with a tool and language, they had not used before. Also the expected degree of detail of the document changed with the need to follow the metaphors. Thus, complexity of the requirements provider team's task increased. Second, both teams now worked with the same tool.

Resulting Changes In consequence, co-evolution of the process happened in two changes: *Capgemini process change 1* and *Capgemini process change 2*, as illustrated in Fig. 13.1 (#1).

Capgemini Process Change 1

Immediately after *Capgemini MDE change 1*, an evolution of the process started: the team roles changed. Originally, the whole requirements provider team was used to write and change the document. However, due to the MDE change, most team members stopped working on the model, while one of the team members specialized and became an expert in the new modeling language and in applying the metaphors.

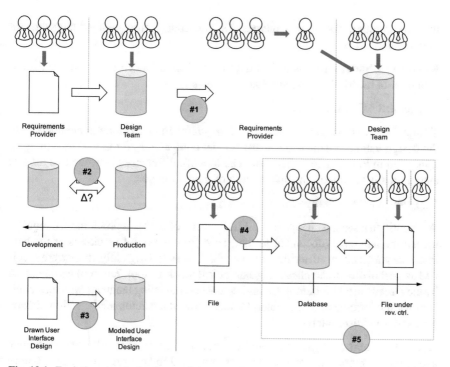

Fig. 13.1 Evolution steps in the Capgemini case study

The other team members developed the habit to approach the new expert when they required changes to the document. This way, the roles in the requirements were providing team split up. Over the years, more team members were trained to participate in modeling. However, the separation in modeling specialists and (textual) business requirements authors endured. A smaller change was that, due to the increased level of detail in the provided document, the communication of the two teams improved when misunderstandings occurred.

Capgemini Process Change 2

A second process change in response to *Capgemini MDE change 1* did not happen immediately, but developed approximately 3 years later. Over time, both teams started to work collaboratively on one model of the software specification. The potential for this change arose when the MDE change made both teams working within the same development environment. A benefit from this second process change was an acceleration, since bottlenecks in one team could better be absorbed. In addition, the design team found opportunities to earlier influence decisions thus reducing risks during development, which also led to improvements regarding the overall cost.

Resulting Situation In consequence, the effort for model merges increased. Thus, it became necessary to merge versions of the model that arise from changes made by both teams. However, model merging is a nontrivial tasks that cannot be automated to the same degree as for instance merges of source code. Consequently, a huge amount of manual effort is involved.

Resulting Changes To this end, this process change indeed triggered itself a co-evolution in the MDE: *Capgemini MDE change 2*.

Capgemini MDE Change 2

To improve the situation that arose from *Capgemini process change 2*, members from the design team implemented a small "model comparator" for the MDE setting, as illustrated in Fig. 13.1 (#2). This tool can identify differences between two models automatically to support the manual task of model merging.

Capgemini MDE Change 3

We identified a second change to the MDE setting of the team providing the requirements: the language (document format) used for creation of mock-ups of the user interface was exchanged, as illustrated in Fig. 13.1 (#3). Originally, these were specified as a set of drawn sketches using a graphical mock-up tool. This tool was replaced by the already used UML tool. Changing tool and modeling language were prerequisites for the introduction of a generator that allowed the automated creation of code for the desired user interface.

Resulting Situation Again, the requirements provider team faced the need for new skills. Furthermore, the mock-up models now need to be more precise than before to enable the code generation.

Resulting Changes *Capgemini MDE change 3* triggered the two process changes *Capgemini process change 3* and *Capgemini process change 4*.

Capgemini Process Change 3

As for *Capgemini MDE change 1*, in consequence of *Capgemini MDE change 3*, some team members specialized to be able to create and modify the mock-ups in the required quality.

Capgemini Process Change 4

As a further consequence to the *Capgemini MDE change 3*, a member of the design team permanently joined the requirements provider team in the role of a consultant. Thus, a mixed team was created.

Capgemini Process Change 5

Another process change that affected the MDE setting was that the design team grew over time. Furthermore, the team was globalized, leading to a distribution of the team across three countries and two continents.

Resulting Situation Initially, all members of the design team worked on the same models that were located in a version management system. However, this approach did not scale for the grown and globalized team.

Resulting Changes In consequence, *Capgemini MDE change 4* was triggered, as illustrated in Fig. 13.1 (#4).

Capgemini MDE Change 4

To cope with the scaling problem resulting from *Capgemini process change 5*, it was decided to migrate the model to a database. For each release, a new database was created. Note that this co-evolution decision was a well-aware trade-off, where it was accepted that the security of logging and check-in mechanism is lost.

Capgemini Process Change 6

Since the hot phase of development is over and the system became more and more stable, the team size was reduced. Sometimes new features are developed in small co-located teams working intensively on the model.

Resulting Situation This occasional change in the team structure, enables the use of version management systems, such that their advantages could be used, leading to *Capgemini MDE change 5*, as illustrated in Fig. 13.1 (#5).

Capgemini MDE Change 5

In response, for some mini-projects, the database was substituted by version management systems again.

13.4 Co-Evolution at AUTOSAR

The second case study has been performed in collaboration with AUTOSAR, a worldwide development partnership standardizing software interfaces and data formats for automotive software and systems modeling. Contributors to AUTOSAR are distributed worldwide and across a variety of companies and organizations.

13.4.1 Introduction to Case Study

The standard, i.e., the product of AUTOSAR, largely consists of informal textual documents and semiformal models. The documents are informal in that they have no formally defined syntax or semantics. Semiformal models follow a syntax, in most cases an XML syntax defined by AUTOSAR itself, but have no formally defined semantics. The XML language is referred to as AUTOSAR XML or ARXML. Parts of the documents and most of the semiformally defined models are generated from UML models. Hence, the case study focuses on modeling, model transformations, generation, and related activities in the standardization work. All activities are embedded into the globally distributed development process of the standard.

AUTOSAR Development and Change Management Approach
The AUTOSAR community develops the standard in a non-agile process.
Changes are agreed on by a change control board. The implementation of
changes is monitored by the AUTOSAR change management. The development is subdivided into phases such as concept elaboration, implementation,
and finalization. There is only one phase of each kind between two subsequent
releases, so the process is non-iterative.

The documents are maintained by approximately 100 document owners, who are
technical experts responsible for a single document or a small number of documents.
Most of the documents address a specific subdomain such as communication or OS.

On the contrary, the modeling is performed by a limited number of about 10–
20 modeling experts. These experts model APIs, configuration parameters and the
syntax of ARXML for multiple or all subdomains, and are responsible for the transformation of models to artifacts that are embedded into documents and to the semiformal deliverables of the standard is automated. The transformation tools are operated,
configured, and maintained by about five tool developers in the *Technical Office*.
Figure 13.2 depicts roles, documents, and artifacts in the *model-based specification*

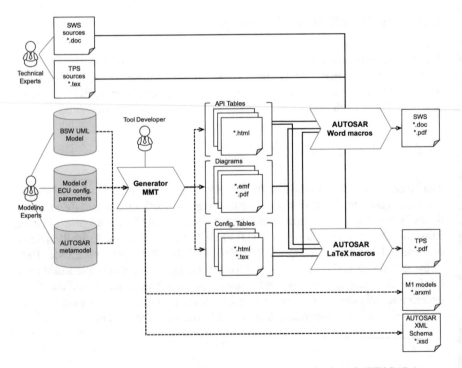

Fig. 13.2 Roles, documents, and artifacts in the model-based specification of AUTOSAR (*source*
own work)

of AUTOSAR. The structural AUTOSAR models consist of three parts, all defined in Sparx Systems' Enterprise Architect:

- A model of the basic software modules and APIs according to a UML profile for component and class diagrams (BSW UML model)
- A model of configuration containers and parameters for electronic control units as UML object diagrams (ECU configuration or EcuC model)
- The metamodel of data formats for exchange between two parties that use AUTOSAR

A change to the standard typically impacts both models and documents. In this case, technical experts and modeling experts agree on the respective changes. A modeling expert then implements the agreed changes in the model. The generator (developed and configured by the tool developers) transforms the changed model to *generated artifacts*. In this step, it generates diagrams and tables to be integrated into the documents, and XML representations of the models, which are delivered as parts of the standard. The results of the generation process are stored in a repository.

One of the technical experts, the document owner, applies the agreed changes to the document sources. Also, he uses Word or LaTeX macros to update diagrams and tables in his document. The latest version of the artifacts can be automatically downloaded from the repository. In case a generated artifact is used in multiple documents, the high degree of automation of these steps substantially facilitates keeping contents consistent across document boundaries.

The changes to AUTOSAR documents and models (except for editorial ones) are performed according to a change documentation process and agreed on by a change control board. In the implementation phase of an AUTOSAR release, the models may change daily or even multiple times a day. A new AUTOSAR release or revision is published approximately twice a year. The latest release contains approximately 800 changes to the standard of which about 200 impact at least one model.

13.4.2 Observed Co-Evolution

The following cases of co-evolution were identified in the AUTOSAR case study.

AUTOSAR MDE Change 1

The first captured change in the AUTOSAR setting was the introduction of modeling. The rationale behind this change was to keep redundant information, such as type structures and operation signatures, consistent across several documents of the standard.

Resulting Situation Utilizing modeling within the heterogeneous team, where all team members were allowed to manipulate the models, led to frequent merges of changes applied by different people. However, as mentioned before, model merging is nontrivial and leads to considerable manual merge efforts. Also, as the UML profile evolved, modeling became unfeasible to be done by the technical experts alongside their work on the documents.

Resulting Changes In consequence, *AUTOSAR MDE change 1* triggered the two process changes *AUTOSAR process change 1* and *AUTOSAR process change 2*.

AUTOSAR Process Change 1

It took several years, but, eventually, the high efforts of parallel modeling (resulting from *AUTOSAR MDE change 1*) led to the decision to reduce the number of persons that change the model. Thus, the roles were changed, such that the Technical Office is responsible for BSW UML model and the AUTOSAR work package "Methodology and Configuration" that maintains the EcuC Model and the metamodel. This makes about 20 modelers with clearly defined responsibilities rather than 100 document owners modifying the models before.

AUTOSAR Process Change 2

To ensure that changes of generated artifacts meet the requirements of the technical experts, and that only intended changes are delivered, a review activity was added as a consequence of *AUTOSAR MDE change 1*. All artifacts provided by the modeling experts pass a review by the technical experts before they are incorporated into the documents.

Resulting Situation However, due to the high number of generated artifacts (hundreds of diagrams and even thousands of tables, both in multiple file formats), a full manual review of the artifacts became unfeasible, soon.

Resulting Changes Thus, *AUTOSAR MDE change 2* was triggered.

AUTOSAR MDE Change 2

To bring back feasibility to the review process (introduced in *AUTOSAR process change 2*), the modeling experts use diff tools for the generated artifacts.

AUTOSAR MDE Change 3

The tool chain shown in Fig. 13.2 turned out to produce slightly different results in different environments. In the first step, the personal computer of one modeling expert was used as a reference system. For published documents, only artifacts produced on that machine were used, making the team dependable on the availability of the modeling expert's computer. To improve the situation, the reference system was moved to a permanently available continuous integration (CI) server. Over time, additional tasks were deployed on this system, e.g., build documents from LaTeX sources or software builds.

Resulting Situation Due to the new importance of the CI server, the need for its dependability increased and, with that, the need for clearly defined responsibilities.

Resulting Changes In consequence, *AUTOSAR process change 3* was triggered.

AUTOSAR Process Change 3

To address the increased need for dependability on the CI server (*AUTOSAR MDE change 3*), responsibility for its operation and maintenance were defined changing roles and responsibilities. The Technical Office was appointed to operate and maintain the system.

13.5 Co-Evolution Drivers and Lessons Learned

In the following, we present the results of the systematic analysis of the collected data: the identified *co-evolution drivers*, *observations* on co-evolution, and *lessons learned* for process managers. Table 13.1 summarizes the identified cases of co-evolution.

13.5.1 Initial List of Co-Evolution Drivers

The case studies show that co-evolution of MDE and processes happen. But why are changes in an MDE setting followed by changes in the process and vice versa? We analyzed the case studies to gain an initial list of co-evolution drivers. These drivers can be needs or additional burdens that arise as result from evolution of the software process or an MDE setting and are addressed and absorbed by the co-evolution. Similarly, co-evolution drivers might be potentials for improvement.

Co-evolution drivers are in focus for two reasons: First of all, they help us understanding reasons and motivations for co-evolution and—hopefully—predicting co-evolution in future. A second reason is that co-evolution drivers, in combination with the knowledge about respective MDE and process changes, can help us learn about the so far scarcely understood relationship between software processes and MDE settings.

13.5.1.1 Overview of Co-Evolution Drivers

In this section, we introduce the initial list of co-evolution drivers that we have identified within the two case studies. Furthermore, we provide a map of aspects in MDE settings and processes that might be connected by co-evolution drivers.

Driver 1 (High additional manual effort). The first driver we identified is an increase of manual effort, which can be caused by new tasks or increased effort for already existing tasks. This driver occurred, for example, in the AUTOSAR case study and led to the co-evolution of the MDE setting in response to the introduction of a review activity (*AUTOSAR process change 2 & AUTOSAR MDE change 2*).

This driver often seems to concern the effort for merging of models, as for the co-evolution in response to *AUTOSAR MDE change 1* and *Capgemini process change*

Table 13.1 Summary of observed evolution propagation

Causes change ID	Description	Effects change ID	Description	Time until reaction	Co-Evolution driver
AUTOSAR MDE change 2	*Introduction of Modeling*	*AUTOSAR process change 1*	*Introduced access rights restriction:* reduction of set of people permitted to change models	Approx. 4–5 years	D1 (high additional manual effort)
		AUTOSAR process change 2	*Introduced review activity:* for generated documents	Approx. 3 years	D2 (quality of automated results)
AUTOSAR MDE change 3	*Introduction of Continuous Integration System for Generation*	*AUTOSAR process change 3*	*Definition of Responsibilities* for system operation and maintenance	Approx. 1 year	D5 (uncertain responsibilities)
Capgemini MDE change 1	*Exchanged tool and modeling language for a diagram*	*Capgemini process change 1*	*Changed roles and document access:* 1 team member became 'expert'; other team members stopped working on the model	immediate	D3 (skill mismatch)
		Capgemini process change 2	*Shared artifact:* both teams (heterogeneous skills, different companies) started to work on the same model	Approx. 3 years	D7 (arising optimization potential)
Capgemini MDE change 3	*Exchanged tool and modeling language for a diagram & Introduction of generation based on the model*	*Capgemini process change 3*	*Changed roles and document access:* single team members became 'experts'; other team members stopped working on the model	immediate	D3 (skill mismatch)
		Capgemini process change 4	*Creation of mixed team:* A member of team 2 joined team 1 permanently	immediate	D3 (skill mismatch)
AUTOSAR process change 2	*Introduction of Modeling and Artifact Reviews* comparison of generation result against expected results	*AUTOSAR MDE change 2*	*Introduction of diff tools and automation* to simplify review	Approx. 3–4 years	D1 (high additional manual effort)
Capgemini process change 2	*Shared artifact* 2 teams (heterogeneous skills, different companies) started to work on the same model	*Capgemini MDE change 2*	*Introduction of differencing (model weaving) tools* to support difference identification	Approx. <1 year	D1 (high additional manual effort)
Capgemini process change 5	*Changed team size/ team globalization* no more all at one location/country	*Capgemini MDE change 4*	*Changed technology for model storage* from SVN to DB	Approx. 2 months	D4 (mismatch in scalability)
Capgemini process change 6	*Team size and cooperation* small temporary teams in very close collaboration	*Capgemini MDE change 5*	*Changed technology for model storage* bring model temporarily back to SVN from DB	Immediate (preplanned)	D6 (solution enabling)

2. In the first case a change in the used tooling (i.e., introduction of modeling) led to this additional effort. The situation was solved by changing the roles' access rights. Interestingly this driver describes a subjective mismatch, which can even occur and lead to co-evolution when the overall manual effort is reduced. For example, the *AUTOSAR process change 2* was a response to the added modeling and generation steps (*AUTOSAR MDE change 1*), meaning that overall the manual creation of the documents was substituted by an automated creation and a following manual review activity. Nonetheless, the additional review activity was judged for its effort.

Driver 2 (Mismatch in expected and actual quality of automated results). We observed this driver in the AUTOSAR case study, when a generator was introduced (*AUTOSAR MDE change 1*). Only during the use it became clear that there is a mismatch in the expected stability of the generator result and the actual stability. In consequence, the process was adapted by adding a manual review activity.

Driver 3 (Skill mismatch). Another driver that seems to be very common, is a mismatch between the skills required for a technology and the skill set of a team. This can happen when teams are confronted with new technologies. Two example cases happened in the Capgemini case study, where such changes in the modeling languages and tooling happened twice to one of the teams (*Capgemini MDE change 1* and *Capgemini MDE change 3*). In response, in both cases, the role structure of the team changed as well as the interaction to the second team.

Driver 4 (Mismatch in scalability). A less surprising driver is the "mismatch in scalability" when (modeling) tools do not sufficiently scale with team size and structure. For example, in the Capgemini case study a change in the team size and also in the team's distribution pattern led to this mismatch (*Capgemini process change 5*). The mismatch was resolved by changing in the tool setup.

Driver 5 (Uncertain responsibilities). A further driver is the uncertainty concerning responsibilities that can occur if new technical solutions are introduced, especially when teams are very heterogeneous (as for *AUTOSAR MDE change 3*).

Driver 6 (Solution enabling). Similar to the mismatch in scalability, also a mismatch between the required and actual performance of tools can be a reason to change the tool set up evolution. However, in the Capgemini case study it did not appear as a co-evolution driver, since the mismatch existed just before the respective evolution step. In contrast, the process evolution enables a solution of this mismatch (*Capgemini process change 6*), since after this process change the team size was small enough to allow the usage of a version management system.

Driver 7 (Arising optimization potential). Finally, a second co-evolution driver that concerns potentials is the occurrence of new optimization potentials. In the Capgemini case study this happened when a modeling language used by one of the teams was changed to the modeling language that was used by the other team too (*Capgemini MDE change 1*). This change led to the potential to safe transformation effort by allowing both teams to work on the same artifact. About 3 years after the initial change it was decided to use this potential (*Capgemini process change 2*).

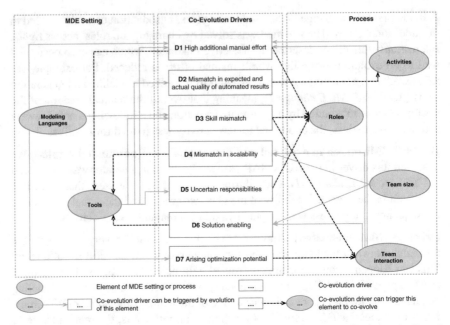

Fig. 13.3 Map of identified co-evolution drivers as well as so far found affecting and affected elements in MDE settings and processes

13.5.1.2   A Map of Co-Evolution Drivers

Figure 13.3 illustrates how the different identified co-evolution drivers connect elements of the process and MDE setting. It can be seen that evolution in tools, activities, and team interaction trigger co-evolution drivers as well as they are triggered by co-evolution drivers. Further, for at least one co-evolution driver we found that it can be triggered from both sides, MDE setting and process. Since this map only illustrates impacts that happened in the two case studies, it is to be expected that there are further co-evolution drivers. It is also possible that here the identified co-evolution drivers can be triggered and can trigger more MDE and process aspects than observed so far. For example, process documents might be affected by MDE evolution.

13.5.2   Observations on Co-Evolution

We could make some general observations and consider them helpful for researchers and practitioners to better understand co-evolution of processes and MDE.

Unintended Change Accommodation The first observation we made is that the team structure and roles can be subject to an "unintended evolution accommodation" when the MDE setting changes. This happened twice in the Capgemini case study when the used tool and modeling language changed for one of the teams. Both times, one or a small number of team members became experts in the new language, while other team members changed their behavior and stopped to change the models directly. In one of the cases an additional *intended* change happened to the team structure: a member of another team joined the affected team as a mentor. In contrast to the other case, not only one but multiple team members adopted the expert role. This observation might be taken as a hint that a proactive introduction of mentoring can help control the unintended impacts to the team and role structure.

In all observed cases, where the MDE setting was co-evolved, these changes had been subject to developer's or management's decisions. This observation points toward a need to more actively maintaining and protecting an established process tailoring.

Sensitive Teams Another direct observation is that most process changes involved in co-evolution concern team structure and roles. Five out of eight observed process changes concern the team structure and two concern the interaction between teams. Indeed, only one of the process changes concerns activities in the process. Thus, a first impression is that the roles and team structure are those process parts most sensitive toward changes in the MDE setting.

No Reaction by Language Evolution Interestingly, for situations where the MDE setting is changed in response to process evolution, we could observe manipulations of the tool set only, while overall both, the sets of modeling languages and tools, caused co-evolution in the process.

Dominant Negative Drivers We can observe that co-evolution drivers are in most cases mismatches or experienced disadvantages. Only in two cases the co-evolution drivers were enablers for solving mismatches or even for optimization.

Cascading Effects Co-evolution can lead to cascading effects: the co-evolution of process or MDE can trigger further co-evolution actions. We observed such cascading effects in both case studies. In the AUTOSAR case, introducing a generator for figures (*AUTOSAR MDE change 1*) led to a co-evolution of the process, which was the introduction of a review activity (*AUTOSAR process change 2*). However, this caused further co-evolution of the MDE, where a differencing tool was introduced to support the review activity. Similarly, in the Capgemini case study, a change of the modeling language and tool (*Capgemini MDE change 1*) opened the potential to remove the need to transform information from one artifact to the other. This opportunity was used by co-evolving the process, such that two teams now work on the same shared artifact (*Capgemini process change 2*). This, however, led to another change to the MDE setting (adding a tool for identification of model differences). In both cases, the cascading co-evolution was driven when the co-evolution of the process led to extra manual effort.

Bidirectional Co-Evolution Drivers Furthermore, we observed that the same evolution driver in even very similar situations can be triggered by different changes. We found a situation that occurred in both case studies as a consequence of evolution (of process in the one case (*Capgemini process change 2*) and of MDE in the other (*AUTOSAR MDE change 1*)): a larger group of developers with different skills was accessing the same model. In consequence, the need for model merging increased, which resulted in a "high additional manual effort," compared to the respective situations before. In the two cases different solutions had been chosen:

- In the AUTOSAR case the process was adapted by regulating the responsibilities and rights to access the model.
- In the Capgemini case a tool for the identification of model differences was introduced to the MDE setting to reduce manual effort.

13.5.3 Lessons Learned for Process Managers

Finally, based on the identified drivers and made observations we collected three lessons learned that can directly help process managers.

Lesson 1 (**There are always two adjusting screws to choose from: the process and the MDE**). The existence of bidirectional co-evolution drivers shows that changes in both, MDE and process, can cause drivers, but also relaxed them. Thus, process managers have the choice when responding to a co-evolution driver. Note, this also means that, e.g., an MDE change can be answered with another MDE change (even if we did not systematically cover such situations with our investigation method).

Lesson 2 (**Consider the risk of cascading effects when planning co-evolution**). Due to cascading effects, changes in the MDE might not only lead to changes in the process, but to follow-up needs for tools, which can cause extra cost. Thus, process managers should consider the occurrence of *cascading effects* of co-evolution steps when triggering evolution of the MDE setting or process. For example, when planning evolution in the MDE setting, it is not sufficient to only consider potential needs for a co-evolution of the process. Moreover, it needs to be considered if process changes trigger other evolution drivers.

Lesson 3 (**Look out for arising potentials**). While most co-evolution drivers identified so far concern problems, we found an example showing that co-evolution can also be performed to gain benefits: in *Capgemini MDE change 1* opened the potential to safe manual model transformation effort. This opportunity was exploited by changing the process, such that two teams collaboratively work on shared models. The takeaway for process managers is to not only consider co-evolution when disadvantages arise, but to actively reconsider whether co-evolution can lead to improvements.

13.6 Discussion

In this section, we discuss generalizability and additional implications of our results.

Completeness of Co-evolution Drivers Surely, the choice of the two case studies impacts the number of evolution steps as well as the number and form of found cases of co-evolution. Similarly, due to the method of data collection, we cannot exclude that there are smaller co-evolution impacts to the process or MDE setting that have not been captured here. This might be the case when these effects are so small that they are only recognized by some team members and are not further communicated within the team and company. With these two points, we cannot expect that the list of identified co-evolution drivers is complete. However, due to feedback rounds on the interview notes and our close cooperation with the respective companies, it can be assumed that we did not find something that did not happen. Thus, the gained data is sufficient to gain some initial insights on existing forms of co-evolution and to create an initial list of drivers, as it is the aim of this paper. We hope that the investigation of further case studies will allow us to complement the list of co-evolution drivers in future.

Generalizability With only two case studies, it is difficult to draw conclusions on the generalizability of the found insights to companies with other sizes or different domains. It thus cannot be concluded that the observed co-evolution drivers would lead to co-evolution in all cases or that the observed co-evolutions are representative. Already our small set of examples shows that the same co-evolution driver might lead to different reactions.

Uncovered MDE–Process Relations As discussed in Sect. 13.2, state-of-the-art research identified already single relations between MDE and processes. Since co-evolution bases on the interrelation of MDE and processes, the insights in this chapter can point to further, so far uncovered, relations. For example, we saw for the first time a relation between the reliability of automation solutions in MDE and manually performed quality assurance activities. Furthermore, we could actually observe an interrelation between the scalability supported by (MDE) tools and the team size. Finally, we saw that an extra phase or activity can lead to the deployment of a tool to reduce the effort of this phase. However, within an initial setup of MDE it is seldom tried to support all tasks with automation immediately. Thus, is there a difference in the mentality when it is about improving new tasks compared to familiar tasks? It would be interesting to investigate in future work, whether during evolution changes happen that would not happen in an initial design.

Offside Process Evolution It can be observed that our findings on triggered process changes go further than known forms of process evolution, where process tailoring is often considered rather static to a project or caused by evolution of process standards. In contrast, the process changes found here happened during the projects. They had not been triggered by process improvement activities and were no adoptions of changed process standards. It might be interesting to focus in future more on the question whether there are more possible causes for process change.

13.7   Conclusions

In this chapter, we presented two industrial case studies on co-evolution. Our first important finding is that our working hypothesis can be confirmed: co-evolution between MDE and process actually exists in practice. We could observe that this co-evolution works in both directions, i.e., can affect both MDE and process. Further, we could observe eight cases, where evolution of MDE triggered or was triggered by process changes.

On this basis we extracted an initial list of co-evolution drivers and analyzed what MDE and process elements had affected or had been affected by these drivers. Though this list cannot yet show a complete picture, it gives an initial insight into how co-evolution of MDE and processes looks like.

In addition we summarized some observations on the co-evolution and lessons learned that can help process managers to better handle co-evolution and even to recognize arising changes. Finally, we discussed our results in context of existing findings on the interrelation of MDE and software processes, which showed that the observed co-evolution indeed uncovers relations between process and MDE that have so far not been discussed in literature.

13.8   Further Reading

In the following, we provide some hints on related literature about process and MDE evolution, as well as on the interrelation of software process and MDE.

Process Evolution How process standards evolve was, for example, studied by Ocampo et al. [22], who investigated the case of ECSS.[2] A well-known approach toward software process improvement is the Capability Maturity Model (CMM), which describes different levels of maturation of processes. An example case study how the CMM helped to improve processes at Motorola was described by Diaz et al. [4]. Other works on process change that are closely related to software process evolution concern process tailoring and software process lines. Process tailoring aims at adapting processes to the need of a specific company and project, for which it is typically applied [12, 19]. Software process lines aim at supporting the task of tailoring a process [24]. How such software process lines can be realized with the help of variability operations was presented in [15] by example using different variants of the V-Modell XT.

Two approaches for modeling and planning process tailoring can be found in this book. In Chap. 11, Benner-Wickner et al. present how case management techniques can be used to reach process flexibility and in Chap 10, Fazal-Baqaie and Engels present the idea of assembly-based method engineering (MESP).

---

[2]European Cooperation for Space Standardization http://www.ecss.nl.

MDE and MDE Evolution Readers who are interested in Model-Driven Engineering can find a basic introduction to the concepts of model-driven engineering is given by Kent [13]. A more detailed introduction can be found in the book "*Model-driven software development: technology, engineering, management*" by Völter et al. [26]. Finally, some works on assessing and describing the state of practice had been published by Hutchinson et al. [11], Gorschek et al. [6], Liebel et al. [17], and Torchiano et al. [28].

Evolution in context of MDE has mainly been studied with focus on the evolution of (design) models during software evolution, as summarized by Mens et al. [20]. Van Deursen et al. [29] summarize different forms of evolution starting with "metamodel evolution," which is also often referred to as language evolution. Language evolution can happen for all kinds of (modeling) languages. For example, the UML changed around all 2–3 years in the past. Studies in this area focus on the question, what metamodel elements change, as by Herrmannsdoerfer et al. [10]. Besides metamodel evolution, Van Deursen et al. describe also "platform evolution" (e.g., when the version of a used tool changes) and "abstraction evolution," which refers to the addition of new modeling languages to an MDE setting.

Multiple elements of an MDE setting often have to change together to stay compatible ("co-evolution"). Meyers et al. [21] describe different scenarios of co-evolution between models, metamodels, and transformations. Finally, in our previous work [8], we studied how the structure of MDE settings changes on several case studies of MDE settings.

Interrelation of Process and MDE Staron [27] and Whittle et al. [30] found independent of each other that there is a possibility that a newly introduced MDE setting leads to changes on the process or process tailoring. Asadi and Ramsin [2] surveyed six methodologies that have been specifically designed for the OMG standard MDA [25]. This is a hint that there is a certain awareness for mutual constraints of MDE setting and process.

To learn more about the question whether and how standard processes can actually be used with MDE, in our previous work, we surveyed nine literature proposals for usage of standard processes with MDE [7]. The found proposals ranged from complete process reuse, via adaptation of process roles (e.g., Loniewski et al. [18]), up to adaptations of the process structure. For example, Kulkarni et al. [16] add a meta-sprint to Scrum to cope with MDE tasks that are more time consuming. However, there seems to be no systematic knowledge about what process changes are necessary and how this depends on the concrete combination of MDE techniques, chosen. In this chapter, we found for the two case studies that evolution in the MDE setting can trigger changes in roles, team structure, and fine granular changes in activities, such as addition of review tasks. However, we could not observe changes in the process phases. This is a hint that such big process tailoring occurs probably seldom during evolution, where both, process and MDE setting, are changed rather incrementally.

Besides explicit proposals and approaches for MDE processes, there are several qualitative investigations on MDE usage in case studies from practice. Some of them include insights that concern the used processes:

- In a case study with an international IT service provider Heijstek et al. [9] identified 14 factors in MDE usage that can impact architectural processes. They found that required skills and communication changed, e.g., models enabled requirements engineers to create parts of the system. Furthermore, they observed an increased need of collective code ownership when MDE was introduced. The authors trace this back to the fact that (a) less and more complex code is written and (b) developers often need to touch code from other projects. In this chapter, we saw that models shared amongst a heterogeneous team can be a pain factor that even leads to access restrictions for different roles. This seems to be in contrast to a result of Heijstek et al. Explanations can be that (a) diversity of roles was lower in the case study investigated by Heijstek et al., (b) the frequency of changes to be expected per model is lower in Heijstek's case study, or (c) Heijstek's insights refer not only to models, but mainly to code, while the found conflicts in our case concern models, only. It is indeed possible that both, our and Heijstek's, findings represent two independent forces that arise from the MDE setting and counteract each other when it comes to their impact on the process.
- In an interview study, Aranda et al. [1] found that the introduction of MDE led to a change in the division of labor at General Motors. This happened since non-software engineers were now enabled to take over parts of the work of the software engineers. The observation of Aranda et al. [1] and Heijstek et al. [9] that the division of labor might change with the introduction of MDE fits to co-evolution we observed in *Capgemini MDE change 3*. However, in this case it was not caused by the introduction of modeling itself, but by a change in the MDE setting, which caused the same modeling tool and language being applied in two teams (cf. Sect. 13.3).
- Whittle et al. [31] found that MDE can help to bring development of software in-house. As a reason they argue that outsourced development often concerns simple, well-defined tasks. These however, are the first once that are candidate to automation, too. This insight of Whittle et al. could be confirmed by Burden et al. [3] in a study with three large companies. Furthermore, Burden et al. found that MDE enables domain experts to work together with developers. The results of this chapter show that this might in some cases not just be a new option, but rather a need, as in *Capgemini MDE change 3*, were a member of one team moved to the partner team, to support them in modeling. However, our results also show that the introduction of a new modeling language can lead to split up of former homogeneous roles within a team, as caused by the driver *mismatch skills* in *Capgemini MDE change 1*.

Acknowledgments We would like to thank Frank Altheide for providing additional information about the history of AUTOSAR.

References

1. Aranda, J., Borici, A., Damian, D.: Transitioning to model-driven development: What is revolutionary, what remains the same. In: Model Driven Engineering Languages and Systems. Lecture Notes in Computer Science, vol. 7590, pp. 692–708. Springer, Berlin (2012)
2. Asadi, M., Ramsin, R.: Mda-based methodologies: an analytical survey. In: Proccedings of the European Conference on Model Driven Architecture: Foundations and Applications, pp. 419–431. Springer, Berlin (2008)
3. Burden, H.k., Heldal, R., Whittle, J.: Comparing and contrasting model-driven engineering at three large companies. In: Proceedings of the International Symposium on Empirical Software Engineering and Measurement, pp. 14:1–14:10. ACM, New York, USA (2014)
4. Diaz, M., Sligo, J.: How software process improvement helped motorola. IEEE Softw. **14**(5), 75–81 (1997)
5. France, R., Rumpe, B.: Model-driven development of complex software: a research roadmap. In: Future of Software Engineering, pp. 37–54. IEEE, Washington, DC, USA (2007)
6. Gorschek, T., Tempero, E., Angelis, L.: On the use of software design models in software development practice: an empirical investigation. J. Syst. Softw. **95**, 176–193 (2014)
7. Hebig, R., Bendraou, R.: On the need to study the impact of model driven engineering on software processes. In: Proceedings of the International Conference on Software and System Process, pp. 164–168. ACM, New York, USA (2014)
8. Hebig, R., Giese, H.: On the complex nature of mde evolution and its impact on changeability. Softw. Syst. Model. pp. 1–24 (2015)
9. Heijstek, W., Chaudron, M.R.V.: The impact of model driven development on the software architecture process. In: Proceedings of the EUROMICRO Conference on Software Engineering and Advanced Applications, pp. 333–341. IEEE, Washington, DC, USA (2010)
10. Herrmannsdörfer, M., Benz, S., Jürgens, E.: Automatability of coupled evolution of metamodels and models in practice. In: Model Driven Engineering Languages and Systems. Lecture Notes in Computer Science, vol. 5301, pp. 645–659. Springer, Berlin (2008)
11. Hutchinson, J., Whittle, J., Rouncefield, M., Kristoffersen, S.: Empirical assessment of mde in industry. In: Proceedings of the International Conference on Software Engineering, pp. 471–480. ACM, New York, USA (2011)
12. Kalus, G., Kuhrmann, M.: Criteria for software process tailoring: a systematic review. In: Proceedings of the International Conference on Software and System Process, pp. 171–180. ACM, New York, USA (2013)
13. Kent, S.: Model driven engineering. In: Integrated Formal Methods. Lecture Notes in Computer Science, vol. 2335, pp. 286–298. Springer, Berlin (2002)
14. Kleppe, A.G., Warmer, J., Bast, W.: MDA Explained: The Model Driven Architecture: Practice and Promise. Addison-Wesley Longman Publishing Co. Inc., Boston (2003)
15. Kuhrmann, M., Fernández, D.M., Ternité, T.: Realizing software process lines: Insights and experiences. In: Proceedings of the International Conference on Software and System Process, pp. 99–108. ACM, New York, USA (2014)
16. Kulkarni, V., Barat, S., Ramteerthkar, U.: Early experience with agile methodology in a model-driven approach. In: Model Driven Engineering Languages and Systems. Lecture Notes in Computer Science, vol. 6981, pp. 578–590. Springer, Berlin (2011)
17. Liebel, G., Marko, N., Tichy, M., Leitner, A., Hansson, J.: Assessing the state-of-practice of model-based engineering in the embedded systems domain. In: Model-Driven Engineering Languages and Systems. Lecture Notes in Computer Science, vol. 8767, pp. 166–182. Springer, Berlin (2014)
18. Loniewski, G., Armesto, A., Insfran, E.: An agile method for model-driven requirements engineering. In: Proceedings of the International Conference on Software Engineering Advances, pp. 570–575. IARIA Inc. (2011)
19. Martínez-Ruiz, T., Münch, J., García, F., Piattini, M.: Requirements and constructors for tailoring software processes: a systematic literature review. Softw. Qual. J. **20**(1), 229–260 (2012)

20. Mens, T., Blanc, X., Mens, K.: Model-driven software evolution: An alternative research agenda. In: BElgian-NEtherlands software eVOLution workshop (BENEVOL) (2007)
21. Meyers, B., Vangheluwe, H.: A framework for evolution of modelling languages. Sci. Comput. Program. **76**(12), 1223–1246 (2011)
22. Ocampo, A., Münch, J.: Rationale modeling for software process evolution. Softw. Process: Improv. Pract. **14**(2), 85–105 (2009)
23. OMG: Unified Modeling Language (UML) ver 2.5. OMG Standard Document Number: ptc/2013-09-05, Object Management Group (2013)
24. Rombach, D.: Integrated software process and product lines. In: Unifying the Software Process Spectrum. Lecture Notes in Computer Science, vol. 3840, pp. 83–90. Springer, Berlin (2006)
25. Soley, R.: Model driven architecture. OMG White Paper 308, Object Management Group (2000)
26. Stahl, T., Voelter, M., Czarnecki, K.: Model-Driven Software Development: Technology, Engineering, Management. Wiley, New Jersey (2006)
27. Staron, M.: Adopting model driven software development in industry – a case study at two companies. In: Model Driven Engineering Languages and Systems. Lecture Notes in Computer Science, vol. 4199, pp. 57–72. Springer, Berlin (2006)
28. Torchiano, M., Tomassetti, F., Ricca, F., Tiso, A., Reggio, G.: Relevance, benefits, and problems of software modelling and model driven techniques-a survey in the italian industry. J. Syst. Softw. **86**(8), 2110–2126 (2013)
29. van Deursen, A., Visser, E., Warmer, J., Tamzalit, D.: Model-driven software evolution: a research agenda. In: Proceedings of the CSMR Workshop on Model-Driven Software Evolution, pp. 41–49 (2007)
30. Whittle, J., Hutchinson, J., Rouncefield, M., Burden, H., Heldal, R.: Industrial adoption of model-driven engineering: are the tools really the problem? In: Model-Driven Engineering Languages and Systems. Lecture Notes in Computer Science, vol. 8107, pp. 1–17. Springer, Berlin (2013)
31. Whittle, J., Hutchinson, J., Rouncefield, M.: The state of practice in model-driven engineering. IEEE Softw. **31**(3), 79–85 (2014)

Chapter 14
Monitoring and Controlling Release Readiness by Learning Across Projects

S.M. Didar Al Alam, Dietmar Pfahl and Günther Ruhe

Abstract Releasing software on time, with desired quality while staying within budget is crucial for success. Therefore, product managers should proactively know which release readiness attributes are not performing sufficiently well (i.e., bottleneck factors) throughout the development cycle and consequently may limit readiness of the software release. We present the Cross-project Analysis for Selection of Release Readiness attributes (CASRR) method to help project managers in (i) systematically studying and analyzing release readiness attributes across multiple projects, (ii) selection of release readiness attributes for monitoring which have previously been shown to become bottlenecks in similar projects in the past, and (iii) learning how bottleneck occurrences are influenced by project characteristics. We applied CASRR to two Open Source Software projects, and analyzed six release readiness attributes in 34 similar projects over a period of two years. Continuous integration rate, feature completion rate, and bug fixing rate are observed as the most frequent bottleneck factors. Bottleneck occurrences of the monitored release readiness attributes are significantly influenced by the maturity of a release. Furthermore, the continuous integration rate is found to be significantly influenced by the team size.

14.1 Introduction

Software Product Management, as defined by Ebert [7] as *"the discipline and role, which governs the software product (or solution or service) from its inception to the market/customer delivery in order to generate biggest possible value to the business."*

S.M. Didar Al Alam (✉) · G. Ruhe
Department of Computer Science, University of Calgary,
2500 University Drive NW, Calgary, AB, Canada
e-mail: smdalam@ucalgary.ca

G. Ruhe
e-mail: ruhe@ucalgary.ca

D. Pfahl
Institute of Computer Science, University of Tartu, J Liivi 2, 50409 Tartu, Estonia
e-mail: dietmar.pfahl@ut.ee

© Springer International Publishing Switzerland 2016
M. Kuhrmann et al. (eds.), *Managing Software Process Evolution*,
DOI 10.1007/978-3-319-31545-4_14

is a key success factor for companies [17] that facilitates timely production and faster product acceptance in market [8]. In the competitive commercial software market, software companies struggle to integrate advanced software product management techniques to monitor and control their development processes and product releases. Thus, the ultimate goal is to ensure competitiveness and business success. The key is to develop high-quality products in time and within budget [1], and to release software the moment it is ready. A *software release* is commonly defined as the deployment of the software product to market, or as the process of delivering the product into the operational environment for the consumers to utilize [15]. Successfully releasing quality software in-time heavily depends on the underlying development cycle. In this chapter, we investigate the readiness of a software release. Instead of measuring release readiness merely for the deployment process, we measure release readiness throughout the complete development cycle of a release.

A product, or a major version of the product, can only be released when it is ready. In fact, a slip in the release can cause millions of dollars in lost revenue. Alternatively, if delivered early, the product might face a lack of proper testing and low quality. In software product management, a product manager is responsible for deciding the product release content, time frame, price, and completing business cases regarding the technical aspects of the product [8]. The dilemma product managers often face is how "ready" the product is to release, and whether more time needs to be spent on feature development, testing, re-work, or process improvement. The problem is commonly known as the "stopping rule" problem [9]. Release decisions should not be made ad-hoc. Product managers should use information related to the product's readiness for release. At any point in time during the development cycle, the measurement of release readiness helps project managers assess the status of the product for release and facilitate release decisions. Release readiness is a time-dependent attribute of a software product release. It aggregates a portfolio of the release process and product measures to quantify the status of the software product for release.

It is important to proactively identify which release readiness attributes are not performing sufficiently well (so-called bottleneck factors) during the phases of software development cycle. These attributes are likely to limit release readiness. In a previous publication [6], evidence for the existence of common patterns in bottleneck factors were found, which suggested that identifying underlying patterns of bottleneck occurrences will aid the understanding of such factors. The presented method called *Cross-project Analysis for Selection of Release Readiness attributes* (CASRR) supports the systematic investigation and analysis of release readiness attributes across multiple projects. CASRR identifies the most frequently occurring bottleneck factors (BF). Further analysis of bottleneck factors identifies (cluster-specific) patterns of bottleneck occurrences. The objective of CASRR method is to identify release readiness attributes, which are more prone to become bottlenecks and limit release readiness. In addition, CASRR facilitates understanding the influence of project evolution and project characteristics on the occurrence of bottleneck attributes. We assume iterative as well as traditional software development with release cycles over a month period are the primary beneficiary of applying the CASRR method. Agile software development techniques (e.g., Scrum) should not apply CASRR method for short-term one/two-week sprints. Instead, CASRR should be applied for major client releases spanning several sprints to identify and understand release readiness and bottleneck factors.

To support our presented method, we comprehensively studied related work and identified state-of-the-art concepts, such as approaches, metrics, tools, and empirical evaluation regarding measurement, monitoring, and controlling release readiness. We also identified the importance of monitoring and controlling release readiness throughout the development cycle of a release. Previously conducted exploratory case study research [6] established the importance of systematically studying and analyzing bottleneck factors across individual projects to reveal their characteristics.

In the absence of proprietary projects for analysis, we applied CASRR method for two Open Source Software (OSS) projects hosted in GitHub repository. In OSS projects, applying CASRR creates a sense of higher visibility and better control. Selected projects *GoldenCheetah/GoldenCheetah*[1] and *Mbostock/D3*[2] are, respectively, desktop and web-based software. Furthermore, we selected an extra set of 34 OSS projects for our analysis—equally distributed across desktop and web-based software domain. We selected six established release readiness attributes applying the GQM paradigm and monitored their performance in retrospective over a two-year period for each project. Our analysis focused on identifying most frequent bottleneck factors and the influence of project characteristics on their occurrence. Continuous integration rate, feature completion rate, and bug fixing rate are observed as the most frequent bottleneck factors in both domains. These factors are responsible for more than 80 % of all bottleneck occurrences. In addition, we identified project characteristics (e.g., project size, team size, and project phase) that significantly influence the occurrence of bottleneck factors. The results of analysis facilitate continuous monitoring of release readiness attributes throughout the development cycle, understand their nature in different project contexts, and achieve improved software release by proactively controlling them.

The rest of the chapter is organized as follows: Sect. 14.2 presents the background and context of this chapter. In Sect. 14.3, we presented the CASRR method. Section 14.4 applied the CASRR method with respect to OSS software hosted on GitHub. Section 14.5 presents summary of the research and our contributions.

14.2 Background and Context

Release readiness is a relatively young area of research in Software Engineering. We found few articles, which attempt evaluating release readiness of which most have taken unique approaches and used metrics for evaluating release readiness. To explore existing approaches and support motivation for our presented method, we

---

[1] Available from: https://github.com/GoldenCheetah/GoldenCheetah.

[2] Available from: https://github.com/mbostock/d3.

studied the most relevant articles in release readiness research. We briefly discuss the state-of-the-art concepts of measuring, monitoring and controlling release readiness in this section.

Existing approaches in literature and industry focused on different phases of the development cycle while evaluating release readiness. Due to this difference, these approaches have chosen a different set of metrics in release readiness evaluation. We broadly categorized these approaches in four categories (A1–A4). Table 14.1 lists all four categories along with a brief description. The table also lists the percentage of the articles falling under each category. We collected different metrics used in the studied approaches and classified them in four dimensions including *implementation status*, *testing scope and status*, *source code quality*, and *documentation scope and status*. In Table 14.2, we list these dimensions along with examples of metrics used.

We identified the frequency of articles falling under different categories or applying different dimensions based on their publication years. The bubble chart in

Table 14.1 Existing release readiness evaluation approaches are categorized in four categories. Their brief description and percent of studied articles in each category are listed here

	Categories	Description	% of articles
A1	Checklist-based approach	Check a set of RR criteria at the end of release cycles and extensively rely on subjective questions [13, 17]	22
A2	Testing metrics-based approach	Consider testing-related metrics only (e.g., test passing rate, defect find rate) and build various RR indicators [12, 14, 21]	43
A3	Defect prediction model-based approach	Consider remaining defects as a major indicator of RR. Build prediction model for remaining defects [16, 22]	22
A4	Multi-dimensional metrics aggregation-based approach	Evaluate a portfolio of product, process-related metrics, and aggregate them into a single measure of release readiness [2, 18, 19]	11

Table 14.2 Categorization of release readiness attributes

	Dimensions	Overview of related release readiness attributes
D1	Implementation status	Attributes related to feature implementation, change request implementation, coding effort, continuous integration, build trends, etc.
D2	Testing scope and status	Attributes related to defect finding, defect fixing, test coverage, test effort, etc.
D3	Source code quality	Attributes related to code review, coding style, code smells, refactoring, code complexity, etc.
D4	Documentation scope and status	Attributes related to user manual, design documents, test specification, test case documentation, etc.

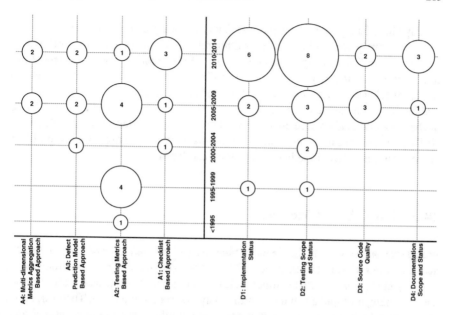

Fig. 14.1 Publication frequency of articles regarding approaches' categorization (*left*) and using metrics from different dimensions (*right*)

Fig. 14.1 summarizes the frequency of articles with respect to their publication year. In the left part, we present the different categories regarding the approaches presented in Table 14.1, and on right side, we present the different dimensions of metrics as listed in Table 14.2.

The checklist criteria and questions in category A1 are useful to assess release readiness at the end of a release cycle. However, software companies need to establish their own process and objective measures to use them effectively. Most of the criteria are subjective and available for evaluation only in the late stages of the release cycle. Category A2 is focused on the testing phase and to provide support for making confident release decision at the late stages of the development. These approaches cannot support product managers in continuous evaluation of release readiness. Category A3 proactively evaluates release readiness with an exclusive focus on remaining defects. Release readiness should represent the overall status of the project at any particular point in time during the release cycle in a quantitative way. The overall status of the project may depend on additional attributes such as satisfaction of bug fixing, satisfaction of test coverage, satisfaction of codebase stabilization, satisfaction of feature implementation, satisfaction of test pass rate etc. Therefore, exclusive consideration of remaining defects partially measures release readiness. Category A4 provides a broad overview of release readiness. These approaches depend on objective measures from various aspect of the software product. However, ad-hoc selection of metrics and misunderstanding their comparative importance can generate misleading release readiness evaluation.

Gaps in existing approaches motivated us to develop a comprehensive approach for continuously monitoring and controlling release readiness. Continuous monitoring and controlling multiple attributes is extremely resource intensive. Therefore, it is important to identify which release readiness attributes have higher chances to represent release readiness. In the majority of cases, metrics for evaluating release readiness were either selected ad-hoc or based on experience or gut-feeling. None of the reviewed studies emphasized a systematic identification of release readiness attributes for release readiness evaluation. In this chapter, we emphasize this problem and present the CASRR method as a proposed solution.

14.3   The CASRR Method

In this section, we present the *Cross-project Analysis for Selection of Release Readiness attributes* (CASRR) method. Product managers continuously measure and monitor project attributes, to ensure timely release and success of the product. Monitoring and analyzing multiple attributes continuously is resource intensive. Therefore, it is important to identify which attributes have greater influence on project success and therefore worth continuous monitoring. CASRR provides a systematic way to identify release readiness attributes, which have higher chances to limit release readiness as bottleneck factors. It helps identify a small subset of available release readiness attributes for continuous monitoring and save resources. In addition, it demonstrates how bottleneck occurrences are influenced by project evolution and different project contexts. We present an overview of the CASRR method in Fig. 14.2 using a flowchart and discuss details of the method and its phases in subsequent sections.

14.3.1   Preparation

The CASRR method identifies release readiness attributes, which may become a bottleneck factor and influence product release success. The product manager selects a project P, which she wants to monitor and control release readiness throughout the development cycle. We recommend that the product manager will perform some preparation steps for her project P prior to using CASRR method. In the following, we briefly discuss the preparation.

First, the product manager characterizes project P. Here, characterizing means identification of unique project characteristics, which are (i) easy to identify without an in-depth project analysis, (ii) possible to estimate prior to the development cycle, and (iii) influence the development cycle. Project size, number of previous releases, number of developers, duration of the release, maturity of the project, the domain of the project etc. are few examples of characteristics that can characterize project P. Characterizing project P helps select similar projects from repositories and learning across projects.

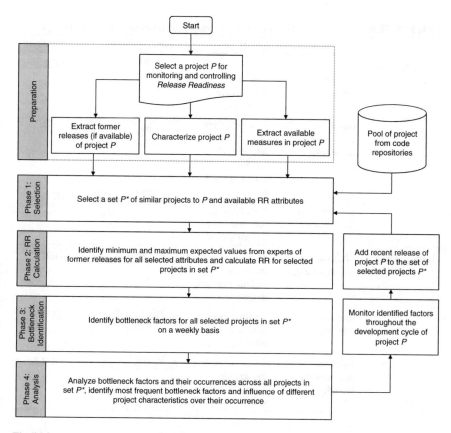

Fig. 14.2 Overview of the presented method Cross-project Analysis for Selection of Release Readiness attributes (CASRR)

Second, the product manager extracts available measures of project P. For example, the status of feature implementation, which is measured on a weekly basis by a metric called feature completion rate (FCR) as defined in Eq. 14.1 (see also Table 14.3).

$$FCR(k) = \frac{\text{ImplFeaturesToWeek}(k)}{\text{RequestFeaturesToWeek}(k)} \qquad (14.1)$$

We collect the number of features implemented (*ImplFeaturesToWeek*) up to week k and the number of requested features (*RequestFeaturesToWeek*), respectively, based on total number of features closed and opened until week k in a given repository. Feature completion rate refers to the completed features. Therefore, it might not measure the progress of implementation most accurately. However, it is a good-enough metric to measure project progress. We assume, for project P we have an

Table 14.3 Details of six selected release readiness attributes (structured according to GQM)

Dimensions	Attributes	Questions	Metric definitions	Acronym
Implementation status	Status of feature implementation	To what extent feature requests are completed	$\frac{ImplFeaturesToWeek(k)}{RequestFeaturesToWeek(k)}$	FCR
	Status of continuous integration	To what extent continuous integration (CI) requests are completed	$\frac{ComplCIRequestInWeek(k)}{ComplCIRequestToWeek(k)}$	PCR
	Status of improvement completion	To what extent improvement requests are completed	$\frac{ImplImproveToWeek(k)}{RequestImproveToWeek(k)}$	ICR
Testing status	Status of defect finding	To what extent the testing activity reducing defects	$\frac{FoundDefectsInWeek(k)}{FoundDefectsToWeek(k)}$	DFR
	Status of bug fixing	To what extent detected bugs are fixed	$\frac{SolvedBugsToWeek(k)}{IdentBugsToWeek(k)}$	BFR
	Status of source code stability	To what extent the source code is becoming stable	$\frac{CodeChurnInWeek(k)}{CodeChurnToWeek(k)}$	CCR

available set of metrics (denoted by M). Extracting these metrics helps in selecting a subset of release readiness attributes that CASRR method can investigate across similar projects.

14.3.2   Phase 1: Selection

The CASRR method is a systematic approach to foster learning across projects. In preparation of using CASRR, we characterize project P. Identified characteristics of P help select a set of similar projects P^*. These projects serve as basis for learning. We assume similar projects will show similar trends in release readiness attributes towards the success of a product release. Analyzing previous projects assist in anticipating potential bottlenecks in similar new projects. Along with project selection, we need to set the observation period. A "longer" observation period is aimed to result in better analyses but consumes more resources. By default, we use two years of retrospective analysis as observation period. Based on the availability of projects and resources, product managers may change this period.

The product manager can select similar projects from one or multiple code repositories. Previous releases of project P (if available) are considered in P^*. Characteristics of P drive the selection of similar projects. For each selected project, we collect the required raw data for the selected set of release readiness attributes. We select release readiness attributes based on the organizational goals and customer expectations. However, this may vary from project to project. Table 14.2 presents four major dimensions for release readiness. These are different aspects of the software product described by a set of possible attributes to evaluate release readiness. One or more metrics quantitatively describe a particular release readiness attribute. The product manager must choose a set of release readiness attributes that are common among all the projects in P^*. To help project managers, we suggest applying the *Goal Question Metric* (GQM; [3]) paradigm. GQM is effective in designing a measurement program that can evaluate release readiness. Release readiness attributes corresponding to questions of GQM achieve the respective measurement goal. Available data associated with each question quantitatively answer them.

As an example of this process, we selected six attributes (Table 14.3) using the GQM paradigm from two major dimensions (i.e., implementation status and testing scope and status) [6]. The attributes and measures taken in this example are highly context specific. According to our previous research [6], these attributes represent 60% of attributes known as influential from comprehensive industry guidelines[3] available. In case of projects from the same repository (e.g., GitHub), the number of overlapping attributes is expected to be higher compared to projects from different sources. Product managers should consider the trade-off between the number of similar projects selected and number of overlapping release readiness attributes available. We suggest selecting the maximum number of projects with most overlapping release readiness attributes. However, the decision depends on multiple external factors, such as importance of release readiness attributes or maturity of projects, and may vary based on expert opinion.

14.3.3 Phase 2: Release Readiness Calculation

In phase 2, we calculate release readiness for all selected projects in P^*. First, we measure release readiness individually for all selected release readiness attributes in each project for each week. This is called the *Local Release Readiness* (LRR) for individual release readiness attributes. Subsequently, we combine LRR metrics into a *Global Release Readiness* (GRR) metric representing readiness of the entire product release. Based on expert opinion or previous releases, we identify the, respectively, expected minimum and maximum values for each release readiness attribute per project.

---

[3] Available from: http://www.softwareconsortium.com/software-release-readiness-criteria.html.

At any time t, LRR of a release readiness attribute a_i, $LRR(a_i, t)$ is calculated based on the actual value achieved at t with respect to the expected maximum and minimum value to be achieved during the development cycle. This is a normalized value from interval $[0, 1]$, where 0 and 1, respectively, represent the expected minimum and maximum values. We measure LRR throughout the development cycle and the value resides somewhere between the two extreme points. We define LRR as follows:

Definition 14.1 (**Local Release Readiness**) We assume that project P with duration of release $[0, T]$ at given week $t \in [0, T]$ have

- A given set of release readiness attributes $A = \{a_1, a_2, \ldots, a_n\}$
- For each release readiness attribute, a corresponding expected minimum and maximum level of values based on previous successful releases or expert opinion are given by n-dimensional vectors $A_{min}(a_i)$ and $A_{max}(a_i)$
- Corresponding actual values of release readiness attributes are given by the n-dimensional vector $A_{actual}(a_i, t)$

Then, $LRR(a_i, t) \in [0, 1]$ is the local release readiness of attribute a_i at week t. It is calculated based on the corresponding value in vector $A_{actual}(a_i, t)$ and expected values of $A_{min}(a_i)$ and $A_{max}(a_i)$ following Eq. 14.2.

$$LRR(a_i, t) = \frac{A_{actual}(a_i, t) - A_{min}(a_i)}{A_{max}(a_i) - A_{min}(a_i)} \qquad (14.2)$$

For any point in time t during the release, the global release readiness $GRR(t)$ metric is defined as the *Weighted Arithmetic Mean* (WAM) for all $LRR(a_i, t)$ values.

Definition 14.2 (**Global Release Readiness**) For a given set of release readiness attributes $A = \{a_1, a_2, \ldots, a_n\}$, the local release readiness of any attribute a_i at week t is represented by $LRR(a_i, t)$, where $LRR(a_i, t) \in [0, 1]$. If $\{w_1, w_2, \ldots, w_n\}$ represents corresponding weights of attributes, the global release readiness is calculated as follows:

$$GRR(t) = WAM(LRR(a_1, t), LRR(a_2, t), \ldots, LRR(a_n, t)) = \sum_{i-1}^{n} w_i \times LRR(a_i, t) \qquad (14.3)$$

We demonstrate the proposed release readiness calculation using a hypothetical example. For $T = 20$ weeks long release of a *DemoProject*, we consider two release readiness attributes: (a) status of bug fixing and (b) status of feature implementation. Objective metrics for evaluating these release readiness attributes are, respectively, bug fix rate (BFR) and feature completion rate (FCR). We already defined these metrics in Table 14.3. Figure 14.3 demonstrates the LRR value for BFR and FCR for the first 10 weeks using bar charts. The curve presents the actual values for BFR and FCR. We identified maximum and minimum expected values for both metrics based on previous releases that are presented using horizontal dotted lines. For each week, we calculate local feature completion rate using Eq. 14.2. For the above example, we consider both feature completion rate attributes as equally weighted. Therefore, the

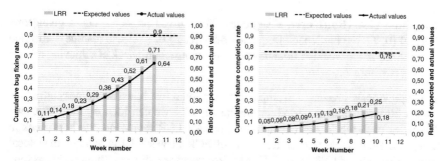

Fig. 14.3 Local RR evaluation (presented in *bars*) for Bug fixing rate (*left*) and Feature completion rate (*right*). The *solid line* curve presents the actual values of BFR and FCR and the horizontal *dotted line* presents the expected values, respectively, for BFR and FCR

GRR at any week t (i.e., $GRR(t)$) is calculated as the arithmetic mean of the LRR value of BFR (i.e., $LRR(BFR, t)$) and FCR (i.e., $LRR(FCR, t)$) at week t.

14.3.4 Phase 3: Bottleneck Identification

Bottleneck factors (BF) are those release readiness attributes responsible for limiting the readiness of a software product release. Factors which achieved a minimum LRR value among all considered release readiness attributes will be referred to as bottleneck factors. Identifying and analyzing bottleneck factors allows product managers to continuously monitor the development cycle and to proactively take action toward controlling them. Resource bottlenecks in project management are a well-understood phenomenon. We transfer this idea from project management to the study of release readiness. We define bottleneck factors as follows:

Definition 14.3 (Bottleneck Factor) For a given project P and a given week $t \in [0, T]$, the *bottleneck factor BF(t)* is a release readiness attribute a_i, which has the lowest LRR value $LRR(a_i, t)$ among all release readiness attributes thus limiting the global release readiness (Eq. 14.3) value $GRR(t)$ at week t.

$$BF(t) = argmin_i\{LRR(a_1, t), LRR(a_2, t), \ldots, LRR(a_n, t)\} \qquad (14.4)$$

Equation 14.4 returns the index of the bottleneck factor. Based on Eq. 14.4, we identify bottleneck factors per week and individually for all selected projects in P^*. We compare the bottleneck frequency for every release readiness attribute in order to understand (i) which release readiness attribute becomes the bottleneck factor more or less frequently and (ii) whether there are certain conditions or contexts which contribute in release readiness attributes becoming bottlenecks. We define the bottleneck frequency as follows:

Definition 14.4 (Bottleneck Frequency) For a given project P and a given time interval $[0, T]$, the bottleneck frequency $BNF(a_i, T)$ of a release readiness attribute a_i is defined as the weekly frequency of a_i becoming a bottleneck in achieving release readiness within T.

In the previously presented example, we monitored two release readiness attributes over a 20-week release period. Applying Eq. 14.4 we can identify the bottleneck factor for each week. For example, in Fig. 14.3 FCR represents the bottleneck at week 10. Here, local release readiness of FCR in week 10 is smaller than local release readiness of BFR in week 10. Multiple release readiness attributes can become bottlenecks in a single week as well. While identifying bottleneck factors, we consider equal weights for all attributes. Therefore, the weighted arithmetic mean in Eq. 14.3 becomes equivalent to arithmetic average, which allows a more simple bottleneck factor identification approach using Eq. 14.4. This simplification helps avoid bias in bottleneck factor identification and analysis of bottleneck frequency.

14.3.5 Phase 4: Analysis

In Table 14.3, we applied the GQM paradigm to select release readiness attributes and corresponding metrics. We selected six release readiness attributes from a larger set of measures extracted from project P. Our selection of release readiness attributes and subsequent metrics was primarily influenced by their (i) availability in selected projects, (ii) influence on release readiness, and (iii) ease of calculation. We identified bottleneck factors within this selected set of metrics using Eq. 14.4. To identify (cluster-specific) patterns of bottleneck occurrence, we conduct a per-domain analysis answering the following questions:

1. What are the most frequently occurring bottleneck attributes (overall and per cluster)?
2. What project characteristics influence the occurrence of bottleneck attributes (overall and per cluster)? Example characteristics considered are:

    - Project size, i.e., to distinguish between bottleneck attributes occurrence in large versus small projects,
    - Project team, i.e., to distinguish between bottleneck attribute occurrence in projects with many contributors versus those with few contributors,
    - Project phase, i.e., to distinguish between bottleneck attributes occurrence in early versus late phases of a release development

Once we collected all data and processed them to phase 3, we start the analysis in order to answer the questions of interest for phase 4.

Note: So far, we have described the investigation regarding bottleneck frequency of release readiness attributes. We provided an exemplary analysis of bottleneck factors across projects based on selected project characteristics. The selection of project characteristics for a particular analysis depends on the context and the goal of the analysis. Experts may consider completely different investigations or project characteristics as more relevant for their analysis based on underlying context or organization.

Based on our analysis results, we identified the bottleneck attributes, which are most important for monitoring and counteracting, per cluster, per project type, and per project phase. This analysis helps with selecting release readiness attributes, which tend to become bottleneck factors. This analysis also helps with understanding the influence of project evolution and project characteristics on the occurrence of bottleneck factors. Selected bottleneck factors are applied in continuous monitoring and controlling of release readiness throughout the release. Monitoring and controlling these bottleneck factors falls outside the scope of this chapter and is subject to future research.

14.4   Proof of Concept

To validate the CASRR method and to demonstrate its applicability, in this section, we present an empirical evaluation. We applied CASRR to different OSS projects. In absence of proprietary projects, we selected two OSS projects for example, one desktop- and one web-based software project for evaluation purpose.

Preparation: We selected two projects from two different software domains as subjects. The selected projects are *GoldenCheetah/GoldenCheetah* and *MboStock/D3*, which are desktop- and, Web-based software projects, respectively. In preparation of using CASRR, we characterized these projects by the *number of commits, number of releases, number of different contributors*, and *project duration in calendar days*. In Tables 14.4 and 14.5, we present these characteristics collected over the total lifespan (i.e., from project start to the end of observation time) of the projects. As a second step, we extract a list of available measures from both projects. Initially, we extract a set of 14 metrics related to the first three release readiness dimensions as presented in Table 14.2. Due to lack of available documentation, we discard extracting measures related to the *documentation scope and status* dimension. After completing both preparation steps, we move toward applying CASRR to both projects.

14.4.1 Phase 1: Selection

In phase 1, we select a set of similar projects based on the characterization of our projects. We have chosen a single repository to select our projects for analysis.

> **Note:** It is hard to quantify the number of similar projects required due to (i) perception of the project manager and (ii) availability of projects. However, as a default rule one should keep ranges flexible to find a significant number (minimum 10) of similar projects.

In this study, we selected 32 projects from GitHub—equally divided into desktop-based (D) and web-based (W) software development projects. Including previous releases of *GoldenCheetah/GoldenCheetah* and *Mbostock/D3*, we analyzed 34 OSS projects in total. Tables 14.4 and 14.5 summarize all desktop- and web-based projects, respectively.

Since all 34 projects are selected from the same GitHub repository, we identified a large set of common attributes among the projects. We applied GQM to select a set of six attributes (shown in Table 14.3) related to release readiness. As mentioned before, the selected attributes cover 60 % of attributes, which are known as influential

Table 14.4 List of 17 desktop-based projects with their characteristics

Project id and name	# Commits	# Releases	# Different contributors	Duration (days)
D1: GoldenCheetah/GoldenCheetah	**4016**	**22**	**41**	**1319**
D2: Ryanb/Can can	419	29	62	1710
D3: Celluloid/Celluloid	1415	45	74	1169
D4: Clinton-hall/NzbToMedia	1472	0	15	581
D5: Fastly/Epoch	345	14	6	385
D6: Berkshelf/Berkshelf	3609	97	81	812
D7: Grafana/Ggrafana	1541	16	70	188
D8: Intridea/Grape	1802	25	151	1450
D9: Joey711/Phyloseq	581	0	5	1046
D10: Mybb/Mybb	1234	37	24	760
D11: Orientechnologies/Orientdb	7731	21	49	590
D12: Owncloud/Mirall	5865	43	42	681
D13: Python-pillow/Pillow	2336	15	95	729
D14: Resque/Resque	1910	70	229	1723
D15: Scikit-learn/Scikit-learn	16816	58	282	1422
D16: SynoCommunity/Spksrc	1754	0	41	1011
D17: Zfsonlinux/Zfs	1408	30	104	1531

Table 14.5 List of 17 web-based projects with their characteristics

Project id and name	# Commits	# Releases	# Different contributors	Duration (days)
W1: Mbostock/D3	**3207**	**173**	**78**	**1393**
W2: Att/Rcloud	2842	12	11	712
W3: Automattic/Socket.io	1293	89	68	1589
W4: Locomotivecms/Engine	2209	36	80	1429
W5: FortAwesome/Font-Awesome	573	14	28	869
W6: Gravitystorm/Openstreetmap-carto	595	29	29	598
W7: H5bphtml5/Boilerplate	1340	24	175	1641
W8: Hawtio/Hawtio	5920	51	45	594
W9: Highslide-software/Highcharts.com	4109	71	31	1498
W10: Hypothesis/H	3851	9	18	831
W11: Jashkenas/Backbone	2629	21	228	1379
W12: MayhemYDG/4chan-x	5151	192	35	1017
W13: Adobe/Adobe	13887	53	225	958
W14: Moment/Moment	2050	36	204	1160
W15: Imathis/Octopress	808	1	103	1683
W16: Travis-ci/Travis-ci	3602	232	94	1241
W17: Webbukkit/Dynmap	1738	67	14	1295

for project success. In order to cover both, functional and non-functional aspects of release readiness, we assess those release readiness attributes that satisfy certain goals related to the implementation and test status in each project.

14.4.2   Phases 2 and 3: Release Readiness Calculation and Bottleneck Factor Identification

As previously demonstrated, phases 2 and 3 are meant to calculate the release readiness and to identify the bottleneck factors. After identifying project characteristics, similar projects, and release readiness attributes, we started collecting the raw data for each release readiness attribute from the selected projects. We collected data for all projects over a two-year observation period (with few exceptions). Following Eq. 14.2, we calculate the LRR value on a weekly basis for all release readiness attributes over all selected projects. To reduce bias in identifying bottleneck factors, we applied equal relative weights for release readiness attributes across projects. We consulted two senior developers from local software companies to decide the expected minimum and maximum values for each attribute. Furthermore, we selected the minimum and maximum values individually for each project based on minimum and maximum values derived from the two-year observation period.

For each project, one or more bottlenecks were identified. We consider release readiness attribute(s) with lowest LRR (Eq. 14.4) value in each week as the bottleneck factor. Following the definition of the bottleneck frequency (BNF) shown in Sect. 14.3.4, we calculate the BNF of a release readiness attribute occurring as bottleneck over the whole observation period.

> **Note:** For the purpose of the demonstration, we primarily relied on the bottleneck frequency data and performed multiple analyses across the selected projects. However, the analysis is not limited to bottleneck frequency. Experts can perform a CASRR-based analysis with respect to other measurable criteria, e.g., how one bottleneck transfers to another one or how bottlenecks group together over the observation period.

14.4.3   Phase 4: Analysis

Phase 3 calculates individual LRR values along with identifying bottleneck factors and the frequency of occurrence. Figure 14.4 shows box plots for the bottleneck frequency of all release readiness attributes across all selected projects. For each release readiness attribute, the range of bottleneck frequencies is given for both desktop- (D) and web-based (W) projects. For example, we observed that the mean value for the release readiness attribute *PCR* became a bottleneck across all projects for above 70 time in D-type projects and above 80 times in W-type projects over the observation period.

Once we collected the information for each project of how often a release readiness attribute occurred as a (potential) bottleneck, we conducted further analyses. By following the plan presented in Sect. 14.3.5, we first aim to identify common patterns

Fig. 14.4 Bottleneck frequency of the six release readiness attributes for D- and W-type projects

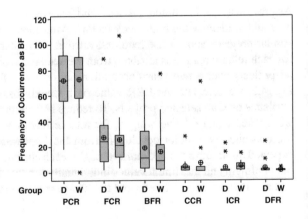

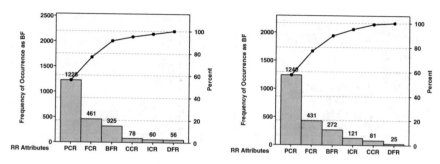

Fig. 14.5 Pareto charts for bottleneck frequencies in desktop-based projects (*left*) and web-based projects (*right*)

of bottleneck frequency, i.e., whether some release readiness attributes occur more frequently than others, or if there is a difference between the rankings of release readiness attributes in the two considered software domains. Figure 14.5 shows the Pareto charts for both project types. We identified similar bottleneck frequency patterns and rankings among both domains. In particular, the same three release readiness attributes (PCR, FCR, and BFR) account for more than 80 % of all bottleneck occurrences. Furthermore, a ranking of the three most frequently occurring bottleneck factors is similar in both domains. This implies that product manager can focus on controlling the top-most release readiness attribute(s) if resources are scarce.

Next, we are interested in whether the occurrence frequencies of bottleneck factors differs depending on certain project characteristics. In the presented case, we focused on the three project characteristics *size* (measured as number of commits), *team dispersion* (measured as number of different contributors), and *release development phase*. In order to determine the early and late phase of a release development of a project, we split each release development into two equal parts—early and late phase. For example, if 16 releases were observed for a project (see column number of releases in Table 14.4), we will consider 16 early phases and 16 late phases, respectively, and we can count how often a certain release readiness attribute became a bottleneck in each of these phases, which also represents the evolution of software projects to a certain extent.

We applied the *Mann–Whitney U Test* for non-parametric statistical testing to check whether occurrence frequency differs significantly per release readiness attribute for a given project type. Figure 14.6 shows the split of occurrence frequencies for all six release readiness attributes regarding size, team dispersion, and release development phase on a per-project-type analysis.[4] In summary, we found three different patterns:

---

[4]The symbol '**' next to the release readiness attribute name indicates that the occurrence frequency of the respective attribute is significantly different at an alpha-level of 5 %.

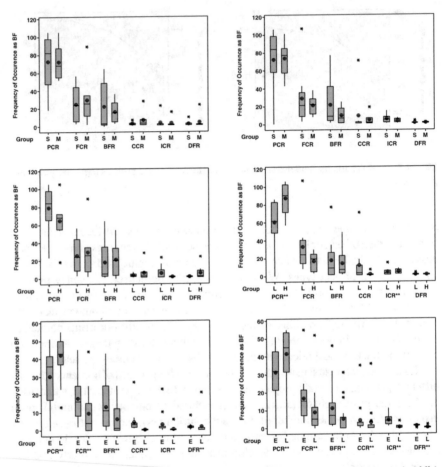

Fig. 14.6 Frequency of occurrence of bottleneck factors by project size (*top*), project team (*middle*), project phase (*bottom*); grouped by desktop-based (*left*) and web-based (*right*) projects

1. Distinguishing projects with regards to size does not show any significant difference in the occurrence frequency of bottleneck attributes in both domains
2. Distinguishing projects with regards to release phase exhibits significant difference in the occurrence frequency of bottleneck attributes for all release readiness attributes in both domains
3. Distinguishing projects with regards to team does not show any significant difference for desktop-based projects but shows significant difference for release readiness attribute PCR for web-based projects

Considering release phases as a representation of project evolution, this analysis demonstrates that bottleneck occurrence for all selected release readiness attributes changes in accordance with the project's evolution.

In our example, all release readiness attributes have presented an almost uniform behavior depending on project types and characteristics. However, this may not always be the case. Therefore, it is of certain interest to highlight the release readiness attribute that in total occurs most frequently as a bottleneck, i.e., PCR. The benefit of such an analysis is that a company with large project portfolios (and related repositories) can use the analysis outcomes to focus their effort spent on monitoring release readiness attributes where it really matters. In other words, it facilitates in understanding the differences between monitoring the bottleneck factors for different project types and different project-related criteria.

14.5 Conclusion

The success of a software release depends on complex decisions related to stakeholders, constraints, features, resources, and many more. Product managers often need to choose between quality, release time, and functionalities of the product. Even a slightly early or late release may result in significant loss or even a complete failure. Therefore, ad hoc decisions or those based on gut feeling can put the project and the organization into risk. Collecting analytical data by continuously monitoring the development cycle can give product managers better insight into a project and its current status, which will result in more astuteness in decision making. However, this process is extensively resource consuming. In order to systematically identify attributes, which have a higher likelihood to limit the product readiness thus using limited resource wisely, we proposed and evaluated the CASRR method in this chapter.

This chapter and the CASRR approach are presented to help product managers in their release decisions by delivering four different contributions: First, we present a systematic way to learn across similar projects. The presented approach guides product managers in focusing on monitoring resources where they are more effective. Second, our approach identifies bottleneck factors early. This will proactively address possible resource limitations and recommend appropriate actions to manage them. Third, we validated our presented method using OSS projects. The evaluation revealed some important conclusions with respect to OSS projects. Finally, we systematically studied related articles, summarized their key findings, and categorized them in meaningful groups. This helps to direct future research in this domain.

We applied our presented CASRR method to two different OSS software development domains. We selected 17 desktop-based and 17 web-based software projects for analysis, which resulted in three major conclusions: (i) We analyzed projects in different groups based on size, project team, and project phase. We found significant differences in the frequency of bottleneck factors in achieving release readiness among different groups for the selected project types, (ii) we found differences between the attributes studied in this chapter and the domain we considered to select our projects, and (iii) project characteristics and project evolution influence bottleneck occurrences.

Since these conclusions are context-specific, it is yet not possible to generalize them for proprietary software. However, the conclusions help with evaluating release readiness and recommend meaningful actions. Applying CASRR supports the detection of the most influential bottleneck factors in a project and the identification of how project characteristics influence the variation of bottleneck factors. Proactively using this information helps project teams to better manage their resource allocation. With the future improvement of this method, we will be able to better monitor and control releases with effective use of assigned resources.

14.6 Further Reading

In this chapter, we presented the CASRR approach to identify release readiness attributes, which can better measure release readiness. In different articles, authors have chosen different attributes to evaluate release readiness. The choice of release readiness attributes was mostly ad-hoc or based on experience and gut feeling. In most cases, these articles did not apply a systematic and comprehensive study across different projects to identify release readiness attributes. In this section, we briefly discuss some of these related publications (Table. 14.6).

In [20], Staron et al. proposed the *time-to-release* indicator for agile development. They identified time-to-release using the Eq. 14.5 based on *number of defects*, *defect removal rate*, *test execution rate*, and *test pass rate*. The value for all metrics in Eq. 14.5 are based on the past four weeks of a release cycle. However, only a single release readiness indicator value cannot provide proper insight into the complexities involved in the decision-making processes of software releases. Assumptions such as traceability between test cases and requirements, and traceability between test cases and work packages etc., limits the applicability of this approach to other domains.

$$Time\ to\ Release = \frac{\#\ defects}{defect\ removal\ rate - (test\ execution\ rate - test\ pass\ rate)}$$

(14.5)

At HP labs, researchers developed a method to assess release readiness for embedded systems [14]. They identified and applied four objective metrics *code turmoil*, *test passing rate*, *defect find rate* and *number of open defects*. Researchers used Spider Charts to visualize and compare the metrics of the current project with past projects. This helps the management understand the risk associated to each metric to deliver the product on the predefined release date. In another approach, researchers estimate the remaining defects [16, 22] to evaluate release readiness and considered a set of source code-related metrics, such as *depth of the inheritance tree*, *responsibility of a class*, *number of parents of a class*, and so forth. They collected data from different layers (e.g., data access layer, presentation layer, and business logic layer) and provided prediction model based on neural networks. Based on the prediction

Table 14.6 List of former articles and details of their performed case study along with purpose of the study, research method and applied metrics in these case studies

Reference	System under study	Research method	Metric applied	Purpose of the study
[17]	DataFinder (a RDBMS product)	Case study	Open and close bug rates, percentage of test passing, and test coverage, task productivity rates, feature productivity rates	Reviewing the actions and measurements taken for the assessment of the readiness of the product ship
[16]	Warehouse management applications and networked information system	Case study	Source code metrics collected from Warehouse management applications	Verify accuracy of the defect prediction model and to quantify the relative importance of the source code-related metrics
[10]	Electronic design automation products	Case study	Defect find rate, severity 1 open defects, and weighted defect density	To validate the metrics used for determining RR of the software product
[5]	75 product release in Motorola	Case study	Failure free testing hours	To validate the proposed zero-failure model for achieving RR
[14]	HP LaserJet product	Case study	As number of open defects, test passing rate, defect find rate, and code turmoil	To validate the RR metrics and approach
[20]	Ericsson products	Action research	Number of defects, defect removal rate, test execution rate and test pass rate	Evaluating time-to-release as key RR in indicator

model, they identified the number of remaining defects along with the amount time required for release.

The majority of the discussed articles does not provide proper tool support—if at all, some kind of visualization was mentioned. Tool support allows product managers to evaluate the approach and to judge its usefulness. Apart from that, we found two companies integrating a release readiness analysis component as a supplementary feature of their main product. For instance, Borland's TeamInspector [4] extracts metrics related to code analysis, test coverage, standard compliance, and build trends to evaluate release readiness. PTC integrity [11] from MKS software extracts and visualizes metrics related to functionality, standard compliance, and budget and schedule to verify release readiness. Some former articles presented case studies in industry setup. These articles evaluated their approaches in industry and discussed their experiences. In Table 14.6, we summarize the most relevant case studies on release readiness along with their article citation, the purpose of the study, the system under study, research method, and metrics applied in the study.

Acknowledgments This work was partially supported by the Natural Sciences and Engineering Research Council of Canada, NSERC Discovery Grant 250343-12, Alberta Innovates Technology Futures and by the institutional research grant IUT20-55 of the Estonian Research Council.

References

1. Ashrafi, N.: The impact of software process improvement on quality: in theory and practice. Inf. Manag. **40**(7), 677–690 (2003)
2. Asthana, A., Olivieri, J.: Quantifying software reliability and readiness. In: Proceedings of the International Workshop Technical Committee on Communications Quality and Reliability, pp. 1–6. IEEE, Washington, DC (2009)
3. Basili, V.R., Caldiera, G., Rombach, H.D.: The goal question metric approach. In: Encyclopedia of Software Engineering. Wiley, New Jersey (1994)
4. Borland: Teaminspector 2008. http://techpubs.borland.com
5. Brettschneider, R.: Is your software ready for release? IEEE Softw **6**(4), 100–104 (1989)
6. Didar Al Alam, S.M., Shahnewaz, S.M., Pfahl, D., Ruhe, G.: Monitoring bottlenecks in achieving release readiness: a retrospective case study across ten oss projects. In: Proceedings of the International Symposium on Empirical Software Engineering and Measurement, pp. 60:1–60:4. ACM, New York, NY, USA (2014)
7. Ebert, C.: The impacts of software product management. J. Syst. Softw. **80**(6), 850–861 (2007)
8. Ebert, C.: Software product management. IEEE Softw. **31**(3), 21–24 (2014)
9. Gokhale, S.: Optimal software release time incorporating fault correction. In: Proceedings of the Annual NASA Goddard Software Engineering Workshop, pp. 175–184. IEEE, Washington, DC (2003)
10. Johnson, M.A.: A case study of tracking software development using quality metrics. Softw. Qual. J. **4**(1), 15–31 (1995)
11. Larman, C.: Agile and Iterative Development: A Manager's Guide. Addison-Wesley Professional (2003)
12. McConnell, S.: Gauging software readiness with defect tracking. IEEE Softw. **14**(3), 135–136 (1997)
13. Microsoft: Plan the release readiness review meeting. http://technet.microsoft.com/en-us/library/cc526651.aspx Accessed 2014
14. Pearse, T., Freeman, T., Oman, P.: Using metrics to manage the end-game of a software project. In: Proceedings of the International Symposium on Software Metrics, pp. 207–215. IEEE, Washington, DC (1999)
15. Port, D., Wilf, J.: The value of certifying software release readiness: an exploratory study of certification for a critical system at jpl. In: Proceedings of the International Symposium on Empirical Software Engineering and Measurement, pp. 373–382. IEEE, Washington, DC (2013)

16. Quah, T.S.: Estimating software readiness using predictive models. Inf. Sci. **179**(4), 430–445 (2009)
17. Rothman, J.: Measurements to reduce risk in product ship decisions. http://www.universityalliance.com/info1/whitepapers Accessed 2014
18. Satapathy, P.R.: Evaluation of software release readiness metric [0,1] across the software development life cycle. Tech. rep., Department of Computer Science & Engineering, University of California (2007)
19. Shahnewaz, S.M.: RELREA-an analytical approach supporting continuous release readiness evaluation. Master's thesis, University of Calgary (2014)
20. Staron, M., Meding, W., Palm, K.: Release readiness indicator for mature agile and lean software development projects. In: Wohlin, C. (ed.) Agile Processes in Software Engineering and Extreme Programming. Lecture Notes in Business Information Processing, vol. 111, pp. 93–107. Springer, Heidelberg (2012)
21. Ware, M., Wilkie, F., Shapcott, M.: The use of intra-release product measures in predicting release readiness. In: Proceedings of the International Conference on Software Testing, Verification, and Validation, pp. 230–237. IEEE, Washington, DC (2008)
22. Wild, R., Brune, P.: Determining software product release readiness by the change-error correlation function: on the importance of the change-error time lag. In: Proceeding of the Annual Hawaii International Conference on System Science, pp. 5360–5367. IEEE, Washington, DC (2012)

Chapter 15
The Effects of Software Process Evolution to Technical Debt—Perceptions from Three Large Software Projects

Jesse Yli-Huumo, Andrey Maglyas and Kari Smolander

Abstract This chapter describes a qualitative study with the goal to explore and understand how software process evolution affects technical debt. We investigated three large software development projects with a long development history with the aim to understand how software processes had evolved during the life cycle and how this evolution affected technical debt. We observed how companies had changed their software processes as well as the reasons, benefits, and consequences of these changes on technical debt. The main driving force for the software process evolution was business pressure from management to increase productivity and become cost-efficient. However, these changes were also the source of technical debt. The results show that software process evolution has a clear effect to technical debt. Software process evolution can be used to decrease technical debt by adopting new methods, tools, and techniques. However, software process evolution includes several challenges. These challenges have a possibility to decrease the productivity and quality of new software processes and technical debt might increase.

15.1 Introduction

The software industry struggles with increasing competition and time-to-market requirements in delivering new solutions to customers. Companies must be able to deliver their solutions faster than competitors to receive a share of the market [6]. In order to be fast, companies should enhance their software development processes and practices to achieve the best ways to produce quality software on time, within

J. Yli-Huumo (✉) · A. Maglyas
School of Business and Management, Innovation & Software, Lappeenranta University of Technology, P.O. Box 20, 53851 Lappeenranta, Finland
e-mail: Jesse.Yli-Huumo@lut.fi

A. Maglyas
e-mail: Andrey.Maglyas@lut.fi

K. Smolander
Department of Computer Science, Aalto University, P.O. Box 15400, 00076 Aalto, Finland
e-mail: kari.smolander@aalto.fi

© Springer International Publishing Switzerland 2016
M. Kuhrmann et al. (eds.), *Managing Software Process Evolution*,
DOI 10.1007/978-3-319-31545-4_15

budget, and for the right market [27]. However, software development processes are not easy to change [4] or manage (see also Chap. 10 and Chap. 9 in this volume). If the new processes do not align to the organization and its way of working, serious consequences may follow. Decreasing quality and productivity can be the result of new software development processes if they do not align with the company's way of working. When omitted quality and productivity issues start to have effect on a software development project, it can be a sign of "technical debt."

The technical debt metaphor is related to shortcuts and workarounds in meeting urgent demands [35]. Implementing shortcuts to the system architecture incur "debt" that must be eventually paid back. If this debt is not properly managed, it might accumulate as "interest," affecting the overall quality of the developed software systems [42, 43]. Although technical debt has negative consequences in a long term, it can be used as a competitive advantage in a short term [26]. Time-to-market and constant customer feedback through releasing software faster than competitors allow companies to gain a bigger market share [26].

This chapter describes a qualitative study that had a purpose to explore and understand how software process evolution affects technical debt. We investigated three large software development projects with a long development history with the aim to understand how software processes had evolved during the life cycle and how this evolution affected technical debt. We observed how companies had changed their software processes as well as the reasons, benefits, and consequences of these changes on the technical debt.

The rest of the chapter is organized as follows. Section 15.2 provides the background and the research process related to this research. Section 15.3 introduces the results analyzed from the gathered data. In Sect. 15.4, we discuss about the results. Section 15.5 concludes the paper, and Sect. 15.6 provides further reading related to the chapter's topic.

15.2 Background and Context

The term "technical debt" was first introduced in 1992 by Ward Cunningham as a situation where a long-term code quality is traded for a short-term gain [13]. Technical debt can be compared to finance debt [1]. Similar to finance debt, technical debt incurs interest, which come in the form of the extra effort that we have to pay back in the future [1]. Often technical debt is related to the source code of the software, where a shortcut or a workaround is taken in order to save time. However, taking shortcuts and workarounds can happen in multiple stages of software development life cycle [38]. In the requirements phase, lack of documentation or lack of requirements can cause requirements debt [29, 44]. Architectural flaws in the design phase can also increase design debt [5, 38] and structural debt [44]. In a testing environment workarounds in running and writing test cases can also incur test debt [44] and automation debt [9].

In addition, technical debt is not always caused by intentional decisions to gain short-term advantages. Technical debt can be divided into two main categories:

intentional and unintentional technical debt [28]. Intentional technical debt incurs when company makes a strategic decision to cut down; for example, the feature quality in order to be able to release the product on time to customer. Unintentional technical debt forms unknowingly, when for example, a junior coder writes lower quality code that needs to be refactored later.

Companies change and evolve their software processes to improve software quality and reliability, employee and customer satisfaction, return on investment and time-to-market [12, 27]. Software process improvement (SPI) is used to improve productivity, quality, schedule, customer satisfaction, and return on investment [2, 17, 18, 23]. Overall, the current research on software process evolution consists of studies about the benefits and consequences of software process improvement. However, their relationship to technical debt has not been studied. In this study, we focus on contributing to the research of technical debt by studying the reasons, benefits, and consequences of software process evolution and their relationship on taking shortcuts and workarounds and provide empirical results by studying three real software projects.

Case study was selected as the research method for the study. Case study is a way to investigate an empirical topic by following a set of pre-specified procedures [41]. According to Verner et al. [40], case studies provide "a systematic way of looking at events, collecting data, analysing information, and reporting the results." Case study method involves an in-depth examination of a single case or a multiple number of cases [40]. According to Yin, it "investigates a contemporary phenomenon within ins real-life context, especially when the boundaries between phenomenon and context are not clearly evident [41]." We followed the guidelines of Yin [41] to conduct the case study process in this research. The process consists five different stages [41]:

1. Designing the case study
2. Preparing for data collection
3. Collecting the evidence
4. Analysing the case study evidence
5. Reporting the case study

The first stage of the case study process was to design and identify the research strategy for the case study. In this study, our focus was on the software process evolution and technical debt. The goal was to understand how software processes had evolved during the life cycle and how this affected to technical debt. We decided to use the exploratory case study method with semi-structured interviews [31] that are frequently used as a data collection technique in software engineering studies [20].

The second stage for the case study process was to prepare the data collection. In this stage, we designed the procedures to conduct interviews and contacted the key persons in the chosen cases. The interviews were designed to investigate the reasons, benefits, and consequences of software process evolution to technical debt, rather than what are the qualities of technical debt in the source code. Therefore, we arranged interviews with people from multiple different backgrounds (business and technical). Since this study was a part of a bigger research program, the selection of the companies was primarily dictated by the list of partners. The selected cases for this study were three large companies in the data communications industry. The primary reason for the selection of these three specific cases was their long product history. We believed that a product with long development history would include more software process changes and it would provide us with more empirical data about the research topic.

Case A is a software development project that develops a self-service channel for customers and automated processes for the company employees. The company is a large telecommunications company and employs currently about 4,200 people and has about 2.3 million customers. The company expects to make significant economic savings with the project. The project was challenging because the company had multiple background systems in use and the goal was to combine these all in a single system. The project started in the beginning of 2007 with developers from a middle-sized software company and other external consultants related to the system integration. The system has been developed since then and the project is still running today. The system is being further developed with additional features and it currently has around 1 million lines of code and integration to over 70 background systems.

Case B is a software product developed for controlling and monitoring telecommunication systems. A large data networking and telecommunications equipment company have conducted the project. The company has around 58,000 employees and the organization size for the studied project is around 1,500 people. More than 320 customers are using the product. The project was started in 1992 and is still running today with multiple yearly releases. The product has currently around 50 million lines of code and it has faced several technology and operational system transitions during its life cycle.

Case C is a software development project conducted by a large company that provides communication technology and services. The company has currently around 1,15,000 employees and customers in over 180 countries. The goal of the project was to develop a product that connects different networks together. The development of the product started in the beginning of 2000 and since then it has been developed further with new features brought or requested by customers. However, at the moment the product is facing the end of its life cycle and includes currently mainly maintenance work.

Table 15.1 shows the overview of the cases. Even though all of the case companies are working in the same industry area, the Case A, as a smaller company, is somewhat different compared to the other two cases. Also the development of Case A started several years later compared to the Cases B and C.

The third stage of the case study process was to collect the evidence from the selected case companies. We conducted 17 semi-structured interviews with the snow-balling technique [7] during March–October 2014. The interviews started from our key contacts from each of the selected cases and the next interviewees were referrals from the previous ones. We were able to interview people from various organizational positions and investigate the research topic from the viewpoint of software developers to managers. The interviews lasted from 31 to 105 min with an average of about 50 min. Table 15.2 presents the roles of the interviewees in this study.

Table 15.1 Overview of the selected cases

	Case A	Case B	Case C
Industry sector	Telecommunications	Telecommunications equipment	Telecommunications equipment
Company profile	Retail and wholesale fixed-line and mobile telecommunications services, internet services	Mobile broadband, consultancy and managed services, multimedia technology	Mobile and fixed broadband networks, consultancy and managed services, TV and multimedia technology
Company size	Large	Large	Large
Employees	4,200	58,000	115,000
Case project	Self-service system for customers	Network monitoring and controlling system	System for connecting networks
Project start	2007	1992	2000
Project end	Still continuing	Still continuing	Still continuing
Lines of code	Approx. 1 Million	Approx. 50 Million	–

Table 15.2 The roles of interviewees

ID	Case	Role
A1	A	Software architect
A2	A	Project owner
A3	A	Project owner
A4	A	Senior software consultant
A5	A	Software architect
B1	B	Technical project manager
B2	B	Software architect
B3	B	Software architect
B4	B	Manager of R&D department
B5	B	Project manager
C1	C	Line manager
C2	C	Manager of release verification department
C3	C	Software testing
C4	C	Manager of maintenance department
C5	C	Software developer/technical coach
C6	C	Innovation and business architect
C7	C	Software developer

The fourth stage of the case study process was to analyse the collected data. The total amount of transcribed qualitative data for analysis was over 150 pages. After the data collection, data was analysed with a special tool for qualitative data analysis (Atlas.ti[1]). In the analysis process, we used similar procedure to open coding in grounded theory [11]. First, we read and examined through all of the transcribed interviews and related content. During the analysis, we categorized the parts related to software process evolution and technical debt into labelled concepts. Then, these data labels were grouped and linked together and we formed categories and subcategories. We used these categories to analyse the results.

15.3 Identified Scenarios of Software Process Evolution and Technical Debt

The last stage of the case study process was to report the gathered and analysed results. During the interviews our focus was to gather information about the history of the software process evolution in the case companies. Our goal was to identify situations during the interviews where companies had to change the software process for some specific reason and learn the reasons and effects behind it. We were able to identify scenarios of software process evolution in the studied cases. The interviewees described us real situations from the cases that had happened in the past or very recently. In this section, we present five scenarios and explain the context and environment in which the software process change happened and how it affected to the technical debt.

15.3.1   Scenario 1: A Need for More Frequent Releases

In Case C, the company made a decision to adopt agile methods after developing the product for several years with the waterfall model. The management of company felt that waterfall development model was not suitable to have frequent releases to customers. The customers required releases monthly, but the company was not able to accomplish that. The waterfall model was too rigid for inter-departmental cooperation and caused delays. The company could not organize the process of switching to agile methodologies on their own, so the decision was to hire a consultant team from another company to train people in agile software development processes and practices. The software process change was challenging during the first year and the project encountered several problems. The agile methodologies included a set of new practices and it was challenging for teams in the project to learn them. The change of methodology also encountered some resistance in the beginning and everyone in the project was not excited about the new ways of working. This resulted in a situation where some of the project members were using the waterfall model, while others were using agile methods.

---

[1] Available from: http://atlasti.com/.

Statement (C4). *People reacted differently, some people thought it is good and some were resisting. So at that point also you have to respect the people who are resisting. The most important thing is that there is need for everyone's contribution. So the thing that you cannot force every person in to the same mold. Some people require more time for change. There have been cases where some people stayed in their offices and did systematic work even though other people were in different room working together.*

In the beginning of the adoption, the productivity of development teams dropped. Previously, with the waterfall model people were assigned to certain jobs based on their competences. The change to agile methods created teams that were focusing on bigger components of the product and people needed to educate themselves to these new components they had never worked before.

Statement (C7). *The productivity dropped for a while during the change. Before the change there was more focus on certain sections that there was competence gathered to certain section and it was really specific. So at the same time when this change was done to this agile way of working, there was a request or actually a demand that teams could focus on bigger sections instead of specific ones. So the effect here was that we needed to learn new things and sections we had not learned or touched before. So this took a lot of time.*

The change also started to have an effect on the quality of the product. The line manager in the project explained a situation where the change of the development methodology started to have a negative effect to the architectural design of the product.

Statement (C1). *We used Scrum discipline and moved to this sprints style, so the architecture went to totally wrong direction at the beginning. Consultants said that the architecture will create itself with the new methodology. So the architecture started to create itself with a method where teams are doing little pieces and it keeps evolving by itself. However, it did not become this sustainable architecture.*

The scalability problems with the architecture resulted to the situation where further development was not anymore possible and the company had to refactor and redesign the whole architecture from the beginning after a year. This also resulted to significant extra costs.

Statement (C1). *We had to take a timeout and stop for a while and start to do the architecture with small team from the beginning. This is how we created a new core for the architecture and we have continued to build around that. The technical debt that formed in the beginning was that we started to develop it wrong, or with wrong methodology. Everybody knew how it should be, but it never became like that. We lost almost a year because of technical debt. 20 people and one year, 60 Euros an hour, so you can calculate from that. I think that we also lost many years in other parts of the product because of this.*

The reason for the bad architecture was that the teams formed at the beginning were not built according to project members' competence and it started to show as low quality solutions. In addition, the new process was still challenging to the people in the project to use.

Statement (C1). *It was that you could choose your own teams pretty much and friends were searching for their friends. There was not a knowledge that what a team should consist, but like I said that the architecture demands people with high knowledge about networks and everything. So they have to be strongly included to the architecture and after that it is possible to expand to other features. But this was not the case and there were like five teams doing pieces of the architecture and there is this collaboration of technical debt.*

However, around one year after the change, the benefits of making the process change started to show. The project teams started to learn the use of new methodology, which resulted to increased productivity and quality.

Statement (C1). *Now you can say that there are clear signs that defects have dropped and productivity has gone up. These are hard to measure, but still there are clear indications to it. We can make several releases in a year that was impossible in the past. However, you can't deny that our productivity dropped during the change of the methodology at the beginning.*

In this scenario, the need for software process change was caused by a need to answer to the requirements coming from the markets and customer. The company would not be able to keep the customer satisfaction and competitiveness in acceptable level with existing software processes. Therefore, the company was forced to change its software development process from waterfall to agile to increase the release cycles and provide faster product development. However, the adaptation to the new software development methodology was challenging and caused a large amount of technical debt to the product architecture during the first year, mainly because of lack of competence regarding the new processes. The company had to rewrite the whole architecture, which caused significant economic consequences. When the competence in agile methodologies increased after several months, the company was able to increase the number of yearly releases. The use of new software processes also started to show as increased productivity and decreased number of defects.

15.3.2   Scenario 2: A Problem with Installation Time

In Case B, the company also decided to switch their software development methodology from waterfall to agile. The reason for the switch was the growth of the product. Before the change, the company was able to do one release each year. It was not an option anymore in the current market. The company needed to be faster in their development in order to meet the business needs of the customers and therefore it decided to try another development methodology.

Statement (B4). *When the product started to grow, like networks and systems to grow, so this meant that different data elements that product was supporting started to grow exponentially. So previously we worked like that we release once a year that includes every supporting items and then we just wait again a year. So the world changed and network technology changed, so instead of ten we could talk about fifty different versions. So this meant that releasing schedules for different versions to customers had to be changed.*

The biggest problems with waterfall model were the slowness and unwieldiness, because the development was layered to so many different places. One of the problems mentioned by the interviewees was that with the waterfall model it took one month for teams to get newest releases in use.

Statement (B2). *Whenever team B released a new version, it took one month for team A to take the new version to use. There were lots of manual things in the process on how you install the new versions. Things changed and then the team A guys complained that "you haven't uploaded the documentation" and team B of course was like "What are you talking about, we have not changed anything." So there was a lot of bad build communication between those sides. They were taken sides and defending their own positions. I guess they were not playing in to the same goal.*

The company did not have any experience previously in using agile methodologies except some small web development projects in the past. The decision was therefore made to acquire a consultant company to train and conduct the needed software process change. The change was started slowly by organizing workshops with teams in multiple sites. The adoption of agile methodologies took a long time and it was difficult for the consultant company to cause a change the culture of the organization. However, after three years the company was able to use agile development methodology for the project without singe help from the consultant company.

The process change had a significant effect to the installation time of the product. Before the adaptation of the agile methodology, the installation time of the product to the customer was estimated to take around ten hours. The reason for the installation time was that previously the processes for the installation required a lot of manual activities and the process was not automated that well. When the consultant company was able to add agile methodology practices and processes and co-operation between teams after three years, the installation time was dropped to around two hours, which started to benefit the company economically.

Statement (B2). *So suddenly when we had this really fast cycle time, fast continuous integration, that was neutral, it was shared by every team on these levels. They could see logs on every system, automated test runs took from half hour to maybe four hours. Everyone could see the reports in the same way, so there was no one to blame. Actually it kind of switched the operation model from where people were in their own cycles to "now we have to fix these together." It was fun to see that there was no coaching or like trying to push people that you should now talk to these guys.*

But instead they were like calling each other's instead of sending emails. So to get whole organization into continuous delivery and manage to get whole organization into sync, which was really nice to see.

In this scenario the company needed to change the software development methodology to answer to the growth of the product. The growth of the product meant that the company had to provide to customers more frequent releases instead of just one or two a year. The size of the organization was extremely large and the adoption of a new software development method was challenging. It took three years for the company to implement the processes and practices. When the company was able to implement the new software processes, the productivity and yearly releases increased and technical debt started to decrease.

15.3.3   Scenario 3: Problem with Organizational Architecture

In Case A the project encountered organizational architecture problems that started to have an effect on the project and product. The company that ordered the project did not have own software development unit and the product development was commissioned from two subcontractor companies. The first subcontractor company had participated in the previous projects with the company and had vital information about the background systems related to the product. The subcontractor company took care of the back-end coding and automation of business processes. The second subcontractor was a well-known software development company and it was acquired to take care of the front-end coding and the user interface. However, this separation of the teams started to generate problems for the project from the beginning.

Statement (A4). *So there were people doing this web user interface and people doing this process automation. There were different teams working for these two, people from different companies with little bit different management processes. We had own repository and they had own repository. So even if you have full access to other team repository, it is still different thing to code something there. So the main thing was that the architecture was really off at some points because of this.*

The separation of the project teams started to affect the quality of the product. There were cases where the other team started to develop low-level features for their own use, instead of waiting for a better solution from the other team. Because of this, the company that ordered the project started to use these low-level features in their business processes. This resulted to the situation where same solutions had been made to different locations with multiple different styles.

Statement (A4). *When they were doing the user interface for their own usage, it was taken in use everywhere. Because there was integration between these, it enabled features that clearly had business benefits. So the company started to use this, instead of waiting that it will be made version suitable for customers. So this was done really roughly, but it was enough for internal use. This resulted to situation where the other* *team started to serve themselves. Well we were not really competitors between these teams, because they were not doing anything for this web user interface, but they were doing their own. Also if they made some API here, we started to use it also and that API did not fit as well as possible to here. But this is basically the Conveys law that results to situations where the best possible solution is not used.*

The communication and processes between the two teams were unsynchronized and the separation of the two teams started to affect the quality of the product. The two teams were not using the same processes and the management of the teams did not work with each other. One team was, for example, focusing a lot on quality of the code, while other team was trying to implement solutions as fast as possible. This resulted in situations where one team had to wait for the releases of the other team for the use. After realizing the issues with the architecture of the product and project, the company that ordered the product decided to make changes to software processes. The decision was made to break down the separation of the teams by creating new teams that included people from both of the previous teams.

Statement (A5). *In 2009 there was an attempt to get rid of this separation, so the answer for this was feature teams that still is a really good idea. So basically we had teams that included people from both teams. So the purpose was that when we have this line from back-end to front-end and teams should be able to everything related to that.*

The process change had a positive effect on the productivity of the project. The removal of the separation of the development teams started to make the software processes between teams unified. The change also started to effect to the quality of the product, since now all teams started to be included to the development of both front-end and back-end, when developers from two companies started to work in same teams. This increased, for example, the knowledge of single developers who had worked previously only for the front-end, because now they had to also develop the back-end.

Statement (A5). *The idea to remove this separation, I think that this was really good step that was taken. This helped a lot and after this we moved that every team was in their own Scrum cycles and we had long time that we had demos and this connected people and this was really good thing.*

In this scenario the company started to incur technical debt at the beginning of the project by implementing challenging organizational architecture for the project teams. The built organizational architecture started to effect the project, which resulted to a lack of productivity that transferred to bad quality solutions in the code base. The reason was that the development teams were not synchronized under same software processes and it made the product architecture complex. However, when the companies noticed that the amount of technical debt started to increase, they decided to change the organizational architecture. Improvement in the organizational architecture started to show as increased productivity, when all the development teams used a same software development process. This software process change started to reduce the amount of technical debt.

15.3.4 Scenario 4: Addition of a New Development Team to Another Country

In Case A the company needed to cut down development costs of the project. In order to do that, the company decreased the number of teams and replaced them by recruiting one new team to another country, where the development costs were cheaper. Another reason for the change was that the top management of the company thought that the product had reached a certain level of completion during first four years of development and the project needed less resources to continue. The subcontractor company that had developed the product from the beginning expressed their concerns to the top management of the company that the process change would bring challenges and problems with the addition of a new team without any experience with the project.

Statement (A4). *The pattern here is that some people in the management think that the system is ready. Even though there is active coding being made all the time with same amount of people. Actually it is also challenging to do changes in the current system, because when you are writing new code, you cannot change the old that much. So even though the system is already completed, even though it is being improved, the management thinks that this can be done with less resources. So it is kind of sad that this thing has been going on few years, and we thought that this process change was ludicrous and it is not going to work at all.*

Adding a new team to another location required many changes to the processes and existing teams needed to adapt to the new ways of working. The company improved their communication structure by adding video conferencing possibilities between the teams working in different locations. The company sent senior developers with a wide knowledge of the product to educate the new team about the development and software processes used previously. Also at the beginning, the company assigned the development of easier features to the new team instead of complex and challenging ones. These kind of activities helped the new team to be able to adapt to the existing processes that the project had been used before the addition of the new team.

However, the software process change also created many problems that had an effect to the project. When the new team was added to the project, it started to decrease the productivity.

Statement (A5). *The project suffered a lot because suddenly there was this bigger team coming from another country and they joined the project without knowing anything and their competence was variable. So basically we had good thing going in the current agile method and suddenly how would this kind of a big change fit in to this process. Here our productivity went basically to zero. So basically from a technical debt point of view, it went to that there were components that did not know anything. So how to integrate this and there was a huge code base already consisting technical debt and just randomly take people to code this.*

The reason for the lack of productivity was that the time of senior developers who went to educate the new team instead of developing or improving something in the product. The new team did not have previous knowledge about the project or the code base and it started to show as additional requests to senior developers.

Statement (A2). *The problem has been that when there are those support request coming and it is showing here as a decrease in productivity. There were some estimation that in some point 25 % of the senior coders' time went to helping because there are lots of questions coming and there has been some single cases where the quality of the code has been terrible and we had to rewrite or revert.*

Another effect of the process change was the decreasing quality of the code base. The quality started to go down since the people had limited knowledge about the code base and its history, which made the development harder. A consultant in the project felt that the overall quality of the code base started to go down.

Statement (A4). *This leads to situation that the base is being destroyed little by little. The code will change to more complex and hard to understand and harder to maintain. Quality starts to go down slowly. So in that sense the technical debt starts to grow. There are these easy technical debt like for example that one thing is in wrong place or something is done with wrong framework and so on. But then there is this general level of code that goes down all the time.*

In this scenario, the company had to add a new development team to another country to cut down the development costs of the project. When the older development team was replaced with a new development team, it started to increase the amount of technical debt. The reason was that the new development team did not have competences of working with the project. It started to show as lack of productivity and quality. This way the technical debt started to increase and older teams had to fix and educate the new development team that also decreased their own productivity.

15.3.5   Scenario 5: Switching from Scrum to Kanban

In Case A, the project had been using Scrum since the beginning of the project. However, the company needed a change and Scrum software development methodology was switched to another agile methodology called Kanban. The reason for the process change was that the company encountered problems with the project teams' cooperation when using Scrum. The work in the project was divided into two teams with two backlogs that caused problems and confusion to the development in the project. Another reason for the change was that in Scrum the company was using, the development was based on 2-week sprints. The company felt that having deadlines every 2 weeks increased the amount of unfinished work and technical debt.

Statement (A4). *Sprint is being planned and one of the driven forces is that team must engage to it. Sprints are 2-weeks long, so what do we do if things are not being* *ready? There is something unexpected, something was planned wrong, and this thing is not capable to be divided into 2 week job. So we just force it through to be ready. So when there is this deadline every two weeks and the sprint model combined with version management that includes unfinished work. These things might occur technical debt, because there is no time. Also you can't do any fixing stories to next sprint, because you might look bad if you have to fix something.*

The software development methodology change to Kanban had a positive effect to the project and technical debt. The teams focusing only on certain parts of the product were removed and the project became a common goal for everyone. The process change also increased the knowledge of project members, since they were now able to take part in multiple development tasks, instead than focusing only on some certain area.

Statement (A3). *We do not have separate teams anymore and everyone is doing what just happens to be in work line. Basically like whoever just finishes work just takes the next story from the backlog and it gets planned and groomed. So this thing removed the fighting and teams were not blaming each other anymore and there are no team silos. Everyone knows something about the project now even if it is different side of the project you are not working.*

The effect of the process changes was that the amount of unfinished work started to decrease. The project teams were able to create better solutions and do more refactoring when the sprints and deadlines used previously in Scrum were not that tight anymore. Kanban also gave the project more flexibility to change the backlog that was difficult previously.

Statement (A2). *Also one good thing in Kanban is that when in Scrum there are these sprints that are really closed and it is really hard to add stuff in there. In Kanban it is possible to change after every story if that thing was not good. You might notice that some feature is much more valuable to customer that something done at the moment.*

In this scenario, the company had a problem with the agile development methodology they were using. The problem was that the frequency of deadlines was too high, which started to increase the amount of not-so-good solutions, because there was not always enough development time. The change of agile methodology removed the concept of hard deadlines and the development time for features was increased. This started to reduce the amount of technical debt and the company was able to pay back the technical debt more efficiently.

15.3.6 Summary of Scenarios

In Table 15.3, we summarize the scenarios observed in the studied cases. We identified and developed categories for types, reasons, challenges, issuesk and benefits of

Table 15.3 Summary of scenarios

	Scenario 1	Scenario 2	Scenario 3	Scenario 4	Scenario 5
Type of process change	Software development methodology	Software development methodology	Organizational structure	Organizational structure	Software development methodology
Reason for process change	Lack of frequent releases, time-to-market	Lack of frequent releases, time-to-market	Project teams	Too high development costs	Project teams, technical debt
Challenges for process change	Lack of competence, team resistance	Lack of competence, needed time for change, size of organization, cultural change	Other companies and teams	Multi-location, other companies and teams	Lack of competence
Issues during process change	Architectural quality, scalability, decreased productivity	Decreased productivity	–	Decreased productivity and quality	–
Benefits of process change	Increased productivity, quality, competence	Increased productivity, quality	Increased productivity, quality, competence	–	Increased productivity, quality, competence
Effect to technical debt	Increased at the beginning. Decreased at the end	Increased at the beginning. Decreased at the end	At the beginning technical debt was high. Decreased at the end	At the beginning technical debt was low. Increased at the end	At the beginning technical debt was high. Decreased at the end

software process change and how they affected to technical debt. Types of software process changes in studied cases can be divided into two groups: *software development methodology* (Scenario 1, 2, and 5) and *organizational structure* (Scenario 3 and 4). *Software development methodology* changes included situations that were done to change the processes, techniques, and tools in the project. *Organizational structure* changes were situations done to change the structure of the organizational units in the project, such as addition of a new team, changing the structure of current teams, and outsourcing/offshoring the software development to another company or country.

The main reason for companies to conduct software process changes in Scenarios 1 and 2 was the *lack of frequent releases* and *time-to-market* that forced companies to change their *software development methodologies* to provide more releases to customers and adapt to changing markets and technologies. In Scenarios 3 and 5, the issues with *technical debt* and *project teams'* structure and co-operation made companies to change their *organizational structure* or *software development methodology* to increase the productivity and quality. In scenario 4, *too high development cost* forced the company to make changes to current *organizational structure* by replacing current development teams with new and cheaper teams.

The biggest challenge for conducting the process change was usually *lack of competence* (Scenario 1, 2, and 5). Companies did not have information or knowledge regarding the new process that made the adaptation difficult and often companies had to hire consultants from another company to educate and administrate the process change. The process changes also encountered sometimes *team resistance* (Scenario 1) and not everyone was willing to learn new ways of working. In addition, all case companies were large size, which meant that *size of organization* (Scenario 2), *needed time for the change* (Scenario 2), *cultural change* (Scenario 2), and other companies and teams (Scenario 3 and 4) created more challenges on adapting new software processes than in SMEs.

The adaptation time to the new software process created issues and problems to the project. The biggest issues during the adaptation time were *decreased productivity and quality* (Scenario 1, 2, and 4). The decreased productivity and quality then led to the *architectural quality* and *scalability* issues (Scenario 1), because it forced the development team to take technical debt to keep the release windows the same.

However, after the adaptation time the companies started to have benefits of the new processes. In Scenarios 1, 2, 3, and 5, the software process change started to show as *increased productivity, quality, and competence*. Companies were able to make releases more frequently and the amount of defects started to decrease. Also, the level of knowledge of project team started to increase regarding new processes and it increased the level of competence.

The software process change had also significant effect to the technical debt. *At the beginning technical debt was low* in Scenario 4, but the business reality forced company to change its current processes. The process change was not the most optimal and caused *decreased productivity and quality*. This was the reason why technical debt *increased at the end*. Sometimes (Scenarios 3 and 5) already *at the beginning technical debt was high*, because the current processes were lacking in productivity and quality and company was in a need for improvement. Companies conducted a successful process change and the level of productivity and quality increased and technical debt got *decreased at the end*.

Challenging period of the software process change regarding technical debt was the adaptation time. In this period technical debt was *increased at the beginning* (Scenarios 1 and 2). The more time adaptation took, more technical debt the project incurred. Low competence regarding the new software process during the adaptation time caused decreased productivity and quality. Omitted productivity and quality then transferred to the practices and methods. This led to situations where decreased productivity was compensated with workarounds and shortcuts to keep releases cycles same as before. However, when the competence level regarding the new processes started to increase, the technical debt *decrease at the end*.

15.4   The Relationship Between Software Process Evolution and Technical Debt

In this section, we discuss the results gathered from the three studied software projects. The discussion focuses on understanding the relationship between software process evolution and technical debt based on our findings.

15.4.1   Common Causes for Software Process Evolution and Technical Debt

Both software process evolution and technical debt were caused by business reasons and decreased productivity. The business needs often force companies to change their software development processes, even though the level of productivity and quality in the current processes might been satisfying [10]. The quality of the software process is connected to the quality of the software process [8]. Because the technology, business environment, and company circumstances are chancing all the time, there is a need for improving also software processes [8]. In our study, we observed situations where time-to-market, customer demand or technology change forced companies to make a change in the current software processes to be more efficient (Scenarios 1 and 2).

Business needs also increase technical debt. Multiple other studies [21, 26] have shown that when companies were acquiring time-to-market benefits by delivering faster the product to the customer, it required shortcuts and workarounds to the product. Shortcuts and workarounds were not necessarily dangerous to take in short-term, because they could advance the product release and therefore increase the time-to-market and customer satisfaction. However, if companies never fix these shortcuts and workarounds, it can lead to extra costs, productivity issues and omitted quality, because the code base turns overcomplicated [42].

Another reason for software process evolution and technical debt to happen was decreased productivity. Often when companies were experiencing that current software processes were not producing enough results and the quality of the product started to go down, there was a need to make a process change. Decreasing productivity forces companies to take shortcuts to keep up the release window that increases technical debt.

15.4.2   Relationship of Competence and Motivation to Software Process Evolution and Technical Debt

Changing and improving software processes requires resources, motivation and competence [3]. The top management of the company does not necessarily understand challenges and resources required to conduct a successful software process change that would benefit the project and product [27]. Instead, they might just think that changing one experienced team in the project to a cheaper team from another country will lead to the same productivity and quality (Scenario 4) or that changing release cycles from once a year to once a month is easy to implement (Scenario 1). The study conducted by Morten Korsaa [22] shows that over 70 % of the software process improvement projects fails because of poor understanding of the process. The reason is that companies have to educate employees to the new software processes and learning is an important prerequisite to improve software development practices [39].

Learning and education time for the new software processes takes time and the results are not showing instantly to the management. Changing the whole organizational structure of software delivery or adaptation to software development methodology with new techniques and practices is not easy to conduct and requires a lot of time to show the actual results [37]. The resistance of project members to change practices is also a challenge with software process improvement [25]. We identified these same issues, when changing from waterfall model to agile methodology or adding a new development teams from another country. It meant that suddenly project members had to start work with different methods and tools and learn new ways to communicate, which had a huge effect to motivation and productivity that in some cases led to technical debt (Scenarios 1, 2, and 4).

In Scenario 4, the lack of competence of new development caused motivation issues to existing development teams and led to significant decrease in productivity, when technical debt needed to be paid back constantly. It would have been interesting to know, if the company would had stayed with the old development teams, instead of recruiting new and unexperienced team, if the current extra costs coming from technical debt could compensate the costs of more expensive development teams that were removed to cut down the development costs.

15.4.3 Challenge of Adaptation Time in Software Process Evolution

The big source for technical debt during the software process evolution was the adaptation time to new processes. During the adaptation time, the productivity often went down, because company had to go through the learning and education period (Scenarios 1, 2, and 5). When the productivity dropped during the software process change it meant that project members had to compensate the decreased productivity with shortcuts and workarounds in their activities to meet the deadlines coming from business goals. Taking a shortcut in the code base of the product or leaving test cases untested to reach the deadline to customer was not dangerous in short-term. According to Eisenberg [15], the customer and business management is more interested on the delivery day of the feature than the quality of the code base. This is the reason why it was accepted sometimes to have lack of productivity in the processes, as long as the features were going to customers in time. However, when these shortcuts and workarounds started to accumulate during the software process change, it started to hurt the overall quality of the product (Scenario 1 and 4). New shortcuts and workarounds had be taken on the top of solutions already consisting of technical debt, because the release cycle of the product remained the same. This way it was risky for companies to work with the same deadlines during the process change. This was the reason why the management of technical debt was important during and after the adaptation of software process change. This way companies had a possibility to reduce technical debt long-term effects to the product and create sustainable and healthy products.

15.4.4   Successful Software Process Improvement and Technical Debt

One study has shown that software process improvement can be used to improve time-to-market and advantage over competition, while increasing the productivity and quality [24]. We found similar results and the case companies used multiple different ways to improve their software processes to increase the efficiency. The companies acquired new teams, changed the existing teams, tried new software development methods, techniques, and tools to change the software delivery process and were able deliver the product quicker and with more quality to the customer.

The studied companies were able to use these new processes to increase the productivity and quality in the project. Increased productivity gives companies more time to focus on refactoring and improving the existing code base, because now the new software processes might take technical debt more in consideration (Scenario 5). Also, the increase in quality and the code base made development easier and the amount of defects will drop during the development. We observed situations (Scenario 5) where the successful change to new software development methodology made technical debt more visible to the company and they were able to reduce it more efficiently.

15.5   Conclusion

In this study, we explored how software process evolution affects technical debt. We used qualitative case study approach recommended by Yin [41] to understand how software processes have evolved in the selected three large case companies. We conducted 17 interviews with professionals from both technical and business background to see the reasons, benefits and consequences of software process evolution to technical debt. We found that often the reason for software process evolution can be business related, where the company has to improve their current software processes in order to gain more advantage over competition and time-to-market. Overall, software process evolution is often considered as a positive thing toward better development processes. However, companies rarely think of its negative consequences and resistance to change. Our inquiry into the practice of three large development organizations revealed that the evolution of software processes affects technical debt accumulated in the code base and can decrease the software quality in short-term. However, if the company takes no steps to manage the technical debt, it may finally have a dramatic effect to the software development and maintenance processes.

15.6 Further Reading

Everett and McLeod [16] define software development life cycle as a "series of stages within the methodology that are followed in the process of developing and revising an information system." The classical software development model is the waterfall [33]. The model typically consists of five stages: (1) requirements; (2) design; (3) implementation; (4) testing; and (5) maintenance [33]. Other software development models such as the spiral model, V-model, incremental model, prototyping model have been developed after waterfall model [30]. Also the use of agile development methodologies that emphasize iterative and incremental way of software development has spread throughout the software industry [32, 34]. In addition, using building blocks from both agile as well as other classical methods is popular, see also Chap. 9. Therefore, software development processes have been evolved for a long time but companies are still interested in finding better models, practices, techniques, and tools for their software development.

The benefits of software process improvement are the reason why companies change and evolve software processes. However, improving, changing and managing software processes include also a lot of challenges [36] (see also Chaps. 10 and 9 in this volume). Beecham et al. conducted an empirical study with twelve software companies that shows that companies aiming at improving their software processes are experience challenges especially in organizational, project and software development processes [4]. According to Dybå [14] successful software process improvement depends on (1) business orientation as the extent to which SPI goals and actions are aligned with explicit and implicit business goals and strategies, (2) involved leadership as the extent to which leaders at all levels in the organization are genuinely committed to and actively participate in SPI, (3) employee participation as the extent to which employees use their knowledge and experience to decide, act, and take responsibility for SPI, (4) concern for measurement as the extent to which the software organization collects and utilizes quality data to guide and assess the effects of SPI activities, and (5) learning strategy as the extent to which a software organization is engaged in the exploitation of existing knowledge and in the exploration of new knowledge [14]. An unsuccessful software process improvement starts to affect the quality and productivity of the software development project [19]. The lack of productivity and quality can be seen as a source for "technical debt" [42].

Acknowledgments We would like to thank the companies that took part in this research and all the interviewees who shared valuable information related to the studied cases. This research has been carried out in Digile Need for Speed program, and funded by Tekes (the Finnish Funding Agency for Technology and Innovation).

References

1. Allman, E.: Managing technical debt. Commun. ACM **55**(5), 50–55 (2012)
2. Ashrafi, N.: The impact of software process improvement on quality: in theory and practice. Inf. Manage. **40**(7), 677–690 (2003)
3. Baddoo, N., Hall, T.: Motivators of software process improvement: an analysis of practitioners' views. J. Syst. Softw. **62**(2), 85–96 (2002)
4. Beecham, S., Hall, T., Rainer, A.: Software process improvement problems in twelve software companies: an empirical analysis. Empir. Softw. Eng. **8**(1), 7–42 (2003)
5. Brown, N., Cai, Y., Guo, Y., Kazman, R., Kim, M., Kruchten, P., Lim, E., MacCormack, A., Nord, R., Ozkaya, I., Sangwan, R., Seaman, C., Sullivan, K., Zazworka, N.: Managing technical debt in software-reliant systems. In: Proceedings of the FSE/SDP Workshop on Future of Software Engineering Research, pp. 47–52. ACM, New York, NY, USA (2010)
6. Carpenter, G.S., Nakamoto, K.: Consumer preference formation and pioneering advantage. J. Mark. Res. **26**(3), 285–298 (1989)
7. Charmaz, K.: Constructing Grounded Theory, 2nd edn. Sage Publications, London (2014)
8. Clarke, P., O'Connor, R.V.: An approach to evaluating software process adaptation. In: O'Connor, R.V., Rout, T., McCaffery, F., Dorling, A. (eds.) Software Process Improvement and Capability Determination. Communications in Computer and Information Science, pp. 28–41. Springer, Berlin (2011)
9. Codabux, Z., Williams, B.: Managing technical debt: an industrial case study. In: Proceedings of the International Workshop on Managing Technical Debt, pp. 8–15. IEEE, Washington, DC (2013)
10. Coleman, G., O'Connor, R.: Investigating software process in practice: a grounded theory perspective. J. Syst. Softw. **81**(5), 772–784 (2008)
11. Corbin, J., Strauss, A.: Basics of Qualitative Research: Techniques and Procedures for Developing Grounded Theory, 3rd edn. Sage Publications, Thousand Oaks (2007)
12. Cugola, G., Ghezzi, C.: Software processes: a retrospective and a path to the future. Softw. Process: Improv. Pract. **4**(3), 101–123 (1998)
13. Cunningham, W.: The WyCash portfolio management system. In: Addendum to the Proceedings on Object-oriented Programming Systems, Languages, and Applications, pp. 29–30. ACM (1992)
14. Dybå, T.: An empirical investigation of the key factors for success in software process improvement. Trans. Softw. Eng. **31**(5), 410–424 (2005)
15. Eisenberg, R.J.: A threshold based approach to technical debt. ACM SIGSOFT Softw. Eng. Notes **37**(2), 1–6 (2012)
16. Everett, G.D., McLeod, R.: Software Testing: Testing Across the Entire Software Development Life Cycle. Wiley, New York (2007)
17. Gibson, D., Goldenson, D., Kost, K.: Performance results of CMMI-based process improvement. Research Report CMU/SEI-2006-TR-004, Software Engineering Institute, Carnegie Mellon University (2006)
18. Harter, D.E., Krishnan, M.S., Slaughter, S.A.: Effects of process maturity on quality, cycle time, and effort in software product development. Manage. Sci. **46**(4), 451–466 (2000)
19. Herbsleb, J., Zubrow, D., Goldenson, D., Hayes, W., Paulk, M.: Software quality and the capability maturity model. Commun. ACM **40**(6), 30–40 (1997)

20. Hove, S.E., Anda, B.: Experiences from conducting semi-structured interviews in empirical software engineering research. In: Proceedings of the International Software Metrics Symposium, pp. 10–23. IEEE, Washington, DC, USA (2005)
21. Klinger, T., Tarr, P., Wagstrom, P., Williams, C.: An enterprise perspective on technical debt. In: Proceedings of the Workshop on Managing Technical Debt, pp. 35–38. ACM, New York, NY, USA (2011)
22. Korsaa, M., Biro, M., Messnarz, R., Johansen, J., Vohwinkel, D., Nevalainen, R., Schweigert, T.: The SPI manifesto and the ECQA SPI manager certification scheme. J. Softw.: Evol. Process 24(5), 525–540 (2012)
23. Krishnan, M., Kellner, M.: Measuring process consistency: implications for reducing software defects. Trans. Softw. Eng. 25(6), 800–815 (1999)
24. Laanti, M., Salo, O., Abrahamsson, P.: Agile methods rapidly replacing traditional methods at nokia: a survey of opinions on agile transformation. Inf. Softw. Technol. 53(3), 276–290 (2011)
25. Lepmets, M., Ras, E.: Motivation and empowerment in process improvement. Systems. Software and Service Process Improvement, Communications in Computer and Information Science, vol. 172, pp. 109–120. Springer, Berlin Heidelberg (2011)
26. Lim, E., Taksande, N., Seaman, C.: A balancing act: what software practitioners have to say about technical debt. IEEE Softw. 29(6), 22–27 (2012)
27. Mathiassen, L., Ngwenyama, O.K., Aaen, I.: Managing change in software process improvement. IEEE Softw. 22(6), 84–91 (2005)
28. McConnell, S.: Technical debt-10x software development. http://www.construx.com/10x_Software_Development/Technical_Debt (2014)
29. Ojameruaye, B., Bahsoon, R.: Systematic elaboration of compliance requirements using compliance debt and portfolio theory. In: Salinesi, C., van de Weerd, I. (eds.) Requirements Engineering: Foundation for Software Quality. Lecture Notes in Computer Science, vol. 8396, pp. 152–167. Springer International Publishing (2014)
30. Pressman, R.S.: Software Engineering: A Practitioner's Approach. McGraw-Hill, New York (2005)
31. Robson, C.: Real World Research: A Resource for Users of Social Research Methods in Applied Settings. Wiley, New York (2011)
32. Rodríguez, P., Markkula, J., Oivo, M., Turula, K.: Survey on agile and lean usage in finnish software industry. In: Proceedings of the International Symposium on Empirical Software Engineering and Measurement, pp. 139–148. ACM, New York, NY, USA (2012)
33. Royce, W.W.: Managing the development of large software systems: concepts and techniques. In: Proceedings of the International Conference on Software Engineering, pp. 328–338. IEEE, Washington, DC (1987)
34. Salo, O., Abrahamsson, P.: Agile methods in european embedded software development organisations: a survey on the actual use and usefulness of extreme programming and scrum. IET Softw. 2(1), 58–64 (2008)
35. Seaman, C., Guo, Y., Zazworka, N., Shull, F., Izurieta, C., Cai, Y., Vetro, A.: Using technical debt data in decision making: potential decision approaches. In: Proceedings of the International Workshop on Managing Technical Debt, pp. 45–48. IEEE, Washington, DC, USA (2012)
36. Shaikh, A., Ahmed, A., Memon, N., Memon, M.: Strengths and weaknesses of maturity driven process improvement effort. In: Proceedings of the International Conference on Complex. Intelligent and Software Intensive Systems, pp. 481–486. IEEE, Washington, DC, USA (2009)
37. Sureshchandra, K., Shrinivasavadhani, J.: Moving from waterfall to agile. In: Proceedings of the Agile Conference, pp. 97–101. IEEE, Washington, DC, USA (2008)
38. Tom, E., Aurum, A., Vidgen, R.: An exploration of technical debt. J. Syst. Softw. 86(6), 1498–1516 (2013)
39. van Solingen, R., Berghout, E., Kusters, R., Trienekens, J.: From process improvement to people improvement: enabling learning in software development. Inf. Softw. Technol. 42(14), 965–971 (2000)

40. Verner, J., Sampson, J., Tosic, V., Bakar, N., Kitchenham, B.: Guidelines for industrially-based multiple case studies in software engineering. In: Proceedings of the International Conference on Research Challenges in Information Science, pp. 313–324. IEEE, Washington, DC, USA (2009)
41. Yin, R.K.: Case study research: design and methods. Sage Publications, Thousand Oaks (2003)
42. Yli-Huumo, J., Maglyas, A., Smolander, K.: The sources and approaches to management of technical debt: A case study of two product lines in a middle-size finnish software company. In: Jedlitschka, A., Kuvaja, P., Kuhrmann, M., MännistÖ, T., Münch, J., Raatikainen, M. (eds.) Product-Focused Software Process Improvement, Lecture Notes in Computer Science, vol. 8892, pp. 93–107. Springer International Publishing (2014)
43. Zazworka, N., Shaw, M.A., Shull, F., Seaman, C.: Investigating the impact of design debt on software quality. In: Proceedings of the Workshop on Managing Technical Debt, pp. 17–23. ACM, New York, NY, USA (2011)
44. Zazworka, N., Spínola, R.O., Vetró, A., Shull, F., Seaman, C.: A case study on effectively identifying technical debt. In: Proceedings of the International Conference on Evaluation and Assessment in Software Engineering, pp. 42–47. ACM, New York, NY, USA (2013)

Index

© Springer International Publishing Switzerland 2016
M. Kuhrmann et al. (eds.), *Managing Software Process Evolution*,
DOI 10.1007/978-3-319-31545-4

Printed in the United States
By Bookmasters